THE SHAPE OF THE GOSPEL

THE SHAPE OF THE GOSPEL ✢ *Interpreting the Bible Through the Christian Year*

Merrill R. Abbey

Nashville • **ABINGDON** Ⓐ **PRESS** • New York

To a noble company who have blessed me
through the life and work of Garrett Theological Seminary

my teachers in the 'twenties
my students in the 'sixties
my colleagues in ministry across the years

Preface

Through the Christian Year successive Bible lessons trace the mighty acts of God which give shape to the gospel. The Christian message is not seasonal, but the seasons help to hold to the light the varied facets of its one jewel. Underlying each season is an aspect of the gospel which—though not confined to a season—focuses attention during one period upon an element in the Christian faith and life which cannot be lost if the total message is to be truly heard. Following the ordered progression of these respective emphases, the Bible reader or worshiping congregation is led to a whole and balanced understanding of the faith.

A good lectionary guides such orderly reading. Offering an Old Testament lesson, an Epistle, and a Gospel for each Sunday or special observance, it relates parts of the Scriptures to one another and to the developing shape of the gospel. Although the Bible readings used here follow the lectionary of the United Methodist Church, adopted in 1964, they are not bounded by denominational interests. The lectionaries of the various denominations have extensive overlappings, using many of the same Bible readings within any season, often achieving virtual unanimity in their selections for a given day; and the United Methodist lectionary draws extensively on this common treasury. On nineteen Sundays of the year, at least one lesson is shared unanimously in the lectionaries rooted in the traditions of the Episcopal, Lutheran, Roman Catholic, and United Methodist churches. Thirty-one of these lessons are shared, on the same day or in the same season, with at least one of the other traditions named. The two-year provisional lectionary of the United Presbyterian Church uses fifty-one passages, and that of the Church of the Brethren fifty-five, on the day for which this lectionary appoints them, or on another day of the same liturgical season. It is thus apparent that what is studied here deals with the common Christian message.

Whoever would understand the Christian faith, or grow in the experience it nurtures, must enter into its interpretation of life in three dimensions—biblical-exegetic, prophetic-practical, and liturgical. Into each dimension a careful use of the lectionary can be a helpful guide.

Apart from Bible study, the student of the faith is left to his subjective devices or to the fickle whims of society and the currents of the times. Christian faith has a history, lore, and thought-structure of its own, for which the Bible is the basic norm. To neglect systematic study of this foundational material is to drift into vague religion-in-general and to lose the particularity of authentic Christian faith and life. Yet consecutive reading of the Bible "from cover to cover" is not the most helpful approach to such study. A good lectionary guides the reader through a sequence of strong key passages whose cumulative force is broadly representative of the total biblical message. By such studies as are presented here, these passages are related to their context in the time from which they came and in the unfolding drama of the Bible. Through such historical study, and through the exploration of meanings in the original languages and in parallel translations, the reader is aided in tracing the forthright reality of their declarations.

Yet Christian faith is not backward-looking. It studies the Bible in order to understand the emerging new day in truer perspective. In Karl Barth's familiar term, the Christian studies with his Bible in one hand and today's newspaper in the other. Or as Gerhard Ebeling has pointed out, we get the intent of any Bible passage only when we move through *exposition* of what it said in its time to *execution* of its insight for our own. Any valid study must keep this prophetic-practical focus on the interpretation of our life now.[1] Hence the attempt of this book to explore the present dynamics of each Bible passage and its bearing on contemporary concerns.

A great liturgical tradition gives structural unity and dramatic movement to exegetic study and prophetic execution of the biblical text. Each season fixes attention on one aspect of the message long enough to give it forceful impact, yet the seasons advance with a dynamic movement that avoids monotony and gives color and balance to the total message. Apart from such guidance, few readers could escape the overemphasis on some doctrinal or practical interests, and the blindness to others, that are inherent in individual subjectivity. Nothing so promotes wholeness and excitement in the pulpit or classroom as live, informed participation in such dynamic movement. In the exploration of the successive liturgical seasons this book seeks to aid the reader's entrance into this creative drama of the Christian year.

The minister, teacher, or serious reader using the lectionary can be helped by a compact commentary which sets a given day's reading in perspective. The interpretations offered here serve this purpose by (a) relating each lesson to its biblical context, (b) viewing the selected passage in the light of its contribution to the developing drama of the Christian Year, (c) seeking to show how the truth in the passage holds the mirror to us where we stand—to reveal the meaning of our life in this living moment.

In a work of this nature—228 Bible passages studied in a single volume —it is obviously not possible to treat the respective lessons in full technical detail. For such studies the reader must turn to major Bible commentaries. Yet each study offered here is based on an extensive exegetical examination of the passage, from which enough selected data have been drawn to light up a central theme.

---

[1] Space in these pages does not permit the fuller development of the idea and methodology suggested by the term "prophetic-practical focus." This aspect of the study and teaching of the Bible is of cardinal importance, however. I have dealt with it elsewhere at length and from varied perspectives. See esp. the discussions of "double analysis" in *Preaching to the Contemporary Mind*, pp. 41-45; *Living Doctrine in a Vital Pulpit*, pp. 42-48; and *The Word Interprets Us*, pp. 20-26, 77-79.

Where such a biblical theme encounters a need in the ongoing life of the person or congregation to be served, an idea for personal meditation, teaching, or preaching emerges. Such ideas properly vary with time, place, and changing needs. For that reason no stock sermon outlines or teaching plans can have general validity. The minister, teacher, or serious reader must recognize the encounter of scripture and need, narrow and sharpen an idea, phrase it in a theme sentence, and develop its meaning for the current experience he or his people confront. The following pages are designed to help in this essential work. They present the kind of initial struggle with an idea that launches the studious reader on a fruitful personal encounter with a Bible passage, or the preacher or teacher on the preparation of a creative sermon or lesson.

Acknowledgment of my indebtedness is an obligation gladly undertaken, but tracing out the myriad sources on which these studies draw is all but impossible. In the reference notes I have attempted to identify all direct quotations. Beyond such conscious use of material, however, lie the contributions of an innumerable company to whose life and thought I have been gratefully exposed through the years, and on whose treasures I have been nurtured. Many of these are my teachers, students, and colleagues, to whom the book is dedicated. Others are the authors by whom I have been instructed, or the parishioners who have fed my insight as I have tried to serve them as pastor. Specific acknowledgment can be made to President Orville H. McKay and the administration of Garrett Theological Seminary for a sabbatical leave which permitted freedom to draw the previous studies of the lectionary passages together into a first draft, and to Mrs. Eve Messner for her diligence and care in adding to the work of a busy office the heavy burden of typing most of the manuscript and supervising the work on the remainder. To all these I extend thanks and acknowledgment of the indispensable nature of their assistance. Through all the effort I have been sustained by my wife's unfailing interest in the long project, without which it could not have come to completion, and for this I renew my thanksgiving.

MERRILL R. ABBEY

Evanston, Illinois
Kingdomtide 1969

Guide to Abbreviations

Throughout the text of this book, respective English translations of the Bible are designated by the following abbreviations:

AB — *Anchor Bible,* William Foxwell Albright and David Noel Freedman, general editors (Garden City, N.Y.: Doubleday).

AT — *American Translation,* Old Testament, J. M. Powis Smith, editor; New Testament translated by Edgar J. Goodspeed (Chicago: University of Chicago Press, 1931).

CPV — *The Cotton Patch Version of Paul's Epistles,* Clarence Jordan (New York: Association Press, 1968).

GNMM — *Good News for Modern Man,* The New Testament in Today's English Version; basic text translated by Robert G. Bratcher (New York: American Bible Society, 1966), following the 1969 text.

JB — *The Jerusalem Bible,* Alexander Jones, editor (Garden City, N.Y.: Doubleday, 1966).

KJV — King James Version of 1611

KT — *The New Testament, A New Translation,* R. A. Knox (New York: Sheed and Ward, 1944).

Knight — *Deutero-Isaiah,* A Theological Commentary on Isaiah 40–55, George A. F. Knight (Nashville: Abingdon Press, 1965).

MT — *A New Translation of The Bible,* James Moffatt (New York: Harper, 1935).

NEB — *The New English Bible,* A Joint Committee under the chairmanship of Alwyn Winton (Oxford University Press and Cambridge University Press. Second edition, 1970.)

PT — *The New Testament in Modern English,* translated by J. B. Phillips (New York: Macmillan, 1958).

RSV — *The Holy Bible, Revised Standard Version* (New York: Division of Christian Education of the National Council of the Churches of Christ in the United States of America, 1946 and 1952).

TCNT — *The Twentieth Century New Testament* (New York: Fleming H. Revell Company, 1904).

TMT — *The Torah, A New Translation according to the Masoretic Text* (Philadelphia: The Jewish Publication Society of America, 1962).

VWS — *Word Studies in the New Testament,* by Marvin R. Vincent (New York: Scribner, 1924).

Except where otherwise indicated, the text followed throughout is that of the Revised Standard Version.

Contents

KINGDOMTIDE

SPECIAL DAYS

ADVENT SEASON

Advent launches the drama in which God's mighty acts pass in annual review. "The prophecies are fulfilled, and the new Age is inaugurated by the coming of Christ"—so the New Testament kerygma declares. The Christian year dawns in expectancy based on this fulfillment by the Lord of history. It is no mere anticipation of the festival of Christmas. Rather it is a penitent, obedient waiting for the God who acts. His advent is ever imminent, since he is history's Lord.

A threefold anticipation marks the season with joyful waiting: for the coming of the Lord in the flesh even as Israel awaited the promised Messiah, for his coming in Word and Spirit, and for his ultimate coming according to the Christian hope of his victorious appearing in an eschatological encounter.

Expecting him so, we are summoned to prepare. From the earliest days of the church's observance Advent has been—as the violet or purple altar color now reminds us—a season of penitence. Even before Christmas was kept as a separate festival, Epiphany (January 6) was observed in celebration of our Lord's birth and baptism, a day which naturally became a time for Christian baptisms. Those who were to be baptized kept a period of fasting and daily church attendance in preparation, a pattern for our Advent and its proper mood of mingled joy and penitence.

19

While the secular community, for its own purposes, exploits Christmas in advance, the Church keeps this season in the penitent mood of the twelfth-century hymn-prayer:

"O come, O come, Emmanuel,
And ransom captive Israel."

FIRST SUNDAY IN ADVENT

Forerunners of Renewal: Malachi 3:1-7b

Advent begins with a promise that could almost have been designed with seekers of church renewal in mind: "the Lord whom you seek will suddenly come to his temple." It has a corollary: "Behold, I send my messenger to prepare the way before me" (vs. 1). It is as if the prophet were declaring that, when renewal comes, it is not of man's doing but of God—yet not of God alone, for a messenger is sent to prepare the way. That truth is still timely.

In Malachi's day, about 450 B.C., morals were loose and religious duties neglected. He leveled his indictment against widespread adultery (3:5), though the reference may be more particularly to the marrying of pagan foreign wives. The consequent decline of family religion violated Israel's covenant with God (2:10-12). Perjury and exploitation of the underpriviliged had become epidemic (3:5). Against such betrayals of the faith, not unfamiliar in our time, Malachi lifted his witness.

He could not force the dawning of the new age, but he could help to prepare the conditions. To whom does he refer as he announces, "Behold, I send my messenger to prepare the way before me"? (3:1) Perhaps to Elijah, who was to come (4:5), or an angelic messenger, or to Malachi himself. Individual messengers pass; the call for obedient response continues. It came to John the Baptist and to the courageous faithful who prepared the soil of the Reformation; it comes to us. The church has wealth and numbers but languishes for vibrant life and persuasive witness. Malachi points to elements of renewal which could be crucial now.

Renewal involves *cleansing.* "For he is like a refiner's fire and like fullers' soap; he will sit as a refiner and purifier" (vss. 2b-3a). The forerunners of renewal are not comfortable promoters of togetherness. John the Baptist was not (Luke 3:4-17), nor was Luther, nor Wesley. Not by accident did persecution and mob action gravitate to these messengers. In the face of drives to success measured by acquisition and status, God's witness is still under mandate to "refine them like gold and silver, till they present right offerings to the Lord" (vs. 3b)—offerings of a life of obedience and faith.

Renewal involves *judgment.* There are searching specifics in the warning, "Then I will draw near to you for judgment" (vs. 5). The indictment is directed to "the sorcerers"—practitioners of false, self-centered, magic-mongering religion, of which every generation spawns new variations; to "the adulterers"—whose violation of marriage disrupts all other relationships; to "those who swear falsely"—for no new day can be built on the breakdown of the pledged word; to "those who oppress the hireling in his wages, the widow and orphan"—one basic test of spirituality being its power to generate justice in dealings between employer and employee and between the comfortable and the dependent; to "those who thrust aside the sojourner"—because every society is most severely tested by its dealings with the minorities who do not quite "belong." All these are judged in that they "do not fear me, says the Lord of hosts"; our degree of obedience in basic integrities measures our fear of God.

Renewal involves *return to covenant faithfulness* (vs. 7). God gives fresh life and insight to those who keep faith with the light they have. The final call is forward to a new day, but we cannot advance until we have retraced our steps to the point where we missed the road. A people who do not know God, who complain that he is silent or fear he is dead, need to begin by looking for him where they last met him. A return to forgotten disciplines of faith is the forerunner of advance into God's new day.

Keyed to Expectancy: Romans 13:8-14

Christian faith subjects life in the present moment to the higher standards of God's new day, which may break at any instant. "The night is far gone, the day is at hand. Let us then cast off the works of darkness and put on the armor of light" (vs. 12).

The Scriptures take *time* seriously. Paul drives home his ethical urgency with the reminder, "You know this critical time" (vs. 11 AT). The gospel is no collection of "eternal truths" airily remote from humdrum days; does not view time as a spiral forever turning on itself. "You know this critical time" (*kairos*, time of urgency and action, as we would say, "harvest time," "election time," "time for decision"). Strong reason for this sense of crisis lay in Paul's belief that our Lord would soon come, ushering in a new day. Do we have any such invigorating expectancy?

Advent renews the call, "it is full time now for you to wake from sleep" (vs. 11), to rouse up from the dullness of days that go on in endless, unchanging sameness. It reminds us that God *did* act in the coming of Jesus Christ and the new era he inaugurated; God *does* act in recurring encounters which may break upon us at any moment; God *will* act "in the end of the day, in the end of our life, in the end of the world." Those who live expectantly, between the times of his coming, live by his standards.

Since the time of our world is running out, it behooves us to adopt the ways of a new day dawning. "Let us conduct ourselves becomingly as in the day" (vs. 13). Walter Lüthi likens our care of the natural world, under this expectancy, to a newly painted house he saw on a Swiss road. Against the background of its gleaming new paint, it bears a bold inscription: "Time flies, the end is near; soon the Lord shall appear. Hallelujah." Expecting the end, the owner dares not let his house deteriorate, a logic learned from God who—knowing the lilies bloom for a swiftly passing day—clothes them more splendidly than Solomon in his glory. How many minutes till midnight on the clock of the atomic scientists? In a threatened world the Christian lives by the standards of the expected new day, standards saving for himself and for the world. Our todays are judged by God's future.

"Not in reveling and drunkenness, not in debauchery and licentiousness, not in quarreling and jealousy" (vs. 13)—there is no hope in these. The new day belongs to love—as all days have, though they have not always known it. For "love is the fulfilling of the law" (vs. 10). It is what the law is all about, laws being enacted to safeguard the well-being of others whom we forget to love. In forgetting we let our house of life tumble into disrepair, let the hands of the nuclear clock creep nearer to midnight, let the crises of ruptured relations with those most dear overtake us. But we need not. Our Lord is coming! The times of his appearance are as dependable, as inevitable as are the crises. "Salvation is nearer to us now than when we first believed" (vs. 11). Our todays are empowered by God's future.

Living on the Watch: Mark 13:33-37

"Take heed, watch; for you do not know when the time will come" (vs. 33). So Jesus finally answered the question held in abeyance throughout the chapter. Before he launched into this discourse, Mark's "little apocalypse," the disciples had asked the question, When? Responding to his prediction of doom for the temple, they pressed him: "Tell us, when will this be, and what will be the sign when these things are all to be accomplished?" (vs. 4). He spoke then of the crisis nature of our life, concluding with the simple warning to live on the watch, since we "do not know when the time will come."

The interpreter must approach this chapter warily, and would do well to give attention to such considerations as are found in the *Interpreter's Diction-ary of the Bible* article on apocalypticism. Sherman E. Johnson makes a terse summary of the conclusions to which such a study leads:

(a) Jesus shared with his contemporaries the general eschatalogical outlook. God had made the world and could bring its history to an end when he chose; and the Kingdom of God would surely come. (b) Jesus predicted the destruction of the Temple and the fall of Jerusalem, at least in general terms; the "signs of the times" that anyone could see made this plain. (c) He did not make the definite predictions that are embodied in chap. xiii, for to do so would be to infringe upon God's prerogatives. . . . (d) But he did teach men to be ready at all times for God's judgement and the coming of his Kingdom. This moral imperative is the essential truth of the eschatalogical outlook.[1]

It calls us to live on the watch.

We hear the call over the shoulders of the *scribes* to whom Jesus presuma-bly directed the parable of the doorkeeper (vss. 34-36). Entrusted with the keys of the kingdom of heaven, they neither entered themselves nor allowed others to go in (Matt. 23:13). It was easy to see them in the role of the door-keeper in this parable, left to keep watch over the sleeping household. But what if their Master should "come suddenly and find [them] asleep" (vs. 36)? Not the scribes, now, but we of the church are set to guard the spiritual welfare of society. What if our Lord were to come and find us prayerless,

[1] Sherman E. Johnson, *The Gospel According to Mark* (New York: Harper, 1960), p. 219.

comforming to the sensate patterns of an affluent society, morally careless, spiritually indifferent, asleep?

We hear his call, again, over the shoulders of the *early church*. In days of persecution they found strength in the expectation that their Lord might come at any time, even in hours of darkness—"in the eveing, or at midnight, or at cockcrow, or in the morning" (vs. 35) just before the day breaks. So they weathered the weary night of persecution buttressed by hope and stirred to watchful obedience. And what of us, set in the world in a time of dark doubts and bitter attacks upon our faith? We can bear our witness in the face of adverse odds, kept strong by the conviction that we may meet our Lord in the midst of crisis.

We hear his call, finally, as it comes personally to *each of us*. Life's demands, as varied as our individual fingerprints, call us to posts of duty at which our Lord expects to find us faithful. He requires not success—a creature of circumstances beyond our control—but faithfulness. Temptation springs from ambush; opportunity knocks when we are ill prepared; crucial decisions are required when we feel unsure and unready. Of the handling of such crises our lives are made. In such moments of judgment we confront our Lord.

During World War II, John Baillie reflected on the question, "Who won the First World War for us? What kind of man was he?" Answer: "He was a plain man, awake all night in a ditch." From that apt description of the victor in trench warfare he turned to a more pressing query: "Is that not the kind of man who by the grace of God will always win the battle of life—a plain man on the watch?" [2]

SECOND SUNDAY IN ADVENT

A Gospel with Secular Urgency: Isaiah 11:1-10

Because he dealt with the secular meaning of faith in God, the great Isaiah of Jerusalem has much to teach us who carry the gospel into the secular arena of "man come of age."

The prophet composed this poem for the coronation of a king. On that secular occasion he declared that God makes the ultimate difference. This "shoot from the stump of Jesse" (vs. 1)—vivid title for the new monarch of the Davidic line—was anointed amid prayers that "the Spirit of the Lord shall rest upon him" (vs. 2). God could give or withhold his blessing, and the king ruled under his judgment.

Our freedoms rest on this conviction. Hitler, intoning "Let history be my judge," interpreted the meaning of that cliché by telling his generals: "No one will ask the victor who was right, but only who was strongest." But history cannot *be* the judge; history stands under judgment. Appealing, in hours of decision, to what subsequent history will say is another way of gazing at a crystal ball; it is superstition that gives back only the reflection of our subjective hunch. We need to know ourselves under judgment that asks, not "Who was the strongest?" but, "Who loyally obeyed the Lord of truth?"

[2] John Baillie, *Christian Devotion* (New York: Scribner's, 1962), p. 60.

"The voice of the people is the voice of God"—so runs the inscription on more than one public building. Such an interpretation of democracy needs Isaiah's reminder that there is One who gives or withholds his blessing upon any sovereign, even a sovereign people. The rule of the people is the most equitable way of governing yet devised, but it is not the voice of God! The voice of the people can be dead wrong. Freedom prevails only in societies saturated with the faith that the government, even of the sovereign people, stands under the judgment of God. Apart from this, majorities breed new tyrannies.

Isaiah reminds us, again, that righteousness and goodwill, not might, have the final word. The king's armor is not the prosperity of his nation nor the fierceness of his garrison.

> Righteousness shall be the girdle of his waist,
>   and faithfulness the girdle of his loins (vs. 5).

His future rests on goodwill and faith, not affluence and conquest.

> They shall not hurt or destroy in all my holy mountain;
> for the earth shall be full of the knowledge of the Lord
>   as the waters cover the sea (vs. 9).

The social philosopher Pitirim Sorokin underscored this conviction in his thesis that societies rise out of an idea held as a faith commitment. Growing prosperous, they become preoccupied with sensual enjoyment and lose the disciplined life which the original faith inspired. Then they either rediscover their commitment or fall under the weight of their sensate prosperity.

Isaiah's poem is a treasure of Advent because of the insight which Paul later echoed (Rom. 15:12): "In that day the root of Jesse shall stand as an ensign to the peoples; him shall the nations seek, and his dwellings shall be glorious" (vs. 10). These lines celebrate Israel's faith in a coming Messiah. When Jesus came, he was not a disembodied idea, nor was he a sudden intrusion into history. He came as fulfillment of an expectant faith—though in the very act of fulfilling the vision he transformed it.

Second Coming—or Third Degree? I Thessalonians 5:1-11

"You yourselves know well that the day of the Lord will come like a thief in the night" (vs. 2). Just so, crisis always comes—with the shock of surprise. Be ready, Jesus warned: "the Son of man is coming at an hour you do not expect" (Matt. 24:44). Paul precedes this glimpse of the "day of the Lord" with reference to "the coming of our Lord Jesus" (I Thess. 3:13; 4:15).

Does it all sound strange to modern ears? We know that all things end. Day ends, life ends, the world will end. And our Lord meets us in the one as in the others. How will he come? We cannot pretend to answer. Yet faith holds it incredible that we shall not one day know him better than we know him now. Whether in some ultimate Coming, or in our life with him from day to day, we live in expectation that he will meet us. A message from the Second Assembly of the World Council of Churches declared, "We do not know what is coming to us. But we know Who is coming. It is He who meets us every day and who will meet us at the end—Jesus Christ our Lord." [3]

When? How? Whence? Paul brushes off all such queries as too marginal to matter: "As to the times and the seasons, brethren, you have no need to have anything written to you" (vs. 1). Yet some things do matter greatly.

The day of the Lord interrupts our self-contained secularism. "When people say, 'There is peace and security,' then sudden destruction will come upon them as travail comes upon a woman with child, and there will be no escape" (vs. 3). Despite long expectancy, the beginning of birth pangs is sudden, inexorable, moving to inevitable climax.

"There is peace and security" (vs. 3), we say, counting on the sophistication gained in our "knowledge explosion" to stand by us under all circumstances. The history of science makes it sure, however, that many of today's discoveries will be tomorrow's castoffs. On only one rock-ribbed certainty can we stake our life: "I know whom"—not what—"I have believed and I am sure that he is able to guard against that Day what has been entrusted to me" (II Tim. 1:12).

It is day that comes—not night. "For you are all sons of light and sons of the day; we are not of the night or of darkness" (vs. 5). If we live as who we really are, we need not fear the Lord who comes to us. "For God has not destined us for wrath, but to obtain salvation through our Lord Jesus Christ" (vs. 9). This confidence we threatened moderns can ill afford to lose.

In a one-act play, *The Last Word*, James Broughton lets us overhear the conversation of a husband and wife who have just heard the news that "the bomb" is on its way. With thirty minutes to live, these young secularists seek solace in a bar. "Have we anything to declare?" asks one. Anything worth declaring to each other? Any treasure to declare at a border not national but eternal? The answer is emptiness.

> I've a cloudy soul and a rainy brain,
> a muddy heart, and no very eager vigor. [4]

Recalling how his teacher had advised, "Always remember who you are," the husband confesses: "Now I can't remember who to remember." [5] Because even secularists need some kind of prayer, they turn to the resources they count on, alternately chanting the petitions of a post-Christian litany:

> United Nations, have mercy upon us!
> Elizabeth Arden, deliver us!
> General Motors, have mercy upon us!
> Sigmund Freud, deliver us!
> Batten Barton Durston and Osborn, have mercy upon us!
> In the name of Mutual Life and Cold Storage.
> Amen. [6]

[3] W. A. Visser 't Hooft, ed., *The Evanston Report* (New York: Harper, 1955), p. 3.

[4] James Broughton, *The Last Word or, What to Say About It;* from *Religious Drama 3*, Marvin Halverson, ed. (New York: Meridian Books, 1959), p. 23.

[5] *Ibid.*, pp. 23-24.

[6] *Ibid.*, p. 27.

The young husband asks the crucial question: "Is it the Second Coming? Or the Third Degree?" [7]

Which do we confront as we face our inevitable crises? Life is no permanent possession. Ours is no secure age. To live is to choose among calculated risks. What do the hazards hold—faith or meaninglessness, meeting with our Lord or absurd Fate, the Second Coming or the Third Degree? Christian faith responds, "God has not destined us for wrath, but to obtain salvation through our Lord Jesus Christ."

We can live as people of the Day. Sleep and reveling belong to the night (vs. 7), but the day calls for clear heads (vs. 8). In Paul's time, the coming (*parousia*) of a king or high official on a visit to any community called for elaborate preparations. So, he said, we prepare for the coming (*parousia*) of our Lord in ways appropriate both to his nature and to ours as his people. "Since we belong to the day, let us be sober, and put on the breastplate of faith and love, and for a helmet the hope of salvation" (vs. 8).

Christ Was God's Idea: Luke 1:26-35

No matter-of-fact reading can catch this lyric reality; these lines plead to be sung. They announce events, but their announcement is not pedestrian prose; it is wonder-struck poetry. To say this is not to discount their power to make a difference in our humdrum milieu. A haunting poetic vision has power to dominate the way we think of ourselves and the world, wielding regulatory control, just as "the American dream" tamed a wilderness, begat gigantic men, and still molds world destinies. It need not surprise us, then, that Luke prefaces his careful account of events with this poetic frontispiece.

The angel's word to Mary announces that the coming of Christ is both a human event and a divine event; this very human girl was to be his mother, but in him God would act. When in him the human stream rose to its highest crest, its rising revealed the nature of its Source. "Conceived by the Holy Spirit," says the Apostles' Creed, echoing the lines,

> The Holy Spirit will come upon you
> and the power of the Most High will overshadow you (vs. 35).

"Conceived," says the dictionary, means not only "to become pregnant with," but "to think; form an idea." So! Conceived by the Holy Spirit, Christ was God's idea!

Presumably sung by the earliest Christians as they praised God, this hymn originated in their experience with the Lord. What Jesus did before their eyes and in their changed persons demanded explanation. How could any man do what he did? Pondering the question,

at first they may have said, God sent him. After a while that sounded too cold, as though God were a bow and Jesus the arrow. That would not do. God did more than send him. So . . . they went on to say, God is with him. That went deeper. Yet, as their experience with him progressed, it was not adequate. God was more

[7] *Ibid.*, p. 21.

than with him. So at last we catch the reverent accents of a new conviction, God came in him. That was not so much theology at first as poetry. It was an exhilarating insight and its natural expression was a song.[8]

This faith that "he will be great, and will be called the Son of the Most High" (vs. 32) has an important corollary in tangible affairs centuries long: "and of his kingdom there will be no end" (vs. 33). A cross could slay him, yet a tomb could not confine him. Rome could drench his followers in blood; it could not contain their witness. Successive persecutions could shatter the Christian community; they would only thereby scatter its seed. As the unity of Christendom now disappears in the secularity and pluralism of our post-modern world, it is still true that "of his kingdom there will be no end." So says this Advent message, sharing, with every soul who will hear, the angel's assurance to Mary: "The Lord is with you."

THIRD SUNDAY IN ADVENT

Restored to Unify: Isaiah 62:10-12

"Prepare the way." What way? Startlingly, not "the way of the Lord." "Prepare the way for the people" (vs. 10). The two calls are not in conflict. The poet-prophet who wrote these lines appears to have been a disciple of the great Isaiah of the Exile, meditating at a later period on his teacher's words, "In the wilderness prepare the way of the Lord" (40:3), and reaching the insight that God's way is the way of the fullest restoration of his people. Vividly he sees that God identifies his life with the life of his people, as Jesus later declared: "As you did it to one of the least of these my brethren, you did it to me" (Matt. 25:40).

The interpreter of these lines can see them in their full glory only as he comes to them from the reading of the poetic trilogy found in chapters 60–62, of which they form the conclusion. Without this exegetical preparation, one is almost sure to miss the meaning of the salvation which these closing verses celebrate. In this context it is seen to be the salvation of a people called to the messianic task of unifying all peoples.

Aptly JB titles chapter 62 a "Second poem on the glorious resurrection of Jerusalem." The prophet announces that he is speaking "for Jerusalem's sake," concerned for "her vindication . . . and her salvation" (vs. 1). There is to be "a new name" (vs. 2). Once the people were named "Forsaken" and the land "Desolate," but now God names the people "My delight is in her" and the land "Married" (vs. 4);

> and as the bridegroom rejoices over the bride,
> so shall your God rejoice over you (vs. 5).

God promises that, invasions ended, Jerusalem will be free to enjoy the produce of the land (vss. 8-9). The messianic people is to be restored, and the verses which comprise this lection sing the purpose of the restoration.

[8] Harry Emerson Fosdick, *Living Under Tension* (New York: Harper, 1941), p. 156.

"They shall be called The holy people" (vs. 12) finds explanation in 61:6, where the people are called "the priests of the Lord" and "the ministers of our God." In this priestly ministry they are to "hoist the signal for the peoples" (vs. 10 JB), thus gathering all the scattered ones. Devoted to this ministry, the people are promised salvation (vs. 11) and given the names, "The-sought-after" and "City-not-forsaken" (vs. 12 JB). No individualistic salvation, this is given to those who have been called, redeemed, and companioned as God's covenant people.

In the face of dispersion and defeat, this is a summons to receive gifts of unity from a victorious God who calls his people to be set apart for ministry, redeemed as a community, companioned by the Lord who has renewed his marriage covenant with them. Its promise to the doughty venturers returning from exile speaks vibrantly to three aspects of our contemporary need.

1. To the divisions that rend the life of the church. The returning peoples for whom the "ensign" or "signal" was to be raised were the scattered sons and daughters of Israel now to be reunited for their priestly task. The struggle for the unity of God's people is thus seen as no new or merely human ideal, but a very ancient call which God's blessing underwrites.

2. To the divisions that threaten the life of humanity. In the age of superweapons, war itself has become the enemy menacing the existence of the race; and conflicting sovereignties in an ungoverned world community contain the seeds of war. Yet God is sovereign Lord, who calls the peoples and underwrites the struggle for world unity.

3. To the divisions that inhere in our individualism. "Behold, your salvation comes" (vs. 11) was not a promise to separated individuals in Isaiah's time, nor is it in our own. We have a continuing need to hear the warning of John Wesley, much in the mood of Isaiah, that ours "is essentially a social religion; and that to turn it into a solitary one is to destroy it . . . . I mean not only that it cannot subsist so well, but that it cannot subsist at all, without society,—without living and conversing with other men." [9] God saves men in a social context and underwrites the endeavor to give salvation substance in society.

No Premature Judgment: I Corinthians 4:1-5

"So pass no premature judgement; wait until the Lord comes" (vs. 5 NEB). It is prejudice—pre-judgment—to draw conclusions about persons or situations before they are seen in the light of our Lord's coming. For he comes into every situation, and his coming is one of the most relevant facts.

Paul's incisive declaration concerning divine judgment was spoken into the chaos of conflicting human judgments. To get his bearings, the reader must go back to the beginning of the letter: "I appeal to you, brethren, by the name of our Lord Jesus Christ, that all of you agree and that there be no dissensions among you, but that you be united in the same mind and the same judgment" (1:10). Conflicting opinions had led the Christians of Corinth to form cliques claiming Paul, Apollos, Cephas, and Christ himself as their partisan heads (1:12). Paul countered such schisms with a series of arguments

---

[9] *The Works of John Wesley* (Grand Rapids: Zondervan, based on 1872 edition), V, 296.

capped by the reminder that "all things are yours, whether Paul or Apollos or Cephas or the world or life or death or the present or the future, all are yours; and you are Christ's; and Christ is God's" (3:21b-23). All our judgments rest under his claim who alone can be our Judge.

In such a context, this lesson finds its keynote in the exhortation to "pass no premature judgment; wait until the Lord comes." The passage makes strong assertions about our life.

We are not in control of the truth; we hold it in stewardship for which we shall be called to account (vss. 1-2). "Mysteries" (vs. 1) compares the gospel with the popular religions of the time, which inducted their initiates into a secret lore, hidden from others. MT aptly reads it "God's secret truths." [10] For Paul it was an *open* secret which he gladly shared with all. The stewards of God's truth are required to "be found trustworthy"; on that the fitting commentary is found in the parable in Luke 12:42-46, with its climactic sentence on the steward: "put him with the unfaithful."

Yet we are wont to act as if the truth were ours to judge. Jesse Hill Ford takes us inside the mind of one of his characters musing on death. The meditation occurs at the funeral of the victim of a racial tragedy. The thoughts are those of a man not insensitive to his own involvement, as a responsible citizen, in the tragedy. "They lay him to that long sleep," he tells himself. "And I have laid my integrity to rest with him." [11] Lawyer, churchman, pillar of the community, he is not unfamiliar with the inclusive claims of the gospel. Yet faced with those claims, he concludes, "At least I know that when I die I'm going to walk through that gate marked 'White Only,' be it fire or pearls." [12] In how many areas of our life do we turn from the gospel with a like rebellious claim to pass our own ultimate judgments?

We are not subject to human opinion, whether of the public, our peers, or ourselves (vss. 3-4). The word translated "judged" (RSV) in these sentences carries the implication of *searching inquiry*, variously rendered, "called to account" (NEB), "being examined" (AT), "cross-question" (MT). Paul refuses to be pressured by human opinion. As a steward he is subject only to the opinion of his Master. Before that court he has no need to be continually measuring himself, conforming to a self-image; yet by the same token, his clear conscience is no final proof of innocence. In our conformist age, this freedom simply to be ourselves before God is rare treasure.

We are not judged (here the Greek word changes to one implying *final verdict*) in any other light than that of Christ, whose judgment is rendered in compassion (vs. 5). Paul is saying: It is not my clear conscience—faulty as that may be—that acquits me, but God's compassionate judgment. "The Christian consciousness gives no valid testimony, save as it reflects the great objective verities of the Christian faith." [13] Yet for our final judgment we

[10] From *The Bible: A New Translation*, by James Moffatt. Copyright, 1954 by James Moffatt. Used by permission of Harper & Row, Publishers, Inc.

[11] Jesse Hill Ford, *The Liberation of Lord Byron Jones* (Boston: Little, Brown, 1965), p. 360.

[12] *Ibid.*, p. 364.

[13] Marvin R. Vincent, *Word Studies in the New Testament* (New York: Scribner's, 1924), II, 389.

come before a Father who says, "It is true, you have sinned. But you are my child, proven to be such by your love. Shall not I, your Father, forgive your sin?" [14]

When God's Word Comes: Luke 3:2b-6

Luke quotes from Isaiah 40:3-5 an insight so vital that all four Gospels take recourse to it in introducing the good news that came in Jesus. "The word of God came to John," writes Luke, using the common Old Testament formula for launching a prophet's message, and so linking the Baptist with the prophetic function. More deeply embedded in this passage, however, is the implication that God's Word was coming in that fuller sense of which the Fourth Gospel speaks—the Word made flesh.

When God's word comes, it shows in Jesus the link with *his promised restoration.* The preparation of a way, to which this passage refers, was a recurring figure by which the prophets made graphic the expectation of God's Day of renewal (cf. Isa. 35:8; 49:11; Jer. 31:9, 21; Mal. 3:1). The evangelists all saw in the advent of our Lord the consummation of this hope. We need its assurance now, as Augustine Cardinal Bea reminds us:

It was no accident that good Pope John, nearly every time I met him, repeated with an affectionate smile this single word: "Coraggio." I don't believe that the thought in the Pope's mind was that I lacked courage; rather, he wanted to underline how much courage was needed to face the obstacles which reared up, and are still rearing up, in the path of the Secretariat for the Promoting of Christian Unity—as, for that matter, they reared up in the path of Pope John himself . . . . Which is why I believe the Pope often had to repeat the word to himself.[15]

In this universal need of courage, we are not left to our own devices. God comes to restore. The very sense of his "silence" or "absence" or "death" is a sign of the hunger and need to which a new springtime can come.

When God's word comes, it shows in Jesus the link with a *"baptism of repentance for the forgiveness of sins"* (vs. 3) which John proclaimed as the way of entrance to the promised restoration. It was a call for total reorientation: "Proclaiming baptism as a mark of a complete change of heart" (PT); "Turn away from your sins . . . , and God will forgive" (GNMM).

Can there be any doubt of our need for reorientation? Let one ironic moment of drama stand for the varied particulars that spring to mind—a radio man's own version of the commercial in the midst of grim news, reflecting how we trivialize our confrontations with the ultimate. One passage in his imaginary broadcast of the outbreak of nuclear war runs:

> This is the ten-minute warning
> London is burning
> And Paris in ashes
> —Stand by for an important announcement
> Pop Corn

[14] *Ibid.,* p. 385.
[15] Augustine Cardinal Bea, "Paths to Ecumenism," *Saturday Review,* July 8, 1967, p. 11.

Pop Corn
Predigested Pop
Undemanding Corn
The best diet
Just try it[16]

Thank God, the needed reorientation is possible. Back of the phrase, "forgiveness of sins" (vs. 3 RSV) or "remission of sins" (KJV) stands a Greek word with medical connotation of release from an illness. The same root appears in Luke 4:39 (concerning Jesus' rebuke to the fever that afflicted Simon's mother-in-law—"and it left her"). It appears again in John 4:52 (reporting that "the fever left" the official's son). In vss. 7-14, which follow this lection, John makes specific the feverish attitudes and modes of conduct that need to leave us. Experience underlines what the gospel declares: that the encounter with Christ produces both repentance and the faith that turns life in a new direction. Being God's gifts, not our achievements, both are available to the weakest among us.

FOURTH SUNDAY IN ADVENT

Expecting "God with Us": Isaiah 7:10-14

"Behold, a young woman shall conceive and bear a son, and shall call his name Immanuel" (vs. 14). What Christian can hear these words without overtones of Matthew's nativity story and Handel's lovely aria? But to hurry off to Matthew in our interpretation is to miss the potent thrust of Isaiah. The lectionary can easily betray us into such a loss by its selection of this five-verse fragment to be read out of context. Our focus on the incidental will eclipse the essential unless we fix attention firmly on the whole passage, vss. 1-16. In the end, it powerfully confirms the New Testament's "Immanuel, God with us"; but its real force can be felt only when it is allowed to speak first in its own terms, in the integrity of its Old Testament message.

It portrays a historic crisis in which the prophet counseled the sturdy restraint born of confidence that God controls events. The king invited disaster by desperate policies which ignored that counsel. It calls us to live by the quiet strength that knows when to act and when to wait, because it expects God's coming as a fact of unfolding history, over which he holds sway. Let the story dramatize this truth.

King Rezin of Aram, in the march of his conquests, had enlisted the alliance of King Pekah of Israel (Ephraim in this passage) in a menacing attack on the northern borders of Judah, while two ancient enemies, Edom and Philistia, made raids from the south and east. Terrified, Ahaz, King of Judah, contemplated the pact with Assyria by which he finally purchased survival at the price of independence and religious integrity. Isaiah sought to stiffen his resolve against this wild course, telling him "he must be calm, never quail,

[16] Penn Kimball, "Can We Communicate with Europe?" *Saturday Review,* July 8, 1967, p. 55. Mr. Kimball is quoting a BBC producer's "Epitaph for a Commercial Station."

never be afraid of these two fag-ends of flickering torches" (vs. 4 MT). Both these kingdoms would soon decline; the only real strength lay in fortitude born of faith. To make the injunction unforgettable, Isaiah used a play on words, the flavor of which is best translated,

> If your faith does not hold,
> you will never hold out. (vs. 9*b* MT).

Covering his disastrous faithlessness with scrupulosity in trifles—as many a man still does—Ahaz, quoting the law (Deut. 6:16), refused to ask a sign of God's faithfulness. Whereupon Isaiah assured him that one would be given without his asking. Before a young woman could conceive, bear a son, and wean him, the danger would disappear. Here again, MT reveals the force of Isaiah's thrust: "for before ever the child knows good food from bad, the land whose two kings are your terror shall be desolate" (vs. 16). No wonder she would name the child "Immanuel (that is *God is with us*)" (vs. 14 and footnote). Events, vindicating Isaiah's faith, brought no comfort to the panic-stricken Ahaz, who had drained his treasury (II Kings 16:7-8) to buy Assyrian aid and had "burned his son as an offering" to appease his new master's gods (II Kings 16:3). Faithless desperation in crises both national and personal keeps betraying us into such bad bargains.

But God remained faithful. Ahaz was replaced by his son Hezekiah, whose coming birth may have been the original reference of Isaiah's sign (vs. 14), assuring the continuity of the Davidic throne. The kingdom was preserved as servant to God's Word. Unfolding events, then as now, showed that when our desperation has run its course to its tragic end, God's quiet purpose still prevails; yet in the throes of decision only a daring faith can enable us to stand with him. Every

human situation is problematical until it is actually determined. Washington and its valiant compatriots could have quit at Valley Forge. Napoleon's defeat at Waterloo was not foreordained. The United Nations is not destined to fail. History is written by men, not IBM machines. Human convictions, judgments, and courage are decisive factors in any historical situation. Christians know that. They also believe that God works in and through history to accomplish his purposes.[17]

One of those purposes was his coming in Jesus of Nazareth, so that Isaiah's sign, "Behold, a young woman shall conceive and bear a son, and shall call his name Immanuel," proved true at a time far later and in a degree far greater than Isaiah could know. For supremely Jesus was Immanuel, God with us. On this Sunday deep in Advent we subject our lives, purposes, and plans to faith's expectancy in a God who came, who comes, who will come, and who rules events by his coming.

Awaiting Our Blessed Hope: Titus 2:11–3:7

Scholarly consensus holds that this letter reflects a later period in the life of the Church than that of Paul and Titus. Somewhere about A.D. 95-105, a

---

[17] Wallace E. Fisher, *Preaching and Parish Renewal* (Nashville: Abingdon Press, 1966), p. 157.

writer saturated with Paul's thought and spirit addressed the problems of his day with what Paul might have been presumed to have written if he were still present. We have no proof that the Titus of Paul's time did not serve in Crete, but the Titus here addressed is very probably a symbolic, or at least another, figure. Such historical questions aside, however, the message is addressed to Christian disciples in need of power to face the seemingly impossible.

Titus has been appointed to serve in Crete and has found it an impossible place. Of course it is bad! the letter agrees: "One of themselves, a prophet of their own, said, 'Cretans are always liars, evil beasts, lazy gluttons.' This testimony is true" (1:12-13a). What a place to have to live and work! No wonder Titus needed motivating—even as do we in the dreary round in which some of us wear our duty like a hair shirt. But, the writer adds, "This is why I left you in Crete, that you might amend what was defective" (1:5). Under such an assignment we too would need—do need, in the Cretes where we live and work—compelling reasons for carrying on. Unfolding the reasons, this letter is for us.

One reason is paramount: We are "awaiting our blessed hope, the appearing of the glory of our great God and Savior Jesus Christ" (2:13). The emphasis here is not on the deity of Christ, since most authorities agree that "the glory of the great God and of our Savior" is an equally valid translation, if not a better one. The *stress* rather is on the blessed hope of his appearing. We are not left to "amend what is defective" in Crete by our own solitary efforts. When our strength seems exhausted there is another power to which to turn. He "who gave himself for us to redeem us from all iniquity" (vs. 14) will meet us again. In the power of that certainty we can go on.

So, in the face of the dreadfulness of Crete we can count on the transforming power of God, which "has appeared for the salvation of all men"—even these impossible Cretans! Experience underlines that. "For we ourselves were once foolish, disobedient, led astray, slaves to various passions and pleasures, passing our days in malice and envy, hated by men and hating one another" (3:3). The columns of any day's newspaper document that. Yet out of such human stuff God has already transformed a people chosen as his own, not because of their efforts but because of his mercy (3:5).

What he has done, he can do again. Are Cretans "always liars"? Now they are to learn "to speak evil of no one" (3:2). Are they "evil beasts"? Now they are to "avoiding quarreling, to be gentle, and to show perfect courtesy toward all men" (3:2). Impossible reversal? Not at all. Witness the change effected on missionary frontiers. "You say the Bible is an outmoded book in your country?" said a Sarawak Christian to a young Western sophisticate. "You can thank God it is not outmoded here—or you would not be a guest at this meal, but its main dish." The change depends not on failing men, but on a transforming God who in Jesus Christ has appeared (3:4) and for whose appearing again we wait in hope (2:13).

It is worth noting that "radical" theologies which dismiss this hope are the products of an affluent age in a prosperous land. They optimistically propose to work their secularized miracles of rebuilding by unaided human power. Such thin diet may suffice for easy times, but when men struggle with impossible situations—depression, war, some ultimate personal Crete—those who persist and finally prevail are those who are buoyed up by this "blessed hope, the appearing of the glory of our great God and Savior Jesus Christ." God meets us at our extremities. A classic prayer entreats his coming "in the end of the day, in the end of our life, in the end of the world." Some of us know from our own experience that he comes at the end of our resources, the end of our goodness, the end of our strength, the end of human hope. "The God of hopeless cases." [18] sustains us who live in expectation of his coming to take a hand in our affairs.

On Divine Initiative: Matthew 1:18-25

For this dramatic preface to the Gospel, Matthew sets the stage in Joseph's *mind*—"an angel of the Lord appeared to him in a dream" (vs. 20)—as if to suggest that here are answers to questions the mind must ponder. Who is Jesus? Whence does he come? By what power does he work? All that transpires in the dream underscores one truth: *he came on divine initiative; in him God acts.*

The first Christians did not base this belief on special circumstances concerning his birth. Paul's letters, our earliest written sources concerning the faith, written over twenty years' time, evangelize by every means the great apostle's fertile mind could devise, in the name of a Lord of whom he wrote, "God was in Christ reconciling the world to himself" (II Cor. 5:19). Yet never in all his letters does Paul base that faith on a miraculous birth. Mark wrote the earliest gospel, for readers who could not assimilate it with other gospels in a finished Bible, but must needs get from its unaided testimony all that was important concerning the Christ. Presenting it as "the gospel of Jesus Christ, the Son of God" (Mark 1:1), Mark did not think a miraculous birth important enough to the faith even to include a birth story.

It remained for Matthew and Luke, almost a generation later, to convey in their nativity accounts the church's maturing reflection on the questions, Who is Jesus? Whence does he come? By what power does he work? When Matthew set down these reflections in Joseph's dream, he was primarily concerned to record our Lord's birth not as a biological but as a theological truth.

One of the most vital Christian leaders of this century was delayed in espousing the faith in his youth because that distinction had been blurred. One day he met the eminent theologian, William Newton Clarke. Later he wrote of that interview that Clarke

soon had me talking about my problems. Troubled about the virgin birth of Jesus, I remarked that I could believe that Jesus was spiritually but not that he was physically divine. "Physically divine?" said Dr. Clarke with a quizzical inflection. There was dead silence for a moment and then I said: "That is nonsense, isn't it?" "Of course it is nonsense," he answered; and then added in effect that if I would start by seeing that any divinity in Jesus must consist in his spiritual quality, I might get somewhere.[19]

[18] The phrase is found in *The Ten Commandments and You,* by Harold Edwin Berg (Philadelphia: Fortress Press, 1964), p. 57.

[19] Harry Emerson Fosdick, *The Living of These Days* (New York: Harper, 1956), pp. 55-56.

That is where the earliest Christians began. "She will bear a son, and you shall call his name Jesus, *for he will save his people from their sins*" (vs. 21), said the angel in Joseph's dream. That is a spiritual achievement, doing in the realm of our most crucial personal struggles what only God can do. "O Israel, hope in the Lord," the psalmist wrote; "he will redeem Israel from all his iniquities" (Ps. 130:7, 8). What men looked to God alone to do, they found in experience that Jesus had done for them. He saved them from their sins—for which Matthew uses the Greek word *hamartion*, literally "missing the mark." Many a man, then and now, who has been missing the mark of what he knew he was meant to be, has been released by Jesus to grow into his full humanity. Christ, who did that for us, came on divine initiative. In him God acts.

Matthew found a symbol of this truth in the quotation he lifted from the prophecy of Isaiah:

> "Behold, a virgin shall conceive and bear a son,
> and his name shall be called Emmanuel

(which means, God with us)" (vs. 23). Why does Matthew quote "virgin" from a passage in which Isaiah (7:14 RSV) reads "young woman"? The prophet's Hebrew word, *almah*, does not carry the necessary connotation of "virgin," but means simply "young woman." Matthew, however, knew the passage through its Greek translation, where the translator had used *parthenos*, which could mean "young woman" but generally meant "virgin." To Matthew's tradition this suggested a fitting symbol of the meaning of Christ's life: he came on divine initiative; in him, as in no other, God acts.

By whatever symbol we represent it, that is the compelling truth about him as each of us can experience it. He sets us free from sin and self to become what God intends us to be. There is only one condition. For us, as for Joseph, what begins in the realm of the mind must be completed on the field of obedient act. His dream completed, "when Joseph woke from sleep, he did as the angel of the Lord commanded him" (vs. 24). Over that route any man can find Christ's liberation. As John later reported the Master's words, "If any man's will is to do his will, he shall know whether the teaching is from God" (John 7:16).

CHRISTMASTIDE

Long before Christmas was celebrated, Christianity burst on the world as an Easter faith. The weekly observance of Sunday as the Lord's Day is a constantly recurring "little Easter." The Resurrection transformed the cross from a dread gallows to a symbol of victory and life eternal. Had there been no Easter, there would have been no New Testament; Jesus would have been another martyred prophet, and from his death no good news could come. So powerfully did Easter engross the attention of the early Christians that the first generations of the church gave no thought to the celebration of the nativity.

Inevitably, however, Christians turned to the keeping of a day of grateful remembrance of Jesus' birth, and that not merely for sentimental reasons. The celebration became a powerful weapon against surrounding paganism. In A.D. 274 the Emperor Aurelian introduced at Rome the festival of the Invincible Sun, a pagan observance which, because of a mistake in the calendar calculating December 25 as the winter solstice, fell on that day. Amid the revelry and vice of this bacchanalia, sometime prior to A.D. 336, Christians began to observe the day as the birth not of the sun-god but of Christ, the Sun of Righteousness.

Not only in Christian resistance to paganism, but in the safeguarding of the church's teaching against heresy, the Christmas festival served a purpose far beyond sentiment and glitter. The Gnostics, on the one hand, taught a doctrine that made Christ's full humanity a mere seeming, since they believed divinity too holy to touch mere bodily life on our soiled earth. The later Arian doctrine, at the other extreme, contended that the human Jesus was adopted into divinity. It became important to the church to have a festival devoted to the celebration of our Lord's Incarnation, fully human and fully divine. The festival now takes its place in the life of the church as a season of joy with the vital function of teaching the true meaning of the Incarnation.

CHRISTMAS DAY

Theme for Trumpets: Isaiah 9:2, 6-7

"The Christian message," Gerald Kennedy observes, "is no longer played on a trumpet but on a violin. It is a soothing, gentle lullaby. . . . Religion becomes a spiritual aspirin tablet for a divine glass of ovaltine." Such qualities are symptoms of sick religion, to which this song of Isaiah, orchestrated for trumpets, brings a tonic response.

It was written to grace an occasion for trumpets. For the anointing of one of Israel's kings—possibly the good King Hezekiah—may have brought forth this messianic hymn. But its measures contain more than mere boastful nationalism; it promises the endurance of the Davidic throne as an instrument of God's service in leading a covenant people called to be his witnesses.

Since the first century, Christians have sung it as a coronation song for the Lord Jesus, as the echoes in the hymn in Luke 1:32-33 give evidence. In our day it is so wedded to the music of Handel's *Messiah* that we cannot read it in the flat voice of daily speech. Christians of the first century, or of the twentieth, know in Christ an experience beyond the power of common prose to describe. Small wonder that in shaping the vehicle for its expression they have had recourse to this ancient coronation hymn. For what Christ means to those who have met him in more than a nodding acquaintance on sentimental occasions can only be expressed in terms of coronation. See what this ancient theme for trumpets proclaims about him.

He comes as light. "The people who walked in darkness have seen a great light" (vs. 2), sang Isaiah, remembering the reign of Ahaz with its impoverishment through disastrous alliances, its chaotic breakdown of public morality, its witchcraft and pagan teaching, of which he could say: "Surely for this word which they speak there is no dawn" (8:16-22). Referring today to "shadowed lands"—lands of war, refugees, poverty, or lands of paganism—we echo Isaiah: "on those who live in a land of deep shadow a light has shone" (vs. 2b JB). If the coming of Hezekiah meant *that* to a people who had been through the darkness of the reign of Ahaz, the coming of Christ into any life brings light more resplendent. Isaiah described the end of horrible warfare as part of that light (vss. 3-5, omitted from this lection). Can we be in earnest about our "Prince of Peace" (vs. 6) without making strenuous efforts to follow him to that light? But "peace," for ancient Hebrews or for modern Christians, is more than war's termination; it is a new quality of living, in harmony with ourselves, with others, and with God. Christ brings that.

Christ comes as royal Son. "To us a son is given" (vs. 6), sang Isaiah, since at his coronation the king was believed to become in some special sense God's son as leader of a messianic people (cf. Ps. 2:7, in another coronation hymn). In a sense far more significant Christ comes as God's Son, revealing his nature and acting in his power. To the first-century mind it was a "scandal" that the *universal* God should be proclaimed as coming in a *particular* man—carpenter, Galilean outlander, crucified. Some present-day theologies, scandalized in the same way, talk vaguely of God incarnated in "humanity." They miss the light of the real Incarnation, for "humanity" is vague and general and offers no norm for the understanding of God or ourselves. "Humanity" is everybody and nobody; and such an incarnation is part pantheism and part nihilism. But the real Incarnation is God coming in the sharp particularity of the character, ministry, death, and resurrection of Jesus; and that is a light in which we can walk with understanding and joy.

Christ comes as the summation of greatness. Isaiah sang of a

> Wonderful Counselor, Mighty God,
> Everlasting Father, Prince of Peace (vs. 6).

What a golden age the reign of such a monarch would be! Those who have best known Jesus have found in him such a likeness to all this that it has sung its way into the Christmas liturgies of all churches. Do we still know him well enough to find in him the supreme gifts? One eighth-grade class did not. Asked to name the ten most important people in history, the 32 pupils listed 137 nominations; and when the tabulations were finished, the three first places went to Lincoln, Washington and Benjamin Franklin, with Jesus in fifth place. Were the children recording the values our society had taught them? Can such a society be Christian? Can it be healthy?

Christ comes as King forever and ever. Of the stability of Hezekiah's just order, sang Isaiah ,"there will be no end" (vs. 7). In a way far surer, we can say that of Christ. William Temple put it truly: "When we serve Him in humble loyalty, He reigns; when we serve Him self-assertedly, He reigns; when we rebel and seek to withhold our services, He reigns." [1] His reign does not depend on our vote; history is the record of his judgments. Happy are they who faithfully obey his rule.

From Peril to Promise: Galatians 4:1-7

Christmas has not come for us until we can read these words as personal history: "When the time had fully come, God sent forth his Son, born of woman, born under the law, to redeem those who were under the law, so that we might receive adoption as sons" (vss. 4-5). This *adoption* is God's new

[1] Quoted in *Twelve Baskets Full*, by Margaret Applegarth (New York: Harper, 1957), p. 26.

Day for us, this *redemption* is the Nativity grown personal, this *time fully come* is Christmas personally come true.

Kyle Haselden has argued that whenever preaching is true to its calling it presents the *peril* in which we stand, the *promise* that lies before us, and the *Alterant* who can make the difference.[2] This passage demands such proclamation.

Consider the *peril*. Apart from Christ we are "slaves to the elemental spirits of the universe" (vs. 3). Much is packed into the phrase, as its various possible translations imply. AT renders it "slaves to material ways of looking at things"—and the nineteenth century's "nature, red in tooth and claw" was never a more fierce jungle than we make with our *materialisms*. JB reads "elemental principles of this world" and explains in a note that this refers "to the elements that make up the physical universe . . . ; Paul uses the phrase to indicate both the Law that minutely regulated the use of these elements . . . and the spirits that used the Law . . . to dominate the universe"—and we know from tragic experience something about the suprapersonal structures (corporations, unions, political parties, governments) that indulge in such *manipulation to dominate*. VWS shows that the Greek implies, among other things, "elements of Nature" or "personal, elemental spirits"—and while our *drives and impulses* that can take matters in their own hands are not quite the same thing, they are not greatly different. What a catalog of perils! Yet the sum of the matter is that they tell the truth about us; this is who we are. Only as we see ourselves in this stark reality can we know the wonder of the promise-come-true in Christ's nativity as personal experience.

Consider the *promise*. Throughout this passage Paul pursues the figure of a child not yet come of age, living under the promise of full freedom to enter into his inheritance. But the figure is redoubled: the bondage is that of one who really is a slave, and the inheritance is that of one who has been both set free and adopted as an heir. The biographies of all mature Christians testify that we can be freed from "the elemental spirits" that bind us, to become inheritors of a full life. In the face of the worst we can find the reconciliation that knows God no longer as dreaded Master but as "Abba! Father!" (vs. 6). We never know what release that spells until we hear Jesus, in Gethsemane, praying, "Abba, Father, all things are possible to thee; remove this cup from me; yet not what I will, but what thou wilt" (Mark 14:36). Entering his prayer "clean forspent, forspent," he came from it "well content." He could face the worst that evil, death, and the devil could do to him, and win his victory. We can meet life's darkest passages with a like wholehearted acceptance, but not without an Alterant to change the peril to promise.

Consider the *Alterant*. "God sent forth his Son . . . to redeem . . . , so that we might receive adoption as sons" (vss. 4-5). By God's act in Christ all this comes about, as the closing line underscores: "You are therefore no longer a slave but a son, and if a son, then also by God's own act an heir" (vs. 7 NEB). Powerless to achieve this freedom for ourselves, we receive it by God's act in Christ. When we are *redeemed from the peril* and *adopted into*

[2] Kyle Haselden, *The Urgency of Preaching* (New York: Harper, 1963), pp. 42-70.

the promised relation by Christ's nativity, accepted in our personal response to him, God's *time has fully come* and Christmas is earth-changing reality.

Event Prolonged in Meaning: Luke 2:1-20

"It had all happened as they had been told" (vs. 20 NEB)—that is stark, sheer *event*. "The shepherds returned, glorifying and praising God for all they had heard and seen"—that is life-renewing *meaning*. Luke has written an exquisite blend of history and art, happening and significance, the once-transpired and the always-present. With a historian's care, he dates and localizes the event by correlation with the reign of Augustus and the administration of Quirinius (vss. 1-2). Whether or not we can fully know "the historical Jesus," his career is historic actuality. Christian faith takes history seriously. God comes in event—supremely in events that center in Jesus, the Christ.

Luke weaves the wonder of this story with the warp of event and the woof of interpretative meaning. Augustus, Quirinius, Jesus were sober history. But could film catch the image of the multitude of heaven's host, or magnetic tape record their hymn of proclamation and praise? Yet these elements of history and poetry join to report what the church found by experience to be true and what the centuries verify. *Event prolonged in meaning declares that God's good news came to common men to free them from fear into joy and wonder.*

The story of the angels and the shepherds (vss. 8-14) puts in unforgettable picture the startling truth that God came—and comes—to common men going about their secular affairs. The shepherds were engaged in a common business of the region; and our faith—whose Lord was a carpenter, its first witnesses fishermen, and its greatest theologian and missionary a tentmaker—began by showing at the Nativity that God does not reserve his visitations and insights nor scholars and clergy. Moreover the shepherds belonged to "the people of the land" (*'Am Ha'arez*), "the common people who were too burdened with making a living to be much concerned about ritual purity";[3] and Jesus persisted in taking the side of such common people against the privileged Pharisees. "This crowd, who do now know the law, are accursed" (John 7:49), sneered the Pharisees. But the shepherds, who belonged to that class, received the angels' visit; and Jesus identified himself with such people at cost of crucifixion. That should prompt long thoughts in a day of social revolution.

God's good news of a Savior is designed to free the shepherds—and us—from fear (vss. 10-14). The Savior has been born, "Christ the Lord" (vs. 11). The phrase is meaningful. "Christ" is the Greek equivalent of the Hebrew "Messiah," and of messiahs there had been—and are—many, most of whom have left a trail of blood. But this Messiah "is also called 'Lord,' a title the O.T. reserves for God. A new era is beginning."[4] Our time knows its multiplied messiahs: scientism, education, legislation, various ideologies.

[3] Article on 'Am Ha' Arez, *Interpreter's Dictionary of the Bible* (Nashville: Abingdon Press, 1962), I, 106-7.
[4] *The Jerusalem Bible* (Garden City, N.Y.: Doubleday, 1966), footnote to Luke 2:11.

Finite, they make infinite claims; and so, repeatedly, they bring tragic consequences. Conflicting with one another, they multiply misery as they complicate conflict.

One typical "messiah" of our time is our trust in armaments.

To an alarming extent, our national economy is being tied to our national defense, so that the time may come when we can no longer afford to disarm. . . . Nations which depend on huge military establishments to maintain their economy cannot afford to be peace loving. They need always to search for enemies in order to justify their defense expenditures.[5]

Like the shepherds, we can be freed from fear only when we know a Messiah who is *the Lord* even of such areas of our common life.

God's good news came to common men to free them from fear into joy and wonder. So they "returned, glorifying and praising God" (vs. 20). The mood of such joy is the prevailing atmosphere of the New Testament. The presence of such joy is the seal of validity in authentic Christian life. The absence of such joy is the denial of our witness, as Nietzsche reminded us in his jibe that he might believe in the Savior when we Christians began to look like the saved! One of England's angry young men shouts the demand:

Sing you silly sod! . . . Sing that a flower is a flower and the world is a wedding. Sing because we are. . . . Even if we are going to be annihilated that was no reason to die before we died. Sing to wake the living and the dead. Just sing. Say yes to life. Yes, yes, yes, and yes again.[6]

Good advice! But do we have within us the resources for such joyful affirmations? There is one proven source. "Let us go over to Bethlehem and see this thing that has happened, which the Lord has made known to us" (vs. 15).

FIRST SUNDAY AFTER CHRISTMAS

The Audacity of the Gospel: Isaiah 42:1-9

With students and other youth home for the holidays, the Sunday after Christmas offers many a church unusual opportunity to challenge the mind of its young people. We may well begin with a recognition of the difficulty of faith in our time. Three lost presuppositions can be cited. Our time has lost the sense of God as the "living, sovereign, Holy One of the Bible." It has lost the "sense of community, of the fact that God works with us through a covenant." And it has lost a "view of nature and history" in which we can "see the hand of God at work . . . ; the world has become greater than our picture of God."[7]

[5] Berg, *The Ten Commandments and You*, pp. 54-55.
[6] Bernard Kops, as quoted in *James Bond's World of Values*, by Lycurgus M. Starkey, Jr. (Nashville: Abingdon Press, 1966), p. 75.
[7] Three lost presuppositions cited by David S. Schuller, *Emerging Shapes of the Church* (St. Louis: Concordia, 1967), p. 33.

Rather than face these difficulties by argument or accommodation of the gospel to their positions, let us confront them with the audacious counter claim that stands at the heart of the Christian faith: *God calls the Church of Christ to the mission of sharing a true way of life with all men.* How can we dare to take such a position? This bold statement from Isaiah provides some answers, rubbed smooth by centuries that provide a kind of verification of their claim.

God calls a servant people, unlikely though that seems. "Behold my servant, whom I uphold" (vs. 1), the prophet begins. Who is this servant? The context has just named him: "But you, Israel, my servant" (41:8). We do not know by half how audacious that is until we see that Servant Israel was a defeated, captive people living in exile, and that the prophets had assured them that this fate was God's punishment for their national sins. Yet, Isaiah dared to say, even in exile God would use this people as his witness. Through the exile God would make this once proud people tender, strong, and pure for his service. The subsequent history of Israel shows how much of the best of that people's witness did come from this shattering experience.

It may be necessary to add that this was not *political* Israel, then or now, but Israel as a community of faith. As centuries went on, that faith hardened until in Jesus' day its great message of God's love had been trivialized by Pharisaic excesses. When Israel as a total people, or even in the "remnant" of which the prophets spoke, had failed to be the Servant Isaiah depicted, Jesus answered the call. These nine verses can be read as a description of him! Audacious as it seemed for one lone man to assume such a mission for the world, twenty centuries of history record how truly he fulfilled the call. Its fulfillment was and is possible, however, only because there is a continuing people incorporated into him—his church, the "new Israel," the continuing servant people. If the claim is audacious for us, it was audacious for Israel and for our Lord before us. True for them, it can be true for us.

God sets his servant people to witness to a true way of life. The word "justice" which occurs three times in vss. 1-4 translates the Hebrew *mishpat,* a word with no exact equivalent in English. "Justice" is a convenient way of saying it, but we should be alerted to the rich complexity of its meaning by the variety of other terms used by various translators: "right," "true religion," "judgment," "the true way of life." Specifics of the task are spelled out in vs. 7: to bring sight to the blind and freedom to those imprisoned in darkness—to release "darkened lives from prison" (MT). Note the daring claim that the servant "will not fail . . . till he has established justice" (*mishpat,* the true way of life) "in the earth"—audacious for exiled Israel, audacious for Jesus, but vindicated by the centuries-long spread of the message. It is still audacious. Though the Church's 980,000,000 Christians seem a great force, a world population approaching four billion at the rate of 120,000 persons a day is a formidable objective. Under God that is our call.

God underwrites this audacious call by the vitality of a great faith. Why do we suppose that we can fulfill the assignment? Because of the greatness of the God who calls us to it (vss. 6-7). In the face of the glitter of Babylon's pagan worship, Isaiah proclaimed the God who alone exists, through whom all else exists, who will share his praise with none; and that is still our testimony. The insights this faith had prompted in the prophets had warned of this judgment by exile, and the God whose past insights had been vindicated would now do a new thing (vs. 9). He calls his servant people to work in the quiet, healing, growing ways to which the future belongs, the prophet declared; not by the fanfare of noisy voices "heard in the street" (vs. 2), but by the kindness that will hurt no weak thing (vs. 3) and the teaching testimony that opens blind eyes (vs. 7). Picturing that in terms of the most idealistic service of Peace Corps, mission, the helping and healing professions, and of every true Christian, you see the audacity and power of the servant whom God calls today.

By This We Know: I John 4:9-16

A school principal, according to Halford E. Luccock, once called to inquire about Christmas hymns usable in a school program. All that she had been able to find, she said, were "so theological." From her viewpoint the answer was not very reassuring: "Christmas is a pretty theological affair." When it ceases to be theological, it becomes cheaply sentimental or vacuously empty.

The Christmas message of God's sending his saving love in Jesus, his Son, is nowhere more succinctly stated than in this passage. "By this we know that we abide in him and he in us," it declares, "because he has given us of his own Spirit" (vs. 13). As the context makes clear, this Spirit is not vague or undefined. We know him in the historic person of Jesus and in the present experience of a love which is not our achievement but a response to God's love as it has been given to us. "It appears," writes C. H. Dodd, "that it was the author's intention to lead up to a conclusion affirming the certainty of the faith, at a moment when many minds were made doubtful or hesitant by the doctrinal disputes which had broken out." [8] Now, in another time of uncertainty born of theological dispute, it speaks strongly to us.

It assures us that *we can know God in Jesus*—a welcome word in a day troubled by feelings of God's "absence" or "death." "In this," it begins, "the love of God was made manifest" (NEB: "disclosed"; JB: "revealed"; MT: "has appeared"; PT: "the greatest demonstration"), "that God sent his only Son into the world, *so that we might live through him*" (vs. 9, italics added). To the historic witness in the life, death, and resurrection of Jesus is added the *personal experience of new life,* a convincing fact. And this new life has its own specific content: out of our hatred and indifference we are brought to love; in that change of ethical climate we know God. For God is the emphatic first word in the Greek of vs. 12, so that MT follows the authentic word order—"God no one has ever seen; but if we love one another, then God remains within us, and love for him is complete in us." Not doctrinaire speculations or airy mysticism, but history and ethical transformation—both anchored in Jesus Christ—are the roots of our knowledge of God.

This message assures us, again, that *the God known in Jesus is present reality.* Much of the talk of the death of God deals with the *kenosis* passage (Phil. 2:7) as if it—and the implication drawn from it, that God so emptied himself into Jesus that at Bethlehem God the Father ceased to exist—were the only seriously theological text in the New Testament. John's characteristic word, here and throughout his writings, is that "God sent his only Son into the world" (vs. 9). That deserves at least as much attention as a forced interpretation of *kenosis*.

Death-of-God talk often deals with the Incarnation as if, having little to do with the historic reality of Jesus, it were a vague incarnation of God in humanity in general. A leading proponent of "radical theology" writes: "Once granted that *Existenz* in our time is swallowed up in a radically immanent mode of being, then the Christ who is an 'answer' to our condition must be a wholly immanent Word that is fully detached from the Jesus of history." [9] The New Testament not only accepts nothing of such a docetic, disembodied Christ; considerable portions of it, including this epistle, were written to refute that doctrine. This passage ties the Incarnation firmly to the historic Jesus: "Whoever confesses that *Jesus* is the Son of God, God abides in him, and he in God" (vs. 15, italics added).

A litany once used in a Chicago church indicates something of where the theology of incarnation in humanity-in-general can lead. It prays: "O God, who is all men; O God, who smells and has no place to bathe; O God, who is a bum, a chiseler, who is lazy; O God, who hangs on street corners, who tastes the grace of cheap wine and the sting of the needle . . ." [10] The motive of such a prayer is the laudable intent to identify Christian concern with the most rejected members of urban society, but it misses the distinctions that need to be made between a God who is *with* man in caring and redeeming love, and a God who "*is* all men." Begin with such a God, and you have no basis for ethical judgment, no standard ever again for any clear thinking about the God you have lost in a sentimentally homogenized mass. This strong Christmas lesson keeps all the human concern without that theological bankruptcy.

This message assures us, finally, that *the God we know in Jesus as present reality is attested by authentic witnesses*. "We have seen and testify" (vs. 14) that all this is true, the writer declares. Its firsthand quality is emphatic. Many a man and woman in every Christian generation can join the testimony to undeniably real events in which all this surges in their own pulses in ways that can be tested and verified. For he heals the malady of our sinfulness; God "sent his Son to be the expiation for our sins" (vs. 10). Westcott well says of the verb used in the Greek text that its implication "is not that of appeasing one who is angry, with a personal feeling, against the offender; but of altering the character of that which, from without, occasions a necessary alienation, and interposes an inevitable obstacle to fellowship." [11] For God's love in Jesus Christ releases in us an answering love that changes the whole climate of our life.

[9] Thomas J. J. Altizer, *Radical Theology and the Death of God,* co-author William Hamilton (Indianapolis: Bobbs-Merrill, 1966), p. 11.

[10] The Rev. Archie Hargraves, First Congregational Church of Chicago, as reported in *The Christian Century,* July 21, 1965.

[11] Vincent, *Word Studies in the New Testament,* II, 325.

The Revolutionary Reality of Christmas: John 1:1-14

"And the Word became flesh and dwelt among us" (vs. 14)—that could become present, revolutionary reality for some of us now. Even for those who do not believe this good news, it must be plain that it *would* be important if it were true. The divinity of Christ is not a fabric of naïve legend, but a profound and penetrating philosophy.

John sums it up in a sentence: "No one has ever seen God; the only Son, who is in the bosom of the Father, he has made him known" (vs. 18; though the lection stops at vs. 14, John's prologue is an indivisible unit extending through this verse). God is the unseen reality on whom all things depend; yet, though we could not live without him, we can live without recognizing him; just as you can see everything through your eyes, but never see them. You catch them fleetingly in the mirror, always in the same position; but, save for that one position, staring straight at you, you never see them. The means of all your seeing, themselves unseen! So it is with God; though we live in him, we do not see him.

Jesus is the clue to his character. Until we meet Jesus, God is abstract. We reason and make inferences about him; we come to fragmentary understandings of his ways, but we do not know him. "No one has ever seen God"; yet in Jesus all of God that can come into a human life, all of God that needs to come into a human life, became flesh and dwells among us.

Being true, this good news is vastly important. God is not too holy for common life, but takes his place squarely in the midst of it. "The Word"—the eternal Logos, truth, reason, mind, purpose, back of all creation—"the Word became flesh."

"Flesh," as John Wesley remarked, "sometimes signifies corrupt nature; sometimes the body; sometimes, as here, the whole man." [12] And to our present-day studies nothing is plainer than that the whole man is a rich and complicated interaction of body, mind, and spirit. The body, with its hungers, sex urges, weariness, its satisfactions and its needs, is a basic ingredient of the whole personality; and God was not too holy to take his place in the midst of all this. By so doing he shows us that our bodies are not of themselves unclean, but can be instruments through which mind and spirit reach their highest levels of achievement.

Many a man thinks of God as above the struggle of our stormy life. Then this good news bursts upon us, that "the Word became flesh and dwelt among us." Manger child, carpenter, cross-bearer, he knows our limitations. He understands our struggles. He has shared our weakness. He cared enough to take it upon himself. Nothing could be so uncalculating as God plunging into human life! He did not come because of a neatly proven argument that if he loved us enough we would love him in return. He came when, at the very least, he knew crucifixion was an open possibility; or, as the New Testament declares, when he knew it was inevitable. Yet he came, not because it would pay, but because in the nature of the case, love does such things. How vastly different from our scheming plans!

[12] John Wesley, *Explanatory Notes Upon the New Testament*, edition of 1788, comment on John 1:14.

True and important, this good news is the foundation of all our hope. For it says: We are not left to struggle alone for the fulfillment of what we know we ought to be. As John put it, "From his fullness have we all received, grace upon grace" (vs. 16).

It is not a matter of our doing; if it were, there might be something in our wistful word, "If only I could!" But it does not depend on us alone. "From his fullness have we all received," says John, obviously speaking out of some depth of experience. Nothing is plainer in the repeated experience which spans these centuries than that we are not left on our own in this matter. We hunger, and yearn, and pray, and expect, and try, and fail, and try again; but on the other side, God is at work, giving us the courage and the will and the transformed desire.

One grace after another, that is the classic Christian experience. We make a decision to give ourselves to Christ, knowing only part of where it leads; and he gives us victory over a small temptation, and then a greater, and a greater. He helps us break an old habit and then leads on to a new concern for others. He compels us to be honest and then lures us further to be generous. Thus he leads us from one victory to another, "grace upon grace."

A famous psychiatrist once wrote concerning a patient, "These people say they *cannot;* their friends say they *will* not; we doctors know they *cannot will.*" Have we been like that—going on in our mediocrity, accepting our crippling habits, our paralyzing moods, our failure to grow into what God meant us to be? We need not! "Grace upon grace," Christ is the present liberator of those who cannot will.[13]

SECOND SUNDAY AFTER CHRISTMAS

The Best to the Brave: Zechariah 2:10-13

"For sudden the worst turns to the best to the brave," sang Robert Browning as he contemplated the pangs of death. The truth in the line does not rest on unsupported human courage; bravery that endures is underwritten by faith. That is the importance of this prophetic oracle for us as a New Year begins. Knowing that uncertainties and dangers await us, we welcome this word of tested assurance spoken by Zechariah.

Perils at flood tide threatened him and his people. Poverty had left its mark upon them. "There was no wage for man or any wage for beast," he recalled, "neither was there any safety from the foe for him who went out or came in; for I set every man against his fellow" (8:10). Responding, the prophet offered faith's promise that "My cities shall again overflow with prosperity, and the Lord will again comfort Zion" (1:17). Having known national defeat and uprooting, the people faced new threats. They saw the life they had made for themselves in the land of their exile menaced by still further conquests to come (vss. 6-9). Into this complex of troubles Zechariah

[13] This exposition of John 1:1-14 is condensed from Merrill R. Abbey, *Encounter With Christ* (Nashville: Abingdon Press, 1961), pp. 148-56.

injected his tonic faith that, despite all appearances to the contrary, God's better age was about to dawn—an age in which joy and gladness would drive out the memory of past distress. "Sing and rejoice, O daughter of Zion; for lo, I come and I will dwell in the midst of you, says the Lord" (vs. 10).

To his age, and to ours, the prophet declared that *God comes in the worst times to bring the strength of hope to those who trust him.*

Faith assures us that in the worst times God is present. "I come and I will dwell in the midst of you"; this recurring theme binds this passage together. It is a fitting theme for Christmastide, as we renew our awareness of God's coming to dwell among us in Jesus Christ. A columnist, inquiring into the saving habits of working girls, found that they are saving little. "Money saved," the report said, "is for dreams, and nobody is having dreams today. They're having nightmares." The story then appealed to the bravery of pioneers who, amid greater dangers, opened the frontier. It forgot to say that the pioneers possessed a rugged faith that underwrote courage. For courage in our uncertain times we need to build on the faith that hears God say, "I come and I will dwell in the midst of you."

God, present amid the worst, strengthens hope of a better future. Repeating God's promise—"I will dwell in the midst of you"—Zechariah looked forward to a better day for the nations. "And many nations shall join themselves to the Lord in that day, and shall be my people" (vs. 11). As Isaiah of the Exile had believed in God's use of this dark experience—"I will give you as a light to the nations, that my salvation may reach to the end of the earth" (Isa. 49:6)—so Zechariah believed God was building a better future.

Hope of the better future prompts witness that builds with him. "He has roused himself from his holy dwelling" (vs. 13), proclaimed Zechariah, certain that God was coming from his heavenly temple to dwell with his earthly people. "And you shall know that the Lord of hosts has sent me to you" (vs. 12a), he declared, certain that he was called to the witness that would help to assure God's better day. This is still faith's outcome. Out of the nightmare of Auschwitz Eli Wiesel came, saying, "I am the witness who will not let you rest. I am the conscience come to trouble you. I have seen it, and I have been spared to make the world remember, lest it sink below the waves of unrelieved brutality."

Rabbi David Polish recalls an inscription found on a concentration camp wall: "I believe in the sun even when it does not shine. I believe in love even when it is denied to me. I believe in God even when He hides from me." [14] That kind of witness helps to build the future it believes in.

He Holds Our World Together: Hebrews 1:1-12

"He reflects the glory of God and bears the very stamp of his nature, upholding the universe by his word of power" (vs. 3a). Here is the functional heart of this vital passage. If a single proposition can gather up its treasure, it may be summarized as saying: *God spoke his final word, performed his cen-*

[14] David Polish, *The Dead Cannot Praise God* (Evanston: Beth Emet Foundation, 1967), p. 8.

tral act in Jesus who is the Christ, to reconcile our estrangement and purify our sins.

In Christ, God spoke not his first but his culminating word. He came as no stranger. "In many and various ways God spoke of old to our fathers by the prophets" (vs. 1). Through Amos and Micah he issued a stern ethical demand:

> But let justice roll down like waters,
> and righteousness like an ever-flowing stream
> (Amos 5:24).

Without this true and necessary word our thought of God would remain cheap and our life tawdry. Yet it called to a steep ascent of heaven too strenuous for our poor powers. Law, important and needed first word, required another for its completion: "The law was our custodian until Christ came, that we might be justified by faith" (Gal. 3:24).

Through Hosea God spoke the welcome word of love. Yet the story of suffering love in Hosea's household was not sufficient to point to the love of God. Another word was needed: "For God so loved the world that he gave his only Son, that whoever believes in him should not perish but have eternal life" (John 3:16).

Through the prophet of the Exile, God spoke of the suffering servant. Commanding the vision, heartbreaking the disappointment of its unfulfilled hope. The haunting, elusive lines sang themselves in the heart as a cry of unanswered need until Calvary made them a song of gratitude that Christ "emptied himself, taking the form of a servant . . . and became obedient unto death, even death on a cross" (Phil. 2:7-8).

This lesson from Hebrews declares that God *has spoken.* In Christ he has given his ultimate revelation of himself. "In these last days he has spoken to us by a Son, whom he appointed heir of all things" (vs. 2). Christ is fully man, the gospel insists, yet in him God acted. The New Testament records never suppress his human qualities. His birth and childhood, his temptations, his hunger and thirst, his weariness, his sorrow and weeping, his suffering and death make that evident. Yet these documents assert unanimously that in him we witness God's act. Heb. 1:2 is typical in making God the subject of the verbs: God "has spoken"; God "appointed" him his heir.

God acted in Jesus, who shared our lot. In his humanity he moved amid uncertainties; he walked, as must we, by faith. In prayer he was dependent on the Father. Standing with us in all things, he can be our Savior. As the Letter to the Hebrews reminds us: "We have not a high priest who is unable to sympathize with our weaknesses, but one who in every respect has been tempted as we are, yet without sinning" (4:15).

From this truth see two all-important outcomes. The first is that God's Word in Christ holds our life together. "He reflects the glory of God . . . , upholding the universe by his word of power" (1:3). Just when any soul's universe is most threatened, he most saves. During World War II, hearing of a village where no pastor remained and all authority had disintegrated, where the women had been victimized by horrors that often followed invasion, one of Germany's great scholars went to give them protection and such reassurance as he could, gathering them in the church and school, where with their children they slept in the straw. Leading their evening prayers, he assured them that "He who bore our human shame from the very day of His birth was now among them, among those who had been shamed. If they were open to Him, they could experience His presence better than in hours of supreme spiritual loftiness." [15] Far from speculation for quiet moments in an ivory tower, this great doctrine, most at home in life's darkest deeps, draws us to one who holds our world together.

God's word in Christ not only upholds our universe, it reconciles our estrangement. "When he had made purification for sins, he sat down at the right hand of the Majesty on high" (1:3b). With these words the thought moves from Bethlehem's manger and the Incarnation to Calvary and the Atonement; yet the two are observed aright only as they are held together. We hopelessly miss the depth, power, and high truth of this doctrine unless we remember whose birth we celebrate. We miss the Word God spoke uniquely in him unless we hear it as a Word from a Cross. [16]

Holy Heritage: Luke 2:21-32

Older forms of the Christian year have a festival early in January for which this is the proper lesson—the festival of the Circumcision and Naming of Jesus. This Gospel lesson for such a day makes three vital stresses.

First it shows Jesus' link with the faith of his people through the Law in which he was reared, as symbolized in the rites of circumcision (vs. 21) and purification (vss. 22-23) central to this lesson. Thus we are reminded of the holy heritage from Israel that was important to Jesus, and through him is important to us. How singularly inappropriate in the light of this is the grotesque phenomenon of anti-Semitism among Christians. Men have rationalized it by pseudo-scholarship, both biblical and anthropological, and have thereby laid the foundations for the barbaric indecencies of Dachau and Auschwitz. Yet Jesus was born into a Jewish family, nurtured in the religion of Israel, loved the synagogue and temple to the very end, and built his church on a first band of followers who were Jews, every one. As Christians we are bound in insoluble brotherhood with the people of Israel.

Second, it shows Jesus' entrance into the enduring hope of Israel. "This man was righteous and devout, looking for the consolation of Israel" (vs. 25), says this lesson concerning the aged Simeon. The poetic passage which follows focuses on the song of Simeon, typical of Jewish saints looking toward the messianic age. His hope was realized in Jesus more fully than he could know; for through Jesus the faith in the revelation of God, precious to Israel, spread to the pagan world. It was enlarged as Jesus put his stamp of fulfillment upon it, yet with powerful emphasis he declared: "Think not that I have come to abolish the law and the prophets; I have come not to abolish them but to fulfil them" (Matt. 5:17). The law has this permanence because "its

[15] Helmut Thielicke, *Out of the Depths* (Grand Rapids: Eerdmans, 1962), p. 47.

[16] This exposition of Heb. 1:1-12 is a condensation from Merrill R. Abbey, *Living Doctrine in a Vital Pulpit* (Nashville: Abingdon Press, 1964), pp. 113-22.

position is one of principle. In other words, the epochs are separate, but there is no break between them, for the elements in the former one persist into the next.[17] We live in the power of the grace Christ bestowed, but we live by the light of the law he loved and interpreted.

Third, it shows Jesus' fulfillment of the expectation of the salvation of all peoples (vss. 30-32).

The Christian gospel is indeed *a light for revelation to the Gentiles*. It affirms the reality of God—the God of Jesus Christ. It declares that man is a child of God and has value in his sight, and that this is true of all men regardless of nationality, race, color, or class. It affirms the reality of moral laws binding upon all men and all nations. It stands for human rights and fundamental freedoms. It stands for moral decency, for the sense of obligation, for good will in every human relationship, for mercy, compassion, the spirit of forgiveness and reconciliation. It stands for things without which human life becomes cruel, corrupt, insecure, and all but unbearable.[18]

[17] Hans Conzelmann, *The Theology of St. Luke* (New York: Harper, 1960), pp. 161-62.

[18] Ernest Fremont Tittle, *The Gospel According to Luke* (New York: Harper, 1951), p. 23.

EPIPHANY SEASON

Celebrated in Asia Minor and Egypt since the second century, the Epiphany Season was the second of the liturgical seasons to emerge, preceded only by the period now known as Eastertide. Like Christmas, Epiphany preempted a pagan festival of the winter solstice, in this case the birth of the god Aeon, which had been celebrated on January 6 because of a calculation of the solstice as falling on that day, which had been carried forward since 1996 B.C.

The word "Epiphany" comes from the Greek word which means "appearing," usually applied to a visible manifestation of a hidden deity. It is the word translated "appearing" as II Tim. 1:10 speaks of the power which God "now has manifested through the appearing of our Savior Christ Jesus"; and as I Tim. 6:14 looks forward to "the appearing of our Lord Jesus Christ." Hence, as alternative titles of the day—Feast of the Manifestation or Feast of the Appearing of Christ—suggest, its stress falls on God's revelation through Christ.

Originally a celebration of our Lord's birth and baptism, it underwent change after December 25 came to be celebrated as the nativity festival. In the East, Jesus' baptism still held the Epiphany focus; late in the fourth century the *Apostolic Consitutions*, listing times of rest from labor, directed: "Let them rest on the festival of Epiphany, because on it a manifestation took place of the divinity of Christ, for the Father bore testimony to Him at the baptism." In the West the Epiphany emphasis fell on the visit of the Wise Men, who came some time after the nativity, finding the holy family, not at the inn manger but in a house, and precipitating Herod's slaughter of infants under two years of age, which suggests a possibly extended time lapse. This revelation to Gentile visitors keynotes the dimension of the faith as mission, leading to a note of missionary concern in worship and preaching. It points to enlarged horizons in applying the gospel: to understanding between faiths, as the occurrence of Brotherhood Sunday in this season suggests, and such recognition of full dignity across chasms of color as Race Relations Sunday inspires.

FIRST SUNDAY AFTER EPIPHANY

The Eternal's Splendor: Isaiah 60:1-3, 6b

Greeting Epiphany on wings of song—

> Light of the world, we hail thee,
> Flooding the eastern skies;
> Never shall darkness veil thee
> Again from human eyes—

the Christian world echoes this ecstasy of Isaiah, which MT aptly renders,

> Arise, be glad, your light is dawning,
> the Eternal's splendour rises upon you (vs. 1 MT).

Darting in and out, all through the message of the Epiphany season, three elements—light, God's good news for all people, and the outreach of Christ to all—are bound into the one declaration that *the light of God's self-revelation in Jesus Christ brings good news to all peoples.* Each of the lessons for this first Sunday of the season introduces one of these elements. This prophetic rhapsody celebrates light—"the Eternal's splendour" dispelling our darkness.

God's light, it says, dispels the *darkness of the human predicament.* In the parallelism of Hebrew poetry "your light has come" stands in apposition with "the glory of the Lord" (vs. 1). God's approach as light is no strange figure. Ezekiel introduces his visions with the dazzling brightness of God's appearing:

And upward from what had the appearance of his loins I saw as it were gleaming bronze, like the appearance of fire enclosed round about; and downward from what had the appearance of his loins I saw as it were the appearance of fire, and there was brightness round about him (Ezek. 1:27).

As if in echo, Pascal recorded "FIRE!" in bold capitals as the pivotal word in his etching of the mystical vision so important that he carried its reminder sewed in the hem of his doublet.

Beyond mysticism, this light is ethical. Isaiah ties it firmly to "righteousness" (58:8) and declares:

> If you pour yourself out for the hungry
> and satisfy the desire of the afflicted,
> then shall your light rise in the darkness
> and your gloom be as the noonday (58:10).

That such a charitable spirit has not always gone with doctrinaire theism is sadly true. "The God-believers," James A. Pike declares, "are shown to be more unethical in direct proportion to their orthodoxy." Faith may not *cause* "closed, judgmental, hating personality deformity," he adds, but such persons are "more likely to cling to the supports belief in God represents." [1] Between such atrophied remains and the light of great faith, however, there is the contrast of midnight and noon. When faith brings light, it is ethical through and through.

It comes as the light of peace dispelling the *darkness of the nations.* Though "thick darkness" covers "the peoples," God's "glory will be seen" (vs. 2). For the darkness in which men grope their way, as Isaiah saw, is a yearning lack of "justice" and "righteousness" (59:9-10).

> Justice is turned back,
> and righteousness stands afar off;
> for truth has fallen in the public squares,
> and uprightness cannot enter (59:14).

How strangely modern! In such darkness we can know little peace, domestic or international. Writing on the tragedy of urban disorder in the summer of 1967, a thoughtful observer seems to be offering commentary on Isaiah. "These," he says,

were not so much race riots as "place riots": anguished acts of frustration from an isolated, nihilistic, Dickensian backwater of our affluent, urbanized, computerized society. Here, masses of essentially penniless and powerless residents—Negro, Puerto Rican, Mexican-American, and "mountain white"—in growing numbers have been compelled to endure such indignities as hearing the screams of their children being bitten by rats at night while city and state governments look away and Congress . . . "cynically laughs" a $20,000,000-a-year rat control bill off Capitol Hill. [2]

"Nations shall come to your light," Isaiah declares. The light of justice, righteousness, and truth is their deep need, met not by Israel's achievement—unless in the secondary sense of the gift of the witness—but by God's gift.

God's light dispelling the darkness of the human predicament, the light of peace driving out the darkness of the nations, calls for the light of dedication to illumine the *darkness of selfishness.* As the nations come seeking the light,

[1] James A. Pike, *If This Be Heresy* (New York: Harper, 1967) as quoted in *Saturday Review,* Sept. 16, 1967, p. 45.

[2] "American Tragedy, 1967," an editorial by Alfred Balk, *Saturday Review,* Sept. 16, 1967, p. 34.

they bring the contributions of their treasure (vss. 4-6a) and dedicate them to "the praise of the Lord." Without such dedication, no peace can endure. That should be clear to present-day Americans. If the earth's total population could be seen as a town of 1,000 souls, 60 persons would represent the United States, 940 all the rest. The 60 Americans would receive half the income and 15 percent of the town's food supply. These 60 "would have 12 times as much electricity, 22 times as much coal, 21 times as much oil, 50 times as much steel, and 50 times as much equipment as all" their 940 fellow-townsmen.[3] In such a division, the dedication of a large portion of our goods to the well-being of the rest of the world is not optional largess; it is essential if the world is to walk in the light of neighborly relations, not in the dark of unending and all-destructive strife.

To say that Isaiah's vision was "eschatological" is not to move it to some safely distant future. Eschatology is future only in the sense that no passing present exhausts it; every present is under its judgment. Whether in Isaiah's 538 B.C. or in the present of crucial decision in which we stand, we are under summons: "Arise, shine; for your light has come" (vs. 1).

Together in the Promise: Ephesians 3:1-12

"That through the Gospel the Gentiles are joint heirs with the Jews, part of the same body, sharers together in the promise made in Christ Jesus" (vs. 6 NEB)—so ringingly this epistle trumpets the Epiphany theme *that the light of God's revelation in Jesus Christ brings good news to all peoples.* The whole burden of this passage is the concern God has laid on the apostle's heart for the Gentiles (vss. 1, 6, 8)—a term also appropriately translated "pagans" (JB) or "heathen" (AT). By extension it becomes "all men" in vs. 9. The message of Christ is God's good news to all men everywhere.

See the *nature* of this news. God's ultimate purpose, it dares to say, is the victory to be won by his children in the church over all the powers of the universe, "the principalities and powers in the heavenly places" (vs. 10). The language of an obsolete cosmology need not detain us here.

Paul understands the "Powers" as, on the one hand, "the framework of creation, preserving it from disintegration . . . the dyke which prevents the chaotic deluge from submerging the world"; and, on the other hand, as that which stands between us and life of freedom as children of God. They are the framework which prevents a world without Christ from disintegrating; but in Christ they are robbed of their absolute power over men.[4]

The structures of nationalism, corporate ownership, and organized religion are approximations in our time for Paul's "powers." In dealing with the darker depths of personality revealed to Freudian man we are face to face with a modern version of the "principalities." With a cosmology light years removed from Paul's, Albert Einstein nonetheless stands with Paul at the heart of the

---

[3] Bennett Cerf, *Laugh Day* (Garden City, N.Y.: Doubleday, 1965), p. 472.

[4] Lesslie Newbigin, *Honest Religion for Secular Man* (Philadelphia: Westminster Press, 1966), p. 138, following *Christ and the Powers,* by Hendrikus Berkhof.

matter in his judgment: "It is easier to denature plutonium than to denature the evil spirit in man." To these powers which enthrall us comes the good news of victory through "the manifold wisdom of God" (vs. 10).

See also the *source* of the news. It is not an achievement, but an inheritance, not the accomplishment of an ambition but the acceptance of a promise. "It means that pagans now share the same *inheritance*, that they are parts of the same body, and that the same *promise* has been made to them, in Christ Jesus, through the gospel" (vs. 6 JB, italics added). Paul has this news to share by virtue of his "insight into the mystery of Christ" (vs. 4)—insight obtained not through his genius but through the "revelation" referred to in vs. 3, the word made known "to his holy apostles and prophets by the Spirit" (vs. 5). These distilled theological statements are historically true; it is through the experiences, of which Jesus is the fountainhead and the unfolding life of the church the medium, that these insights have spread abroad in the world.

By doing away with the old opposition of Jew and Gentile Christ had begun the work of reconciliation; he had established a centre from which it could extend and fulfil itself. If men could only apprehend all that was involved in the fusion of two opposing elements in the Christian church, they would have a key to the whole eternal purpose of God.[5]

See finally the *medium* of the news. At the outset of this passage Paul is writing literal facts about his dealings with a gospel held in trust. He is "a prisoner for Christ Jesus on behalf of you Gentiles" (vs. 1). It is exactly his proclamation that *Jesus* is the Christ that has involved him in his troubles. The idea of a *messiah*—a Christ—was everywhere acceptable; but the presentation of *Jesus*, with his biting specifics, in this role, was the offense. Paul had compounded his difficulty by proclaiming this message to the *Gentiles*. Rome would not have bothered with him as merely a Jewish sectarian, but had found him impossible to ignore as a disturbing teacher of his ideas in various pagan centers.[6] So he lived under the mandate of "the stewardship of God's grace that was given to me for you" (vs. 2).

As the undeserving beneficiaries of this good news, children of ancestors who were among the Gentile pagans to whom the mission brought new life, we too have this message only in stewardship. Bishop Lesslie Newbigin speaks out of the depths of his participation in this enterprise when he says:

Mission is more than church extension. It is that daring act of self-emptying which mirrors and in a true sense re-enacts the self-emptying of the Son of God. It is the Christian going out, leaving familiar forms and words behind him, becoming a child who cannot speak till someone teaches him the alphabet, but believing that the God who raises the dead can take his nothingness and create out of it something new, a manifestation of the life of Jesus in the idiom of a new people and a new culture.[7]

[5] E. F. Scott, *The Epistle of Paul to the Ephesians*, Moffatt New Testament Commentary, p. 186.

[6] *Ibid.*, p. 182.

[7] Newbigin, *Honest Religion for Secular Man*, p. 118.

We are part of that stewardship because we are "sharers together in the promise."

The Rising of His Star: Matthew 2:1-12

"We observed the rising of his star, and we have come to pay him homage" (vs. 2b NEB). That universal paean rings through this story with which Matthew prefaces the gospel. At this point Matthew is more theological than historical. Who were these "wise men from the East"? What were their names? their countries? their racial backgrounds? Matthew is not concerned with such questions. He has a theological purpose in mind, for which this beautiful story serves as symbolic medium. How do we identify the star of Bethlehem? He is not setting out to tell us someting about the nature and action of a heavenly body, but to show us the universal Lordship of the Christ. The Epiphany proclamation, that the light of God's self-revelation in Jesus Christ brings good news to all peoples, speaks definitively through this drama—chosen as the Epiphany gospel in every great liturgy of Christendom. The manifold nature of "the rising of his star" provides the dramatic excitement.

Here the star of *the Christ of the universe* is rising. From time to time new theories are propounded in an attempt to domesticate this star in the body of astronomical knowledge. It is proposed, for instance, that a known conjunction of planets might have produced this effect, or that this was one of the recorded appearances of Halley's Comet. But Matthew is not writing that kind of material. This star was no aloof voyager in galactic space, but a guide which took part in the affairs of earthly pilgrims, going "before them, till it came to rest over the place where the child was" (vs. 9). "Obviously the evangelist is thinking of a miraculous star; it is futile to look for a natural explanation" (JB footnote to vs. 9).

By enchanting poetry of faith he is hailing the Christ of the Universe. He etches in a picture what Paul conceptualized:

In him all things were created, in heaven and on earth, visible and invisible, whether thrones or dominions or principalities or authorities—all things were created through him and for him. He is before all things, and in him all things hold together (Col. 1:16-17).

The principles that give unity and meaning to our life, and that link us with the visible universe, come to fullest expression in him. The "wise men," or "magicians" (MT), or "astrologers" (AT and PT) who study such things bring their homage to him. So this gospel addresses its word, in our day, to *scientism*. Religion need not quarrel with *science*, but Christian faith has found one of its most vigorous rivals in scientism's assumption—often made by those not firmly grounded in the sciences—that science provides final powers and ultimate guides which make faith unnecessary. The Epiphany gospel challenges that supposition.

Here the star of *the Christ of the Jews* is rising. "Where is he who has been born king of the Jews?" (vs. 2) the wise men asked. Herod feared, plotted, murdered because one born under such portents might claim his throne. For counsel he turned to "the chief priests and scribes of the people" (vs. 4) because these experts in matters of religious law could best inform him concerning the messianic hope. In reply these counselors appealed to a quotation from Micah 5:2. Two reflections emerge from all this: (1) Jesus fulfilled these prophetic expectations but enlarged and transformed them; he was crucified because, a generation later, other leaders viewed the matter much as Herod had; in his death he accomplished far more than a martyred messiah of the Maccabean type ever could. (2) Christians still have a witness to offer to their Jewish brothers, but—such are the tragedies of bloody centuries of pogroms, prejudices, and persecutions—we cannot for a long time offer it other than by the indirection of loving respect for them and their faith, and humble faithfulness to the Christ who was "born king of the Jews."

Here the star of *the Christ of all nations* is rising. We asked in the beginning, "Who were the wise men?" To that question there is only one significant answer: they were Gentiles, representatives of pagan nations outside the Covenant. Jesus was *their* Lord, the Lord of all men. So "they fell down and worshiped him" (vs. 11). With subtle artistry Matthew weaves into the picture threads from Isaiah 60:6*b*,

> They shall bring gold and frankincense,
> and shall proclaim the praise of the Lord.

For in the prophet's vision, men would come from the ends of the earth to lay their treasure before God. "Gold and frankincense and myrrh" (vs. 11*b*) here dramatize the fulfillment of that vision in the coming of the Christ who belongs to all men.

So the Epiphany message portrays "the rising of his star" on all areas of experience. (1) As Christ of the universe, he challenges our scientism; (2) as Christ of the Jews, he stands at the center of all history; (3) as Christ of all men, he sends us on mission to all the world.

SECOND SUNDAY AFTER EPIPHANY

Redeemed to Be Redeeming: Isaiah 49:8-13

To distill the yeasty figures of this lection in one terse proposition: *God frees the bound, whom he then upholds as he uses them in freeing others.* The prophet's faith, as he meditated on the specifics of a desperate historical situation, led him to this conviction concerning his people, despised and dispirited in exile. It has both summons and assurance for us now.

To rejected people comes the enrichment of the redeemed. MT, in harmony with the Dead Sea Scroll, recasts vs. 8 from the prophetic perfect into future tense: "I will answer you, and aid you when the day for rescue dawns." Knight renders it as present: "Now is the day of salvation; I have come to thine aid." The force of it all is that, with Cyrus at the gate, upsetting such securities as the exiles have found in their adjustment to the life of Babylon, God is offering assurance that this is a meaningful time—a *kairos,* to borrow New Testament vocabulary—a time of decision and opportunity in which he will act to free his people. In finding their freedom they will bring enrichment to the common life; the obscure line, "to apportion the desolate heritages" (vs. 8) may be read, "re-peopling desolate places" (MT), or "and assign you the estates that lie waste" (JB). The suggestion is that of the earth scorched by evil, which God will renew for his people.

Human experience provides its own documentation of this prophetic insight. Out of centuries of slavery and rejection Negro people have brought the enrichment of our culture embodied in the spiritual, in the work of a host of black poets and artists, and in the fresh implementation of faith embodied in the nonviolent struggle for human rights which—despite eruptions of violence by those not committed to the program—may yet bring a new creative strategy to our explosive age. The church, too, has been most creative in periods when persecution drove it underground. Influence out of proportion to numbers has emanated from the peace witness of the Quakers and from the unpopular disciplines of other small, rejected sects. To the church in a day of declining acceptance and increasing trouble and threat to its life, this is a word of summons and assurance. We can hold the faith resolutely in the conviction that to the rejected comes the enrichment of the redeemed.

But this is not the end of the matter. The redeemed are made the redeeming. In a disputed line, which MT omits and JB sets in parentheses, the prophet reports God's declaration that he has given these rejected redeemed ones "as a covenant to the people" (vs. 8). Quite apart from questions of textual accuracy concerning the phrase, the idea is emphatic in the whole poem. In vs. 6, God has been heard to say, the mere *preservation* of *Israel* is "too light a thing";

> I will give you as a light to the nations,
> that my salvation may reach to the end of the earth.

The redeemed are to relay God's liberating word, "saying to the prisoners, 'Come forth' " (vs. 9).

For the saving activity of God is visible only as we see men breaking down prison bars, or venturing into the dungeons beneath the public buildings of Babylon or Birmingham, there to meet with a stench and a filth that appalls. Yet without this human action God's purpose could not advance. On the other hand, God takes the initiative in love.[8]

To the contemporary faithful this says vigorously that the Church is true to itself and its mission only when it is at the work of liberation: (a) from the bondage of sin; (b) from the fears inherent in the animism and superstition encountered on many missionary frontiers; (c) from exclusions from human rights, from employment and opportunity, and from the dignity of unrestricted housing.

When the redeemed are made redeeming, God gives them his aid. Even "on all bare heights shall be their pasture" (vs. 9). God will make his mountains not obstacles but highways for their return (vs. 11). These assurances of the care of the divine Shepherd must not be sentimentalized. This is no prom-

---

[8] George A. F. Knight, *Deutero-Isaiah, A Theological Commentary on Isaiah 44–55* (Nashville: Abingdon Press, 1965), p. 189.

ise of easy peace of mind, no blanket assurance of the fruits of positive thinking; it is the conviction that God sustains those who dauntlessly go forth on mission. Martin Niemoeller, in solitary confinement in a Nazi prison, exemplified it. Taking his ordination seriously even there, he daily chose a text from each Testament to whisper to fellow prisoners who came near enough in their exercise walks to hear him through a crack above his door. Thereby, he not only served them in their captivity, but kept his own sanity and strength in the process. Physically emaciated, but grown gigantic in spirit to bless the postwar age, Niemoller offers living witness to the protection of the redeemed made redemptive.

Sundered—United—Reconciled: Ephesians 2:11-18

On the eve of the reunion of the three largest bodies of American Methodism, a fraternal delegate spoke words which now prick the conscience of Christendom:

Possessing as we are supposed to do a gospel of love toward God and all men and living under the constant assurance of available heavenly resources of untold and unsuspected extent, if we cannot find ways of ending strife among ourselves it ill behooves us to chide governments and rulers and armies and navies for war and misery and crime and endless suffering.

Even more disturbing was the question he asked: "Why should anyone believe that Christ is the hope of the world when the Church, his own broken, hurt body, connot heal its own wounds?" [9]

To these facts of separation, union, and reconciliation in Christ, this Epistle addresses a daring proposition: *Christ draws us to each other across tragic chasms of separation as he reconciles us to God.*

The Epistle begins where, apart from Christ, each of us must—with the tragic *fact of separation.* It reminds the Ephesians, as representatives of all who have come out of a pagan Gentile world, that their existence apart from Christ is atomized and lonely—"strangers to the covenants of promise, having no hope and without God in the world" (vs. 12). That describes the culture of our pagan forebears, before the Christian mission reached them. More immediately, it describes our own society, as the somber pages of any metropolitan newspaper report it. More intimately still, it traces whole movements of our personal lives as, immersed in the secularism of our time, we stray from Christ. Here JB is startlingly suggestive: "You were immersed in this world, without hope and without God." Lonely, bereft of meaning, bloody with strife, we recognize the familiar, tragic facts of separation.

Joyfully the Epistle leads on to the empirical *fact of unity* in Christ. "But now in Christ Jesus, you that used to be so far apart from us have been brought very close, by the blood of Christ" (vs. 13 JB). Being in Christ is a real state, an event, effected by the offering of his life as Messiah. If the Ephesian letter is from Paul himself, its author had firsthand knowledge of

[9] James H. Straughn as quoted by Albert Outler, *That the World May Believe* (New York: Joint Commission of Education and Cultivation, Board of Missions of The Methodist Church, 1966), pp. 4-5.

"the dividing wall of hostility" (vs. 14) which separated the court of the faithful from the court of the Gentiles in the Jerusalem temple; for Acts 21:28 records how charges that he had violated that division precipitated the arrest that led to Paul's final imprisonment in Rome. But unity in Christ was a fact as solid as this historic division; Jews and Gentiles bound to the one Lord found unity with each other, the law being "annulled" as he created "out of the two a single new humanity in himself" (vs. 15 NEB). The peace he brought was not a victory of one over the other, or a conversion of one to the other's position, but a new humanity including both—a humanity foreshadowed in the church.

To this empirical fact the World Council of Churches points, both by its existence and work, and by the Message of its Third Assembly.

We believe that the unity which is both God's will and his gift to his Church is being made visible as all in each place who are baptized into Jesus Christ and confess him as Lord and Saviour are brought by the Holy Spirit into one fully committed fellowship, holding the one apostolic faith, preaching the one Gospel, breaking the one bread, joining in common prayer, and having a corporate life reaching out in witness and service to all who at the same time are united with the whole Christian fellowship in all places and all ages in such wise that ministry and members are accepted by all, and that all can act and speak together as occasion requires for the tasks to which God calls his people.[10]

Beyond the facts of separation and unity, the Epistle culminates in the healing *fact of reconciliation*. Christ's purpose in the cross was that he "might reconcile us both to God in one body" (vs. 16). Not only drawn to *each other*, we are reconciled *to God*; indeed, it is only in one body that we can come to God and only in God that we can be one body. Psychiatrists trace the pathology which organizes hatred against scapegoat groups to our submerged hatred of ourselves. Unable to live with such self-loathing, we displace it on others. Back of this sickness of self-hatred, some psychiatrists say, is a man's hatred of his father, whom he sees extended in himself. The healing of our tragic hatreds must begin in a reconciliation that reaches far back. He who is first reconciled to his heavenly Father has come to the strategic center of all other reconciliation.

Sharing Borrowed Light: Matthew 5:14-20

Many a youth, haunted by a call to the ministry, has held back with a reluctance born of fear of his inability to live the exemplary life essential to this calling. Many a Christian hesitates to make overt witness on similar grounds. Yet our Lord is unequivocal: "You are the light of the world" (vs. 14).

The demand would be impossible if it required such shining in our own right. There is no such light in us, apart from Christ, as the Epistle to the Ephesians emphatically reminds us: "For once you were darkness, but now you are light in the Lord; walk as children of light" (Eph. 5:8). The light we share is borrowed, and one cannot approach the injunction in this gospel

[10] *The New Delhi Report,* Third Assembly of the World Council of Churches (New York: Association Press, 1962), pp. 116-22.

lesson apart from another word of our Lord's: "I am the light of the world; he who follows me will not walk in darkness, but will have the light of life" (John 8:1). In this reflected light we bear the witness that fulfills the prophecy: "I will give you as a light to the nations, that my salvation may reach to the end of the earth" (Isa. 49:6). To be deterred from witness by our fearful mistrust of our capacity to be exemplary persons is to miss the meaning of the gospel. Christian faith has never dreamed of assuming such a preposterous claim for ourselves. Precisely the opposite is the case. We can be witnesses only because we are frail, failing, sinful persons *whom God makes new.* We are to let our light shine in order that men may "give glory to [our] Father who is in heaven" (vs. 16).

Since the witness is not in our own right, there is no exemption from its demand. The little parables of the city on the hill and the lamp on the stand are so firmly entrenched in the gospel message that they occur in all three of the Synoptics. I Peter echoes their demand for witness through clear and open life: "Let all your behaviour be such as even pagans can recognize as good, and then, whereas they malign you as criminals now, they will come to see for themselves that you live good lives, and will give glory to God on the day when he comes to hold assize" (I Peter 2:12 NEB).

"Clergymen," reports the news account of a Washington investigation, "are bad auto insurance risks because they tend to drive with the attitude that 'the Lord will provide.'" It is against such shirking of personal responsibility on grounds of misapplied faith that both I Peter and the Sermon on the Mount raise their warning.

Here, as at all points in the Sermon on the Mount, we must read christologically. This call to be so exemplary in our witness that we become light to the world confronts us with manifest impossibility—impossible for Galilean peasants to whom it was first directed, impossible for modern Christians to whom it still comes. The plain fact is that when we have done our best we are still sinful men and women in whom—despite all that Christ does for us and in us—the taint of defiled human nature persists. But we are sinful beings *who have been accepted!* Christ has accepted us through his forgiving act on the Cross. The church has accepted us into its forgiven and forgiving fellowship. God continually accepts us anew by his forgiveness. The old brittle tempers need not persist in us. We can exemplify the light of the relaxed, accepted, forgiven, and forgiving. We are released from the old round of resolutions which defeat themselves by presenting again and again to the imagination the very acts they seek to avoid; for now we live not by resolution but by adoration of a Christ whose genius it is to stamp his image on those who love and worship him.

Having accepted us, failing as we are, he renews the call and sends us on a witnessing mission. He has not come to set aside one least part of the law, he says, but to "complete" it (vs. 17 JB). And he adds that he expects perfect fulfillment and obedience from his disciples. Unless we are better than even the most rigorously faithful of his day, the scribes and Pharisees, we have no part in his reign. The rules are not abolished, but our witness to him calls us to an ethic beyond anything the mere following of rules can achieve—which is the heart of the best that "situation ethics" has to say to us.

THIRD SUNDAY AFTER EPIPHANY

Set Apart to the Lord: I Samuel 1:19c-28

It was Saturday night, and the Salvation Army captain, out on the round of his duties, met a man of the neighborhood making an indulgent round of his favorite taverns—and leading by the hand his four-year-old son. Stopping to chat and to admire the little fellow, the captain proposed that he come next morning and take him to Sunday school. "No, no!" the father replied. "Not for a while yet. He's too young for that." Not too young for tavern education, but only for church school! To whom did the boy belong?

The incident raises issues with which this passage from I Samuel vigorously deals. Boiling the story down to its essentials brings the issues to sharper focus. On the birth of her child, Hannah named him in remembrance that he was given in response to prayer. Through the crucial first two or three years of his life she kept ever before the family the vow that made him God's child, and at the earliest possible time, by the grace of God, she carried her vow into resolute action, dedicating her son to God with irrevocable finality. From the ancient story three issues, current and perennial, emerge.

First of these is the issue of *life as our own versus life under God's claim, our children as ours or as God's trust.* Hannah's answer is plain: "She called his name Samuel, for she said, 'I have asked him of the Lord'" (vs. 20). MT reads: "calling his name Samuel or 'God-asked.'" Though this spelling out of the meaning is not in the Hebrew text and the meaning itself is debated among scholars, MT's suggestion is a reasonable inference from the context. If this was what the name itself implied, what a heritage the boy had in the reminder at each mention of his name that his life itself was an answered prayer!

Whose are our lives? Our age has been fumbling fatally with the question. The proposal that we own our lives, with its corollary of self-interest as the mainspring for the promotion of the general welfare, has not justified its claim. Under it society has deteriorated, economic life has been so burdened that the public interest has had to be protected by increasing governmental restraints, international life has exploded in hot and cold wars whose continuance calls the future of man in question. In revulsion, men have said: Life belongs to the state—personal life has no meaning save as it serves the state; all other values must be subservient to the continuance and the advancement of the interests of the state. From this concept have come purges, regimentation of thought as well as life patterns, blackout of high spiritual values. Having learned from experience some answers that will not work, we have not yet settled the issue as to whose our lives are. Does Hannah's answer suggest the direction we must move? What does it mean, in personal and business affairs, in child-rearing, in education?

A second issue is that of *households preoccupied with personal, secular concerns versus such a home as that of Hannah and Elkanah, keeping vows in confidence that God is the prompter of purposes* (vss. 21-23). The disputed translation of vs. 23 prompts useful reflection. Elkanah said to Hannah, concerning her dedication of the boy, "Only, may the Lord establish his word" (RSV), or "only the Lord establish your words" (AT), or "May

Yahweh bring about what you have said" (JB), or "may the Eternal let you carry out your purpose" (MT). Do we draw distinctions too firmly between our religious actions and God's act? God "lets" us carry out our purpose. Does he, then, "bring about" what we have said, the intention itself being the prompting of the Holy Spirit? Do our answers to these questions need implementation in education? Concerning our attempt at education which is religiously neutral, the late William Temple observed that "if you give to children an account of the world from which God is left out, you are teaching them to understand the world without reference to God. If He is then introduced, . . . He becomes an appendix to His own creation." [11] Hannah and Elkanah challenge such education. Our society has reached no satisfactory common response to the issue.

One other issue emerges: *our tentative and changing dedications versus commitment such as Hannah's, resolute and final.* Despite the suggestion of God's localization in the shrine, there is grandeur in Hannah's purpose: "As soon as the child is weaned"—at age two or three, according to the custom of the time—"I will bring him, that he may appear in the presence of the Lord, and abide there forever" (vs. 22). This was no passing impulse: she persisted in her plan and carried it through over the years (vss. 24-27). Its finality is not adequately expressed in the RSV reading, "I have lent him to the Lord" (vs. 28), but is more fully conveyed in JB: "Now I make him over to Yahweh for the whole of his life," and in AT: "I have dedicated him to the Lord; as long as he lives he is set apart to the Lord." What claim do such fixed commitments still have upon us?

That One Face: II Corinthians 4:1-6

A major Epiphanytide theme rings in this lesson's climactic closing lines: "For it is the God who said, 'Let light shine out of darkness,' who has shone in our hearts to give the light of the knowledge of the glory of God in the face of Christ" (vs. 6). The same God whose word was decisive in the creation of the world—which began with light (Gen. 1:3)—has now become personal "in our hearts"—"has caused his light to shine within us" (NEB). Paul speaks for himself and in some secondary sense for those who share with him the witness of the gospel. There is an inner shining, but it is not purely subjective; it belongs to the same order of experience as God's calling forth of light at the creation, and is not from us but from him. That one "face of Christ" confronts us at crucial points in our contemporary life.

A time dark with uncertainty about God confronts the light of the knowledge we have of him in the face of Christ. Vs. 6 may refer to light Paul saw on Christ's face in his experience on the road to Damascus, but it goes far beyond this; it remained persistently in control of his life's pattern from that time on. This illumination, Paul was sure, was given to be shared—"to *radiate* the light of the knowledge of God's glory" (JB, italics added). Radiating the light of that knowledge, Paul became not only a heroic missionary and eloquent preacher, but the decisive theologian of the ages.

[11] I cannot now identify the source of this quotation from the then Archbishop of York, garnered apparently from a periodical in September, 1941.

One influential mood of our time was expressed by John Haynes Holmes:

> When I say "God," it is poetry and not theology. Nothing that any theologian ever wrote about God has helped me much, but everything that the poets have written about flowers, and birds, and skies, and seas, and the saviors of the race, and God —whoever he may be—has at one time or another reached my soul! . . . I never seem so near truth as when I care not what I think or believe, but only with these masters of inner vision would live forever.[12]

That is lovely sentiment, but in such a time as this, sentiment which does not know what it thinks or believes and can talk only vaguely of "God—whoever he may be," does not help us much. We need some clue more definitive than flowers, birds, skies, seas, and generalized plural "saviors of the race." With Paul, we can find the decisive clue in the face of Christ.

A time when vision is distorted by secularism confronts the light of reality beyond the immediately seen, which we have in the face of Christ. The gospel, Paul declares, "is veiled only to those who are perishing" (vs. 3), people whose "unbelieving minds are . . . blinded by the god of this passing age" (vs. 4 NEB). Which is to say, they are victims of secularism, whose Latin root—*saecularis*—means literally "this age or generation." The secularist has only Now. He is cut adrift from a guiding tradition and from prudent consideration of tomorrow. But Christ "gave himself for our sins to deliver us from the present evil age" (Gal. 1:4). In him "this world," this passing Now, comes under judgment (John 12:31); "the ruler of this world is judged" (John 16:11).

Secularism, says the *Oxford Universal Dictionary*, is "the doctrine that morality should be based solely on regard to the well-being of mankind in the present life, to the exclusion of all considerations drawn from belief in God or in a future state." Paul would have men whose minds are thus blinded made aware of "the light of the gospel of the glory of Christ, who is the likeness of God" (vs. 4b). In him we see God's nature, both as shown in his character and deeds and as operative in his death and resurrection. Through him we know what God is like. The outcome of that understanding is "ourselves as your servants for Jesus' sake" (vs. 5). The witness to the risen and glorified Lord is an integral part of the gospel, and its truth is that gratitude and fealty to Christ make the disciple the servant of all men.

A *time of temptation to short-cuts* confronts the light of a more durable proclamation in the face of Christ, who sustains our ministry. "Therefore," this passage begins—referring to "beholding the glory of the Lord" (3:18)—"Therefore, having this ministry by the mercy of God, we do not lose heart" (vs. 1). Courage for a trying ministry emerges from this knowledge that God has given us the grace of sharing such a message. It controls methods. As Paul declares in vs. 2, one so entrusted can have no part in the shameful practices which deceive or water down the gospel. By an open proclamation of the truth it must be commended "to the common con-

[12] John Haynes Holmes as quoted by Halford E. Luccock, *More Preaching Values in the Epistles of Paul* (New York: Harper, 1961), p. 50.

science of our fellow-men and in the sight of God" (vs. 2 NEB)—a vital reminder to the church in such a time as this.

Silent Years Bear Witness: Luke 2:39-52

This one glimpse of the so-called "silent years" of Jesus' boyhood and youth gives us, not biography in the usual sense, but a statement of the gospel full of strong theological overtones. Its interest lies not in circumstances of the life of the Nazareth family but in the *meaning* that permeates all that relates to Jesus. Against three erroneous views it erects safeguards.

Against all *docetic tendencies,* Jesus is shown as growing up through normal, full-rounded maturing. Apocryphal gospels deal in fantastic stories of boyhood miracles grotesque with whimsical magic; but in this, the New Testament's one reference to the period, Luke turns away from all such embellishments. The two summary statements with which the narrative begins and ends (vss. 40, 52) portray the unfolding of a fully developed human personality. "And the child grew up and became strong and thoughtful, with God's blessing resting on him" (vs. 40 AT) is perhaps the best reading, because the least sententious. It shows a vigorous, normal human growth within a religious household.

Plummer notes helpfully that:

The intellectual, moral, and spiritual growth of the child, like the physical, was *real.* His was a perfect humanity developing perfectly, unimpeded by hereditary or acquired defects. It was the first instance of such a growth in history. For the first time a human infant was realizing the ideal humanity.[13]

Not only did he grow normally, he did so in a cruelly difficult time. During this interval the Jews sent a delegation to Rome to protest the accession of Archelaus, and later sent another to lodge the complaint that led to his being deposed. In these years, Galilee erupted in bloody revolt against Roman rule, put down with mass crucifixions of the revolutionaries. The ethereal conception of Jesus is utterly at variance with this picture of his full identification with us in a rounded, obedient boyhood spanning times of unusual crisis. When Paul relates him to us as "the first-born among many brethren" (Rom. 8:29), he is speaking a language which the gospel corroborates in the fuller statement embodied in this passage.

Against all *anti-Semitism indulged by Christians,* Jesus is shown growing under the nurture of Jewish law, custom, feasts, and traditions. When everything had been done according to orthodox Jewish usage, his parents took him from Bethlehem to Nazareth, the story tells us (vs. 39). They were faithful in their religious duties, bringing him up in the tradition of his people (vss. 41-42). In this story of how the sense of belonging to God took control of him in the identity crisis of early adolescence—at the age when a young Jew became "a son of the Law"—Jesus is shown, fascinated, lingering in the temple at the feet of the teachers, "listening to them and asking them

[13] Cf. Plummer's treatment of this passage in the *International Critical Commentary.*

questions, and everyone who heard him was astonished at his intelligence and at the answers he made" (vs. 47 AT). The Christian debt to and kinship with the temple and synagogue that gave us Jesus is beyond all reckoning.

Against all *tendencies to make him only human,* Jesus is shown at an early age acknowledging his close relation to his heavenly Father. "Your *father* and I have been looking for you anxiously," said Mary; and with subtle nuance he replied, "Did you not know that I must be in my *Father's* house?" (vs. 49, italics added). So he made the identification by which we know him best, as God's Son.

FOURTH SUNDAY AFTER EPIPHANY

Sleeping While Death Stalks: Jonah 3:1-5

Like one frame in a motion picture, these verses glimpse in still fixation one element in the swift action of the parable of Jonah. For the crucial moment one turns to an earlier sentence, so unobtrusive that it might easily be passed by: "But Jonah had gone down into the inner part of the ship and had lain down, and was fast asleep" (1:5b). The raging storm threatened the lives of all the ship's company, including Johah, but he slept while death stalked. Nothing else in the extended parable of Jonah makes any sense apart from that key statement; the parable was written to awaken such sleepers.

There was another who slept in a storm. "The waves beat into the boat, so that the boat was already filling. But he was in the stern, asleep on the cushion; and they woke him and said to him, 'Teacher, do you not care if we perish?'" (Mark 4:37-38.) They were full of anxiety, which "finds its sustenance in the painful events of the past, its occasion in some physical weakness in the present, and its specificity in fear of the unknown future." [14] But he had made his peace with the painful past, had no fear of the future, and could act decisively in the present; so his faith held the answer for their anxiety. Of course he "cared" if they perished! In that regard his capacity to sleep in the storm was poles apart from Jonah's. *He slept while death stalked, secure in a faith that could act; Jonah slept, numbed by insensitivity that evaded action.* The parable is an alarm to disturb the dreams of such slumberers.

They are *asleep to the outreach of faith even to the most unworthy.* So God called Jonah to "go to Nineveh, that great city, and proclaim to it the message" (vs. 2). Its "three days' journey in breadth" (vs. 3) bears marks of exaggeration due to hearsay or storyteller's license; the city wall was eight miles in circumference. Nevertheless it was an important capital of its time. And its wickedness seemed a stench to high heaven (1:2). Paganism found a center there in the temple of Ishtar and in the making of statues of Ishtar that found their way as kingly gifts to the rulers of Egypt. Long before Jonah's time it had been the center of the great power of Sennacherib's Assyrian imperial aggrandizement. From it had come the conquering hordes which brought the northern kingdom of Israel to an end. No wonder Nahum

[14] Paul Tournier, *The Person Reborn* (New York: Harper, 1966), pp. 10-11.

had hurled his denunciation: "Behold I am against you, says the Lord of hosts, and I will burn your chariots in smoke, and the sword shall devour your young lions; I will cut off your prey from the earth, and the voice of your messengers shall no more be heard" (Nahum 2:13). To this unlikely charge Jonah was appointed to preach! Faith has an outreach even to the most unworthy, but Jonah's sleep was symptomatic of his heedlessness.

Who are the sleepers who miss this truth now? What questions does the parable raise for us? Does faith cry to be shared with those we consider enemies? As it drove Jonah to Nineveh and Paul to Rome, must it drive Christian Americans in the third quarter of the twentieth century to Moscow, Peking, Hanoi, not with bombs but with a message of healing reconciliation? Does it call for the compassionate sharing of our faith and its fruits with those whom Kipling brutally branded "lesser breeds without the law"?

The parable was written to disturb the slumbers of those *asleep to the universal jurisdiction of God*. Late and reluctantly Jonah preached: "Yet forty days, and Nineveh shall be overthrown!" (3:4), but only after he had vainly attempted the role of a refugee from God. He had fled "to Tarshish from the presence of the Lord" (1:3), secure in his belief that the jurisdiction of Israel's God stopped at Israel's shore. Even the pagan sailors were better theologians than that! In the storm, "each cried to his god" (1:5) and, when they found Jonah sleeping, shouted: "Arise, call upon your god!" (vs. 6). Better a pagan who believes in many gods but is sure that a man's god goes where *he* goes, than a believer in the one true God, who leaves him behind at the national frontier! Even the pagan Ninevites "believed God; they proclaimed a fast, and put on sackcloth" (vs. 5).

Where do we suppose the boundaries of God's jurisdiction lie? Perhaps at the edge of our parish or denomination, prompting us to answer the call to mission with the rejoinder, "Why foist our faith on people of other lands? They already have a religion, as good for them as ours is for us." Is that assumption more valid for us than it was for Jonah?

The parable seeks to disturb the slumbers of those *asleep to the call of human concern inherent in our faith*. About the heartless Ninevites Jonah "couldn't care less." When they repented at his preaching, he had only complaint to offer: "I pray thee, Lord, is not this what I said when I was yet in my country? That is why I made haste to flee to Tarshish" (4:2). The only joy in the preaching—the coming of the promised destruction—had been snatched from him! So the parable ends with God's burning question, "Should not I pity Nineveh, that great city, in which there are more than a hundred and twenty thousand persons who do not know their right hand from their left, and also much cattle?" (4:11).

So said Jesus: "Blessed are those who mourn" (Matt. 5:4)—those who *care*, those whose faith will not let them sleep while death stalks.

No Place for Pride: I Corinthians 1:18-31

"And so there is no place for human pride in the presence of God" (vs. 29 NEB). To scale the rugged heights of his thought to the promontory of this summit, Paul had to start from the low swamplands of sectarian contention. Parties in the church were vying for preferred authority by appeal to their supposed patrons—" 'I belong to Paul,' or 'I belong to Apollos,' or 'I belong to Cephas,' or 'I belong to Christ' " (1:12). Shocked, Paul set out to answer. What lies before us in this lection is a vigorous part of his argument.

Such divisions, still persisting, are not merely distasteful; they are a tragic denial of a gospel embarked on a saving mission. "For how," asks a leading theologian,

can we convince men that God was in Christ reconciling *the world* to himself, when they see that Christians are not reconciled to each other? How can Christians hope to unite mankind in peace and fellowship when they are still divided among themselves at their own baptismal fonts and communion tables? How can churches that will not risk any loss of their own institutional sovereignty persuade their members to risk more in the ventures of international cooperation? What can churches that look for all the world like avocational or recreational interest groups expect to achieve in the successive crises that are wrecking our secular society in this age of rapid social change? [15]

In similar temper, Paul declares that there is no room for our doctrinaire exclusions of one another. Christ is not divided. At his cross we are all alike insufficient and all alike dependent on him. *These divisions grow out of an overestimate of human wisdom, failing to see that the Cross is God's power, beyond all philosophies to enclose.* To support his conviction he appeals (1) to the fact of the Cross, and (2) to the experience of the church.

Infinitely greater than our wisdom, the Cross is God's power. Those who look at the Cross from the outside, as mere observers, philosophical speculators, see in it only foolishness; but from the inside, as seen by committed, dependent faith, it is the very opposite. Its extreme antithesis to folly is not *wisdom,* as one might suppose, but *power* (vs. 18). Appealing to Ps. 33:10 and Isa. 29:14, Paul asserts that wise men, interpreters of the law, philosophers of the age, all look foolish in comparison with what God *did* on Calvary (vss. 19-20).

"For when the world with all its wisdom failed to know God in his wisdom, God resolved to save believers by the 'sheer folly' of the Christian message" (vs. 21 MT). Paul is not denigrating preaching, as the KJV, "the foolishness of preaching," or its RSV modification seems to imply. He is stressing the saving power of the Christian message. The word *sosai,* "to save," was used in the Greek version of the Old Testament to point to liberation at the Messiah's coming, to salvation from the penalties of the messianic judgment or from the evils which obstruct the messianic deliverance (cf. Joel 2:32). The message of Christ crucified as the power and wisdom of God is all we Christians have to offer, even though "the Jews ask for miraculous proofs and the Greeks an intellectual panacea" (vss. 22-24 PT).

Summing up this first step in his argument, Paul writes, "For the foolishness of God is wiser than men" (vs. 25), not in anti-intellectual diatribe, but to stress that whatever the value of human intellect, it cannot bring

[15] Outler, *That the World May Believe,* p. 13.

us to God. God's initiative alone can do that. We know a person only as he opens himself to us; a personal God, likewise, can be known only as he reveals himself. He does this most fully at the Cross. No denomination or school of thought can make exclusive claim to Calvary.

Not only the fact of the Cross, but the experience of the Church refutes all assumptions of sectarian exclusiveness. At the time of their call these Christians of Corinth (can it be greatly different with us?) could depend on little in the way of what men consider wisdom; there were "not many leading men, not many of good birth" (vs. 26 MT). In a powerful triad, Paul thrice repeats "God chose," setting over against these choices an ascending scale: "to shame . . . to shame . . . to bring to nothing" (vss. 27-28). In our experience we Christians have reason to know that the only thing we can boast of is God's gift in Christ. "For God has made him our wisdom; he is our righteousness; in him we are consecrated and set free" (vs. 30 NEB). Who can deny this plain fact of experience? For our only righteousness is our acceptance in him; our only sanctification is the mature growth he gives, as the Holy Spirit leads us into the fullness of his teaching; our only freedom comes as we walk his narrow way that broadens into life.

So the barriers of our pride fall, and out of our divisions we are brought together in him in whom alone we can boast. What was once an external injunction—

let not the wise man glory in his wisdom, let not the mighty man glory in his might, let not the rich man glory in his riches; but let him who glories glory in this, that he understands and knows me, that I am the Lord (Jer. 9:23-24)—

has been underwritten by personal experience with Christ.

In Quest of the Authentic Jesus: John 12:20-36a

On the file folders in its biographical morgue *The Washington Post* identifies famous people with a single vocational notation ("home run king," "motion picture star"). One of these . . . is marked "Jesus Christ (martyr)." How *do* you classify him? A *Who's Who* of his era would have had difficulty locating him, since the conventional marks of status were not evident. Of low estate, he had no degrees, no club memberships, no publications, no offspring, no institutional ties, no honors.[16]

Ever since Albert Schweitzer wrote his *Quest of the Historical Jesus,* the studious have known something of the difficulties of discovering him in terms of the externals dear to historians and biographers. Yet every generation asks anew the question which "some Greeks" brought to Philip: "Sir, we wish to see Jesus" (vs. 21). In John's use of characters as types, these Greeks represented the world outside the circle who could know Jesus in the flesh. Thus they represent us, and their query is an important question, to which this pericope makes a threefold answer.

First, it says, we can know him as one glorified by crucifixion (vss. 24-

[16] Martin E. Marty, "Naturalistic View of the Nazarene," a book review, *Saturday Review,* Sept. 16, 1967, p. 46.

26). In John's distinctive vocabulary, references to Christ's "glorification" always point to the Cross. When "outsiders" like these Greeks seek to know him, Jesus replies: "The hour has come for the Son of man to be glorified," and explains that life is gained only by those who are ready to lose it. For others, crucifixion is supreme horror; for him it is a glory which we continue to celebrate in the symbolism of baptism as new life for those who have gone down into the waters of death, and in Holy Communion by which his church proclaims "the Lord's death until he comes" (I Cor. 11:26). Across all the centuries it has thus been literally true that we know Jesus as the celebration of his crucifixion changes us from "outsiders" to insiders through baptism in which we are joined with him, and the Supper in which we are bound to him. We know him in this growing fellowship of the Cross.

Second, it continues, we can know him *as one before whose cross the world is judged* (vss. 27-31). This scene is often spoken of as John's version of the Gethsemane story. But characteristically John has resolved the Gethsemane tensions and come to the inner meaning through a generation of experience with his Lord. Here the agonizing search for alternatives has become the calm assurance, "For this purpose I have come to this hour" (vs. 27). The need for guidance from his Father has yielded to the serenity that can say, "This voice has come for your sake, not for mine" (vs. 30). Jesus goes to the Cross with untroubled resolution, knowing that "now is the judgment of this world, now shall the ruler of this world be cast out" (vs. 31a).

We know him only when we see how truly our world comes to judgment at the Cross. The world says, "*Assert* yourself," implementing this prudential maxim in its business, its standards of personal success, its international dealings. But the Cross embodies another counsel, "*Deny* yourself," and wherever there is a good home, an abiding love, a glorious friendship, an artistic creation, or a saintly life, that maxim has become an incarnation. The world says, "Take it *for* yourself," and history is blood-red, the morning paper tear-stained, with the outworkings of that injunction. At the Cross we see one who "took it *upon* himself," and all that binds the world together belongs to his way. The world says, "God *helps* those who *help* themselves." But at Calvary we learn that God *saves* those who *cannot* help themselves. At the Cross the world is judged, and only they know Jesus who know him as the center and source of that judgment upon their lives.

Third, it concludes, we know him *as we walk in his light* (vss. 32-36). In being "lifted up from the earth," Jesus said, he would draw all men to himself. Since Messiah comes to remain forever, his questioners asked, how could he be "lifted up" in death on a cross? Who, then, was he? Jesus answered with what at first seems a sublime *non sequitur*: "The light is with you for a little longer. Walk while you have the light, lest the darkness overtake you" (vs. 35). In reality it is the ultimate answer to the question of who he is and how we know him. When we commit ourselves to him, follow his teaching, stand shoulder to shoulder with him in service, uphold him by the witness of our lives, seek his presence in prayer, celebrate the wonder of the fellowship gathered around him in worship—when we thus walk by his light—we learn who he is.

FIFTH SUNDAY AFTER EPIPHANY

Renewal Requires Repentance: Hosea 6:1-3

You have sought the quick rewards of religion without the long costs, Hosea lamented. "Your love is like . . . the dew that goes early away" (6:4). "He *talks* a good fight," says the pugilist, scornful of his rival's boasts. The people *talk* a good religious renewal, declares Hosea. Its pious ring is its condemnation, for there is no reality behind it. But hypocrisy is always a tribute to real goodness; the counterfeit would not be worth making if the genuine coin were not precious. So this passage is to be read on two levels—the surface piety and the repentance that leads to renewal.

When swollen numbers in church attendance and membership produced talk of a revival of religion, men of insight were not deceived. There is no revival, they said, because there is no depth of repentance. When the shift of focus from *numbers* to *activity* evoked a corresponding shift of vocabulary from "revival" to "church renewal," the depth reality remained unchanged. *Only in repentance that changes both behavior and the climate of our minds is there real renewal of life.* This truth leaves its watermark in every line of this lection.

Its foundation promise declares that renewal of life requires genuine return to God. "Come, let us return to the Lord" (vs. 1), the people were saying, but it was all "like a morning cloud" (vs. 4) on a swiftly clearing day. So their aphorism, "for he has torn, that he may heal us" (vs. 1b) expressed far too light a view of the situation. True as it may be at a deeper level, the "healing" does not automatically follow the "tearing." This easy piety had not penetrated the people's plight to the depth its gravity demanded.

The religious "return" could be real only if it produced ethical reform. Hosea and Amos dealt with the same set of facts: the common people were being trampled, cheated, debased. The rulers were irresponsible, the priests corrupt, the prophets perverse with cultic preoccupation. Amos, shocked by the injustice, denounced public and personal morals. Hosea pursued the diagnosis to another level and demanded a return to Israel's neglected covenant relation to God. Moral rot was the symptom, and moral recovery must be the response; but the disease lay deep in the people's allegiance to false gods. Depending on the wrong ultimates, they came out with the wrong style of life.

> Every man-made god turns out to be an extension of the man who worships it . . . Every god of human creation is designed to make a man feel good without disturbing him . . . Success, power, wealth, popularity, lust, pleasure, and security are worshipped like the ancient golden calf, the powerless, meaningless, pathetic substitutes for God.[17]

So our idolatries falsely finalize incidental goods and treat our finite desires as if they merited ultimate loyalty and trust. "Sooner or later," as H. Wheeler Robinson said of sin in general, this "finds the universe arrayed

[17] Berg, *The Ten Commandments and You*, pp. 18, 20.

against it; for sin is the challenge to the whole of things by the individual man, which is the sheerest and uttermost folly." [18] Return to the Lord at this deep level finds it undeniably true that "he has stricken, and he will bind us up" (vs. 1c).

To those who return, God reveals his love, both stern and steadfast. "After a day or two," the people were staying, "he will bring us back to life, on the third day he will raise us and we shall live in his presence" (vs. 2 JB). Even before Voltaire, they had discovered what an ideal arrangement it is that we love to sin and God loves to forgive! It is all too glib and presumptuous. The time is longer and the way harder than such flippant repentance dreams. God's steadfast love is the rock on which Hosea's ministry—and all true faith—is built; but it is love that redeems at a cost, as the tear-drenched story of Hosea's redemption of Gomer demonstrates. For such costly redemption there is no cheap acceptance.

So the end of the matter is that God's love evokes response at depths that revitalize our life. "Let us know, let us press on to know the Lord," the people intoned; but it was all too trivial and cocksure: "his going forth is sure as the dawn" (vs. 3). It was too sweetly pleasant: "he will come to us as the showers." To know the Lord is a precondition of renewal. But we do not find him by "pressing on." We can know him only as he reveals himself—in tragic history such as Hosea's with Gomer, or Christ's on Calvary. This knowledge lies "far beyond intellectual apprehension. It is a knowledge which is possible only in a personal relation in which the entire existence of the knower is involved. To know God is to respond to him in faithful love and to have the whole of life determined by the understanding of oneself and one's fellow men that becomes possible in this relation." [19]

Christ's Happy Warrior: Colossians 1:21-29

"It is now my happiness to suffer for you" (vs. 24a NEB). Paul was writing in summation of his ministry: "This is the gospel which has been proclaimed in the whole creation under heaven; and I, Paul, have become its minister" (vs. 23b NEB). He could hardly contain the wonder of the treasure entrusted to him—a great gospel, a great ministry, a great joy. To this threefold wonder Christ calls his happy warriors who minister in his name.

They are *entrusted with a gospel of total reconciliation* (vss. 21-23a). For the call to the ministry comes, as Paul Scherer once observed, from a world that is committing suicide. The human condition is the ground of the need, the chaotic plight in which we "once were estranged and hostile in mind, doing evil deeds" (vs. 21)—a shiveringly graphic picture of our embittered world. Paul saw estrangement gripping the *whole cosmos* (vs. 20), but most tragic among *men*, who have power to choose their way, and so have guilty responsibility for it. Hostile to God, we are estranged from his creatures, our fellowmen.

But Christ "in his body of flesh" (vs. 22) has so fully shared the human

---

[18] H. Wheeler Robinson, quoted in *The Interpreter's Bible*, VI, 554.

[19] J. D. Smart, article on Hosea, *Interpreter's Dictionary of the Bible*, II, 652.

condition that his reconciliation to the Father and to all sinful men pioneers a way for our reconciliation. In his accepting death he endured and overcame the worst that our hostility can do. The outcome of this gospel is that we are made "dedicated men, without blemish and innocent in his sight" (vs. 22 NEB)—an amazing change from the original human plight. For its accomplishment we need to "adhere to the foundations and stability of the faith" (vs. 23 MT). So the call to preach this gospel of total reconciliation is an imperative one.

Christ's happy warriors are *entrusted, too, with a ministry to carry forward Christ's work* (vss. 24-27). To one who knows and loves Christ, it is a joy to enter into his labors, even at painful cost. "This," wrote Paul, "is my way of helping to complete, in my poor human flesh, the full tale of Christ's afflictions still to be endured, for the sake of his body which is the church" (vs. 24 NEB). He "is not saying that he thinks his own sufferings increase the value of the redemption (since that value cannot be increased) but that he shares by his sufferings as a missionary in those that Jesus had undergone in his own mission." [20] Suffering is the Christian's call, not his punishment. It has value in helping to complete the work of Christ, a work of salvation finished in itself, but continued through "his body, that is, the church" (vs. 24).

What a long way this work brings those for whom it is done—from those "estranged and hostile in mind, doing evil deeds" (vs. 21) to the outcome of the "mystery" or "open secret" (MT), "which is Christ in you, the hope of glory" (vs. 26). The ambiguity of "in you," which JB and MT translate "among you," is suggestive. The Greek is open to both readings. "In you," in the sense of *within*, carries the connotation of Eph. 3:17—"that Christ may dwell in your hearts through faith." "Among you" accords well with "how great among the Gentiles are the riches" (vs. 27). Both meanings are true of the outcome of this ministry; the enrichment is both inward and social.

Christ's happy warriors are *entrusted with a nurturing task*—"that we may present every man mature in Christ" (vs. 28). In this pastoral calling, we have a responsibility to "*every* man"; Paul repeats the phrase three times in one sentence, to stress the inclusiveness of the gospel as contrasted with the exclusive secret rites of the Gnostics who were troubling the church. It is a stress worth preserving. "Him we proclaim, warning every man and teaching every man in all wisdom, that we may present every man mature in Christ" (vs. 28). That is our great commission—to warn, to teach, to present mature.

A great gospel of reconciliation, a great ministry to carry forward Christ's work, a great joy in nurturing every man to maturity—no wonder Christ's warriors are the happy ones!

Christians in a Non-Christian World: John 1:19-30

To speak of a non-Christian world is to recognize reality. Old unities once known as "Christendom" have broken up in what many now call a post-Christian age. Large areas of business, governmental, and social life operate

[20] *The Jerusalem Bible,* note on Col. 1:24.

on pagan assumptions. Amid population explosion on a world scale, evangelism and mission do not keep pace with population growth; despite rapid increases in the number of Christians, the church becomes a dwindling minority in the human mass. What is the role of Christians in a non-Christian world?

In John the Baptist we have a classic paradigm. For though he, not privileged to become a disciple of our Lord, was not a Christian, he was the first man to point a non-Christian world to Christ. In this gospel pericope we have three fruitful suggestions concerning our role.

First, the Christian in a non-Christian world *can be a voice*. AT, JB, and NEB alike translate John's self-identification by the indefinite article, "I am a voice crying aloud in the wilderness, 'Make the Lord's highway straight' " (vs. 23 NEB). To John, the popular preacher, had come the urgent demand for more information about himself. But, he replied, *he* did not matter. Who am I? "I am a voice."

It is a good role. Good for a minister called to be a "servant of the Word." Harry Emerson Fosdick, one of the greatest ministers of this century, could write a significant chapter of his autobiography under the title "Ideas That Have Used Me." Good, too, for a layman called to make daily decisions that create the conditions of labor and of family, community, and world life. One pastor reminded his parishioners that in the town hall and the centers of trade they daily made decisions based on prudential considerations rather than gospel principles, so that in them the church was "present but without voice." In a non-Christian world nothing is more needed than for every Christian to be a voice.

Second, the Christian in a non-Christian world *can awaken men to an unseen Presence*. "Among you," said John, "stands one whom you do know" (vs. 26). Our missionary witness once went to the non-Christian world assuming that we "brought Christ" to them; it must now go in the realization that Christ is already there. Of every missionary frontier, whether abroad or at home, that is true. Christ is *there*, among us as one whom we do not know. In a non-Christian world it is vital for every Christian to awaken men to his presence.

Third, the Christian in a non-Christian world *can point to a Savior*. "Behold, the Lamb of God, who takes away the sin of the world!" (vs. 29). We may well be shy and reticent about witness that calls to other men to follow him as *we do;* our imperfections are too glaring for that. But there is no need for reticence about inviting others to accept him whom *we need*. A visitor to a church in a Caribbean outpost was shown a collection of choice needlework on ecclesiastical vestments and altar appointments, done by women who had come into the Christian life out of the depth of paganism. As a memento of his visit, he was given a dozen purificators made by former prostitutes! The gift was symbolic. Christ *makes* such changes; we *need* such changes. Though we cannot call men to be like us, we can come to them "as one beggar telling another beggar where to find bread." It is incumbent on Christians in a non-Christian world to invite others to know him without whom we cannot live.

SIXTH SUNDAY AFTER EPIPHANY

Never Learn to Live Like Pagans: Jeremiah 10:1-7

One couplet of MT's free poetic reading of this passage sounds the keynote for the whole:

> Never learn to live like pagans,
> dismayed at portents in the sky. (vs. 2)

Historical scholarship suggests that the poem presumes a time and place different from Jeremiah's principal ministry in Jerusalem. Occupied with problems and temptations more sophisticated and cosmopolitan than those of pre-exilic Israel, it confronts the paganism of Babylon. Perhaps that is why it aptly interprets our life amid the sophistication of our post-modern world.

"Dismayed by portents in the sky"—the phrase ticks off the pagan, now as then. For astrology, with its roots in the ancient pagan world, recurs in all pagan periods. Too sophisticated for simple belief in God, many a post-modern fills the central void by catch-as-catch-can devices, of which the newspaper horoscope is one. "Pagans are dismayed at them," MT reads the redoubled following line—a spine-shivering reminder of the horrors that ensued in ancient paganism—or when Hitler, star-led, loosed his terrors.

"For the customs of the peoples are false" (vs. 3). The line is apt in this RSV reading. Adaptation to a prevailing paganism is no guarantee of truth or right. Salvation by census, security by survey, is a false hope. JB may be correct in translating, in place of "the customs," "the Dread"—a reference to a pagan idol—and reading the line, "Yes, the Dread of the peoples is a nothing" (vs. 3a JB). In the wake of theologies under the spell of Nietzsche, the suggestion of nihilism is forceful. "God is dead," and at the center of life is Nothing.

Even post-modern man, with his knowledge explosion, cannot live with Nothing enthroned at the core of his being. Inevitably believing in *something*, he believes by chance when he refuses to believe by commitment. Whenever the thirteenth of the month falls on Friday, the nervous humor of cartoon and human interest story in metropolitan dailies belies his uneasy search for meanings beyond the positivism he professes. The custom that hotels have twelfth and fourteenth floors, but no thirteenth, tells the truth about how superstition rushes in to fill the gap of a lost faith. If God is dead, Chance is not. On a recent Labor Day, nearly half a million Americans at twenty-seven racetracks wagered $28,647,672. At Aqueduct 67,878 New Yorkers bet well over $5 million, and at Arlington Park 36,330 Chicagoans hazarded almost $3 million—the urbane life of "the secular city" in the two largest urban centers being little protection against the wiles of Chance in an age of the enthronement of Nothing. And beyond the racetracks, supermarket "bingo" and merchandizing "sweepstakes" add the concealed price of a wager to commodities in nearly every category. As if in comment on post-modern as well as ancient nihilism, the poet-prophet adds, "But their rites are inane" (vs. 2d MT).

"They have to be carried" (vs. 5), he observes, looking at the idols that

fill the void. Such is the burden of the absurdity of worshiping, or placing dependence upon, what owes its existence to us. It is all "the work of craftsmen
. . . propped with nails and hammer, to keep it from falling!" (vs. 4
MT). Even so our secular securities—superior arms, expanding economy,
political panaceas, pleasure-filled leisure, hard-bought success. When God is
dead, these are our faiths. "They have to be carried."

How starkly this contrasts with the faith that carries us! With such a
faith, the poem moves on to celebrate "thee, O Lord; . . . for among all the
wise ones of the nations . . . there is none like thee" (vss. 6-7). One of John
Updike's characters, a man of ninety-four, comments aptly. A young
sophisticate has been attacking the faith of a group of simple men. Then the
old man replies:

When you get to be my age—and I shall pray that you never do, I wish it on no
one, but if you do—you shall know this: There is no goodness, without belief.
There is nothing but busy-ness. And if you have not believed, at the end of your
life you shall know you have buried your talent in the ground of this world and
have nothing saved, to take into the next.[21]

So "never learn to live like pagans"!

Dramatis Personae for a Missionary Epic: Acts 8:26-35

Christian faith on mission unfolds the epic of the ages. Once well called
"the March of Eleven Men," it began with the ragged remnant of the once
hopeful band who followed a crucified leader. Based in one of the smallest,
least populous countries in history, it built amid the ruins of the crumbling
Greco-Roman society a civilization that circled the world and spanned the
millennia. Moving out of the sparsely peopled West into the dense population
masses of the East, it breathed its ferment into religions far more ancient,
and became the largest body of believers in any single faith, numbering more
than a fourth of all the people of the globe. Even for those who have no
primary commitment to Christ, such an epic is absorbing drama.

For this epic today's lection provides the basic *dramatis personae*.
Sometimes called the first Gentile convert, the Ethiopian in this story is not
properly so identified; his pilgrimage to Jerusalem marks him as at least a
Jewish proselyte, leaving Cornelius secure in his place as the first Gentile
Christian (Acts 10). The passage before us has a deeper bearing on the
Christian epic. It reflects the *first evangelistic method*, the early wide *spread
of the gospel*, and its *theological center*. These are well interpreted through
the *dramatis personae* here gathered.

Here we meet the *Inquiring Outsider*. We know three significant facts
about the Ethiopian eunuch. He was a man of large responsibility (vs. 27);
the faith has appealed, in every age, to men of ability. A eunuch, under the
Law, was excluded from the "assembly of God"; Christianity welcomes those
deprived of full standing elsewhere. Having been on pilgrimage to Jerusalem,

---

[21] John Updike, *The Poorhouse Fair* (New York: The Modern Library,
1965), pp. 92-93.

he was reading the prophecy of Isaiah as he returned; faith speaks to the inquiring mind. These are central items of the strategy of the gospel in any age.

We meet, second, the *Christian Opportunist*. Philip did not wait to preach a sermon in an assembled congregation; he answered a question on the road. He moved quickly into a conversational opening. Kenneth Scott Latourette has pointed out that in its first swift spread into all the urban centers of the Mediterranean world, faith in Christ was carried not by professional missionaries but by businessmen in their travels. It could be so again. Unprecedented numbers of businessmen, diplomats, soldiers and sailors, tourists, students and scholars on fellowships abroad are also *Christians*. Suppose they knew and trusted their faith sufficiently to move quickly into conversational opportunities, what a surge of growth might come again in the Christian epic through the ministry of the Christian Opportunist!

We meet, finally, the *Suffering Savior*. The Servant delineated in Isa. 53 fascinated and perplexed the Ethiopian outsider, "and beginning with this scripture [Philip] told him the good news of Jesus" (vs. 35). So at the outset of the epic, Christians found a key to the understanding of Jesus in the Suffering Servant become Savior. This central figure of the drama still captivates. Hardly a year passes without a new book about him from the pen of a major secular scholar or literary artist. Significant novels as different as Faulkner's *The Sound and the Fury* and Ken Kesey's *One Flew Over the Cuckoo's Nest*, eschewing all sentimental biblicism or overt preachment, make their savior figures—startlingly different in mood—in the unmistakable image of the Suffering One, surprisingly like him in numerous ways and in a multitude of details. Even the secular world is still hungry for the Suffering Savior.

Inquiring Outsider, Christian Opportunist, Suffering Savior—the cast of the drama is gathered. On with the epic!

Dare to Live: John 4:7-26

"There came a woman of Samaria to draw water. Jesus said to her, 'Give me a drink'" (vs. 7). Stumbling uncertainly today, weighed down by yesterday and tomorrow, how like us she was! If you had told her she was about to become a convincing person who had found something that could win her fellow townsmen to a new way of life, she would have laughed her scornful, mirthless laugh. Yet the event turned out exactly so, as the stranger she met by the well helped her to abandon the quest for a life someone could give her, and simply dare to live.

It began when this appealing stranger asked her for a drink. The conversation is worth picking up (vss. 9-14). Using the same word, they talked of vastly different things. To her, water was a necessity laboriously carried from the well. Not unlike us, she thought most naturally of comforts and interests close at hand.

Sherwood Eddy, vigorous missionary crusader for pioneering causes through a long generation, recalls how such preoccupation almost drowned out God's call to him in his youth. Recollecting college days, he says, "Like most of the men, I heard no missionary call; for with self-centered plans and ambitions thundering in our ears, we were simply not within calling distance." Could that be a picture of us?

Speaking of "living water," how much more than a creature comfort Jesus offered! But the woman's mind moved only the short distance from the water to the well. An honored ancestor, Jacob, had dug it; let no stranger belittle the gift of so great a man. Jacob, indeed, had dug the well of the community's faith. To the degree that religion had a place in this woman's life, she treasured its tradition as a spiritual heirloom from Jacob and such worthies of the remembered past.

For Jacob, faith had been an epoch-making adventure, unlocking new discoveries, remolding him from the crafty supplanter into the man of God whose spiritual strength would bless a whole people. But for this woman no sharp excitement of creative renewal remained. Could that be our case, too?

All this Jesus tried to break through with his request, "Give me a drink." Sometimes God involves us in more of life than we anticipate, by awakening us to a religion of things we can do for him. So Jesus, purposing what he might give the woman, began with something she could do for him. So God's call got through the preoccupation of the young Sherwood Eddy. When he heard at last, he gave himself completely. With exhausting exertion, through endless unrelenting days he labored at his calling, until complete breakdown plunged him into bottomless, terrifying depression.

One morning in 1897, he lay in bed too spent to get up, telling himself that if he did he would have no message worth giving to anyone. Then, almost as if from an audible voice, it came to him: "Every one who drinks of this water will thirst again, but whoever drinks of the water that I shall give him will never thirst: the water that I shall give him will become in him a spring of water welling up to eternal life." Suddenly he knew! The disciplined life had its place, but it was not the whole gospel. There was a power he could have if he would accept it. He rose from his bed with his energy restored, never to break again, and through a long generation to live on the growing edge of social and spiritual advance, as one of the most moving personalities of his time. Many years after, he testified: "This promise has proved literally true for nearly half a century and I believe it will prove eternal truth so long as I keep drinking of this water of life (the life of God in the soul of man, shared with his fellow-men)."

Isn't it strange, what barriers we throw up to defend ourselves against him? Wanting his gifts, we are afraid of him. Perhaps a bit more of the conversation with the Samaritan woman will help us to see ourselves more clearly (vss. 15-20). She plunged into the old, tired religious argument. For this stranger had brought the conversation round to matters too painful to discuss. Desperate for escape, she took an age-old course—flight from God into religion.

Jesus would have none of it. From a religion of escape, he invited the woman—can you doubt that he invites us?—to a religion of reality. He said to her, "God is spirit, and those who worship him must worship in spirit and truth" (vs. 24). Some of us might begin now to dare to live. Out of our traditionalism into a fresh experience, out of our hideouts from conscience into a real facing of all life's issues, we might come now to an encounter with

Christ, who stands for utter reality. As the conversation came to its thrilling close, it happened so to the Samaritan woman.

She said to Jesus, " 'I know that Messiah is coming (he who is called Christ); when he comes, he will show us all things.' Jesus said to her, 'I who speak to you am he' " (vss. 25-26). The divine visitation would surely come someday, but not now. Like us, she looked to a wistful some other time. Jesus brought her up short. The time is now, he declared. "I who speak to you am he." About his presence there is no question. He meets so many men and women in transforming encounter that the burden of proof rests on those who say he will not come to them. But does he have the vote in the living *now*—not enshrined in yesterday's fond memories or tomorrow's wistful hopes? [22]

SEVENTH SUNDAY AFTER EPIPHANY

God Veils His Power: Habakkuk 2:18-20; 3:2-4

Viewing the lectionary in ecumenical perspective, it is well to note that for large sections of the universal church the third Sunday before Lent, or Septuagesima, opens the sub-season of pre-Lent. Its keynote gospel is the parable of the laborers (Matt. 20:1-16), from which it takes its theme of wages and grace. When Epiphanytide is shortened by an early Easter, these sister churches thus omit the requisite number of Sundays *before* this seventh, keeping the three Sundays next before Lent as a fixed period of observance. While the United Methodist lectionary does not demand such treatment, it might be appropriate. The lections for these pre-Lent Sundays are apt for the purpose.

This Old Testament lesson, seen in its context, is useful for pre-Lent. The theme of wages and grace stands here in one of its basic sources, "the righteous shall live by his faith" (2:4b). The theme of trust amid adversity is never more beautifully stated than in 3:17-18 with its affirmation that though "the fields yield no food, . . . yet I will rejoice in the Lord." "The Lord is in his holy temple; let all the earth keep silence before him" (2:20) is one of the best loved introits and a familair call to worship. In this liturgical use it has lost its initial word, "But," and that word restored makes this great verse climactic and dramatically powerful in Habakkuk's prophecy. For what we have here is a hard-won conviction wrought out in long wrestling with an agonizing problem.

The time is desperate. "Outrage and violence, this is all I see, all is contention, and discord flourishes. . . . The wicked man gets the better of the upright, and so justice is seen to be distorted" (1:3b, 4b JB). Chaos reigns not only internally in Judah, but in the sweep of Chaldean conquests and the harsh duties they exact. Why does God permit such arch-wickedness? Habakkuk laments. "O Lord, how long shall I cry for help, and thou wilt not hear?" (1:2).

[22] This exposition of John 4:7-26 is condensed from Abbey, *Encounter With Christ*, pp. 47-54.

A first answer suggests that God is not passively *permitting* but actively *using* the Chaldeans, even though these pagans do not know it. Their "own might is their god!" (1:11). Nevertheless, they are unwittingly God's instrument of judgment upon Judah: "O Lord, thou hast ordained them as a judgment; and thou, O Rock, hast established them for chastisement" (1:12).

From this answer another troublesome question emerges. How can a good God ally himself with a wicked servant? "Why dost thou look on faithless men, and art silent when the wicked swallows up the man more righteous than he?" (1:13). Answer: this is no lasting victory the Chaldean is winning; it cannot stand. "He whose soul is not upright in him shall fail" (2:4a). Furthermore, there is another day coming: "But the righteous shall live by his faith," or as the RSV note suggests, "by his faithfulness" (2:4b).

As if to spell this out, there follows the series of taunts, of which 2:18-20 is climactic. The first sets the tone: "Trouble is coming to the man who amasses goods that are not his" (2:6 JB). He collects numerous enemies who will arise against him and exact retribution (2:6-8). For the nation that seeks to make itself invulnerable by plunder, there is trouble in store (2:9-11). He who "builds a town with blood, and founds a city on iniquity" will come to ruin, for God's own glory will finally cover the earth (2:12-14). The Chaldean must finally drink from the cup he has forced on others: "The violence done to Lebanon will overwhelm you" (2:16-17).

In all these ways the pagan will learn the uselessness of his self-contrived gods. "Woe to him who says to a wooden thing, Awake" (2:19). The dumb stone cannot arise. Such a god teaches nothing: "Can this give revelation?" (vs. 19). "Can that give any guidance?" (MT). It is "a false guide" (2:18 MT) or "a teacher of lies" (RSV). Nothing in itself, it enourages false dependence on the self-made standards that have prompted its contrivance. In contast, see the glory of God: "But the Lord is in his holy temple; let all the earth keep silence before him." God is sovereign Lord of history, despite all appearance to the contrary.

The psalm that follows (Chapter 3) may well be from the hand of a later poet, but this does not matter. It expands the conviction at which Habakkuk has arrived over a hard road. God is Lord not only of history but of the cosmos. Events have sometimes veiled his power but cannot negate it. The heavens and the earth, likewise, are full of his glory; the very light is a veil of his presence—"and there he veiled his power" (3:4). Even destitution and adversity are but veils he wears, so that in the midst of them "yet I will rejoice in the Lord. . . . God, the Lord, is my strength" (3:18-19). Thus set in its full context, today's Old Testament Lesson speaks to every age, for the adversity and the religious perplexities it propounds are always with us.

Creative in Crisis: I Peter 2:4-10

"But you are a chosen race, a royal priesthood, a holy nation, God's own people" (vs. 9)—imagine saying *that* to little companies of slaves and persecuted nobodies huddled in the back streets of cities dotted around the Mediterranean! Enduring purge and bloodbath, this letter insisted, they were still important and, amid crisis, could be creative. As the event turned out, the absurd claim was vindicated. The future lay not with the impressive pagan culture that oppressed them, but with the faith and way for which these witnesses stood.

The resources which this held out to them can be important to us in our age, for which crisis has become a way of life. *From Christ, it says, we receive both the call and the capability to be a creative community in the midst of crisis.* For this general letter to the church stands as a basic charter of the Christian community in all ages and is a part of our heritage and marching orders.

It shows us, first, that Christians do not exist as isolated individuals, but from their diverse sources are drawn together as a united people of God. Like "living stones," which no longer lie scattered about, we are to be built "into a spiritual house." We are called to "a holy priesthood, to offer spiritual sacrifices acceptable to God through Jesus Christ" (vs. 5). Piling figure on figure, the writer shows our corporate unity—a new temple, a new priesthood—dynamically affecting the world of which we are a part. The *calling* of the church as a priesthood of all believers stands structurally at the heart of our faith. An isolated Christian, not committed to this community of concern, is a contradiction.

The letter shows, second, that as a new temple, a new priesthood, we have a sacrificial and transforming witness to make. "A chosen race, a royal priesthood, a holy nation, God's own people"—the titles once reserved for the people Israel are now applied to the church. The new Israel is called to continue the unfulfilled mission of the old, to "declare the wonderful deeds" of God, especially in the new Exodus by which he has led us "out of darkness into his marvelous light" (vs. 9). Once we were "no people," existing as we did in our uncommitted separateness outside the fellowship of faith, but now we are "God's people" (vs. 10). The Greek term translated "people" is *laos,* root of our terms "layman" and "laity." As the root indicates, our terms do not properly connote the untrained and less committed nonprofessional, but *the people* who make up the vital witnessing body of the concerned and the creative.

We have a great story to tell; for whereas once we "had not received mercy," now we *have.* As recipients of mercy, we can have nothing self-consciously superior in our testimony. "Nothing separates us more from one another than being right when someone else is wrong and insisting on acting accordingly." [23] Knowing we were once "no people," that we are what we are only because we "have received mercy," we can give only the creative witness that stands beside our brother man admitting our own guilt and our thanksgiving that God meets our need.

The letter shows, third, that in this new temple our lives are held together and given meaning and strength by Christ, who is our cornerstone, "that living stone, rejected by men but in God's sight chosen and precious" (vs. 4). The figure is borrowed from two Old Testament sources: (a) Ps. 118:22, which is part of a thanksgiving for God's salvation from distress, and seems to be a proverbial recognition that the rejected stone can become the cornerstone which ties the building together. New Testament writers saw in it an

---

[23] Helmut Gollwitzer, *The Demands of Freedom* (New York: Harper, 1965), p. 115.

allusion to Christ, and so used it in all of the Synoptic Gospels, in Acts and Ephesians, and in this passage. (b) Isa. 28:16, which is an oracle against the rulers of Jerusalem, who have contracted a covenant to serve strange gods in exchange for their protection—though the Lord offers the real cornerstone, the true foundation. Unbelievers see in Christ only something to reject, but in their rejection they stumble over the values that are real and indispensable in him; while Christians find in him the cornerstone that gives design, meaning, and strength to our lives (vss. 7-8). In his teaching, his transforming friendship, and his vital presence lies our *power* to be the creative community we are *called* to be in the midst of crisis.

No Secondhand Christ: John 1:35-51

Typically for the Fourth Gospel, this lesson deals with meanings at more than one level. There is surface event, conversational remark, individual character; but beneath these lie the universal experience, the double meaning, the wide category of persons. At this second level, the passage points out, *each of us can and must meet Christ for himself, at firsthand, in a life-changing religious experience.*

Jesus' first words in the Fourth Gospel are reported in this passage. Significantly they are the question, "What do you seek?" (vs. 38). "In a real sense they raise the fundamental religious problem, both of the Gospel itself and of human experience generally. By accepting Jesus' invitation to go with him to his abode (1:39), the disciples have discovered (or are in the process of discovering) the goal of their religious quest." [24] Three key questions, addressed by the new disciples to Jesus, unlock the meanings to which the quest leads.

First they asked: "Where are you staying?" (vs. 38). How can we find you? How can we be with you? At the deeper level of meaning, "they learn where Jesus really dwells, that is to say, in the realm of eternal life, and they associate themselves with him in the sense that they are no longer of 'this world' (cf. 17:14)." [25] The recurring response, "Come and see" (vs. 39), is first heard in reply, as if Jesus were saying that he is not to be known theoretically by secondhand telling, but only by those who see at firsthand. The upshot was that Simon got a new name, representing a new nature, a new being (vs. 42). Finding Jesus at this deeper level, one becomes a new man.

Nathanael asked: "Can anything good come out of Nazareth?" (vs. 46). That is, can Jesus' simple origins give rise to anything important? Particularly, can the Messiah come from this town in outland Galilee? Again we hear, "Come and see" (vs. 46), as if Philip was replying: There is no good in merely talking about origins or what *we might expect;* you must have direct *personal dealings with him.* The upshot was that Nathanael had access to an epiphany of "the angels of God ascending and descending upon the Son of

[24] Eric Lane Titus, *The Message of the Fourth Gospel* (Nashville: Abingdon Press, 1957), p. 78.
[25] *Ibid.*

man" (vs. 51, cf. Gen. 28:12). Finding Jesus' deeper origin one is led to God.

Finally Nathanael asked: "How do you know me?" (vs. 48). For he had found himself deeply understood, as many a man finds that the New Testament interprets the meaning of his life. Setting out as a merely curious reader, he is drawn into personal encounter. The day before his execution, a fighter in the Norwegian resistance began such a reading of the New Testament which the prison chaplain gave him. The following day, preparing to meet the firing squad, he said: "I read the book you gave me. From it walked a Man. I go confident of heaven." One who emerges from the pages becomes our friend and, feeling ourselves addressed, we, too, ask, "How do you know me?"

Discovering how fully Jesus knew him, Nathanael replied: "Rabbi, you are the Son of God! You are the King of Israel!" (vs. 49). This moves less in the realm of meeting with a new teacher than in that of direct and authentic religious experience. Of such experience Jesus spoke in his use of the figure of Jacob's dream at Bethel (Gen. 28:10-22), "You will see heaven opened, and the angels of God ascending and descending upon the Son of man" (vs. 51).

Whatever our point of encounter with the figure of Jesus, it becomes the place where the ladder is set for us. There God deals with us, even when we do not recognize him. John Knox recalls young men who have spoken to him of their admiration for Jesus the teacher—and their rejection of any theological dimension of his being. They need no such mediator, they say, for they experience God directly in mystical prayer. Asked to describe the nature of this experienced Deity, they speak of him in terms which, despite their disavowals, Jesus has made a part of their cultural inheritance. Proclaiming their independence of Christ the revealer, they live by the influence of a revelation they have imbibed unawares.

"You shall see [opse, singular] greater things than these" (vs. 50) is changed to "You will see [opsesthe, plural] heaven opened" (vs. 51). So, the syntax of the Gospel seems to say, this assurance belongs not simply to Nathanael, but to all who will hear and meet Christ for themselves.

EIGHTH SUNDAY AFTER EPIPHANY

Where Relativity Stops: Leviticus 19:1-2, 15-18

According to a widely accepted axiom of everyday wisdom, "Everything is relative." [26] John Steinbeck depicts a memorable character all but undone by this sophistry. "Money has no heart," he reflects. And sin? "That's relative too in a relative universe." [27] Remembering the impression of patriotic

---

[26] Cf. "Axioms of Modern Man," by Emil Brunner, in *The Church's Witness to God's Design*, vol. ii of the Amsterdam Assembly Series (New York: Harper, 1948), p. 81.

[27] John Steinbeck, *The Winter of Our Discontent* (New York: Viking Press, 1961), p. 65.

virtue left by his ancestors who founded the family's wealth on commissions to intercept shipping in the wars of 1776 and 1812, he comments: "But to the British they were pirates, and what they took they kept." So he rationalized his own plan for a potentially tragic robbery from which only a last minute turn of circumstance deterred him.

We have learned that no code can adequately prescribe for every contingency and that conduct worked out by rigid application of law is not always good. But we have been learning, too, that ethical thinking which begins with the premise, "Everything is relative," may leave us without a moral guide just when we need it most. Is relativity the last and only word? Where, if anywhere, does relativity stop?

At the heart of the Holiness Code (Lev. 17-26) stands the guiding principle, "You shall be holy; for I the Lord your God am holy" (19:2). The Code prescribes specific conduct in a wide variety of areas, but its lasting contribution is this insight that at the heart of our life stands an inviolable relationship to a holy God. The numinous, whose meaning is somewhat parallel to the holy, has been characterized as "an event, an experience, a place, an object that evokes in us a sense of mystery, of terror mixed with fascination, of the eerie." [28] We are so constituted that, to live fully, we must respond not fractionally but with our whole being, to whatever shows itself as having supreme worth. For the Judeo-Christian faith, this is a holy God. To violate this need of our being is to fragment and decimate our personhood.

This responsible relationship can guide us to right choices amid the decisions which constitute the fabric of our lives.

H. Richard Niebuhr has compared ethical responsibility with the task of "the motor-car driver who must make forty decisions each minute. Neither obedience to rules of the road, nor desire to arrive at his goal, offers sufficient basis for his conduct." The driver is not going to do better by forgetting his goal or by neglecting the traffic rules, but these are not enough. He must meet situations as they arise, must improvise, must exercise his judgment. The task of our society and the people in it is even more challenging, because many of our travels are on uncharted roads where no patterns of traffic have been established.[29]

In the adaptations we are not left to completely unguided improvisation. We belong to a covenant community whose great tradition communicates tested insights out of a past with which we have continuity and at the heart of which stands our relation to God. Here is supreme value demanding whole response, foundational to the health and wholeness of the community and of our own being.

Rooting its ethic in this relation, the Holiness Code arrives at another foundation principle: "Do not deal basely with your fellows. Do not profit by the blood of your neighbor: I am the Lord" (vs. 16 TMT). Though the chapter contains varied directions related to rituals and social structures no longer relevant, this concern for persons is universally vital. What it means to refuse

---

[28] *The Interpreter's Bible*, II, 88.
[29] Roger L. Shinn, *Tangled World* (New York: Scribner's, 1965), pp. 154-55.

"to profit by the blood of your neighbor" in business, labor relations, housing laws, and international dealings is pivotal to significant religion and crucial to human welfare, as much today as in ancient Israel.

If the center of the Holiness Code is its insistence that a holy God requires a holy people, the radius which scans the moral horizon is its declaration, "you shall love your neighbor as yourself: I am the Lord" (vs. 18), or "You must love your fellow, since he is the same as yourself, for I am the Lord" (AT)—implying the integral relation of individuals within the covenant community of which God is the center. It is this sense of the relatedness and wholeness of our life with each other and with God which modern society has lost. "Noninvolvement," "alienation," "anomie"—we have invented numerous terms to describe it. Until our fragmentation is replaced by the dynamic wholeness symbolized by the Holiness Code, no situation ethic can safely guide us.

There is a strong affirmative quality about it. Ex. 23:4-5 serves as a fitting commentary: "When you encounter your enemy's ox or ass wandering, you must take it back to him. When you see the ass of your enemy prostrate under its burden and would refrain from raising it, you must nevertheless raise it with him" (TMT). Neighbor-love which includes the enemy, provides fixed rights for the poor (vss. 9-10), and concerns itself with proper payment of wages (vs. 13) has a creative quality still needed in modern society.

One limitation must be recognized. As it stands, this law is an in-group ethic. MT and AT catch its spirit by reading "fellow-countryman" for the RSV "brother" in vs. 17: "You must not cherish hate against your fellow-countryman" (AT). Even such a limited field of application would be an invaluable forward step for modern organized hate-groups! But it needs such a reminder as Benjamin Franklin offered: "Justice is as strictly due between neighbor nations as between neighbor citizens. A Highwayman is as much a robber when he plunders in a gang as when single; and a nation that makes an unjust war is only a *great gang*." [30] Even more, it needs the broad sweep given it by Jesus in the parable of the Good Samaritan.

Antidote to Aimlessness: Ephesians 4:17-32

"In particular, I want to urge you in the name of the Lord, not to go on living the aimless kind of life that pagans live" (vs. 17 JB). Timely word in an age when whole philosophies are built as bulwarks against the meaninglessness and aimlessness of the common life! This passage delineates the symptoms of the disease and prescribes a cure. Both are on target for our need.

See the *disease* in full clinical detail. Pagans live "in the futility of their minds" (vs. 17). "They are estranged [RSV: "alienated"] from the life of God" (vs. 18 MT). Paganism has made of them something other than they were meant to be. And this has not come about by chance, but is the outgrowth of a total deadening of sensibility which accompanies their pagan values. "They are estranged from the life of God by the ignorance which their dullness of heart has produced in them" (vs. 18 MT). "The man who

[30] Quoted by Starkey, *James Bond's World of Values,* p. 89.

habitually indulges in evil finally loses all the finer sensibilities. What began as a moral failing becomes also an intellectual one. That side of his mind which ought to respond to the higher things has become atrophied." [31]

There is a bitter picture of the neo-paganism of our "post-Christian age" in the line, "Dead to all feeling, they have abandoned themselves to vice, and stop at nothing to satisfy their foul desires" (vs. 19 NEB). Back of the phrase "dead to all feeling" lurks a Greek medical term for paralysis or deadness to pain, which leads E. F. Scott to remark that "pagan vices, as practised in the age of Nero, could only be set down to the utter deadness of the sense of right and wrong." [32] Might we not make some substitutions for "the age of Nero" in that sentence? What about the age of napalm? Age of the Playboy philosophy? Age of alcoholism? Age of racism?

It is pointless thus to diagnose the disease save in preparation to prescribe *treatment*. The therapy involves two steps, the first calling for revolutionary change. The good news of Christ and the style of life to which he leads stand in stark contrast to this pagan pattern (vss. 20-21). A complete change of nature ensues when one's thought and feeling are truly grounded in him (vss. 22-24). As a result, "Your mind must be renewed by a spiritual revolution" (vs. 23 JB). No milder term will suffice to describe the change; for creation has begun again, as the lost image of God is restored in "the new nature, created after the likeness of God in true righteousness and holiness" (vs. 24).

The second step in the therapy is a recognition that "we are members one of another" (vs. 25). As in the Holiness Code (Lev. 17–26) a holy God requires a holy people, knit together in neighbor-love; so, being united to Christ, we become parts one of another. This central reality makes itself felt in numerous particulars. Belonging to the one body of Christ, we must be truthful in our dealings with one another; only a church so united in mutual truthfulness can do the saving work of the Body (vs. 25). We must not persist in anger, since festering anger mortgages future usefulness (vss. 26-27). Turning from ways of getting a living at others' expense, we are to live by honorable toil in order that we may contribute to the welfare of others (vs. 28). "Evil talk" is to be replaced by such speech as builds up others and fits the occasion, bringing the goodness of God to those who hear (vs. 29).

John Wesley gave his Methodist Societies a set of "General Rules" reminiscent of this antidote for aimlessness. Those who desired "to flee from the wrath to come, and to be saved from their sins" were expected "to evidence their desire of salvation,

First: By doing no harm, by avoiding evil of every kind, especially that which is most generally practiced. . . . *Second*: By doing good; by being in every kind merciful after their power; as they have opportunity, doing good of every possible sort, and, as far as possible, to all men . . . . *Third*: By attending upon all the ordinances of God." [33]

---

[31] E. F. Scott, *Moffatt New Testament Commentary, ad loc.*

[32] *Ibid.*

[33] *The Book of Discipline of The United Methodist Church* (Nashville: The Methodist Publishing House, 1968), pp. 50-51.

Here is the same proscription of hurtful conduct, the same mandate to the good that builds up (vs. 28). Here, too, is the capping of all rules of conduct by a certainty that our relation to God is at stake. Offenses against the unity of the brotherhood "grieve the Holy Spirit of God" (vs. 30).

Free in Obedience: Luke 10:25-37

Though William Stringfellow's book, *Free in Obedience*, does not treat this parable, its title compactly describes the Samaritan. Without slavishly following a code, this man is utterly obedient to the law of love. No flaunting of slogans about freedom has any place in his program, yet in the creativity of his response to a need he shows himself a free man.

Many of the older lectionaries number this Sunday not in the sequence after Epiphany but as the Second Sunday before Lent, or Sexagesima. The pre-Lenten cycle carries the motif of a good life which arrives at its goals over this route of obedient love that makes free, I Cor. 13 being a traditional lesson for pre-Lent. This parable caps today's trilogy of lessons in our lectionary, completing the consideration of the freedom of the obedient life which the Old Testament lesson began.

In response to the lawyer's question, Jesus has brought together the two facets of the law of love. "And who is my neighbor?" (vs. 29) the lawyer asks, whereupon Jesus tells the now familiar story. The question was not captious or trivial, since the meaning of the term here translated "neighbor" was in dispute.

It was generally agreed that the term connoted fellow-countrymen, including full proselytes, but there was disagreement about the exceptions: the Pharisees were inclined to exclude non-Pharisees . . . ; the Essenes required that a man 'should hate all the sons of darkness'; a rabbinical saying ruled that heretics, informers, and renegades 'should be pushed (into the ditch) and not pulled out,' and a widespread popular saying excepted personal enemies.[34]

The question at issue was, How far in the community does the demand of friendship run? Where can the line be drawn?

When Jesus told his story, bringing into view first a priest and then a Levite, the rule of climax in the triadic form of storytelling would seem to lead from these two orders within Judaism to a Jewish layman as the third character. It is the flouting of this expectation which gives the story its breathless twist. Instead of such an expected figure, a hated Samaritan appears. So the parable underscores the answer that the line of neighbor-love can be drawn nowhere. Love's law knows no limit. A neighbor is not someone you *have*, but someone you *are*. Being neighborly, you are never without a neighbor.

This kind of goodness, Harold Edwin Berg suggests, is like the disciplined freedom of the jazz musician. There is wide and breathless improvisation, yet the jazz artists are not in chaotic anarchy, going their separate ways in disregard of one another. All are held alike by the *beat*, in "a creative act of faith, improvisation within the boundaries of felt rhythm."

[34] Joachim Jeremias, *The Parables of Jesus* (New York: Scribner's, 1963), pp. 202-3.

True morality, he adds, is like that; it does not ape a code, it responds to the climate of love.

Improvised morality is more rigidly disciplined than any formal code because it rests on faith. The man who demands to be told what to do is precisely the man who does not believe. He must be shown. And his performance will be a still-born reproduction of a sterile code. The moral pioneer can break out of such dull, uncreative conformity into the infinitely more demanding sensitivity of responsible love.[35]

Note well how organically this lesson relates neighbor-love and God-love. Perhaps we should not be surprised that a generation which denied love by apathy, unwillingness to be involved, and organized hatred on partisan, racial, and national levels, should come eventually to proclaim the death of God. It might be better, Carlyle Marney suggests, to speak of "the eclipse of God." "For," he adds, "the God who does not talk to men in the sacred or secular cities of our time may very well be the God who does not talk because he has *said* it. He has no more to say until the Son is heard." [36] Lent will call us to hear him, beginning with his teaching in this crucial parable.

NINTH SUNDAY AFTER EPIPHANY

Hold Fast to Discipline: Proverbs 4:10-18

Hold fast to discipline, never let her go,
keep your eyes on her, she is your life.
(vs. 13 JB)

Not very welcome advice in our time! Discipline looks like a limited notion of life. Popular or not, this couplet catches the flavor of a passage from Proverbs which has commended itself to thoughtful people across the centuries. Not only biblical, it carries overtones of the counsel of many of the most honored thinkers, at least as far back as Socrates. Wisdom so durable deserves a hearing.

On the Sunday next before Lent, the message of this wisdom poem provides an apt transition. Whatever its *original* meaning, the passage on instruction (vss. 10-13) reminds *Christians* of God's revelation (epiphany) of himself in Jesus Christ. The lines dealing with the path of the wicked (vss. 14-17) carry to every sensitive soul a fresh awareness of his own violations and his need of the penitence to which Lent calls. Epiphany as season of light comes to its climax in the promise (vs. 18) of walking in the fully realized light of the maturity God gives.

The lesson speaks first of the *disciplined life of wisdom*. "Hold fast to discipline, never let her go" conveys the practical nature of the wisdom dealt with in the Proverbs—a source of long life and unhampered progress. Yet it is a *lofty* practicality, as Prov. 3:19-20 makes clear, with its keynote: "The Lord by wisdom founded the earth." In 8:22-31, wisdom speaks in the first person,

[35] Berg, *The Ten Commandments and You*, pp. 117-18.
[36] Carlyle Marney, *The Carpenter's Son* (Nashville: Abingdon Press, 1967), pp. 11-12.

underscoring this primordial participation with God in creation, reaching a grand climax which celebrates both the creative act and the joy in all that has been brought forth.

> When he marked out the foundations of the earth,
>   then I was beside him, like a master workman;
> and I was daily his delight,
>   rejoicing before him always,
> rejoicing in his inhabited world
>   and delighting in the sons of men (8:29b-31).

Discipline that admits one to the joy of such workmanship is worth its cost.

One of Wallace Stegner's characters speaks of such discipline over against the current tendency to blot out distinctions. "Some codes," he says, "are better than the codes that displace them; and I believe this is a corrupt age because it accepts everything as equal to everything else, and because it values indulgence more than restraint." [37] Speaking of the death of a man of thirty-seven, who had lived a studiedly undisciplined life, the same character remarks that his

face had given up all its poses and looked merely young, incredibly young, far younger than it had any right to look, the very face of kicks-crazy America, unlined by thinking, unmarked by pain, unshadowed even by years of scrupulous dissoluteness, untouched by life—or by death either—except for a slight discontented droop at the corners of the lips.[38]

End of the road for those who do not "hold fast to discipline"!

For the Christian, all this evokes the image of Christ. Wisdom that was there when the Lord established the heavens (8:27) calls to mind the Word that "was in the beginning with God" (John 1:2) and that "became flesh and dwelt among us" (John 1:14). And wisdom integrally related not so much to meditation as to action in the arena of practical life awakes echoes of Jesus' saying, "If any man's will is to do his will, he shall know whether the teaching is from God" (John 7:17).

The lesson speaks, again, of *wickedness as a deadening of sensibility.* Contrary to the easy assumption that one gains freedom to live more fully by throwing off limitations, it declares that the violation of the restraints of conscience is itself the most limiting of all things. Vs. 19, following this lection, may have stood originally between vss. 17 and 18, and is so placed by both MT and AT.

> The course of bad men lies through darkness dim,
>   they cannot see what makes them stumble (vs. 19 MT).

Vision limited to the immediate and obvious, sensitivity calloused, interests fenced in by self-concern, their perception is blinded and their freedom gone.

In its discussion of the wicked, this passage (vss. 14-17) sharply divides

---

[37] Wallace Stegner, *All the Little Live Things* (New York: Viking Press, 1967), p. 176.

[38] *Ibid.*, p. 185.

them from the righteous, a thing which Jesus in his compassion refused to do. The separation becomes utterly impossible when good and evil, not confined to overt acts, are traced to inner motives and attitudes. Guided thus by his Lord, the Christian must see in this passage less a justification of disdain for the moral lapses of others than a call to penitence for his own stained life.

The lesson speaks, finally, of *the increasing light that falls on the way of the committed,* a light "which shines brighter and brighter until full day" (vs. 18). In a slightly different figure, Gunnar Mattsson speaks of the same experience of enrichment through disciplined dedication, as he writes of a beautiful marriage. "Married happiness," he observes,

is like a tree: it has to grow before you can enjoy its shade. And it doesn't grow if you don't take care of it but run around admiring other plants. It takes many years. If you concentrate your love on a single tree and wait, you can see it grow, and there comes a day when you can lean against it and find coolness in its shade.[39]

In some ways resembling a marriage commitment, the full life found in Christ is the product of such disciplined devotion. It is a personal relation which admits no possibility of "running around admiring" other Lords and other ways of life. Jesus said it is a narrow way that leads to life (Matt. 7:14). Paul saw it as growing into maturity (Col. 1:28; Eph. 4:13). Experience finds it a light that steadily brightens "until full day."

The Persuasion of Power: I Corinthians 2:1-16

Paul departs from our familiar term, "the power of persuasion," to deal rather with the persuasion of power! Not that he boasts of superior might, a mailed fist that ends all arguments, or of that way of imposing our will that we euphemistically call "negotiating from strength." "The word I spoke . . . ," he says, "carried conviction by spiritual power" (vs. 4 NEB).

If that kind of power is available, we need it to bind up the fractured life of our revolutionary age. In the crisis of population explosion, when the growth of the Christian community is outrun by the sheer multiplication of the human mass, we need that power. Amid the fissuring of the common mind in our pluralistic post-modern culture, when preaching lacks the shared presuppositions to make *argument* effective, we need this power that carries the weight of *demonstration.* "The word I spoke . . . carried conviction by spiritual power."

Needs claimant in Corinth resembled our own. In that revolutionary era, marked by a message that changed the life patterns of the Western world, this "conviction by spiritual power" met the needs. When the church was not merely a minority but an all but negligible one, this power made it a creative force. When the Christian message had to challenge a society not only pluralistic but overwhelmingly pagan, this power prevailed. By it these few infectious believers "outthought, outlived, and outdied the pagan world."

What they offered was not argument, but the power of the crucified Christ (vss. 1-5). In ironic contrast to the argumentative sects at Corinth,

[39] Gunnar Mattsson, *The Princess* (New York: Dutton, 1966), quoted from Reader's Digest Condensed Books, Summer, 1967, p. 38.

Paul offered this persuasion of power. "I declared the attested truth of God," he says, "without display of fine words or wisdom" (vs. 1 NEB). His only message was "Jesus Christ and him crucified," literally, "Jesus Christ and this one having been crucified," as if to emphasize a crucifixion now past and swallowed up in the power of the resurrection. So, against their clamorous arguments, another kind of gospel prevailed. "The word I spoke, the gospel I proclaimed, did not sway you with subtle arguments; it carried conviction by spiritual power" (vs. 4 NEB).

To the question, "What makes a church grow in our disturbed world?" a missionary statesman makes a fourfold reply. (1) Being part of the national stream, not in the sense of acquiescent accommodation to rampant nationalism, but in vital participation in the real affairs of the common life. (2) Speaking with courage on issues, not limiting itself to the safety of nostalgia for yesterday or the haven of the inner life. (3) Showing compassion for need. (4) Expecting God's action.[40] Such specifics are the carriers of "conviction by spiritual power" in our explosive age.

What the demonstrators of spiritual power offered was not improvised human policies, but the strategy of the Cross (vss. 6-13). "Wisdom" was available, Paul conceded, but it was for the "mature" who could respond to it; for it was not "what this world calls wisdom" (vs. 6 AT), not the wisdom of "any of its governing powers, which are declining to their end" (NEB). If the powers of this world had known this wisdom of God's hidden purpose, they would not have launched anything so self-defeating as the crucifixion of Christ (vs. 8). What the world cannot give of wisdom, however, God's Spirit imparts as only he can. For just as only a man's highest self-perception can grasp his own nature, so only God's Spirit can reveal himself (vs. 11). "These disclosures we impart, not in the set phrases of human philosophy, but in words the Spirit teaches, giving spiritual truth a spiritual form" (vs. 13 AT).

How does one translate this into actualities of the contemporary scene? Perhaps the missionary statesman quoted above was doing so in the program he laid down in response to the question, "How hold the church together in revolution and explosive change?" His four points call for imaginative expansion. (1) Render sheer obedience to our Lord. (2) Stay on the field where the spoken word is no longer received; serve, think, wait; and while you wait make what witness you can. Rebels who have won out have a lesson for the church; they were disciplined, ready to die, and they smelled victory in the air. (3) Live with joy in casting bread upon the waters. (4) Work with compassion undergirded by competence—without which there can be no adequate witness.[41] By such steps as these we translate the strategy of the Cross for today.

The demonstrators of spiritual power offered, not divisive judgments, but a shared exposure to the mind of Christ (vss. 14-16). The theological and ecclesiastical factions at Corinth, Paul pointed out, had no sound basis for their judgments against each other. They had only the mechanisms of earthbound

---

[40] Summarized from the author's notes of an address by Dr. Tracey K. Jones, Jr., June, 1967.
[41] *Ibid.*

life to guide them. They were *psychikos de anthropos*, "natural man." Such "a material man will not accept what the Spirit of God offers" (vs. 14 AT). A deep change, the coming of the Spirit, is needed before such a man has any way of perceiving these depth meanings. So the judgments of one another inherent in Corinthian sectarianism—and in all human divisiveness—are indefensible. Only one way lies open to the truth in which we need to stand: "A spiritual man . . . is able to judge the value of everything, and his own value is not to be judged by other men" (vs. 15 JB). Central to all this spiritual discernment is not any esoteric "wisdom," but "the mind of Christ" (vs. 16), the "understanding" he gives (VWS); "we share the thoughts of Christ" (vs. 16 AT).

There is no other way out of the confusion and destructiveness of our divisions. Across wide chasms of nationality, race, ideology, and creed, the delegates to the World Council of Churches at New Delhi affirmed our unity in Christ and his mind.

> We confess Jesus Christ, Saviour of men and the light of the world;
> Together we accept his command;
> We commit ourselves anew to bear witness to him among men;
> We offer ourselves to serve all men in love, that love which he alone imparts;
> We accept afresh our calling to make visible our unity in him;
> We pray for the gift of the Holy Spirit for our task.[42]

Power for a New Age: Mark 1:14-22

To those who suffer the pangs of adjusting to an age of rapid change the gospel comes as doubly good news. To such an age it was first announced. This lection for the Sunday next before Lent issues no call to a dolorous march to Jerusalem; it proclaims power to live in a new and changing world. From its three paragraphs three dynamic suggestions emerge.

First, Christ brings the changed outlook required by the new age (vss. 14-15). "The time has come; the kingdom of God is upon you; repent, and believe the Gospel" (vs. 15 NEB). "Time" here is *kairos* (time of crucial decision), not *chronos* (clock or calendar time). The new age, "the kingdom of God," is dawning though not yet fully here; it is "at hand" (RSV), "near" (MT and AT), "close at hand" (JB), "upon you" (NEB). It calls for a complete change—"repent," *metanoeite* (change your mind, turn about), speaking not to the isolated individual but to the common life, the verb being plural. In the strong phrase of Alan Walker's book title, we need "a new mind for a new age." Swift change comes as good news, but only for those who get a new mind to think new thoughts, act from new motives, move in new directions.

Second, Christ brings the changed style of life required by a new human possibility (vss. 16-20). Crucial here are the call, "I will make you become fishers of men" (vs. 18); and the all-out response, "they left their father Zebedee in the boat with the hired servants, and followed him" (vs. 20). This depicts the later missionary work of the disciples and now of the church. Weighing the approach to a modern industrial city, Lesslie Newbigin remarks that it would be "possible to erect a series of fishing stations around

[42] *The New Delhi Report*, p. 322.

that pool and fish for proselytes; but that is not mission." Fishing for Methodists, Anglicans, Baptists, Lutherans is less than fishing for *men*. Our call is to empty ourselves "for Christ's sake in order humbly to learn what kind of community can truly represent his intention for that industrial community," [43] and to advance its growth.

Third, Christ brings the new authority required by the need for a new center of allegiance (vss. 21-22). "Unlike the doctors of the law, he taught with a note of authority" (vs. 22 NEB). The Greek might be literally rendered "was teaching"—as if this may have been a continuing process; his customary mode of teaching was personally authoritative. It still is. He brings an immediacy of authentic insight that shows us ourselves and the meaning of our life. As the episode in vss. 23-28, beyond this lection, makes dramatically clear, he liberates us from the cramping, paralyzing spirits that have made us less than we need to be in this new time.

[43] Newbigin, *Honest Religion for Secular Man,* p. 118.

LENTEN SEASON

In accord with the practice of most evangelical churches, the lectionary followed in this book enters Lent directly from the Epiphany Season, omitting the short pre-Lent observed in Roman Catholic, Lutheran, and Episcopal churches. In common with the whole Church, however, the evangelical tradition devotes Lent itself to spiritual disciplines designed to prepare the faithful for a more fruitful celebration of Easter.

Lent originated in the observance of the Pascha—the Passion and Resurrection of our Lord—for which the early church kept a forty-hour fast beginning on Good Friday. Gradually this became a six-day period of fasting and devotion corresponding with what we know as Holy Week, although it was not until the latter half of the fourth century that Palm Sunday, Good Friday, and Easter came to be observed as separate festivals. The fast of those preparing for Easter baptism and reception into the church was slowly extended to a penitential observance for all Christians. This season dedicated to God in special disciplines was at one time thirty-six weekdays in length, a "tithe" of the 365 days of the year. Its later extension back to Ash Wednesday, making forty weekdays (Sundays, as "little Easters," being excluded from such somber observances) was probably influenced by the remembrance of Jesus' fasting in the wilderness during the temptations on the threshold of his ministry.

Though the detailed remembrance of the events leading to the Crucifixion belongs to Passiontide in the latter days of Lent, the whole season is preeminently devoted to the Church's remembrance of the Cross, not only as unique reconciling act but as ever-present principle in the life of our Lord and as discipline for all who follow him.

ASH WEDNESDAY

Pivotal Penitence: Joel 2:12, 15-17

This is penitence that matters. On its pivot our life turns in two directions—back to harsh events reviewed in a new perspective as judgment, and forward to a better day to be entered in obedient faith.

Joel found meaning in past calamity. Devastation had swept his country. The scorched earth policy of modern warfare is the nearest parallel to the desolation left by swarms of locusts that had come like the invasion of "a great and powerful people" (2:2).

> The land is like the garden of Eden before them,
> but after them a desolate wilderness,
> and nothing escapes them (2:3).

To one reared on stories told by pioneer grandparents, of three successive years of grasshopper scourge on the Minnesota prairies in the 1870s, Joel's poetry has the ring of realism. The calamity, he declared, was not meaningless chance. Crisis demanded decision; it was God's Day. Though "the day of the Lord is great and very terrible" (2:11) it calls, he said, to penitence that can be pivotal.

We too have lived through "years which the swarming locust has eaten" (2:25). Depression came with terrors that still haunt the generation who suffered its ravages. Two world wars shattered the structure of our common life. In "the lonely crowd" of our mass society, conformity, apathy, and secularist assumptions have steadily eroded conscience. Nuclear arsenals have so changed the potential of war that the old question—"Are some men so evil that they must be destroyed?"—has given ground to the insane query—"Are some men so evil that all men must be destroyed?" [1] Beyond the crash of events can we hear a call to penitence?

> "Yet even now," says the Lord,
> "return to me with all your heart,
> with fasting, with weeping, and with mourning" (2:12).

Changed by pivotal penitence which reassesses calamity and crisis as judgment, we can look ahead with foreboding turned to faith. Fertility can be restored to the scorched earth.

[1] Questions phrased by J. Allen Broyles, *The John Birch Society, Anatomy of a Protest* (Boston: Beacon Press, 1965), p. 95.

> Fear not, you beasts of the field,
>> for the pastures of the wilderness are green;
> the tree bears its fruit,
>> the fig tree and vine give their full yield (2:22).

God, whose dependable seasons keep faith with the land, will pour out his Spirit, so that

> your old men shall dream dreams,
> and your young men shall see visions (2:28).

He will hold nations accountable and "enter into judgment with them" (3:2). Though Joel's understanding of judgment bears the color of his nationalism, his faith perceived the accountability of all nations, including his own. A better day would dawn when they were brought to obedience.

God's love is the other face of his judgment,

> for he is gracious and merciful,
> slow to anger, and abounding in steadfast love (2:13).

What Joel could see in a blessed future through the eyes of faith, we can know in realized experience at the foot of the Cross.

This love, freely given, is not cheap. Its judgment turns to hope on the pivot of penitence. "Return to me with all your heart," God requires, "and rend your hearts and not your garments" (2:12-13). True repentance is no mere regret over things past. It is turning, return to God, an about-face. Beginning in mind and emotion, it affects all the practical spheres of our existence, as Helmut Thielicke makes plain in recalling an incident in postwar Germany. Entertained in a home of wealth and taste, he expressed regret at the bombing from which the house had been restored at great cost. "Don't talk about regret," replied the owner. "Even in this loss I experienced the grace of God." As Thielicke marveled at the man's devoutness and humility, the latter went on to say: "God left me with just enough room so that I did not have to take in any refugees after the war." Reflecting on the incident, Thielicke observes that this man's piety and prayer were no sham. He carried social concern into his business. But he had never seen a connection between a housing shortage and a Christian relation to God and neighbor. "He had failed to see that this problem, like every other area of life, is related to the message which he had accepted and affirmed in his heart. His spiritual house stood apart, separated from and unconnected with the rest of his life." [2]

In Lent, season of penitence in remembrance of Christ's Passion, we face the fact that what makes true repentance pivotal is a change of mind and heart which re-establishes such broken connections with the rest of our life.

Christian Discipline in the Secular City
I Corinthians 9:24-27

"I pommel my body and subdue it, lest after preaching to others I myself should be disqualified" (vs. 27). In these words Paul reaches a climactic

[2] Helmut Thielicke, *The Trouble With the Church* (New York: Harper, 1965), p. 11.

point in the section of his letter which NEB captions "The Christian in a Pagan Society." How to live in such a setting is a perennial problem. Ernest Fremont Tittle faced it and wrote *Christians in an Unchristian Society;* Reinhold Niebuhr addressed it in *Moral Man in an Immoral Society;* we confront it as faith's problem in *The Secular City.*

In such settings Christian effectiveness costs discipline. Paul packs this paragraph with pictures pointing to that truth. We are runners in a gruelling race who, like "every athlete," must exercise "self-control in all things" (vs. 25). Fighting a tough opponent, we dare not shadowbox. Paul sets the example: "I bruise my own body and make it know its master" (vs. 27 NEB). Christians who help to change "the secular city" achieve by discipline. But discipline is unwelcome in our indulgent age.

See, for one thing, how discipline, not denying freedom, guides and fulfills it. "Am I not free?" (9:1) Paul asks in the opening line of this chapter. The question dominates all that follows. Elsewhere he has written with passion on the freedom of all Christians; here he notes his added freedom as an apostle. Free to earn his living by preaching, he has made free choice to witness in a costlier way. To preach without obligation to any, he has supported himself by his trade. To remain free to take the risks of the gospel, he has not married. Simply to *preach* the gospel is no virtue for him, but an urgency in which he has no choice. Beyond this *necessity* he has chosen in freedom to lay hard disciplines upon himself, that his witness may be the more winning. So Paul gives a rationale for Christian self-discipline that pommels and subdues our bodies, of which fasting and abstinence are only the beginning. Spiritual athletes are needed in the indulgent secular city.

See, further, that discipline is the price of Christian service. Paul disciplined himself not for his own pious development, but that he might be more useful to others. "I am a free man and own no master," he writes; "but I have made myself every man's servant, to win over as many as possible" (vs. 19 NEB). This is the voluntary principle of the Cross which Jesus called us to take up daily. Paul had a *thorn* of personal suffering he could not evade, and God gave him grace to bear it (II Cor. 12:7-9). He called us to bear necessary *burdens*—our own and others'—as all decent men of good will must do (Gal. 6:1-5). But he knew his Lord called him to the free act of taking up a *cross,* a service and a witness of which the disciplined life of self-restraint, and the simplification of expenditures of time and substance for the sake of truer stewardship, are part of the price.

See, finally, that discipline trains us for a serious race. Olympic athletes keep training to win "a perishable wreath." In our secular city, likewise, many a man undergoes rigorous discipline for business success or achievement in the arts. If all this for "a perishable wreath," Paul reasons, how much more for "an imperishable." In the secular city the cost is high: a whole world of affluent baubles gained and a soul lost; men and women depersonalized in the anonymity of the computer age; multitudes lost in the murky uncertainties of relativistic ethics. Winning the struggle for the imperishable also costs. For some, it costs a fast in protest against destructive evils. For others, it requires fasting which shares a little of the pain of hungry multitudes. For all, the discipline is worth its price.

Living Open to the Real: Matthew 6:16-21

"When you fast" (vs. 16)—hearing Jesus say that, we indulgent heirs of affluent society and soft Christianity fidget and hasten on to other aspects of his teaching. Most Protestants have given little heed to Lent as a fast. We turn rather to the grace of Christ's Cross. "Many Lenten sermons I have heard," a theologian remarks, "have had to indulge in great preliminary huffings and blowings to make it clear that Lent is not a season of fasting in the medieval sense." [3] But suppose it should turn out that some purposeful fasting is a vital way of opening our complacent lives to the reality of the Passion!

Jesus took fasting as a matter of course. He did not plead with his disciples to fast; he assumed they would. In an injunction far transcending exhortation to fast, he began with the actuality that fasting is a baseline from which concerned men and women start. He did not decry the practice: "You fast, not knowing how wrong it is." He did not belittle it: "Although you fast." He made it no minor elective: "If you fast." He took it as elemental: "*When* you fast." Let our over-graced churches take heed.

In every hard command, no matter how much we falter and fail, Jesus is the supreme Doer. Saying "When you fast," he remembered forty days in the wilderness. We may find even minor fasting a thing to argue away in the name of some fancied "inner spirituality"; he was not too spiritual to endure hunger that made the devil's suggestion of turning stones to bread a real temptation. When "he set his face to go to Jerusalem" (Luke 9:51), his flinty steadfastness was reinforced by the concern that had led to and grown with the disciplined life of fasting. Grateful for the forgiveness assured by the Cross, we open ourselves to its reality in the concentration made possible "when you fast."

Fasting is no pious parade of proud virtue. It secretly opens our life to God. It is not "seen by men but by your Father who is in secret" (vs. 18). Bishop Fulton Sheen once remarked that whether you *diet* or *fast*, the result is the same: you lose twenty pounds! But in that case, as Jesus hinted, the sluffed-off poundage is your reward. True fasting, he taught, has no ulterior motive—approval, weight-control, coveted influence. These may result; they do not *motivate*. Fasting opens life to God—by deepening our awareness of the misery of the hungry in whom he confronts us, and by hunger pangs which become a continuing call to prayer. It partakes of prayer's nature: "Your Father who sees in secret will reward you" (vs. 18).

"For where your treasure is, there will your heart be also" (vs. 21). Is our treasure in creature comforts? Reputation for being "religious"? A good figure? Winning friends and influencing people? Then it is exposed to moth, rust, thieves, advancing age, and all other hazards of a precarious world (vs. 19). But there is security for those who, deliberately denying the quest of passing baubles, keep themselves open to the permanently real. They find true security.

I am certain that neither death nor life, neither angels nor principalities, neither the present nor the future, no powers of the Height or of the Depth, nor any-

---

[3] Translator's Note by John Doberstein in Thielicke, *ibid.*, p. ix.

thing else in all creation, will be able to part us from God's love in Christ Jesus our Lord (Rom. 8:38-39 MT).

Living open to the real, they have laid up treasure which earth's changing conditions cannot snatch away.

FIRST SUNDAY IN LENT

Good News for a Tragic Era: Ezekiel 33:7-16

"As I live, says the Lord God, I have no pleasure in the death of the wicked" (vs. 11). Our self-inflicted tragedy sends out shock waves even to God, who seeks to cure it. "Turn back from your evil ways," he pleads, "for why will you die?" Independent of historical questions concerning complexities that underlie the book of Ezekiel, this urgent word impinges on our living present.

It speaks of responsibility. The prophet has been set at a sentinel's post. If those who hear his alarm do not take warning, they become guilty of their own death. If the prophet fails to warn them, their death is his guilt (vss. 8-9). The parable speaks to pastor or preacher, who has no option concerning the truth he shall teach. It is given him; he dares not withhold or dilute it. Even more, this is a parable of the whole Church in a threatened world.

Helmut Gollwitzer highlights this responsibility as he writes:

If the Church seeks the guidance of God's commands in relation to indiscriminate and still unimaginable mass murder that goes by the name of nuclear war, then there is no doubt that God's commands and every page of the New Testament and the name of Jesus Christ stand between us and such participation in mass murder.[4]

To mute the warning, he adds, would be to sabotage our central testimony. It is false to keep silence on the ground that this is "a political problem," as if we could sound our warning only when we have a full-blown political alternative to offer!

The Church has to proclaim the will of God, as made known in the biblical message, in relation to the actual situation existing at a particular time. Thus today it has to state clearly that a nuclear war is incompatible with faith in and obedience to the living God. It has not got to wait to say *that* until it has found a practical method of implementing this fact politically in the atomic age.[5]

Ezekiel's parable thus confronts every Christian with responsibility for his own witness. To visualize the need, read the newspaper with the biblical commandments in mind, asking of each story, "What commandment of God was broken here to result in such misery or such wickedness?"[6] Or scan the

[4] Gollwitzer, *The Demands of Freedom*, p. 39.

[5] *Ibid.*, p. 40.

[6] John H. Baumgaertner, *Declaration of Dependence* (St. Louis: Concordia Publishing House, 1965), p. 88.

amusement page, asking how its values square with the biblical priorities. In a world where the death-wish often seems to ride and rule us, Christians have a warning witness which to withhold is traitorous to the gospel and treacherous to our fellowmen. The witness that bears most weight will be the individual Christian's conviction expressed in action at the points of responsible decision-making where, in business, citizenship, and personal relations, he touches the ongoing world of affairs.

God's concern with our tragedy runs, beyond warning, to an invitation to enter life anew through repentance. We need not remain as we are. Just as the good man is not proof against the evil of an unguarded moment, the wicked man is accepted when he repents (vss. 12-15). "None of the sins that he has committed shall be remembered against him; he has done what is lawful and right, he shall surely live" (vs. 16). God reads the heart. He accepts the *person*, not the sum of the deeds. He looks, not at cast up accounts, but at the present direction in which a man is moving. Spoken in the plea of the prophet, this truth is acted in the Cross and in our Lord's acceptance of the worst—even the eleventh hour worst: "Today you will be with me in Paradise" (Luke 23:43).

When the Spiritual Is the Real: I John 2:1-3, 15-17

Exclaiming, "It's too good to be true!" we may be jubilant but our words are cynical. "In this perverse world," they seem to say, "such good things don't happen." The First Letter of John, far from cynical, suggests a similar skepticism about some expressions of religion. For some "spirituality" substitutes doctrine and sentimentality for the earthy substance of character verified by performance. Such religion, says this letter, is too *spiritual* to be true!

The passage before us teaches complementary parts of a single truth: Never suppose that what God has done for us through Christ softens the demand for plain obedience; but never suppose, either, that simply by resolving and putting our will into it we can live a life acceptable to God. *Obedience*, the word this too "spiritual" religion needs most to hear, makes full sense only in the context of God's *gift* in Christ.

In that context this reading begins: "My little children, I am writing this to you so that you may not sin; but if any one does sin, we have an advocate with the Father, Jesus Christ the righteous" (vs. 1). "We have one to plead our cause with the Father" (NEB) aptly interprets the meaning of the Greek *parakletos* (Advocate) as one who takes our side in court. Our cause needs pleading! The claims of character laid on us by God's commands are as difficult to surmount as a mile-high wall in the path of a mountain climber.[7] Who of us has scaled that steep ascent? "If we say we have no sin," this letter declares, "we deceive ourselves, and the truth is not in us" (1:8). Gone-wrongness disrupts our life.

Christ not only sets this mile-high wall before us by demanding a higher righteousness that includes the outer act; beyond the deed, he commands even the unspoken thought. He meets the high demand as no other ever has.

[7] Cf. Eduard Thurneysen, *The Sermon on the Mount* (Richmond: John Knox Press, 1964).

Yet, for all his perfection, he accepts and forgives us in our failure and sin. Accepted, forgiven, loved, we are drawn to love in return. His love sets us in a new, right relation to God, our brother, and ourselves. In this dynamic sense "he is the expiation for our sins" (vs. 2). His prayer on the Cross, "Father, forgive them" (Luke 23:34), eternally pleads our cause.

But forgiveness renews the need to obey. Do we really *belong* to the company of the forgiven? There is one way to tell! "Here is the test by which we can make sure that we know him: do we keep his commands?" (vs. 3 NEB). Imperfect though we be, are we on the way? Have we stopped rationalizing our disobedience? Do we keep returning in response to his call? "Whoever claims to be dwelling in him, binds himself to live as Christ himself lived" (vs. 6 NEB).

There are those who would smother this call under a theology that separates him from us. "We cannot take His life without reserve as an example," they say, "for He was uniquely the only divinely begotten Son of God, on a divine mission." [8] True when it finds in his divinity power to live as he lived, Christian faith turns false when, exalting him to another sphere, it excuses our failure. Such faith, says this New Testament letter, is too "spiritual" to be true.

Beyond bogus "spirituality," faith builds on the dependably real. Obedience finds reinforcement, seeing a creature world stripped of its glamorous disguise. "Do not love the world" (vs. 15) translates *kosmos* in the sense of worldly life alienated from God.

Do not set your hearts on the godless world or anything in it. Anyone who loves the world is a stranger to the Father's love. Everything the world affords, all that panders to the appetites or entices the eyes, all the glamour of its life, springs not from the Father but from the godless world. And that world is passing away with all its allurements, but he who does God's will stands for evermore (vss. 15-17 NEB).

Where is "the real joy of good living" (as the hucksters say)? Not in "everything the world affords" (the slick ads notwithstanding). Not in "all that panders to the appetites" (food, drink, status). Not in what "entices the eyes" or "all the glamour of life"—perfect description of "the Playboy philosophy." That "philosophy" fills the magazine with two million dollars' worth of advertising, showing itself a philosophy of wanting, getting, spending as you please. It declares that "a man's morality, like his religion, is a personal affair best left to his own conscience." The trouble is that when *each* considers morality to be doing as he pleases, *all* must bear the brunt of the resulting anarchy. No wonder "that world is passing"! Glamor fades, appetites pall, energies decline. Meanwhile, considering what we choose to do as strictly "a personal affair" crumbles the mortar that holds society together.

"But he who does God's will stands for evermore." Living by integrities that outlast changing fashions, insights that give lasting joy, and resources

[8] Joseph R. Schultz, *The Soul of the Symbols* (Grand Rapids: Eerdmans, 1966), p. 62.

from great depths of durability, such a man has found reality in obedience, the only spirituality that stands up under strain.

Christus Victor: Mark 1:9-13

In these swift lines we see a battle jointed. In the Cross and Resurrection it will end in victory over the whole kingdom of evil. Note the embattled forces: Jesus, the Spirit, Satan, wild beasts, the angels. Formidable contestants!

"The Spirit immediately drove him out into the wilderness" (vs. 12). But he was already there! "In the wilderness" he was baptized (vs. 4). More symbolic than geographical, "wilderness" here connotes the wild solitude with "wild beasts" (vs. 13) and turbulent, terrible forces hurled against him. To modern city dwellers "wilderness" spells escape from the din of traffic and the conflicts of men, as when William O. Douglas writes of how cities need "a wilderness at their back door, where a man can go and once more find harmony and peace in his inner being." [9] In the wilderness Jesus achieved "harmony and peace" only on the far side of deep disturbance.

"Most contests, from bridge to tennis, are not *won,* but *lost,*" writes a newspaper columnist. "The victor is simply the one who makes the fewest errors, not the one who makes the most brilliant plays." [10] Yet Jesus *won* his contest. All his life, from this solitude to that final one of Gethsemane and Golgotha, he stood alone against the concentrated power of evil. "Angels ministered to him" (vs. 13), but only after he had won his victory. As Matthew's fuller statement is at pains to show: "Then the devil left him, and behold, angels came and ministered to him" (Matt. 4:11). What he won is promise that in our own temptations we fight a foe who, for all his rage and bluff, is already defeated. Vanquished in the wilderness, routed at the Cross! After these strategic victories, we can hold the line.

For the successive assaults of the battle we must turn to Matthew (4:1-11), in many lectionaries the lesson for the First Sunday in Lent. There we see a fight for the kingdoms of the world. Satan offered realms in exchange for Jesus' allegiance, a bid later renewed by the party of the Zealots. In an unstable land their threat of armed revolt carried power. Leading such forces, one man with the fierce convictions and burning energies of Jesus could have overturned kingdoms. In Hitler's case one man did, fabricating the Nazi might from a defeated, disarmed, isolated Germany. Jesus denied that demonic option.

He won by another method. Scorning both Machiavellian violence and pseudo-religion that would test God by a leap from the pinnacle of the temple, he chose to stand or fall by the power of love. The choice led to the Cross where, exposed to the worst the kingdom of evil could do, he won the battle begun in the wilderness.

Who was this gallant victor? Our elder Brother, setting the example for us? Our Teacher, showing us the true resources? Yes, and we need to follow

[9] William O. Douglas, *My Wilderness: East to Katahdin* (Garden City, N.Y.: Doubleday, 1961), p. 189.

[10] Sydney J. Harris, *Chicago Daily News,* Sept. 30, 1965.

him and learn from him. But the voice from heaven hails him as far more: "Thou art my beloved Son" (vs. 11). This victory is won at a cosmic summit. We face the assaults of evil with trust that, in the strength of his conquest, it is possible to "withstand in the evil day, and having done all, to stand" (Eph. 6:13).

SECOND SUNDAY IN LENT

Living Faith and the Death of God
Exodus 33:18-23

What does this passage, portraying a God so anthropomorphic that we are allowed to see his back but not his face, have to say to us in an age when some theologians talk about the death of any God at all? It may say much about the *kind* of God who is dead. Moses had been asking for a claim on God. Confronted with his difficult assignment, he asked, "How shall it be known that I have found favor in thy sight, I and thy people?" (vs. 16). His demand, "I pray thee, show me thy glory" (vs. 18) had amounted to a request for full disclosure of God's nature. In this pivotal experience Moses learned that he was not dealing with a god who delivers himself into the hands of even the most devout. He is not their possession, delivering special favors, leaving them in control with no margin of mystery.

He denies such control: "You cannot see my face; for man shall not see me and live" (vs. 20). We have passed through a period when much religion aimed at ends of our own designing. Religion was commended as a good thing because it would stabilize society, strengthen democracy, defeat Communism, promote success, guarantee peace of mind. A few weeks before the 1965 outbreak of the "death of God" controversy, the Harris Survey reported that 97 percent of the American people profess belief in God. It also reported that more than half the people "hardly ever feel concern" about the pollution of rivers and streams, about the strictness of our immigrant exclusion laws, or about the treatment of Jews in the United States; that more than one-third of the people "hardly ever feel concern" about our food surplus in a starving world, about conditions of life in our slums, or about the way Negroes have been treated. Believing in God, from one-third to one-half of us professed not to care about his creation or what happens to his other children! Do we want God only for our own ends? Like Moses, do we ask for a God who will show us that we "have found favor" in his sight, a God who will fully disclose himself for our benefit? This passage declares that no such God can be found.

When this caricature dies, real faith in the living God can be born. Always beyond us, he has vital dealings with us. "I will make all my goodness pass before you" (vs. 19a) summarizes the biblical understanding of God's revelation. We know him in his "goodness," his acts. He delivered Israel at the Red Sea; he continued a covenant relation with a servant people; he was known most fully through the acts of Jesus Christ. We can know him still by his "goodness" in blessing us. Yet he remains sovereign, saying: "I . . . will proclaim before you my name, 'The Lord'" (vs. 19b). He is not our intimate, not the object of our investigation, not our convenient servant; he is forever Lord beyond us and above us. We cannot control him by cult pieties or by any favors we do for him. His word is rather, "I will be gracious to whom I will be gracious, and will show mercy on whom I will show mercy" (vs. 19c). God blesses in accord with his own nature and will, not because we have worked out a bargain. So Paul observed in quoting this passage (cf. Rom. 9:15-16).

Though we cannot know all of God, we can know all we need: "You shall see my back; but my face shall not be seen" (vs. 23). This is the word of a God who goes before us. Called to a demanding work, Moses would find a God he could control irrelevant. Yet dealings with a God who led on had become a life-and-death matter. In living issues in the world of affairs, we too have dealings with a God who leads. We see his back, but not his face!

"I will put you in a cleft of the rock; and I will cover you with my hand until I have passed by" (vs. 22)—how poignant the words for those who sing,

> Rock of Ages, cleft for me,
> Let me hide myself in thee.

For, in the Christ to whom that prayer is addressed, God draws near.

Negotiator of a New Agreement: Hebrews 12:18-29

"But you have come . . . to Jesus the negotiator of a new agreement" (vss. 22a, 24a AT). These words form the watershed of the passage. "Agreement," more contemporary than "covenant," is no more accurate. "Agreement" has overtones of a "deal" between equals. The passage corrects that misconception. Comparing the old and new "agreements," the passage confronts us with God's sovereign power, our crucial need to respond in faith, and our fragile life, as driving us to him who is unshakable.

The God known under the old agreement (vss. 18-20) inspired awe. Men met him at a sacred mountain so filled with numinous terror that the Law decreed, "If even a beast touches the mountain, it shall be stoned" (vs. 20, cf. Exod. 19:12-13). But now "it is no tangible blazing fire that you have come up to, no blackness and darkness and storm, no trumpet blast and voice whose words made those who heard them beg to be told no more" (vss. 18-19 AT). This kind of terror has passed, but God has not abdicated the sovereign power it represents.

With the passing of the old agreement there is still need for the kind of control upon our life for which it stood. Rene Carpenter speaks of such a need in her life. "It has little to do any more with the Heavenly Father of my childhood prayers," she confesses, and less with cozy prayer circles or parish coffee hours. Rather, she says, "I need the altar—not too close from where I sit, but approachable—so that I may take my awe and questionable state of grace as companions there to kneel and receive the mysterious." Then, speaking of the varied movements of worship, she adds: "The motions are necessary to fill the gaps of not believing."[11] No Space Age sophistication outgrows the need to sustain faith by basic acts of allegiance to a God recognized in the awe of great worship.

Though God, known under the new "agreement" is less terrifying, obedient faith in him is no less crucial. There is joy in the new relation, as the mounting figures testify (vss. 22-24). Christ's new covenant opens the way to a new order of life, "the city of the living God"; to an angelic host, in company with the Church Victorious, celebrating before God who judges all; and to "upright men now at last enjoying the fulfillment of their hopes" (AT). Climaxing the whole joyful scene is "the sprinkled blood that speaks more graciously than the blood of Abel" (vs. 24). For Abel's blood cried out from the ground (Gen. 4:10) for *vengeance*, but Jesus offered his blood as "poured out for many for the *forgiveness* of sins" (Matt. 26:28). With that change a new age dawned.

Under old or new agreement, we are still responsible to a sovereign God. Just as there was no escaping the warning of a God who spoke in the worn-out terms of the tangible, there is no escaping him who speaks in terms more personal (vs. 25).

Any mention of the word "God" nowadays immediately produces a herd of sophisticates who with one voice cry aloud, "Now what do you mean by *that* word?" Unaware of what is hidden—the darkness, the light, the mystery, the freedom—they have no other question to ask. But asking it manifests that they have not seen the reflection of that dimension of reality in which we feel ourselves humbled, threatened by judgment, subject to redemption.[12]

No new "agreement," condition, or age sets such realities aside.

All that shows us how fragile we are drives us to God, who is unshakable. He will shake heaven and earth, bringing the treasures of the nations to his temple (vs. 26; cf. Hag. 2:6-7). Amidst persecution, the writer to the Hebrews experienced such shaking, but he was sure that those who belong to Christ can live by the realities of "a kingdom that cannot be shaken" (vs. 28). We still live in such need, shaken by successive threats of nuclear annihilation, famine in the wake of population explosion, poisoning by atmospheric pollution, being robotized by chemical and electrode manipulation, or rendered obsolete by computers. Amid such hazards, happy are those who live in touch with "a kingdom that cannot be shaken."

The Finality of Christ: Matthew 17:1-9

If in any real measure it is not possible to get within hearing and seeing distance of the man Jesus, then talk about the finality of Jesus Christ is simply futile. The crux of the finality issue is whether or not in Jesus Christ men confront and are confronted by the transcendent God whose will they cannot manipulate, by whose judgment they are bound, and with whose intractable presence in their midst they must inevitably reckon.[13]

[11] *Chicago Daily News*, Nov. 23, 1967.

[12] Samuel H. Miller, *Man the Believer* (Nashville: Abingdon Press, 1968), p. 124.

[13] D. T. Niles, "The Christian Claim for the Finality of Christ," in Dow Kirkpatrick, ed., *The Finality of Christ* (Nashville: Abingdon Press, 1966), p. 14.

This issue confronted the disciples in their experience on the mountain. This issue still confronts us as we seek to make sense of the story.

As all three Synoptic Gospels report it, this scene came a few days after the pivotal conversation at Caesarea Philippi in which the disciples first recognized Jesus as the Christ. Since the Christ-idea was interpreted differently in varying circles, however, they still had to face the question of what the term, newly applied to him, might mean. In an exalted moment on a mountain they began to find the answer.

"His whole appearance changed before their eyes" (vs. 2 PT). They saw him no more as merely familiar friend, honored teacher, adored master. He was transcendently awesome: "His face shone like the sun, and his garments became white as light" (vs. 2). Matthew describes Jesus here as, like the awesome angel who rolled the stone from the door of the tomb, dressed in garments of light (vs. 2; cf. 28:3). Dealing with experiences the senses cannot grasp, this does what we must always do in such cases—resort to the language of sense as metaphor.

"There appeared to them Moses and Elijah, talking with him" (vs. 3). What the founders of law and prophecy in Israel had to say threw light on him. "Talking with him" suggests a profound interchange between the meaning of his life and the great religious tradition in which they stood. Excitedly responding, Peter proposed to make booths for Moses, Elijah, and Jesus. Some interpreters associate this with the booths of the feast of Tabernacles and the idea that the new Age of the Messiah had already dawned. Or Peter may have been suggesting three centers of religious authority: the law, the prophets, and Jesus.

If so, a voice from a cloud emphatically rejected the idea. "This is my beloved Son," it commanded; "listen to him" (vs. 5). The voice from a cloud is a familiar biblical figure for a word from God (Matt. 24:30; 26:64; Exod. 19:16). The disciples prostrated themselves as men who had met God, but Jesus characteristically "touched them, saying, 'Rise, and have no fear'" (vs. 7). Then, other centers of authority surpassed, "they saw no one but Jesus only" (vs. 8). As they came down the mountain, he spoke of the experience as a "vision" and suggested that after he "was raised from the dead" it would help them interpret the message with which they were entrusted (vs. 9).

The issue joined is vital. Tracey K. Jones notes the Hindu contention that "there is no final way, but that all religious truth is relative and tentative. The Hindu will compromise on everything else but not on this basic assumption that all religions are in the final analysis the same." [14] Many a modern, not thinking of himself as a Hindu, shares that basic assumption. Yet we need an overarching authority to give us purpose. As a popular columnist observes, "When people believe there is no purpose in the universe, they will fabricate a purpose of their own—and it will usually be a bad one." [15] The history of the twentieth century is strewn with fabricated purposes, to which the finality of Christ is the most tenable answer. All other authorities surpassed, "listen to him."

[14] Tracey K. Jones, *Our Mission Today* (New York: World Outlook Press, 1963), p. 121.
[15] Sydney J. Harris, in *The Chicago Daily News*, Sept. 30, 1965.

THIRD SUNDAY IN LENT

As if We Owned the Cosmos: Amos 7:7-10, 14-16a

"We dare not strut through the cosmos with our hats on, as if we owned the place." [16] These words, addressed to an international conference of scientific planners, have much in common with those of Amos in this vivid lesson.

Amos speaks first of a plumb line which shows the nation Israel in danger of falling. The figure takes on impressive emphasis as we see it reiterated in prophetic writings. In II Kings 21:13 the emphasis is on the impartial rigor with which God applies his moral law to all peoples: "I will stretch over Jerusalem the same measuring line as over Samaria, the same plumb-rule as for the House of Ahab" (JB). Isaiah emphasizes the moral nature of the test:

> And I will make justice the measure,
> integrity the plumb-line (28:17 JB).

The Lamentations that followed the fall of Jerusalem stressed the inexorable finality of God's judgment.

> With a line he measured it, and did not withdraw his hand
> until he had completely overthrown it (2:8 JB).

So here, Amos is declaring that Israel's moral dereliction will not be spared its judgment on any grounds of cultic observances: "the sanctuaries of Israel shall be laid waste" (vs. 9).

The prophet then confronts popular religion. Amaziah, priest of Bethel, attempts officially to silence this troublesome lay prophet, not only complaining to the king but also directing Amos to "flee away to the land of Judah, and eat bread there, and prophesy there; but never again prophesy at Bethel, for it is the king's sanctuary, and it is a temple of the kingdom"(vss. 12-13). "Get out, you silly dreamer!" (PT), Amaziah addresses him contemptuously, much as the spokesmen of personal piety detached from social concern address those who see the secular relevance of the Christian message today. It is to this that Amos is replying in his denial that he is a prophet or a prophet's son. "I am no prophet, no member of any prophets' guild" (vs. 14 MT)—no professional, no spokesman of official religion, but a man called to speak a burning word of conscience in a situation about which he cannot keep silent. The whole sweep of biblical faith sustains such a word of conscience as a word from the Lord.

Only by forceful amputation can the lection stop at vs. 16a, for this is the introduction of an oracle that, once opened, must be heard. It is the prophet's forecast of the fate awaiting a society that will not hear a moral warning. There will be crime in the streets, Amos declares, as the youth fall by the sword and even the king's wife is treated as a common harlot. "Israel shall surely go into exile away from its land" (vs. 17). So historically accurate is

[16] Reported in *Newsweek*, Oct. 16, 1967, p. 54.

this word that some students believe it the addition of a later writer who could speak in the light of accomplished events. However that may be, the outcome underscored the truth that those who sow the wind of moral irresponsibility reap the whirlwind of national disaster.

In an international scientific conference held in Oslo in 1967, a speaker alluded to the catastrophic slide of mine waste in which 144 persons lost their lives at Aberfan, Wales. One report had noted the accumulated waste as piled and then "banished from thought." " 'Banished from thought,' " said the speaker. "What a lovely phrase. Things banished from the mind later come down to bury us." [17] Reality collects its toll, regardless of our moral fictions or neglect. Amos was no "dreamer"; the truth he saw is the truth history continues to underline with the indelible markings of inescapable events.

Wage Slave or Rich Heir? Romans 6:15-23

"Sin pays a wage . . . but God gives freely" (vs. 23 NEB). With this vivid contrast Paul caps the logic of his rugged discussion of two ways of life. It is his final answer to the question he has raised in vs. 1—"Are we to continue to sin that grace may abound?"—and repeated in vs. 15: "Are we to sin because we are living under the reign of Love and not of Law?" (TCNT). Paul was no armchair mystic, lifted above the moral battle by his doctrine that faith, not law, is the source of our salvation. As the first seven chapters of this letter to the Romans make painfully clear, he was devoted to the struggle to live a good life. He found freedom not *from* the struggle, but *for* it—freedom to be what he had aspired to be, but could not.

You belong inevitably to *something*, he argues. "You *belong* to the power which you choose to obey, whether you choose sin, whose reward is death, or God, obedience to whom means the reward of righteousness" (vs. 16 PT). So! Set free, you can be the fully good and useful person you once struggled fruitlessly to become. On another occasion Paul responded to the "emancipated" mystics who boasted, "For me there are no forbidden things." "Maybe," was his retort, "but not everything does good. I agree there are no forbidden things for me, but I am not going to let anything dominate me." (I Cor. 6:12 JB.) Not a bad rejoinder to an "anything goes" ethic! But now he pushes the matter further. Decide what you belong to, he says, and take the consequences! You can go your own separated way, and live under its compulsions and obsessions; or you can make obedience a way of life and discover what a freedom there is in voluntary discipline. "But thank God that while you used to be sin's workers you later gave *voluntary* obedience to a type of teaching in which you got carried away" (vs. 17 CPV).

It follows that what you belong to *matters*. "You before gave up the parts of your bodies in slavery to . . . greater and greater license" (vs. 19 AT). That was what you belonged to, and it left you no longer a whole person, but only "members" (RSV), "bodies" (NEB), "parts of your body" (AT). In one of Jack London's stories a robbery leads to the killing of the victim, and one of the criminals shrugs it off: "Why worry, he was just meat!" Later, one rob-

[17] *Ibid.*

ber poisons his partner's coffee, and the partner poisons the first man's food, each hoping to be left with all the loot. To such futility the "just meat" philosophy leads! "You gave up the parts of your bodies in slavery to greater and greater license" sounds like a description of the current philosophies of sexual permissiveness—another manifestation of the "just meat" philosophy, finding in a partner a means to passing gratification, not a whole person to be cherished.

"Greater and greater license"—back of that lies the Greek *anomia*, translated "iniquity" (RSV) or "moral anarchy" (NEB). From this root current sociological usage derives the word "anomie," signifying a breakdown or absence of social norms and values, as in the case of uprooted people. Under anomie, vandalism becomes epidemic, violence snowballs, and sex standards disappear. Vance Packard, introducing his huge study of *The Sexual Wilderness*, generalizes that while there have always been violations of sexual mores, "today there are few rules that could command a majority vote if the voting were done by both adults and adolescents. It is not the violations, but the normlessness, that makes the contemporary problem a historically significant one." [18] This is the cost to society, which accrues from "slavery to greater and greater license" (*anomia*). And to the individual, Paul declares, the cost is a tormented conscience and a sentence of death (vs. 21).

But there is another side to the matter. "Bound to the service of God, your gains are such as make for holiness, and the end is eternal life" (vs. 22 NEB). If it is true that "sin pays a wage, and the wage is death"—the piecemeal death of the "just meat" philosophy—it is also true that "God gives freely, and his gift is eternal life," the fulfilled life of becoming a whole person "in union with Christ Jesus our Lord" (vs. 23 NEB).

Mandate to Stewardship: Mark 10:17-27

There was no harshness in Jesus' words, "Go, sell what you have, and give to the poor, and you will have treasure in heaven; and come, follow me." The hard demand merely pointed to a *need* Jesus had read in the man's character: "You lack one thing." It was spoken in the deepest goodwill, for "Jesus looking upon him loved him" (vs. 21). With the hard invitation he opened the way to a full life, but the man "went away sorrowful." His wealth constituted a mandate to stewardship, and he refused it. Rejecting the mandate, he closed the door on his highest potential.

The theme of liberation from human and worldly objects of dependence is, of course, dominant here. These may be material riches, social status, academic honors, popular acclaim, intellectual and esthetic interests, self-conscious moral and religious rectitude, or many other treasures. Whatever dominates our life, getting in the way of the "one" who is "good," who is "God alone" (vs. 18), must be dealt with in such radical fashion as to bring it and all of our life under his control. This broader application of the passage will be dealt with, however, when we come to the parallel in Luke 18:18-30, the Gospel for the Tenth Sunday after Pentecost. What claims us

[18] Vance Packard, *The Sexual Wilderness* (New York: David McKay, 1968), p. 15.

now is the forthright teaching of the passage that the possession of affluence is a mandate to stewardship.

It is our own personal mandate. Anonymously, Jesus' questioner is introduced: "a man ran up and knelt before him" (vs. 17). The Greek underplays his individuality, using only a pronoun—"*one* ran up and knelt"—someone, anyone, *each* one being thus involved. So it talks about us. And we *are* those who have "great possessions," for almost every reader of these words belongs to a little, rich minority of the world's population. If the world's people could be represented by a village of a thousand, in which the wealth were distributed just as it is now on the world scene, nearly half of them, 495 persons, would be eking out a dying existence on less than $100 a year. Roughly two-thirds, or 670 persons, would be subsisting on less than $300 a year. Only 115 people would have as much as $1000 annual income. To belong to that slender company is to be claimed by a mandate.

Jesus' words of challenge and invitation to this man, and to us, call for a clear-cut choice. Either we stand with Jesus, "the man for others," or we stand with the one who for all his great possessions, "went away sorrowful," the man for himself. Jesus presents the man with a claim entirely secular. The question, "What must I do to inherit eternal life?" (vs. 17) seemed to anticipate some "religious" or "spiritual" formula as a response. Instead, Jesus pointed to the *world's* need and declared that only by helping to meet it could the *man's* need be met. But the secular advantages he enjoyed were no longer expendable in a higher quest. They held him, possessed him, and would not let him go. He so lived by them that he could not accept a great opportunity when it endangered them. Whether we stand with him or with Jesus is the crucial question this passage raises.

"Great possessions" in our time are not merely personal. They are the strictly limited resources of our crowded earth. Economist Kenneth E. Boulding foresees the future as dependent on what he calls a "spaceman economy, in which the earth has become a single spaceship without unlimited reservoirs of anything, either for extraction or pollution, and in which, therefore, man must find his place in a cyclical ecological system . . . capable of continuous reproduction of material form." [19] At present rates of depletion and pollution we are rapidly making our spaceship uninhabitable. How we need the grace of God to cut us loose from our selfishness and make us stewards!

FOURTH SUNDAY IN LENT

I Will Hope in Him: Lamentations 3:22-26, 31-33

"The steadfast love of the Lord never ceases" (vs. 22). What a blessed generalization! The poet who wrote the words, however, was speaking to a specific situation of unrelieved gloom. Even here, he was saying,

> the favours of Yahweh are not all past,
> his kindnesses are not exhausted (vs. 22 JB).

[19] *Newsweek,* Oct. 16, 1967.

It is one thing to give assent to a general rule, quite another to know that even in *this* agonizing hour God has not forgotten. Out of this certainty the poet could cry, "Therefore I will hope in him" (vs. 24).

To see the plight of his people is to know the courage of the poet's cry. Five poems of grief over the destruction of Jerusalem in 586 B.C. constitute the Book of Lamentations. Done in the form of an acrostic on the Hebrew alphabet, they seem to say: Here is the whole gamut of suffering and of God's answer to it, "from A to Z." The first poem pictures the stricken city as a lonely widow among the nations, once a princess, now a vassal. Weeping, enslavement, desertion God has made her suffer for her many sins (1:1-5). Filth clings to her clothes, her young people are in exile, starvation stalks; yet in honesty she confesses,

> The Lord is in the right,
> for I have rebelled against his word (1:18).

So faith's sorrow issues in confession.

If God has brought this desolation on Israel, the second poem declares, he himself suffers not only in the downfall of his people but also in the despoiling of his own altars and the silencing of his festivals. Terrible are the ravages of famine. Children cry to their mothers, "Where is bread?" (2:12) until finally

> The hands of compassionate women
> have boiled their own children;
> they became their food (4:10, see also 2:20).

In the face of all this, the official spokesmen of religion have offered only delusive, tinsel optimism instead of the sterner realism which the time demanded (2:14).

In this desperate time, there is power in the hope born of realistic faith: "The Lord is good to those who wait for him" (vs. 25), "to those who trust him" (JB), "to him who craves him" (AT). Such waiting is a determined clinging to God in spite of everything.

> It is good that one should wait quietly
> for the salvation of the Lord (vs. 26).

The word is spoken of those who hold *on* and so hold *out*, to the desperate finish.

There is one reason for such endurance; God will not forsake his covenant with his people. Instead of the Psalmist's wistful query,

> Will the Lord spurn for ever,
> and never again be favorable? (Ps. 77:7),

this poet dares, in the face of all he has suffered, to assert:

> For the Lord will not
> cast off for ever,
> but, though he cause grief, he will have compassion
> according to the abundance of his steadfast love (vss. 31-32).

His "steadfast love" is his covenant-keeping love. He will honor his promise at all costs. Bound, in all honor, to punish his people's faithlessness, he is bound by the same honor to be faithful to his covenant. In this he will not fail.

With his fellow Jews in a Nazi prison yard, Eli Wiesel was forced to watch the hanging of some of their number, among them a child too light to bring mercifully sudden pressure against the noose, who hung struggling for half an hour before death claimed him. Behind Wiesel another prisoner groaned, "Where is God? Where is he? Where can he be now?" Deep within him Wiesel answered, "Where? Here he is—he has been hanged here, on these gallows." [20] Understanding that shocked cry that the God of love is dead, one also remembers that he was hanged on another gallows, on a skull-shaped hill outside Jerusalem, and that his death there was the beginning of new life forevermore. In his sharing of the agony there, he vindicated the cry of a suffering poet six centuries before:

> for he does not willingly afflict
> or grieve the sons of men (vs. 33).

Don't Waste God's Grace! II Corinthians 6:1-10

"As God's fellow-worker, I appeal to you, too, not to accept the favor of God and then waste it" (vs. 1 AT). Describing the posture of apostleship, which provides a pattern for the mature Christian, Paul has just unfolded the grand strategy of God's act of reconciliation in Christ (5:18-21). He gives grace for one purpose only, Paul declares: for reconciliation. Now, in this situation of quarreling within the church, *be* reconciled. Don't waste God's grace!

Frederick C. Grant has rightly observed that the Corinthian letters show Paul on the defensive. For they

reflect one special crisis in Paul's career, one in which his whole mission and character as a Christian leader and apostle were at stake. Paul is on the defensive, and the letters give us, accordingly, an intimate picture of the apostle himself, his mind, his thought, feelings, temperament and personal character. [21]

How these shine in this passage! The catalogue of his sufferings (vss. 3-5) lends weight to the witness of his life: "We recommend ourselves by the innocence of our behaviour, our grasp of truth, our patience and kindliness; by gifts of the Holy Spirit, by sincere love, by declaring the truth, by the power of God" (vss. 6-7 NEB). What a level of "defensiveness"! Looking at our own tawdry, brittle, often vindictive defenses, who is not forced to ask: Why can't we defend ourselves on this level?

For one thing, we use the wrong weapons. Paul has "the weapons of righteousness for the right hand"—sword hand of offense—"and for the left"—shield hand of defense (vs. 7). His ways of witnessing make it clear

[20] Eliezer Wiesel, *Night* (New York: Hill and Wang, 1960), pp. 9-10.
[21] Frederick C. Grant, *Nelson's Bible Commentary* (New York: Thomas Nelson, 1962), VII, 64.

that he is not depending on his own strength but on a strength that can only come from God. It is sheer, tragic loss that we increasingly depend on ourselves and so are left with only our own bitter defenses.

From her experience in the work of the Church of the Saviour in Washington, D.C., Elizabeth O'Connor draws material to underscore our plight. Despite her commitment to the service of community need at all practical levels, she declares that

it is not enough to say the Church must be shaped by the world's need. This leaves the large and heavy question: Which need? Surveys and studies of surrounding communities have not resolved it, for often agreement cannot be reached on a choice from the multitude of possibilities that exist in every situation. There is juvenile delinquency; there are alcoholism, dope addiction, the aged, the blind, the sick, the broken in mind and spirit; there are slums, with all the problems of housing and education; there are nuclear warfare and the problems of automation and leisure; and on and on runs the list. We can go where the action is, or make some surface decision, but this is not what it means to hear a call or to be "sent." It is only to arrive on the mission field with no word from the Lord.[22]

For it is sadly true that we cannot serve such needs in our own strength. Living by our own puny resources amid such needs, we presently find ourselves worn away, embittered, perhaps broken in one way or another, part of the sickness but not part of the cure. Dietrich Bonhoeffer was opposed to using "God as stopgap," but he was not opposed to depending on God's strength as we work in troubled situations. For many, however, his call for a Christianity that is "religionless" in the sense of not *using* God for our private salvation, has come to mean a call to get things *done* in the world without "wasting time" on prayer. To all that, Albert van den Heuvel replies that "a religionless approach to Christianity then merely ends in a plea for humanism, and theology is replaced by anthropology." Such people forget, he adds, that "Bonhoeffer was an aristocrat of discipline, a man with a performed life of prayer, meditation, and Bible study." [23]

Paul makes it clear that these were his sources of strength, too: "by gifts of the Holy Spirit, . . . by the power of God" (vs. 7 NEB). No man has access to such power except through the disciplines of the Spirit. We cannot carry out our assignment as reconcilers by a life absorbed in go-go activity, however good that is. Before we are useful in *reconciling* a troubled world we must *be reconciled* within. And for that, Paul says, *now* is always the time (vs. 2). Don't waste God's grace!

And Not Lose Heart: Luke 18:1-14

Amid the sufferings of the Exile, faithful men had declared that

> It is good that one should wait quietly
> for the salvation of the Lord (Lam. 3:26).

[22] Elizabeth O'Connor, *Journey Inward, Journey Outward* (New York: Harper, 1968), pp. 31-32.

[23] Albert van den Heuvel, *The Humiliation of the Church* (Philadelphia: Westminster Press, 1966), pp. 132-33.

Here Jesus underscores their faith with the question, "And will not God vindicate his elect, who cry to him day and night? . . . I tell you, he will vindicate them speedily" (vss. 7-8). Thus he lends poignancy to the topic sentence of the passage: "And he told them a parable, to the effect that they ought always to pray and not lose heart" (vs. 1).

Praying always remains appropriate; no situation is too "hopeless." This fills in the content of the *waiting* espoused in the Old Testament lesson for today: one "waits" by perseverance in prayer. God is faithful, declares the Old Testament poet. His faithfulness must not be wasted, adds Paul in today's Epistle. A faithful God saves those whose faith is expressed and sustained by persistent prayer, says Jesus in this Gospel. "When the Son of man comes, will he find faith on earth?" (vs. 8).

Joachim Jeremias offers a careful grammatical defense of his translation: "Will not God hasten to the rescue of his elect who cry to him day and night, even if he puts their patience to the test?" (vs. 7).[24] The focal figure of the parable is the judge, not the widow. Vividly cynical, he neither fears God nor regards man. Case-hardened, he ignores the justice of the widow's grievance. But sensitive to pestering, he grants her a verdict to get rid of her nagging. And Jesus dares to make him the figure for God! The purpose, of course, is not comparison of likeness, but contrast of difference. It is the device used in other teaching passages where Jesus makes his point by throwing God's ways with us into sharp relief, as in his question: "If you then, who are evil, know how to give good gifts to your children, how much more will the heavenly Father give the Holy Spirit to those who ask him?" (Luke 11:13). If this cynical judge, who had rejected the widow's plea, at last came to her rescue in order to get rid of her nagging, *how much more* we can expect from God! So we "ought always to pray and not lose heart."

The call receives scant welcome today. Our secular minds assume that what gets done in the world is done by work; prayer has nothing to do with it. Linking cause and effect, stimulus and response, we rule prayer out of the equation. Pragmatically we conclude that overt results are important, and the disciplines that link us with the unseen are irrelevant and wasteful. Quoting Bonhoeffer's stress on "living completely in this world," we opt for a Christianity immersed in activity and scornful of inner and personal disciplines. But it is one thing for Bonhoeffer, bearing imprisonment for conscience' sake, to make light of suffering and discipline; and it is quite another for those already mortgaged to worldly indulgence to be told that a further plunge into this world is what the gospel of grace is all about. Jesus taught a "worldly" life of service to need, but a "religionless Christianity" that supposes the disciplined life of prayer is not part of that service has not really faced the strand of his teaching of which this passage is a sample.

Yet we need to be "religionless," if the Pharisee in the second parable of this lesson represents religion! Here Jesus addresses those who trust not God but themselves and their own righteousness (vs. 9). The Pharisee offered thanks not for anything God had done, but for his own works above and beyond the call of duty. The law decreed an annual fast; he fasted twice a week! The law prescribed major tithes of crops; he tithed every minor crumb

---

[24] Jeremias, *The Parables of Jesus,* p. 155.

that came into his house! Comparing himself with obvious sinners, he felt very smug! Any man who examines his own heart in honesty must know how like that his own religious practices constantly threaten to become. It is far too easy to be more conscious of religion than of God, more grateful for *our goodness* than for *his grace!*

The tax collector could not so easily hide from his conscience. His hands were dirty with dishonest gain. In all candor he cried, "God, be merciful to me a sinner!" (vs. 13). Jesus did not condone his wrongs, but declared that he was "justified rather than the other" (vs. 14). He was forgiven. He was accepted. He was held in the sight of God as now "right," restored to good terms with God. The other man could not be forgiven, for he had not repented. He could not be accepted, for he acknowledged no need of it. He could not be restored to a right relation with God, for he assumed a kind of godlike goodness in himself. So this parable, too, is about the character of God, who, as Jeremias remarks, "welcomes the despairing, hopeless sinner, and rejects the self-righteous." [25]

PASSION SUNDAY

The Old Cost of the Human Redemption
Genesis 22:1-2, 9-13

In a passing line, Robert Penn Warren once spoke of "the old cost of the human redemption"—as if, of course, everybody knows what that cost is. But we do *not* know, and we fumble to find out. We scramble for "success," but it turns out that we are not quite sure what success really is. And is there no redemption for our *failures?* Or what of the successes we win only to eat out our hearts in boredom or disappointment, shocked that success can be another name for lostness?

Whole philosophies have been aimed at solving the riddle of redemption, one pointing the way of pleasure, another the way of stoic indifference, and so on. In today's racial struggle it is just "the old cost of the human redemption" that is contested. What can pay that cost—the ruthless application of power? or winning demonstrations of love?

Surely love must be involved in redemption—love that reaches out to our brother, love that reaches up to God. Yet, swept by seas of rage, how can we find it in us to love? Out of centuries-long experience, faith declares that the springs of love are in God himself and that the most important love, because the most germinal, is the love that reaches us *from* God. It is this love, paying "the old cost of the human redemption," that the testing of Abraham is all about.

Abraham hears God's call and is convinced that he must sacrifice his only son, Isaac. On the way to the sacrificial rites, Isaac asks, "Where is the lamb?" (vs. 7), and Abraham replies with the key saying of the story, unfortunately omitted from the Lectionary reading: "God will provide himself the lamb for a burnt offering" (vs. 8). Restrained at the last moment from the

[25] *Ibid.*, p. 144.

slaughter of his son, Abraham finds a ram caught in a thicket by its horns and discovers that his answer to Isaac was truer than he knew: God *has* provided the lamb. God *does* pay the cost of redemption.

Ancient peoples, prompted by heartache over dangers, losses, loneliness, guilt, believed only the most perfect sacrifice could answer the need and relate them rightly to their gods. Since nothing was more precious than a loved child, human sacrifice seemed the tragic necessity. Prophets protested that this did not please God, but rather outraged him. "Shall I give my first-born for my transgression, the fruit of my body for the sin of my soul?" (Micah 6:7). Law forbade it: "There shall not be found among you any one who burns his son or daughter as an offering" (Deut. 18:10). Psalmists declared God's character the opposite of all this: "As a father pities his children, so the Lord pities those who fear him" (Ps. 103:13). Yet the practice persisted. This story may well have been told as a parable from the life of the most venerated patriarch, giving a theological depth to Abraham's assertion that "God will provide himself the lamb." Who but God *can* provide an adequate sacrifice? Can the finite satisfy the Infinite? Can the unholy satisfy the All-holy?

Sadly, we still offer human sacrifice. When worse comes to worst, we seek to save ourselves by offering our sons in war. War sacrifices children wholesale. Slums sacrifice children. Denial of human rights sacrifices children. Our drive for success sacrifices children. Can the love of God never get through to us to show us the love that ends this futile holocaust?

Like us, Abraham was torn between love of Isaac and obedience to God. Obedience won out. For apart from the integrity of an obedient will, he could give Isaac nothing else of worth. In the experience, he learned that love and obedience have no final conflict, for the God we obey is himself Love. He learned at last that God never intended to exact Isaac's sacrifice, that what he had said in ignorance is *true*: "God will provide himself the lamb." That love, God loving through us, is still the potent force to resolve conflicts in our pressing necessities.

The lection ends with vs. 13, but the story is not ended until God has blessed Abraham, with the added promise: "And by your descendants shall all the nations of the earth bless themselves, because you have obeyed my voice" (vs. 18). The promise came true in the long witness of Israel as a "kingdom of priests" among the nations. It came true in Jesus, a descendant of Abraham. It keeps coming true in the gospel. God required Abraham's willingness to give "your son, your only son" (vss. 2, 16), but God himself "so loved the world that he gave his only Son" (John 3:16). How gloriously true that "God will provide himself the lamb"! Nothing in all the world is so saving as his love accepted.

High Priest of Good Things: Hebrews 9:11-14

Asserting that "Christ appeared as a high priest of the good things that have come" (vs. 11), this passage points to three ways in which he meets our ultimate needs.

First, he deals not with our *acts* but with *ourselves*. The old religious rites had dealt with outer events, with what we had done, "the purification of the flesh" (vs. 13), our "outward lives" (JB). But Christ "offered himself without blemish to God," to "purify your conscience from dead works" (vs. 14). He gave his whole self to accept us at the point most personal to our self, our conscience. It is one thing to forgive a specific deed done; it is quite another to accept a whole person. But this is what Jesus continually did in his encounters with all sorts of persons whom society had rejected. A century ago, Sir Edwin Arnold prayed,

> Lord! make us just, that we may be
> A little justified with Thee.[26]

His words document the failure of the old religious rites, which moved on the level of our *acts*, not *ourselves*, and so left us only "a little justified," not wholly accepted. Our burning need, now as always, is to be accepted fully as persons in a right personal relation. This acceptance Christ conveys.

Second, he deals with our needs by offering, not external sacrifices, but his *whole self*. "He entered once for all into the Holy Place, taking not the blood of goats and calves but his own blood" (vs. 12); so the Old Testament imagery speaks of the offering of life. For in the blood offering it was not the *death* of the victim that mattered, but his *life released* and made available, "for the blood is the life" (Deut. 12:23), and "it is the blood that makes atonement, by reason of the life" (Lev. 17:11). Jesus gave his life, not only on the Cross but in the intense self-giving that characterized all his dealings with persons throughout his ministry. The writer to the Hebrews, repeatedly in previous chapters (2:14-18; 4:15; 5:1-5), has been at pains to stress this fact of Christ's giving of himself in full identification with us. No abstract acceptance will do. It is no academic affair to make the acceptance real. We need a *person* who makes himself fully present, gives himself undividedly. Christ meets this need.

Third, he deals with us in ways that reflect the ultimate reality of God's eternal dealings. The imagery of this passage is drawn from the Old Testament, but much of its philosophic implication is Platonic. Plato's world of visible phenomena was only a shadow of the real world, which for him consisted of "ideas"—those eternal concepts of which *things* were but dim replicas. This passage speaks of Christ as entering into God's presence "through the greater and more perfect tent (not made with hands, that is, not of this creation)" (vs. 11). One catches the Platonic mood even more forcefully, as JB reads: "He has passed through the greater, the more perfect tent, which is better than the one made by men's hands because it is not of this created order"; or Weymouth: "which does not belong to the material creation." The same philosophic understanding appears later in the chapter: "For Christ has entered, not into a sanctuary made with hands, a copy of the true one, but into heaven itself" (vs. 24).

Thus the passage is declaring the Christian conviction that what was seen on the stage of time in Jesus is eternally true of the very nature and life of God himself. He who deals not with our *acts* but with *ourselves*, giving not

---

[26] *Pearls of the Faith*, No. 47, as quoted in *The Oxford Dictionary of Quotations* (Oxford University Press, 1955), p. 14.

external sacrifices but his *whole self*, is an earthly representation of what is eternally *real* in God. He meets our personal need by his personal self-giving as the divine Ultimate.

It Is Expedient! John 11:47-53

There is wide agreement among scholars that this is a "pronouncement story" told as a setting for the sententious words of Caiaphas: "You do not understand that it is expedient for you that one man should die for the people, and that the whole nation should not perish" (vs. 50). The crafty Caiaphas is portrayed as speaking better than he knew. He meant one thing by what he said, but God meant quite another—which is often the case with us.

"This man performs many signs" (vs. 47), said the members of the council. In the ironic complaint John finds a summing up of chapters 2–11, sometimes known as "the book of signs." Throughout these chapters we are told of events which point beyond themselves to deep meanings. John is not chiefly concerned with the events, but with the meanings to which as signs they point. Last among them stands the raising of Lazarus, which in John, unlike the Synoptic Gospels, serves to trigger the crucifixion plot.

Caiaphas and his colleagues find even in such signs no deep meaning, but only a challenge to what is "expedient" for themselves. They fear that the people will believe and rise in messianic fervor, giving the Romans occasion to upset the *status quo* of both temple and nation. With the comfortable of all times, they are disturbed and disgruntled by a gospel that makes a difference in the political world of *here* and *now*. In the name of temple and nation they oppose that gospel to the death.

One of the factors that make the Fourth Gospel fascinating is John's love of double meanings. There is stratum and substratum in the conversations that fill this book. Caiaphas speaks on two levels. On one, he is merely an opportunist saying, "It is expedient for you that one man should die for the people." He is making sure that whoever dies it will not be Caiaphas! But more is involved than crafty insurance of himself and his caste. His is the expediency of the responsible official, the greatest good of the greatest number. The argument is not all wrong; the general welfare must be protected. With strikingly similar attitude we reason about war and civil disorder: some must die to perpetuate the state. But "the greatest good to the greatest number" is a cruelly insensitive instrument for getting at truth that goes beyond counting noses, as the event proved when the high priest's expediency nailed Jesus to a cross.

On the second level, John tells us that Caiaphas is used of God to say something far more important than the cynical expediency he intended. "Being high priest that year" (vs. 49) is phrased not so much to date his priesthood as to stress the authenticity of his prophetic words. He was "high priest *that* year" of all years, year of the world's supreme crisis. In this capacity, John says, he spoke the truth that Jesus' death would have meaning universal and communal, "to gather into one the children of God who are scattered abroad" (vs. 52). Faulty aspirations leading to anxious jealousies had scattered

God's children, according to the Babel parable (Gen. 11:9), but in Jesus that bitter trend would be reversed.

A prayer in the second-century *Didache* reflects this conviction: "We give thanks to you, Our Father. . . . As this fragmented bread was scattered on the mountains, but was gathered up and became one, so let the Church be gathered up from the four corners of the earth into your kingdom." This is the meaning of our Lord's passion. Lifted high on the cross, he draws to him all who can see beyond the event to the saving love it offers. This is the meaning of every celebration of Holy Communion. As the scattered grain is gathered into the loaf, and as the broken pieces belong to *one* loaf, so we belong together in Christ.

Every man confronts a crucial question: At what level do I see Christ? Do I miss him because he disturbs my cozy *status quo,* or do I see his deeper meaning? Do I miss his moral challenge because of what "is expedient," or will I so respond to him that I may be gathered with "the children of God who are scattered abroad"? As he comes to me in events, is it possible that I will *one* thing, while *God* wills quite *another?*

PALM SUNDAY

He Shall Command Peace: Zechariah 9:9-12

Palm Sunday celebrates faith's declaration that Christ is king. He comes not merely as prophet, priest, teacher, hero, martyr; he comes as king. Believers waved palm branches and spread garments to carpet his path because they saw in him a king. But what *kind* of king? Two of the gospels quote Zechariah's poetic vision in answer to this question, and all four have recourse to its symbolism. Presumably it held an important place in the mind of Jesus.

"He shall command peace to the nations" (vs. 10) may be taken as the keynote of the passage. The prophet's perceptive eye has swept the political horizon. Alexander the Great may well have been on the march, his conquests reflected in Zechariah 9-14, and the prophetic faith dared to see in the forward sweep of the conqueror an instrument God was using to work out his purpose.

Before the conqueror, the wealth and fortified power of Tyre is stripped away and "devoured by fire" (vss. 3-4). The other cities of Syria and Phoenicia likewise fall (vss. 5-6), and the Philistines adopt the dietary laws of the Jews and become "like a clan in Judah" (vss. 6-7). In all this conquest, God himself is working his design into history's fabric and preparing the way for the ideal king:

> Then I will encamp at my house as a guard,
>   so that none shall march to and fro;
> no oppressor shall again overrun them,
>   for now I see with my own eyes (vs. 8).

Thus the cruel history of a bloody period is seen by the eyes of faith as preparing the way for the messianic king who "shall command peace to the nations." He will come, "triumphant and victorious," not by earthly might but by the power of God, "humble and riding on an ass." Humility, being the characteristic virtue of the future people of God (cf. Zeph. 3:12; 2:3), properly belongs to their king. The ass is not merely the beast of burden, but the mount of princes. "Jair the Gileadite, who judged Israel twenty-two years . . . had thirty sons who rode on thirty asses; and they had thirty cities . . . ." (Judges 10:3-4). Abdon "judged Israel" and "had forty sons and thirty grandsons, who rode on seventy asses" (Judges 12:14). Though the legitimte prince, Solomon, rode on "David's mule" (I Kings 1:38), Adonijah, the warlike pretender to the throne, "prepared for himself chariots and horsemen" (I Kings 1:5). So comes this prince, peacefully, mounted on an ass, not as a horseman of war.

It follows that the God who guards (vs. 8) and whose intention is peace, "will cut off the chariot . . . and the war horse . . . and the battle bow . . . and . . . command peace to the nations" (vs. 10). "His words make peace" (vs. 10 MT) as he counsels the nations; their warlike postures are relaxed because justice and right guide their mutual relations.

It is significant that, from the varying conceptions of messiahship current in his day, Jesus chose to dramatize this one. The Gospels enshrine it. In its annual Palm Sunday festival the Church proclaims it. Christians have no ready-made blueprint by which peace is built, but we have here a mandate to insist that the way be found. So says Helmut Gollwitzer:

It is not the business of the Church . . . to consider how in a world where nuclear weapons exist and the pre-atomic rules of politics are retained, the politicians can come to terms with the Christian 'No' to nuclear war. The churches have to pronounce this 'No' because it is God's command, thus making clear to the politicians their task, implicit in it, of pursuing their politics without war in an atomic age.[27]

Humility that Exalts: Philippians 2:5-11

If Palm Sunday proclaims Christ as the humble king who brings peace, it is not content to leave the matter there. Not only kingly, he is divine. Paul summarizes the theology of the passion, death, and eternal exaltation of our Lord in this supreme hour. Characteristically, this sublime theology is a spark struck from his clash with a practical problem.

There has been strife in the church at Philippi. Inflated pretensions have become so extreme that even the preaching of the gospel has been tainted by perverted motives: some seek converts in order to swell a faction. From his Roman prison Paul writes this urgent appeal to unity and humility toward one another and before God, begging them not to push their own ambitions but to advance the interests of others (vs. 4). What follows (vss. 5-11) seems to have a liturgical form and to be a magnificent hymn which Paul—whether he composed it for the occasion or is quoting from the liturgical treasury—offers as a theological foundation for the ethic of humility. Giving up what was rightfully his own was Christ's way, he says; it is always God's way; it is the only way to utlimate exaltation.

[27] Gollwitzer, *The Demands of Freedom*, p. 132.

"Have this mind among yourselves, which you have in Christ Jesus" (vs. 5), is not a claim to intellectual reproduction of Christ's thought. Alternate translations catch its intent: "Treat one another with the same spirit as you experience in Christ Jesus" (MT); "Have the same attitude that Christ Jesus had" (AT). What follows shows the central quality of that "mind" or "attitude."

Line by line, the hymn portrays the progression of God's action in Jesus Christ as a divine-human act of humility. "Though he was in the form of God" (vs. 6) means that he possessed "all the attributes that express and reveal the essential 'nature' of God" (JB note). Yet he "did not count equality with God a thing to be grasped." The stress is not on Christ's divinity itself, but upon the fact that—divine as he was—"he did not set store upon equality with God" (MT).

The reminder was needed in Philippi. It is needed now. At a diplomatic reception, Hans Tabor, Danish ambassador to the United Nations and president of the Security Council during one of its most trying crises, suggested the need of such an ungrasping posture. Diplomats, he said, might learn something from the words of a Danish poet:

> The noble art of losing face
> May one day save the human race,
> And turn into eternal merit
> What weaker minds would call disgrace.[28]

Not grasping "equality with God," Paul continues, Christ "emptied himself" (vs. 7). Thomas J. J. Altizer places such stress on this verse as the basis of his "Christian atheism" that it needs a careful second look. We should not depend on a single form of English words as fully translating the meaning. It can be variously translated: "impoverished himself" (TCNT); "made himself nothing" (NEB); "stripped himself of all privilege" (PT). Far from Altizer's metaphysical fixation on a God who ceased to be God, this carries ethical and psychological meaning. It fills in the nature and extent of Christ's self-humbling. It says in conceptual terms what the gospel puts in the narrative of a Christ who, knowing that he had come from God and was returning to God, stooped to wash the feet of his disciples (John 13:3-5). Having been "in the form of God" (vs. 6), he was content to take "the form of a servant" (vs. 7) and became like men.

It was not enough to become a *man* and a *servant;* he even submitted to *death on a cross,* which was believed to carry an ultimate curse (Deut. 21:23). If his humility could go to such lengths, Paul is saying, we can well afford to humble ourselves to give preferment to others.

Such humility is power. "Therefore God has highly exalted him" (vs. 9); the theological statement underscores Jesus' ethical counsel: "He who is greatest among you shall be your servant; whoever exalts himself will be humbled, and whoever humbles himself will be exalted" (Matt. 23:11-12). That, Paul asserts, is not just wise advice to Christian disciples; it is the way things are, eternally in the heart of Christ, in the very life of God. So the humbled one is given "the name which is above every name" (vs. 9), which,

[28] From an account of Tabor's remarks at a New York reception, *Chicago Daily News,* July 13, 1967.

in biblical idiom, declares he is given a dignity, a glory, a nature that stand above all. The outcome is the glory of God the Father (vss. 10-11). Thus the death-of-God perversion of biblical kenosis (he "emptied himself") based on this passage is left without a shred of support in the principal New Testament text of which Altizer makes use. Christ came from *God*, was raised by *God*, returned to *God*, and all "to the glory of *God* the Father."

A Thrust at Life's Center: Luke 19:29-40

In the face of the shouts of praise, the Pharisees' protest, "Teacher, rebuke your disciples," or "check your disciples" (vs. 39 JB), sounds very much like the watchwords of today, "Be cool!" "Stay detached!" Where the deadly sins—pride, lust, wrath, sloth, envy, gluttony, avarice—were once understood as offenses against moral and spiritual integrity, *Esquire* has announced that today's deadly sins are chastity, poverty, anonymity, age, ugliness, constancy—departures from the norm of cool detachment, self-possession, and self-gratification.

To the challenge Jesus replied, "I tell you, if these were silent, the very stones would cry out" (vs. 40). It may have been a proverbial saying; Habakkuk used its idiom in the face of the devices by which the powerful were exploiting the poor:

> For the stone will cry out from the wall,
> and the beam from the woodwork respond (Hab. 2:11).

Both Jesus and the ancient prophet were declaring that some truths rise from such depths of reality that they cannot be silenced; if men do not speak them, earthly events will. This was the truth about the challenges he brought to the center of Israel's life. It continues to thrust at the center of our life.

The narrative action in this account of his entrance into Jerusalem (vss. 29-34) carries the strong impression of a deliberate plan to challenge men in the way most conspicuous, at the political and religious capital. Some scholars offer alternative theories, suggesting that Jesus' words about the colt were for Luke simply evidences of Jesus' omniscience, but the story itself sounds very much as if a careful prearrangement for the use of the colt had been worked out. Vs. 28 is only the latest of a long series of Luke's references to Jesus "going up to Jerusalem" (see 9:51; 13:22; 13:31-33, as examples). In the last of these, he points to his destination and its purpose with the word, "It cannot be that a prophet should perish away from Jerusalem" (13:33). Now we see him deliberately adopting the messianic image of Zech. 9:9-12, as if to demand a decisive judgment for or against him. Opposition had gathered throughout his ministry. If he went on without compromise he would eventually be silenced. He would not let it happen in some obscure country place. Coming to Jerusalem, he brought the issue dramatically to a head.

This challenge at the center sharply raised the question of the nature of power. One popular view of the expected Messiah held that he would come as a conquering king, who would re-establish the throne of David and restore Israel's lost political independence and power. His disciples with their shout,

"Blessed be the King who comes in the name of the Lord!" (vss. 37-38) may well have had such a king in mind. It seems clear that the authorities did, that they feared an abortive clash with Rome, and that one of the pressures that moved Pilate to his judgment was the fear that Jesus or the crowd that gathered around him might hatch something treasonous against Caesar.

In her play, *The Man Born to Be King*, Dorothy Sayers pictures Jesus as here responding to such a misunderstanding of his purpose. The Zealot leader, Baruch, sends Jesus an offer of armed men to take the city. At a named rendezvous there is not only "the ass's colt that is tied to the vineyard door" but "a war-horse saddled and ready." If Jesus chooses the colt, there is no help to be expected from Baruch, but by mounting the horse he can "ride into Jerusalem with a thousand spears." From what we know of the political ferment of the time, the choice is plausible. Jesus chose the ass, and thereby he made evident that he chose power not from spears but from the servanthood that leads to suffering, death, and resurrection.

The choice recurs in constantly new forms. Amid the demonstrations and counter-demonstrations of 1967, a journalist's photograph showed a group of angry young men carrying a large white cross topped with an American flag and neatly inscribed in large letters, "Our goal: Smash Communism—We Support Our President on Vietnam." From the Cross such a mood removes a suffering and dying Christ who came in peace. In his place it puts a nationalism whose goal is to destroy a rival. Some of us, who cannot believe Jesus would endorse modern Communism, cannot believe, either, that to "smash" would be his answer. He knew another kind of power. It led to a Cross—and beyond. At the center of life, where we decide the question of power for ourselves, the Palm Sunday gospel makes its thrust.

MAUNDY THURSDAY

Christian Passover
Exodus 12:1, 3, 6-8, 11, 14, 25-27

Hotly debated as the chronology of Jesus' last week and the timing of Passover and Crucifixion may be, there is an undeniable tie between the Passover and the Lord's Supper. As Maundy Thursday celebrates Jesus' institution of this holy meal, it is fitting that Christians meditate on the Passover festival for which this lection gives directions. For this festival is, as a note in JB observes, "a rehearsal for the Christian Passover." Or as Gregory Dix remarked, "It is simply the feast of the *Christian redemption*, as the Jewish Passover was the feast of the Jewish redemption."

Both are *feasts of remembrance*. "This day shall be for you a memorial day" (vs. 14), "a day of remembrance" (JB and TMT). The Supper, likewise, was instituted by Jesus "in remembrance." But the memory is no mere looking backward, recalling what *was*, allowing it to remain in the historic yesterdays. "It is as well to know," writes G. Henton Davies,

that for the Hebrew the recollection of the past means that what is recalled becomes a present reality, which in turn controls the will. . . . Remembrance is revival for the downcast. . . . Memory revives faith. In turn, in the cultic ceremonies themselves Israel remembers her ancient story, the works of God, his marvelous deeds in times past. Thus cult is sacred memory becoming sacred reality and life for the participants.[29]

There is in vss. 25-27 of this lesson such a present re-presentation of the past event, making it faith's reality present again. Keeping the festival for all time, the people of Israel are to be brought again into the presence of the God of deliverance. This is a model of the way in which Christian celebration of the Lord's Supper rises above memory's recall into holy Presence.

Both Passover and Lord's Supper *celebrate a deliverance.* Israel is directed to eat the meal, clothed and shod for a journey, staff in hand, and "in haste" (vs. 11), to dramatize the liberation of the slave people from Egypt. In a fourth-century Easter sermon, Gregory of Nazianzus describes to his congregation the way the death and resurrection of our Lord effect our deliverance, using colorful imagery of the Passover. "Yesterday," he says,

the Lamb was slain and the door-posts were anointed, and Egypt bewailed her Firstborn, and the Destroyer passed us over, and the Seal was dreadful and reverend, and we were walled in with the Precious Blood. To-day we have clean escaped from Egypt and from Pharaoh; and there is none to hinder us from keeping a Feast to the Lord our God—the Feast of our Departure. . . . Yesterday I was crucified with Him; to-day I am glorified with Him; yesterday I died with Him; to-day I am quickened with Him; yesterday I was buried with Him; to-day I rise with Him. But let us offer to Him Who suffered and rose again for us. . . . Let us offer *ourselves* . . . let us know the power of the Mystery, for what Christ died.[30]

Once we were slaves of sin and death, but every celebration of the Lord's Supper renews our contact with the living reality of deliverance.

Both Passover and Supper approach *deliverance through bitterness.* The people of Israel were told that "with unleavened bread and bitter herbs they shall eat it" (vs. 8), for there had been deep bitterness in bondage. And of a bitter cup of sorrow and suffering Jesus prayed, "My father, if it be possible, let this cup pass from me; nevertheless, not as I will, but as thou wilt" (Matt. 26:39). Not his cup alone, it is now shared with us, as the Communion liturgy reminds us: "Drink ye all of this." For as the model of the Passover traces the way to freedom and joy through the bitterness of bondage, Christian experience discovers in the sharing of our Lord's cup the way to victory and new life.

Heralding! I Corinthians 11:23-26

One of the newer translations restores the lost flavor of rejoicing to this earliest written account of the Last Supper. It reads, "So it is the Lord's death that you are heralding, whenever you eat this bread and drink this cup, until he comes" (vs. 26 KT). Of course *heralding* is a synonym for

[29] Article on "Memorial, Memory," *The Interpreter's Dictionary of the Bible,* III, 344-45.

[30] *Nicene and Post-Nicene Fathers,* 2nd Series (Grand Rapids: Eerdmans, 1955), VII, 203.

proclaiming, the more customary word in the passage; yet the feeling-tone is different. As one dictionary of synonyms savors the nuances of meaning, "We *report* an interview, *reveal* a secret, *herald* the coming of some distinguished person or great event." [31] So! "You are heralding . . . until he comes." Great person and event indeed! That is what the Supper is about.

In the Supper we herald a *great thanksgiving.* Our Lord "took bread, and when he had given thanks, he broke it" (vss. 23-24). "When he had given thanks"—the Greek *eucharistesas*—gives us one of the church's precious names for the feast: the Eucharist. It was, of course, the familiar Jewish thanksgiving at table, but in this setting it became much more. The atmosphere was solemn, but not funereal. It looked toward a great future, "until he *comes.*" We look back to it flooded with the light of Easter and give thanks for that victory won.

Taking the loaf, he said, "This is my body which is for you" (vs. 24). The best Greek texts do not say "broken for you," but simply "for you." That is true of his body because it is true of his whole life as "the Man for others." His body, the church, is for us; his body in the Eucharist is for us; his body on the Cross was for us: "This is my body which takes your place" (AT). Yet he did break the loaf, and we all share in it—one loaf, one life, one body, one church, shared with us. So we *celebrate* the Communion, we do not *mourn* it; for it is the feast of a great thanksgiving.

It heralds a *great covenant.* "This cup is the new covenant in my blood" (vs. 25), he said. The symbolism is that of Moses' act in sealing the covenant with Israel (Exod. 24:5-8), a symbolism borrowed from the practice of kings of the time. A king made covenants with subjects or with lesser chiefs, not on the basis of haggling negotiations but on the basis of the great monarch's free offer. One either accepted the terms of refused them; he could not negotiate them by argument. When they were accepted, a blood ceremony ratified the agreement; and it was such a ratification between God and his people which Moses sealed with the blood ceremony which, though it may offend our modern esthetic sense, was very real in its day. The later prophets looked forward to a new covenant, more intimately real to the inner life, of which God said, "I will put my law within them, and I will write it upon their hearts" (Jer. 31:31-34). The New Testament gets its name from that New Covenant, for the terms are equivalent. We are the people of a New Covenant, a new law written not on stone or parchment but on our hearts. As the Old Covenant made Israel God's people, the New Covenant makes the Church God's people called to a great mission. So we *celebrate* the Communion, we do not merely *perform* its ritual; for it is the feast of a great covenant.

It is, moreover, the heralding of a *great future.* "For as often as you eat this bread and drink the cup, you proclaim the Lord's death until he comes" (vs. 26). Looking forward to our Lord's fuller coming, the sacrament celebrates his presence in the interim. What a word to our common life! Disgracefully, in Corinth, some of the people gorged on Communion meals they brought, while others went hungry. Some drank to the point of drunkenness, the whole affair disorderly. Chapters 11–14 give the picture. Paul wrote

[31] James C. Fernald, *Synonyms, Antonyms, and Prepositions* (New York: Funk and Wagnalls, 1947), p. 50.

this gem on the institution of the Lord's Supper to set the matter straight: their divisions—the one bread; their drunkenness—the cup of the covenant; their selfish gluttony—the shared loaf; their unworthy observance of the feast—the remembrance of the Lord; their unworthy present—a great future full of his presence already beginning.

Are we so unlike the Corinthians that this has nothing to say to us? "The very mention of the breaking," said Bengel, "involves distribution and refutes the Corinthian plan—every man his own." If it spoke to Corinth, it speaks to a modern world of rich and poor nations, refuting our plan too. Sitting at the Lord's table, as George A. Buttrick remarked, we need enough manners to pass the bread. So we *celebrate* the Communion, we do not merely *repeat* a rite; for it is the feast of a great future kingdom already spilling over into the now of his presence, a kingdom where sharing is real.

From Infamy to Glory: Mark 14:17-25

The Last Supper begins in infamy—"one of you will betray me" (vs. 18); it arrives at glory—"new in the kingdom of God" (vs. 25). These extremes mark the outer boundaries of this brief account. Are they not present in every celebration of the Supper?

It begins as a festival of penitent self-examination before the searching scrutiny of the Lord. "One of you will betray me, one who is eating with me" (vs. 18). That can be said whenever the church gathers for Communion. For we betray him, again and again. We never gather except as a company of sinners; forgiven sinners, perhaps, sinners who are growing into maturity in Christ, but sinners who must come for forgiveness, again and again—so that Martin Marty was right when he called us "the company of the daily unburdened."

The twelve in the upper room "began to be sorrowful" (vs. 19); "they were distressed" (MT and JB), or "dismayed" (NEB). The words apply to us and our betrayals, both individual and social. "It is impossible to discuss the Holy Communion today without deciding about nuclear war," a distinguished churchman declared. For Communion focuses the reconciling act of Christ, between us and God and between us and our estranged brothers; and war in the nuclear age is "rebellion against the reality of the atonement." [32] The personal and the social become fused. Dietrich Bonhoeffer, struggling against the Nazi defilement, working at both the personal and the social questions of his day, cared deeply for a right liturgical celebration of communion but declared that all these were so bound in one that "only he who cries out for the Jews dare permit himself to sing in Gregorian," the great musical language of Communion. [33]

In self-examination the disciples asked, "one after another, 'Is it I?'" (vs. 19). Naming no individual, Jesus said as if sharing their sorrow, "It is . . . one who is dipping bread in the same dish with me." That describes all who take the Communion, who share his common dish. Such is our sinfulness: we violate the table fellowship, alienate ourselves as did Judas, break

[32] Gollwitzer, *The Demands of Freedom*, p. 136.
[33] Helmut Thielicke, *The Trouble with the Church*, pp. 84-85.

the covenant bond of loyalty. Refusing to identify Judas, Jesus would not lacerate the fellowship by accusation. Was he not mindful of the need of each of us to ask, "Is it I?" Did he imply that any man sharing the meal could be the sinful betrayer? Before this chapter's close, the disciples sleep when he has left them to watch and pray (vss. 32-42); an anonymous young man, often thought to be Mark himself, flees in panic (vss. 51-52); Peter denies that he ever knew Jesus (vss. 66-72). Do we see ourselves somewhere in the picture? It is deadly serious. Better for the betrayer, Jesus declares, "if he had not been born" (vs. 21).

Beginning as a festival of penitence, the Last Supper ends as a celebration of the kingdom of God. Giving the Supper to exactly this company of betrayers, our Lord gave them his "blood of the covenant, which is poured out for many" (vs. 24). Elsewhere the New Testament has substitutionary language about Jesus' blood sacrifice, but not here. This is covenant language, as alternative translations make clear: "covenant-blood" (MT and TCNT); "my blood which ratifies the agreement" (AT). So he looks ahead to a new life he will share with us when he drinks it "new in the kingdom of God" (vs. 25).

In whatever infamy we come to the Communion, we are granted entrance to his kingdom—its new, cleansed life, its victory over all that robs our days of meaning, its fellowship with our Lord and with all other disciples who gather round him. This promises a new world. C. F. Andrews, gallant missionary, bound by ties of intellectual kinship and shared interests to Mahatma Gandhi, was once asked to compare his bond to Gandhi with his relation to other Christians. "When I kneel at the communion table of my Lord Jesus Christ," he replied, "and beside me is an illiterate Indian peasant I have never seen before, I am closer to him than I could be or ever have been to Gandhi, my friend." [34] To such fellowship, bridging all chasms of race, class, ideology or interest, we are bound in the kingdom which Holy Communion celebrates.

GOOD FRIDAY

A Sight Unheard Of: Isaiah 52:13–53:12

For they shall see what they were never told,
    a sight unheard of (52:15b MT).

That God's Servant could succeed through suffering because God suffered with him and brought glory from it, was a new idea then—and it remains a new amazement in every generation, "a sight unheard of." We recall it on Good Friday because it so exactly describes what was happening in the Crucifixion, but we need to see its roots in another dark historic hour. Until we do, we miss the light it throws on the Cross as no isolated happening on a hill outside Jerusalem.

The writer was that prophet of the Exile whose work, now fused with the writings of Isaiah of Jerusalem, constitutes chapters 40–55 of the book as

[34] Jones, *Our Mission Today*, p. 87.

we know it. In the dark night of Babylonian Exile, he struggled to understand how God could allow his covenant people to fall into this catastrophe. Little by little, he came to see that Israel was a Servant people, through whose sufferings God was showing all men a saving truth they would not otherwise perceive.

> For they shall see what they were never told,
> a sight unheard of.

The poem is cast in the form of dialogue. God's voice is heard (52:13-15), declaring that his fallen servant shall rise, and that both kings and the masses will come to understand a new truth. To this the kings and peoples reply in the long middle section (53:1-9). In the conclusion (53:10-12) the prophet summarizes a new insight into what God is doing in this historic crisis. Though each section invites extended meditation, we can call attention to only one or two essential matters.

The people see God's Servant as they would abhorrently behold a leper. "A man of sorrows, and acquainted with grief" is more accurately translated, "a man of pain, who knew what sickness was" (53:3 MT, closely paralleled by nearly all modern translations). He called forth pity and revulsion. "As one from whom men hide their faces" is the idiomatic way of speaking of a leper. How strange that Israel, God's chosen, could become a leper among the nations. Has their God been overpowered?

Then it dawns on the nations that God has used his Servant to bear a suffering which rightly belongs to all. Can it be that he loves all—not merely his "chosen"?

"But he was wounded for our transgressions" (53:5) should not be understood as substitutionary in some way external to our act. It was through our agency that he suffered, "for our faults" (JB), "because we had sinned" (MT), "by our rebelliousness" (Knight). Throughout this portion of the dialogue most translators replace RSV's "for" with "through." "He fell," the nations confess, "struck down by sins of ours" (53:8 MT).

J. Elliott Corbett makes the meaning current by his paraphrase, through which we, like the people in Isaiah's poem, meditate on another suffering race:

> *"He had no form or comeliness*
> *that we should look at him.*
> His nose was too broad,
> lips too thick,
> hair too curly.
> *And no beauty that we should desire him.*
> Would you want your daughter to marry one?
> *He was despised and rejected by men.*
> He knew a door, not as an entranceway,
> but as a barrier to be shut in one's face . . .
>
> *Upon him was the chastisement that made us whole,*
> *and with his stripes we are healed.*
> As he strode uncowed to freedom,
> our sense of human dignity deepened.

> As his flesh was torn open,
> the bleeding sore of our bitterness healed . . . .

> knowing now no whiteness of skin is purer
> than suffering love.[35]

The prophet's new understanding of what God is doing in this historic tragedy fills the closing lines (53:10-12). God, not defeated nor aloof, is at work amid the suffering, so that when the servant

> had made himself a guilt-offering,
> He might see posterity, might prolong his life,
> And the pleasure of the Lord might prosper in his hand (53:10 AT).

So Israel's suffering serves in the end as a witness by which the nations shall be brought to God. "He bore the sin of many, and made intercession for the transgressors" (53:12).

Jewish suffering remains a perennial tragedy: all the Jews of Jerusalem burned in a synagogue by crusaders in 1099; the charge of poisoning wells in time of plague and the retributions that followed, as in the era of the Black Death; the tortures of the Spanish Inquisition; expulsions wholesale from Spain, France, and England in the fifteenth century; ghetto life haunted by pogroms; the Nazi genocide; and the exclusions and snubs of our own society. Yet through it all the witness persists.

Out of their life came Jesus who, above all others, embodies the role of the Suffering Servant upon whom "was the chastisement that made us whole" (53:5).

A Share in Christ's Victory: Hebrews 10:4-7, 10-23

Victory, announced in the opening chapter of the Letter to the Hebrews, is here reasserted. In both declarations (1:13 and 10:13) there rings the messianic claim of the psalmist:

> The Lord says to my lord:
> "Sit at my right hand,
> till I make your enemies
> your footstool" (Ps. 110:1).

In the opening chapters, the writer admits, we do not yet feel the victory in our grasp; "but we see Jesus," whose victory is a *promise* of our own (2:5-9). Now the writer works out the detail of his assertion that Jesus has won, over the whole kingdom of evil, a victory we can share.

Religious practices cannot win it (vs. 4). As if it were Christ's own words, the psalmist's enumeration (Ps. 40:6-8) of rites that prove insufficient is repeated. "Sacrifices" of animals; "offerings" of meal or cereal; "burnt offerings," the wholly consumed animal sacrifice intended to make peace; and "sin offerings" intended to win expiation—all have failed, for all must be

[35] J. Elliott Corbett, *The Prophets on Main Street* (Richmond: John Knox Press, 1965), pp. 150-51.

offered again and again. If they had ever won a real victory over evil, this constant repetition would be needless.

Albert Camus, in his sophisticated novel, *The Fall,* pictures our experience in similar light. Jean Baptiste Clemence seeks to rid himself of his guilt by endless confessions which serve a twofold purpose. They exteriorize the guilt and so get rid of it. And in confessing, Jean Baptiste shifts his narrative of wrongdoing from "I" to "we," lightening his load of guilt by the realization that all men are guilty along with himself. He can thus draw others into mutual confessions, *relieved* by spreading his guilt thin, and *superior* because he has been first to confess. Yet the ingenious device, he wryly admits, never satisfies for long. When he has ended his session with one confessor he must find someone else with whom to begin anew. If he could again face the crisis which precipitated his fall, he doubts his courage to do other than he did before. Whether practiced by ancient Israel or the modern existentialist, our devices for expiation fall short of victory.

But when Christ had offered his one sacrifice, "he sat down at the right hand of God, then to wait until his enemies should be made a stool for his feet" (vss. 12-13). Steadily was he isolated for the solitary struggle. Attended first by multitudes, in the upper room by the twelve, in Gethsemane by his intimate three, on the Cross he was left utterly alone. There he met all that evil could do to him—physical cruelty, subtle innuendo, slanderous lies, dread forebodings of the dangers to which his followers would be exposed, spiritual agonies of which the cry, "My God, my God, why hast thou forsaken me?" (Mark 15:34) is but an echo. Yet his death, resurrection, and continued life in the world across these centuries testify to a victory complete and final.

Karl Heim likens the victory to the collapse of a dike on the North Sea. Only a small segment of dike may be affected, not vastly important in itself. Yet it is momentous for all the life of the low countries because the incalculable power of the sea surges behind it. In a different figure, Karl Barth writes: "The war is at an end—even though here and there troops are still shooting, because they have not heard anything yet about the capitulation." [36]

We need to hear of it, for it is a victory won for *us* (vss. 15-23). All our sins forgiven, we no longer need the old religious rites (vss. 15-18). Drawing near by faith, we are invited to appropriate the peace of a cleansed conscience. We keep the faith, not in our power, but by the power of him who has made a promise from which he will not depart (vss. 19-23).

Beware the Little Deaths: Luke 23:33-38, 44-46

Carl Sandburg warned us, "Beware the little deaths." We die a little, hour by hour in our compromises, self-seeking, anxiety, and fear, our wasted energies, escapism, and sin. Dying many little deaths, we are like the alcoholic father in Faulkner's story, who saw life as utter futility, man a mere product of climate—"a problem in impure properties carried tediously to an unvarying nil: stalemate of dust and desire." Time, he said, is our misfortune.

[36] Karl Barth, *Dogmatics in Outline* (New York: Philosophical Library, 1949), p. 123.

Obsessed by clocks that ticked life away, he asserted that "Christ was not crucified: he was worn away by a minute clicking of little wheels." [37] To such deluded futility the little deaths can lead.

At "the place which is called The Skull" (vs. 33) men of high and low estate were dying the little deaths. From their eminence "the rulers scoffed at him [Jesus], saying, 'He saved others; let him save himself, if he is the Christ of God, his Chosen One!'" (vs. 35). At their humbler posts, the soldiers "made sport of him" (AT), sneering in their buffoonery, "If you are the King of the Jews, save yourself!" (vs. 37). There was darkness at noon, "the sixth hour" (vs. 44). Darkness here is intended in a spiritual sense. "The sun's light failed" (vs. 45) not in the sense of an eclipse—an impossibility at the time of the Passover full moon—but in the more terrible sense of the deep darkness of the soul that can engulf men and nations, now as well as then. They had died the little deaths until "darkness covered the whole land" (vs. 44 MT). How little they understood! But Jesus, refusing to save himself, died as he had lived, still calling men away from the little deaths of self-seeking to the great death of self-renunciation: "Whoever seeks to gain his life will lose it, but whoever loses his life will preserve it" (Luke 17:33).

Over against their little deaths, his great death proved redeeming. "Father," he prayed, "forgive them; for they know now what they do" (vs. 34). As the marginal note in RSV points out, this saying is omitted from a number of ancient manuscripts. Paul Scherer speculates[38] that some ancient copyists may have omitted it because they were puzzled by it. Whatever the case may be with regard to manuscript texts, it is *like* Jesus to pray thus. It is of a piece with his life. The early church—knowing him best—was so impressed that this was the quality of his great death that Stephen died with an echo of it on his lips (Acts 7:60).

As if in answer, "the curtain of the temple was torn in two" (vs. 45). Like the failing of the sun's light, this interprets a spiritual meaning. The Holy of Holies thus opened to allow access by sinful men symbolizes what the Epistle for today puts in more theological language as its speaks of "the new and living way which he opened for us through the curtain, that is, through his flesh" (Heb. 10:20). His redeeming death showed us God's unlimited forgiveness, opening the way into the divine Presence for the most sinful.

He died the great death, offering faith's ultimate prayer: "Father, into thy hands I commit my spirit!" (vs. 46). For him, as for us, it tokened *faith*, not sight. "I commit" (*paratithemai*) is the word of utter trust used by Paul, concluding his farewell to friends at Ephesus: "And now I commend [*paratithemai*] you to God and to the word of his grace, which is able to build you up and to give you the inheritance among all those who are sanctified" (Acts 20:32). It is the word used of the loaves and fishes when Jesus fed the multitude: he "blessed and broke them, and gave them to the disciples to set before [*paratheinai*] the crowd" (Luke 9:16). So he trusted himself to God, and set himself before God to be used. As Easter's glory was to testify, God honored the trust.

[37] William Faulkner, *The Sound and the Fury* (New York: Random House, Faulkner Reader edition, 1954), pp. 59, 79, 94.

[38] *The Interpreter's Bible*, VIII, 408.

EASTERTIDE

Oldest of the Christian festivals, Easter proclaims the power of the resurrection, celebrated anew every Sunday. For the force which lifted the church above martyrdom's power to silence and projected the Christian mission into all the world, made the first day of every week a "Lord's Day," a "little Easter." "The Great Fifty Days" from Easter to Pentecost formed the first liturgical season, and it was not until medieval emphasis on man's lostness gave pre-eminence to Lent that Eastertide receded to second place. The restoration of a dominant proclamation of Easter's message of God's redemption is needed in the life and worship of the church today.

Throughout the seven Sundays of Eastertide there rings the strong note of the kerygma, that Christ "rose on the third day according to the Scriptures." No festival celebration of Easter Sunday can in itself sound the deeps of the good news of the Resurrection: God's victory over the kingdom of evil; Christ's eternal lordship; the assurance of life no grave can finally cancel; and the power of an endless life for those who, risen with Christ, "seek the things that are above" (Col. 3:1). Seven Sundays are all too short for probing such vital concerns.

In the fourth century, the church marked the fortieth day after Easter as the festival of the Ascension. Falling always on Thursday, it is not widely

132

observed among Protestants. To restore recognition of its important message, this lectionary has placed the Ascension Scriptures on the sixth Sunday of Eastertide. Only the most literal-minded need be deterred by the space imagery. The Ascension celebrates a Christ *liberated from spacial limitations* to be our universal Lord and eternal contemporary. The *ascension of Christ,* not the "descent of man," as G. A. Studdert Kennedy once remarked, gives the key to life's meaning.

EASTER DAY

Opened from the Outside: Isaiah 25:1, 7-9

We beat vainly against many a door that, shutting us in, can be opened only from the outside. Out of such experience these verses from Isaiah were written. Israel was entering the night of Hellenistic dominance whose attempts to force a repugnant foreign faith upon her were to bring on the blood bath of Macabbean revolt. Chapters 24–27 of Isaiah are made up of eschatological visions of a better day, prayers for its coming, psalms of praise in the night.

As, against the grim darkness of a Good Friday background, the Christian world celebrates the dawn of Easter, Isaiah's cry of confidence that God will open the doors from the outside constitutes an apt Old Testament lesson. The Easter mood vibrates in the shout of praise to God:

> for thou hast done wonderful things,
> plans formed of old, faithful and sure (vs. 1b),

a cry more triumphant for its somber background. A scene of stark terror fills the preceding chapter.

> Desolation is left in the city,
> the gates are battered into ruins.
> For thus it shall be in the midst of the earth
> among the nations (24:12-13).

God has overthrown a "fortified city" (vs. 2). Was it Babylon? Nineveh? A Moabite city? Some stronghold razed by Alexander the Great? Each is held possible in some scholarly quarter. The multiple possibilities underscore the recurring human predicament of entrapment. In such a plight, the prophet proclaims, God will be "a stronghold to the poor, . . . a shelter from the storm and a shade from the heat" (vs. 4). Easter, likewise, celebrates the faith that we, who know the entrapment of death, will see its door opened by that same powerful hand. As the ancient faith is based on intimations in history's events, our Easter confidence looks to the momentous event in Joseph's garden, where a tomb stands empty.

Amid the groans and sobs of a persecuted people, this prophet dared to lift assurance that God would end sorrow. "He will destroy . . . the veil that is spread over all nations" (vs. 7). This "covering that is cast over all peo-

ples" reflects ancient mourning customs: at Absalom's death, "David went
. . . weeping . . . barefoot and with his head covered; and all the people
who were with him covered their heads . . . weeping as they went" (II Sam.
15:30). But, the prophet was sure, "the Lord God will wipe away tears from
all faces" (vs. 8). The exiled seer on Patmos, echoing that, faced disaster,
despair, and death with like assurance that Christ's resurrection is a foretaste
of victory for all disciples and their seemingly lost causes. He too sang, "he
will wipe away every tear from their eyes, and death shall be no more" (Rev.
21:4). Its door could be opened from the outside.

God "will swallow up death for ever" (vs. 8), the prophet exulted, taking his imagery from the Caananite myth of the victory of Baal over Mot,
god of death. Does such pagan origin cast a shadow over this vision? Or
does such origin rather underscore its evidence of a universal hunger which
points to reality? Though the *argument* from such longing to its fulfillment is
not conclusive, the *faith* here realized has persuasive force. The primitive
Baal myth is transformed into undaunted conviction that the Lord of hosts
will banish the death born of sin. The Old Testament foregleam comes to
realization as Paul exclaims, from the bright morning of the Resurrection,
"then shall come to pass the saying that is written: 'Death is swallowed up in
victory'" (I Cor. 15:54).

Born of disaster and deliverance, fulfilled in Christ's crucifixion and rising, these insight are verified again and again as the blood of the martyrs becomes the seed of the church. In a letter from prison, Dietrich Bonhoeffer
wrote: "Life in a prison cell reminds me a great deal of Advent—one waits
and hopes and potters about, but in the end what we do is of little consequence, for the door is shut, and it can only be opened from the outside." [1] It
was the Nazi executioner who opened Bonhoeffer's *prison* door from the
outside. Yet *death's* door was opened by a greater hand. Now, a subsequent
generation that did not know him responds to Bonhoeffer's voice as to few
others. Can we doubt the liberation of such spirits into eternity's bright
morning?

Claimed by the Resurrection: Acts 13:26-33

For Paul, to preach Christ was to preach the Resurrection. God's raising
of Christ from the dead set the seal of authority upon him. The good news,
he said, is "that what God promised to the fathers, this he has fulfilled to us
their children by raising Jesus" (vss. 32-33). Faith's issue centered there.
The Resurrection lays upon us a claim calling for reply.

For Paul, Cross and Resurrection were related as question and answer.
What does Christ's death mean? We do not know until the Resurrection
claims us. Is the Cross only another in the world's cruel procession of martyrdoms? No! For the Resurrection is God's answer. It stands as evidence that
our crosses do not have the last word: God does.

So Paul begins with the fact of the Cross. The leaders and people in
Jerusalem, he reports, have not understood the messianic prophecies; their

---

[1] Dietrich Bonhoeffer, *Letters and Papers from Prison* (New York: Macmillan,
1953), p. 95.

condemnation of Jesus, far from discrediting him, has fulfilled the prophecies concerning him (vs. 27). Though they could not substantiate any capital charge against him, "they asked Pilate to have him killed" (vs. 28). There was no surprise in his horrible death; they were only "carrying out all that had been predicted of him in scripture" (vs. 29 MT). The worst they could do served to set the seal of authenticity upon his mission; this was God's way of showing love and power. It remains God's way, and when we scoff at "idealists" and "do-gooders" who work by the power of goodwill rather than "the big stick," we join forces with the crucifiers who set Jesus aside with such finality as they could muster: "they . . . laid him in a tomb" (vs. 29).

Cross and rejection do not set a period to his life. Paul's announcement is unequivocal and emphatic. Modern translations, amid variant wordings of the rest of the story, cannot miss unanimity in the seven stark words: "But God raised him from the dead" (vs. 30). Not once only, but "for many days" he appeared to those who had come with him from Galilee who "are now his witnesses to the people" (vs. 31). So Paul distinguishes between rumor and event. This is not a pictorial way of saying something that is real only in the inner world of mind and emotion. Of mystery cults that say something subjective through the poetry of a dying and rising god there are plenty. This is not one of them. Like the Crucifixion, the Resurrection is an *event* with *witnesses*. As D. T. Niles once remarked, Paul "is talking not about something that had happened to the disciples"—a subjective idea poetically expressed—"but about something that had happened to Jesus." [2] "They asked Pilate to have him killed. And . . . they . . . laid him in a tomb. But God raised him" (vss. 28-30).

God's promise to the fathers has been fulfilled to their children. In raising Jesus from the dead, Paul notes, God validated and said anew what the psalmist understood him to be saying in another context: "You are my Son! Today I have become your Father" (vs. 33 AT). In the letter to the Romans, Paul underscores this contention that Jesus was "designated Son of God in power according to the Spirit of holiness by his resurrection from the dead" (Rom. 1:4).

What thus happened in the realm of event can become important to us only by *faith*. It is of the nature of miracle, which can come to bloom

only when one begins with something quite ordinary. Breakthroughs occur only where there is darkness. Faith is like energy, which is measurable only in terms of resistance, or in the presence of doubt. The sacred reveals itself in the secular. This is the very essence of the Christian scandal of Incarnation: the Word found in the flesh, the *logos* in a man born of woman, the purposes of God manifested in the events of the world. The miracle only happens, it is only achieved, when man adds the dimension and dynamic of his spirit to the waiting world, to the common event, the dark ground of routine.[3]

It is thus that the Resurrection claims us, asking whether we will let the sacred reveal itself to us in the secular. Nothing could be more secular than a Roman execution unless it be a mushroom cloud and a nuclear arms race

[2] In Kirkpatrick, ed., *The Finality of Christ,* p. 17.
[3] Miller, *Man the Believer,* pp. 100-101.

spiraling to nuclear war. God answered the one. Do we have ears to hear his answer to the other? And to "the dark ground of routine" in which the days engulf us?

Rendezvous in Galilee: Mark 16:1-7

"He is going before you to Galilee; there you will see him" (vs. 7). This line takes us in. Crucified in the Jerusalem of the temple and the religious capital, he would meet them in the Galilee of fishermen's boats and humdrum work. Galilee is our kind of everyday place, and the story of the Resurrection as Mark reports it is the promise of a rendezvous in Galilee. Not to privileged disciples was the Resurrection first revealed, but to a group of women outside that inner circle. By such tokens Mark's story testified that the Resurrection reality is for everyday people in everyday places.

The women "bought spices, so that they might go and anoint him" (vs. 1); and so do we. Anointing, last respect to a remembered life, is what we offer him as we dwell on wistful memories of past experiences, or on what he meant to others in bygone generations. It is what we do when we embalm him in creedal statements, entombed behind stained glass, shut away from the realities of our struggling life in a tormented world. But the Resurrection calls us, as it called them, away from all such anointings, to meet him in the weary work and the harsh issues of commonplace Galilee.

The women "were saying to one another, 'Who will roll away the stone for us from the door of the tomb?'" (vs. 3). They felt helpless, as do we in an age when men announce that God is dead. Even a church may unwittingly confirm his decease, as did one whose bulletin board announced the hour of a "Christ is Risen Memorial Service." Our preaching may confirm it, on the one hand, by so much past tense attention to the biblical record that even "Christ is risen" sounds like a memorial of things gone by; or on the other, by a topical plunge into our human solutions of the world's problems that seems to say we can expect no help from God. Neither historical memories nor humanistic resolutions can roll away the stone. Only God can! The Resurrection announces that he is alive to meet us in everday Galilee.

The women found that what they could not do was done for them. "And looking up, they saw that the stone was rolled back; for it was very large" (vs. 4). A messenger "said to them, '. . . He has risen, he is not here'" (vs. 6). Not in anything we can embalm out of yesterday! All that memory and sentimental devotion can find is summed up in the invitation, "See the place where they laid him." The Resurrection looks, not back, but forward: "Go, tell his disciples and Peter" (vs. 7). Especially Peter, heartbroken at his fiasco of denial, thinking all is lost, is beckoned forward to a rendezvous in Galilee!

"He is going before you to Galilee; there you will see him, as he told you" (vs. 7). "Before you!" Wherever you go, he precedes you. He will meet you just around any corner. Galilee—outland of provincials, center of busy tradesmen, homeland of joy and sorrow, temptation and fall, despair and exaltation—was where he would meet them. To that rendezvous the Resurrection invites us.

FIRST SUNDAY AFTER EASTER

We Trust the Answerer: Job 19:1, 23-27

P. T. Forsyth once confessed, "We do not see the answer; we trust the Answerer. We do not gain the victory; we are united with the Victor." Job had reached a like conclusion. Desperately he had sought the answer to the enigma of rampant evil in a world belonging to a good God. To the mind's conundrum he found no answer. Yet there came an answer to life itself: "I know that my Redeemer lives, and . . . I shall see God . . . on my side" (vss. 25-27).

Searching fruitlessly for answers, we too can feel Job's bewilderment in what seemed to be universal desertion and false accusation:

> I cry out 'Murder'!—there is no reply;
> I call for help, and get no justice (vs. 7 MT).

Even God had abandoned him—"it is God who has undone me" (vs. 6 MT). His own family and clan, on whom he had thought he could depend, had turned against him:

> My clansmen have abandoned me,
> my friends are all estranged,
> my kinsmen will not own me (vss. 13-14 MT).

He longed for some way of taking his case to the ages. Time, he thought, would vindicate him if only the appeal could be made.

> Oh that my case could be preserved in writing
> cut with an iron pen on lead,
> or lastingly engraved on stone! (vs. 23-24 MT).

Like many another, he made his "appeal to history." Hitler did that: "Let history be my judge." But in the perplexity of a decisive moment, ages yet unborn offer little guidance. "Let history be my judge" becomes, "Let me go my unguided way today without a judge. If I am wrong, I shall be safely out of reach before the judgment is returned."

Seeing through that, Job assumed a truer stance: "I know that my Redeemer lives." We need to clarify the word translated "Redeemer," the Hebrew go'el, which "denotes primarily the action of the next of kin to recover the forfeited property of a kinsman or to purchase his freedom if he has fallen into slavery." [4] We catch the flavor of the word in the reading,

> Still, I know One to champion me at last,
> to stand up for me upon earth (vs. 25 MT).

Though his own blood kin had failed him, faith assured Job that God would adopt their rejected role. Unable to prove this faith in advance, he took his stand upon it. In echoing mood, Woodrow Wilson believed that only by a faith he could not prove could he find his way through the historic maze in

---

[4] R. C. Dentan, article on "Redeem, Redeemer, Redemption," *The Interpreter's Dictionary of the Bible*, IV, 21.

which he held titanic responsibility. "There are some people who *believe* only as far as they *understand*," he said. "That seems to be presumptuous and sets their understanding as the standard of the universe." [5] Job would set no such limits. Though the answers were beyond his grasp; he trusted the Answerer.

Job dared no such announcement of immortality as comes to us in the wake of the Resurrection. There is brave faith in the lines

> This body may break up, but even then
> my life shall have a sight of God (vs. 26 MT),

but it is not a clear resurrection faith. "Job was not so much concerned with how God was going to work out the ultimate events of life as he was with his own holy call to affirm his own being. And even though death may destroy every visible evidence of being, yet Job will insist that being outlasts death." [6]

He had been burdened by bitterness against fickle friends and against God who had "undone" him. But from "the leaven of malice" he was delivered by faith's reconciliation, praying:

> my heart is pining as I yearn
> to see him on my side,
> see him estranged no longer (vss. 26-27 MT).

In like manner, Jesus prayed, "My God, my God, why hast thou forsaken me?" (Mark 15:34), not as an accusation to an absent God but as a cry to a God present and listening. Passing beyond answers to the Answerer, we too may find reconciliation in the face of life's worst, as we pray: "Grant us so to put away the leaven of malice and wickedness, that we may always serve thee in pureness of living and truth." [7]

On Finding the Right Cure
I Corinthians 15:12-22

"How can some of you say that there is no resurrection of the dead?" (vs. 12). Evidently the Corinthian church was troubled by the questions and denials that plague us. One of the characters in a play by James Saunders puts them bluntly:

What is man but the manifestation of countless diseases and disorders, physical, mental, and psychosomatic, each one struggling for supremacy? An exquisitely balanced system of interacting death wishes. And what is death but the ultimate cure of all these disorders? The disease is life, the cure is death. [8]

[5] Arthur S. Link, *Wilson: The New Freedom* (Princeton: Princeton University Press, 1956), pp. 64-65.

[6] Wesley C. Baker, *More Than a Man Can Take* (Philadelphia: Westminster Press, 1966), pp. 50-51.

[7] From the collect for the First Sunday after Easter, *Book of Common Prayer*.

[8] James Saunders, *Next Time I'll Sing to You* as digested in Henry Hewes, ed., *Best Plays of 1963-1964* (New York: Dodd, Mead, 1964), pp. 147-48.

But, Christian faith replies, that puts it wrong way round. The disease is death, the cure is life made new in Christ. Paul backs that assertion by the argument he develops in this vigorous passage.

Having summarized (vss. 1-11) the basic facts concerning the Resurrection, he proceeded by closely linked reasoning:

> "If there is no resurrection . . . Christ has not been raised" (vs. 13).

> "If Christ has not been raised, your faith is futile" (vs. 17a).

> If your faith is futile, "you are still in your sins" (vs. 17b).

But this was manifest absurdity; for his readers had found new life with a strong flavor of joy and a present experience of victory. Reasoning inversely, their new life had sprung from faith, and their faith stood on the foundation of the Resurrection. "The disease is life, the cure is death"—that mood of alienation and meaninglessness can find reconciliation and meaning in Christ.

"Moreover," Paul's argument goes on, if Christ has not been raised, "those who have died believing in Christ are utterly dead and gone" (vs. 18 PT). At stake in the Resurrection is the issue, not so much of our own precious survival as of the fulfillment or futility of the lives of those dear to us. To write off as unimportant the question of life that survives death is to bypass that issue in a way that denies the best in human relations from the dawning days of the race, as anthropologist Loren Eisely makes plain. Writing of the burial customs of Neanderthal men, he says:

Massive flint-hardened hands had shaped a sepulcher and placed flat stones to guard the dead man's head. A haunch of meat had been left to aid the dead man's journey. Worked flints, a little treasure of human dawn, had been poured lovingly into the grave. And down the untold centuries the message had come without words: "We too were human, we too suffered, we too believed the grave is not the end. We too, whose faces affright you now, knew human agony and human love." [9]

It will not do for us to say that *this* life is all that matters, what lies beyond death being irrelevant. To do so is to relinquish what is most human and humane. Paul replied to that notion: "Truly, if our hope in Christ were limited to this life only we should, of all mankind, be the most to be pitied!" (vs. 19 PT).

From such absurdity Paul turned to fact: "In fact Christ has been raised from the dead, the first fruits of those who have fallen asleep" (vs. 20). "First fruits" assure a further harvest to come. For "he who raised Christ Jesus from the dead will give life to your mortal bodies also through his Spirit which dwells in you" (Rom. 8:11). "He is the beginning, the first-born from the dead" (Col. 1:18). Like Adam, we are all sinners; and, like Christ, we are all candidates for resurrection (vs. 21). "For as in Adam all die" cites Adam (the name in Hebrew *means* "man") as representative man,

[9] Loren Eiseley, *The Firmament of Time* (New York: Atheneum Books, 1966), p. 113.

typical of our life of creature existence and creature death. "So also in Christ shall all be made alive" (vs. 22) is, likewise, a way of saying that Christ represents God's new humanity, Christ's resurrection being the promise of ours.

In a Chinese village, on the eve of the Communist takeover, a young doctor—one of ten Christians in the community—bravely preached the funeral sermon of his wife, who at twenty-eight had died of tuberculosis. To the packed company of Buddhist neighbors he held up two eggs. " 'In this one,' he said, 'is only an egg. If you do not use it, it will spoil. But in the other there is a small chicken. It will soon break out and grow!' " Then, pointing to the stricken body, he continued, " 'You see only her shell. But the life in her has come out and is with Jesus Christ, her Savior and mine.' " [10] Such courageous witness in the hour of grief points to the right cure. For in Christ life is not a disease; death is. And in Christ death is not cure but disease, to which the answer is new life through resurrection.

How Do We Know He Lives? John 20:19-31

"Have you believed because you have seen me? Blessed are those who have not seen and yet believe" (vs. 29). With these words this passage takes its stance exactly where we must. We were not there. We have only what seem incredible stories from witnesses gone beyond access for cross-examination. How can we know that the Resurrection is true? Does a living Christ touch our life today in any way that makes a real difference? To exactly these questions the Gospel according to John—written near the turn of the second century to interpret Jesus to a generation that had not known him in the flesh—is speaking. For that reason it speaks cogently to us. In this passage it says three forceful things to our need.

We know the reality of his living presence, first, by its power to bring peace under turbulent conditions. Three times within this closely packed story Jesus greets the disciples with the words, "Peace be with you" (vss. 19, 21, 26). To be sure, this was a customary greeting of the time. But, in a document that wastes no words, why this threefold reiteration? Our word *peace* translates the Greek *eirēnē,* which in turn is used in the Septuagint to translate the Hebrew *shalom.* To greet another with *shalom* is to offer a comprehensive prayer in his behalf, for the word embraces such blessings as health, strength, security, prosperity, success—not the end of struggle but victory in it. Peace is God's gift. When, on the eve of his crucifixion, Jesus told the disciples, "My peace I give to you" (John 14:27), he added, "not as the world gives do I give to you." When worldly peace seemed most impossible, his peace was given—a gift of harmony with the Father. Later in John's report of Jesus' words in the upper room, he says: "I have said this to you, that in me you may have peace. . . . I have overcome the world" (16:33). That he brought this gift of victorious harmony under the most dire circumstances is the testimony of martyrs in all ages, including those in our century who have faced Nazi and Communist imprisonment in the sense of his presence. Paul, writing from prison, with the promise that "the peace of God, which passes all understanding, will keep your hearts and your minds in Christ Jesus" (Phil. 4:7), is their prototype.

[10] Jones, *Our Mission Today,* p. 123.

We know the reality of his living presence, second, by its power to heal through forgiveness. He said to them, "Receive the Holy Spirit! If you forgive any man's sins, they stand forgiven; if you pronounce them unforgiven, unforgiven they remain." (vss. 22-23 NEB). Some psychotherapists testify that no concept or experience is as therapeutic as forgiveness. There is more to do with sins than to dissolve guilt *feelings*. There is forgiveness for real guilt, and those who have received it know its healing power. Jesus reminds us that such liberating forgiveness is more than human; it is a gift of the Spirit. Yet it comes through Christians who, knowing the living Lord through his present Spirit, deeply accept the sinful brother. With this acceptance comes release; without it, men remain in their sins. To carry healing forgiveness into the world is our mission. Jesus said: "As the Father has sent me, even so I send you" (vs. 21). In that mission and the renewal born of forgiveness, his living presence still makes a mighty difference.

We know the reality of his living presence, third, by its power, within the Christian fellowship, to convince thoughtful questioners that the unseen, present Christ has unbroken continuity with the Jesus of the Gospels. Thomas, like us, did not deny his friends' subjective experiences. Granted this helpful inwardness, he was saying, how does it relate to the continued life of Jesus, who taught in Galilee and died on the Cross? Only if I have the tangible evidence of touching him can I believe. Did Thomas satisfy his demand to touch the wounds? The story does not say so. It does stress what needs repeating in every age: that what we know of Christ is more than disembodied spirit or general ideas. The living Christ is no vague concept, such as men imply when they say, "What matter whether Jesus lived? The ideas released in the world by the New Testament are all that matters." The Christian message is not a set of ideas, but a new life, verified through the *life, death,* and *resurrection* of Jesus.

Within the Christian fellowship, Thomas discovered in present experience a vital continuity with the Jesus he had known. In our time, Thomas Altizer, spokesman of the "God is dead" position, asserts that "contemporary theology must be alienated from the Church." "The theologian," he adds, "must exist outside the Church." His colleague, William Hamilton, agrees that "the theologian does not and cannot go to church; he is not interested; he is alienated." Quoting them, William Hordern asks, "Is there a parable here? Does this say that God will seem to be dead to the man who tries to live his life outside of dialogue within the fellowship of those who know and are committed to God through Christ?" [11] It was so of Thomas. Absent from the fellowship, he remained a skeptic (vss. 24-25). Within the fellowship he found the Jesus of Galilee and Golgotha, convincingly alive.

SECOND SUNDAY AFTER EASTER

Let the Whole Earth Know: Isaiah 12:1-6

"Sing the praises of the Lord, for he has done glorious things,
Let the whole earth know of it" (vs. 5 PT).

[11] William Hordern, *New Directions in Theology Today*, Vol. I, *Introduction* (Philadelphia: Westminster Press, 1966), p. 153.

So sang the prophet, making gratitude for a great deliverance the motive for irrepressible witness. This chapter inserts psalms of praise evoked by the prophecy of liberation which closes Chapter 11, and celebrating God's power to overcome, as Israel experienced it in return from Exile. That God "has done glorious things" was news too good to keep. "Let the whole earth know!"

No date or signature anchors these words to time or place. Belonging to all ages, they are never more appropriate than in the song of gladness that erupts from new life in Christ. Once a song of liberation from exile, they become a shout of freedom from the bondage of sin and death, as we use them in thanksgiving for the victory of the Resurrection.

> Give thanks to the Lord,
> Call upon his name!
> Make his deeds known among all nations (vs. 4 PT).

When we discover resurrection as personal experience, its joy must be celebrated! The experience is open to any man. Who of us cannot share the prophet's thanksgiving?

> . . . for you were angry with me
> And now your anger is past and you have given me comfort (vs. 1 PT).

Where there has been estrangement, reconciliation reigns. The torment of guilt and anxiety has turned to peace. The deadness of life's seeming absurdity has given way to the new pulse of purpose. If we have not found this, we have not entered into our heritage as Christians. Yet it is waiting for us. "Joyfully will you draw water from the wells of salvation" (vs. 3 PT)—that prophecy can be fulfilled for us when we accept our Lord's invitation, issued beside a Samaritan village well and renewed as long as the world lasts: "If you knew the gift of God, and who it is that is saying to you, 'Give me a drink,' you would have asked him, and he would have given you living water" (John 4:10).

Resurrection as personal experience issues in witness and calls to mission. To "let the whole earth know of it" becomes an inner compulsion. If we are content to silence missionary urgency before the argument, "Why foist our faith on others? Their religion is as good for them as ours is for us," it is safe to assume that *our* faith has made no indispensable difference. A faith we can bottle up is less important to us than profits are to a businessman with an urge to advertise. It means less to us than does democracy to a patriot with a passion to propagandize. Such apathy is the telltale symptom of nutritional disease of the spirit. The cure is the new life of the Resurrection.

We can "let the whole earth know" by the witness of workaday life. Witness and wages, justly paid and rightly earned, are woven in one fabric. Witness and racial attitudes are of one piece, not merely because of the moral issue of justice, but because of the theological issue of alienation. Unless we who have been set against each other, black and white, can become one new man in Christ, so making peace (Eph. 2:15), there is no good news to tell.

The message is theological, but the witness speaks through workaday deeds.

There is joy when the victory of the Resurrection becomes our own. If we have missed it, we have treasure yet to claim. If we have found it, we cannot confine it. The only way to keep it is to give it away.

Outliving Ourselves: Romans 6:3-11

When Paul wrote, "But if we have died with Christ, we believe that we shall also live with him" (vs. 8), he spoke to our need to get ourselves off our hands. Obsessed with ourselves, we die a little in our compromised standards, in our bitterness in bereavement, inch by inch as we let disappointment make us cynics. Paul called us to die to the old self, once for all—and outlive it. "If we have died with Christ, we believe that we shall also live with him."

Christian strategy begins by getting rid of the twisted, sick self. "We know that our old self was crucified with him so that the sinful body"—in Paul's usage the body represents the whole self as it is—"might be destroyed, and we might no longer be enslaved to sin" (vs. 6). We have missed the mark of our full humanity, as the Greek word for sin—*hamartia,* literally "missing the mark"—implies. We have given free rein to our animal nature—innocent enough in the beasts, but willful and guilty, because fractional, in men.

A university chemist reports the judgment pronounced on such fractional living by the "knowledge explosion." Man's place in the universe is one of control, he observes, but we can survive to fulfill it only if we learn to control our own "irrational tendencies." We "must have enough responsibility" to fulfill our destiny "without leading to death and self-destruction," the scientist declares.[12] This does little to *solve* our ancient problem, but only documents it! For the irrational permeates our life, taints our wills, makes us more dangerous as technology lengthens our arm, adds power to our fist, sharpens our fangs, multiplies our cunning. Control our irrational selves? With what? The self that is tainted by that very irrationality? Until the old, twisted self dies, we have it on our hands.

We can die in our surrender to Christ. Baptism is the drama of that death. Immersion symbolizes burial beneath the waters, that we may come forth in a new life with Christ; sprinkling merely abbreviates the symbol. "Do you not know," Paul asks, "that all of us who have been baptized into Christ Jesus were baptized into his death?" (vs. 3). Resolutions to control the old self fall short, pointing a way we are powerless to go. In surrender to Christ we accept God's judgment on all that killed him. Seeing it as a judgment on ourselves, we bid a graveside farewell to all that. To whatever degree the old self persists, our surrender "deprives him of his passport and his ration card."

Yet *life* has the last word. "The death he died he died to sin, . . . but the life he lives he lives to God" (vs. 10). The absurd, irrational twist in our nature cost Christ's death, even as it threatens ours; but he lives again, as can we when we identify ourselves fully with him. Faith gives a new self. Con-

[12] Willard F. Libby in a University of Chicago symposium on Man's Relation to the Universe, as reported in the *Chicago Daily News,* April 13, 1965.

science, with its "you ought," ceases to be a foreigner in our thinking, and the old twisted self becomes the foreigner. We know what we belong to, where our homeland is. This is the intent of the Bible's way of speaking of our life "in sin" as replaced by life "in Christ." Not suddenly perfect, we nevertheless know where we belong, and to whom. "So you also must consider yourselves" (vs. 11) Paul enjoins us. A new way of viewing ourselves opens the way to a new existence, "dead to sin and alive to God in Christ Jesus" (vs. 11).

Life for a Dying World: John 6:37-40

"For this is the will of my Father, that every one who sees the Son and believes in him should have eternal life; and I will raise him up at the last day" (vs. 40). If that means what it seems to say, it is good news for us who are doomed. Long aware that all men must die *some* day, we now dread the new weapons by which we may all die the *same* day. Meanwhile the deaths of friends remind us of our slender hold on life. Short of that finality, the feeling of futility—a kind of death-while-we-live—overtakes many of us who dread being made "obsolete" by new machines, new methods, new knowledge, which usurp the work that gave us our sense of worth.

Christ's promise of "eternal life" speaks to our need, first at the point of this fear of being automated out of meaningful existence. In the vocabulary of the Gospel of John, "eternal life" is life to the full, beginning *now*, a lifetime at the level some of us remember from a few red-letter days. Technology cannot give it. For technology multiplies "comforts" and banishes comfort, inflates prosperity and deflates personhood. Sociologists worry lest "eventually we will find the number of jobs lost due to automation will far outnumber those created." Already, they report, many workers "are finding their work loads insufferably light." In Japan there has been an increase in suicides stemming from "automation neuroses." For the United States, they predict, the equivalent result will be a sharp increase in alcoholism.[13]

Yet we can have life which such threats will not defeat. It comes to those who have a self they can live with when other supports are taken away, a cause they can live for that is bigger than a paycheck, and a faith they can live by when the gifts of a technological age let them down. They have what made Kagawa, Schweitzer, Thomas Dooley, Francis of Assisi memorable—eternal life. They have accepted Jesus' promise: "I will raise him up at the last day" (vs. 40). Not that eternal life must *wait until* the last day! But it will *last beyond* it! In our fragile life, our precarious age, this assurance is the lasting deposit of the Resurrection.

"Every one who sees the Son and believes in him" (vs. 40) can possess this gift. There is in Christ a magnetic attraction, an induced vitality, for those who "see" and "believe in" him. We can look at each other, or at him, without *seeing*. Prayer, worship, Bible study are efforts to *see*. But we are not confined to our own efforts; God *intends* this best life for us. "This is the will

[13] Dean J. Champion, of the University of Tennessee, reported in the *Chicago Daily News*, Nov. 3, 1966.

of my Father" (vs. 40), says Jesus, reminding us that all that he has done is not his own will, but his Father's (vs. 38). "This is the will of him who sent me, that I should lose nothing of all that he has given me" (vs. 39). We cannot gain this gift *by* an act of will—or *without* one. We can only expose ourselves to our Lord until we *see* and *believe*.

THIRD SUNDAY AFTER EASTER

On a Day of Whirlwind: Ezekiel 34:11-16, 30-31

"As a shepherd searches for his flock on a day of whirlwind, when his sheep are scattered, so will I search for my flock, and rescue them from all the places to which they have been scattered on the day of clouds and thick darkness" (vs. 12 AT). God, of course, is the speaker in this key sentence of the chapter, and the theme is his restoration of his people after whirlwinds of historic calamity.

The figure of God as shepherd, which fills this lection, is set in sharp relief against the preceding denunciation of false shepherds (vss. 1-10). Not caring for the sheep, they have exploited and fed upon them. So the sheep were scattered, "because there was no shepherd; . . . with none to search or seek for them" (vss. 5-6). For Ezekiel, as for his contemporary, Jeremiah, the shepherds are the rulers of Israel. Jeremiah condemns "shepherds who destroy and scatter the sheep," and promises a king who will come from David's line to establish conditions under which "Israel will dwell securely" (Jer. 23:1-6). From this contemporary use of the figure, and from Ezekiel's dark portrayal of the national misfortunes suffered at the hands of the "false shepherds," it is plainly the kings and rulers of the people who are thus flayed.

Writing amid national collapse and exile, Ezekiel holds out the faith that God will provide the shepherding care in which the national leaders have been derelict. Searching out his flock (vs. 11), he will gather the sheep scattered on such a day of whirlwind as the Exile has produced (vs. 12), bringing them home again from the far lands in which they have been dispersed (vs. 13). There they will enjoy a new national well-being, grazing in lush pastures (vs. 14). It is God and no other—the twice repeated "I" is emphatic in the Hebrew—who will be shepherd-protector to his people (vs. 15). He and no other will seek the lost, the strays, "bandage the cripples . . . put strength into the sick . . . guard the strong and prosperous" (vs. 16 MT).

Not only will God thus protect his people from external danger; he will guard the internal order of his obstreperous flock and set over them a messianic shepherd of the line of David. Then will come a day of peace, prosperity, and blessing, with security from all outward foes (vss. 17-29).

Though the calamity of the Exile has cast doubt upon God's power to protect his own, he will again be known among the nations as Israel's God who is mighty to save (vs. 30). In beautiful summation, Ezekiel concludes: "And you are my sheep, the sheep of my pasture, and I am your God, says the Lord God" (vs. 31).

How, one may ask, does all this apply to Eastertide? First, by providing strong background material for the Epistle and Gospel for this Sunday, which present Christ as the Shepherd who laid down his life for the sheep and who gathered God's new flock in fulfillment of the messianic promise. Second, by suggesting that as God, discredited among the nations by the exile of his people, vindicated himself by restoring them; so he did in the restoration of Jesus after the seeming defeat of crucifixion. Giving new life to believers, he revealed his victorious saviorhood.

This theology of and by the oppressed speaks cogently to those who identify themselves with the black experience. To the oppressed it declares: (1) God's concern for the restoration of the decimated community, (2) the unfailing integrity of his rule in redressing the wrongs of earthly sovereigns, and (3) his power to reverse the disasters of history and to care for his people.

When You Do Right and Suffer
I Peter 2:19-25

In the wake of Dauchau and Auschwitz, our time is painfully conscious of the problem unjust suffering poses for faith. The quantity of today's suffering makes the problem seem qualitatively different, proving that a God who cares is no longer actively real. But, Ronald Goetz replies, it must surely be "rank boastfulness" to suppose that suffering in the past is so much "less dreadful than our own. . . . This is to inflate our ego by trivializing human suffering, and thus human life, in the past." [14]

The point is underscored for one who reads this passage from I Peter with sensitive historical recall. The major part of I Peter embodies a baptismal address intended to help those who were being inducted into a faith which would lead to intense suffering in an age of bitter persecution. One phrase, "when you do right and suffer" (vs. 20), ticks off the cruel paradox they would be forced not so much to *think* out as to *live* out. It does not refer to merely natural evils which every life must risk. These slaves, living under a cruel totalitarian control (vs. 18), had to endure the whimsical, often diabolical rulings of emperors and governors (vss. 13-15). Torture and tyranny were jagged firsthand realities. Yet it never occurred to this writer that unjust, bloody persecution might point to God's abdication of control. On the contrary, he wrote: "Conscious of God's presence, a man who is suffering unjustly bears his troubles patiently" (vs. 19 TCNT).

Support of this faith begins with the conviction that every man wants to live not as an abject victim of circumstances, but as one who manages his affairs with some credit to himself. But "what credit is it, if when you do wrong and are beaten for it you take it patiently?" (vs. 20a). Such patience only keeps the score even! *Unjust* suffering, on the other hand, lets the best in us come out. "If, after doing right, you take your sufferings patiently, that does win the approval of God" (vs. 20b TCNT).

[14] Ronald Goetz article, "God: Love or Death," *The Christian Century*, Nov. 22, 1967, p. 1487.

Such suffering, furthermore, is our *calling!* "For this you have been called" (vs. 21), or "this is your vocation" (MT). Why? Because this is the example set for us by our Lord: "Christ also suffered for you, leaving you an example" (vs. 21). He was sinless; he took no revenge; he *trusted* God's justice, even when he could not *see* it (vs. 23). Where do we find the real revelation of ultimate truth? Do Hitler and his power to inflict torture and death reveal final reality? If so, nihilism and death have the last word. Or do Christ and his capacity to win victory over suffering and death have the last word? Are we overpowered by brutality, with its *quantitative* considerations? Or are we persuaded by the *quality* that is in Jesus?

This passage takes its stand on Christ and goes on to point its reasons. Vss. 24-25, using language directly borrowed from Isa. 53:5-12, are evocative of the historic vindication of the Suffering Servant whose portrait was painted by the prophet of the Exile. There is, moreover, an empirical consideration: Jesus' vicarious sufferings have produced results verified in experience. "By his wounds you have been healed" and are no more "straying like sheep" (vss. 24-25). Having found new life in him, we know his unjust sufferings were not wasted. God's economy of suffering has not met defeat.

This is no counsel of passivity in the face of injustice. From the midst of a suffering population, James H. Cone declares that "black people should not accept . . . injustice as tending to good. It is not permissible to appeal to the idea that God's will is inscrutable or that the righteous sufferer will be rewarded in heaven." [15]

We can return to him as "the Shepherd and Guardian of [our] souls" (vs. 25). Echoing Ezekiel, this affirms that God has the last word in our trials, the word of a Shepherd competent to protect his flock. The Resurrection assures us of this truth. "We have been born anew to a living hope through the resurrection" (1:3) and "are guarded through faith for a salvation ready to be revealed in the last time" (1:5). Cross and resurrection are permanent realities. God stands in the midst of the suffering, sharing their pain. He turns suffering to victory, not in a distant heaven but in the turmoil of earth. And he calls us to stand with the sufferers, for that is where we meet the victorious resurrected Christ.

Now, Take Lincoln . . . : John 10:11-16

In one of its most persistent axioms, the contemporary mind jauntily affirms that "Jesus was a good man. What we need are a lot more people like Him. Now, take Lincoln . . . " [16] On this easygoing creed old liberals, new radicals, and run-of-the-decades popular religionists find common ground. Persuaded by the horrors of slum ghettos, concentration camps, and the computer's threat to personality, they conclude that anything more ultimate than human effort is too much to believe in. Then, with a headlong plunge into optimism, they put their trust in our human competence to remake the world. Jesus, they say, is the ideal of the effort. He is even a helpful teacher of

---

[15] James H. Cone, *Black Theology and Black Power* (New York: Seabury Press, 1969), p. 124.

[16] One of the "Axioms of contemporary proverbial wisdom" from *The Church's Witness to God's Design*, p. 72.

ethical principles. All we need is to create enough carbon copies of him, and the battle is won. "Now, take Lincoln . . ."

This absurd optimism has no standing ground in the New Testament. Such a passage as this lection from John challenges its basic assumptions at three crucial points.

It challenges, first, the assumption that we are adequate self-directive managers of our own affairs. No, says the New Testament—our only source for clear thinking about Jesus—we are more like sheep in need of a shepherd. We need protection, not only against external dangers, but against our own tendencies to stray away from what is best for us. Jesus is "the good shepherd" (vs. 11).

The figure needs to be understood in the light of its cumulative biblical usage. As we have seen, Ezekiel used the figure to depict human life betrayed by bad government, "false shepherds," and brought to a happier historical outcome by God's participation in historical developments; God is the good Shepherd. Jesus, as good shepherd, laid down his life for the sheep (vs. 11*b*). But his death was not the end of the matter, for "God . . . brought again from the dead our Lord Jesus, the great shepherd of the sheep" (Heb. 13:20). For other developments of the shepherd figure see Ps. 23:1; Isa. 40:11; Jer. 23:1-4; Luke 15:4-7.

Ancient thinking about this figure is not confined to the Bible. One of the cynical hecklers of Socrates sneered, "You fancy that the shepherd . . . tends the sheep . . . with a view to their own good and not to the good of himself or his master." But any care that rulers take of their subjects, he countered, is purely for selfish purposes.

The just is always a loser in comparison with the unjust . . . . Wherever the unjust is the partner of the just you will find that, when the partnership is dissolved, the unjust man has always more and the just less. . . . When there is an income tax, the just man will pay more and the unjust less on the same amount of income; and when there is anything to be received the one gains nothing and the other much . . . . Injustice, when on a sufficient scale, has more strength and freedom and mastery than justice[17]

Athens as well as Jerusalem, and Washington as well as Athens, have known the problem of human nature powerless to carry out its dreams of building a better life. New Testament Christianity meets the problem not by futile calls to an ideal we cannot realize, but by the offer of a Lord who can shepherd our wayward impulses and make of us what we could not make of ourselves.

A second challenge turns to the assumption that our *historical knowledge about* Jesus is all we need. No, declares the New Testament faith, such external knowledge *about* him is only a stepping-stone to the real knowledge, our *personal relation with* him. He is the good shepherd who knows and is known by his sheep (vs. 14). No mere intellectual cognition, this is *recognition* based on experience. When the Bible speaks of knowledge in any personal sense, this is its typical understanding, as when Hosea writes:

[17] *The Republic,* Jowett Translation (New York: Random House, 1920), I, 343-44.

For I desire steadfast love and not sacrifice,
the knowledge of God, rather than burnt offerings (Hos. 6:6).

The device of Hebrew poetry makes the second line a parallel statement in apposition with the first, "knowledge of God" equivalent to "steadfast love of him." Christian experience is not chiefly learning *about* Jesus—though of course this is involved—but exchange with him through prayer, worship, and faith's obedience. Francis of Assisi, fearful that the rule of poverty in his order would be modified, disillusioned by the horrors of the Crusades, threatened by loss of eyesight, recovered spiritual power not by new facts *about* Jesus, but by a spiritual encounter *with* him. In it, he was confident, his Lord spoke to him, saying,

Why art thou distressed? Have I so set thee a shepherd over My religion that thou knowest not I am its chief Protector? I set thee over it, a simple man, to the end that those who will, may follow thee in those things I work in thee for an example to others. It is I who have called them; I who will keep and feed them; and I will make good the falling away of some by putting others in their place, in such wise that if these others be not born I will cause them to be born.[18]

This, says the New Testament, is Jesus' typical relation with the disciple. "I know my own and my own know me, as the Father knows me and I know the Father" (vs. 14).

In its third challenge, the New Testament confronts our cocksure assumption that we know how to create community. All we have to do is to get together and draw up plans for a new order! No, this more realistic faith responds, we need to be *drawn* together by our common bond in one Shepherd. Other sheep, in many folds, hear one voice. The one Shepherd will bring them together into one flock (vs. 16). Our dream of community through "a network of technical systems, transportation, and communication" comes out, as Samuel Miller reminds us, with "only an increase of loneliness and a sense of vacuity." [19] Our old optimism, that science and trade would make a new world unity, has yielded to a new realization that trade also sharpens new rounds of mortal competition and science is as likely to accelerate a nuclear "balance of terror" carrying the battle to outer space. John Macquarrie is far more realistic in his echo of the New Testament challenge:

It is the man who prays and is aware of a transcendent reality who, in the long run, is likely to be most concerned with other men as persons; while the man whose mind is fixed on some impersonal ideal, even if it happens to be an admirable one in itself, is the man who can be most inhuman toward his fellows and can use them as means for the realization of his ideal.[20]

[18] Alan Paton, *Instrument of Thy Peace* (New York: Seabury Press, 1968), pp. 39-40.

[19] Miller, *Man the Believer*, p. 70.

[20] John Macquarrie, *God and Secularity*, Vol. III in *New Directions in Theology Today*, gen. ed. William Hordern (Philadelphia: Westminster Press, 1967), p. 58.

FOURTH SUNDAY AFTER EASTER

On Assuming God's Responsibility
Deuteronomy 7:6-11

To make sense of this passage, one must note that it was a part of the marching orders of a people heading into encounter with an engulfing pagan environment (cf. vss. 1-5). This aspect of the matter makes it arresting for us as we move into a proudly post-Christian age. Too often we try to work out our stance in such a time apart from the norms once associated with great religion. "The prospects for the human race are decidedly bleak," says the provost of King's College, Cambridge, if we do not "teach those of the next generation that they can afford to be atheists only if they assume the moral responsibilities of God." [21] Quite an order! Not much in our experience underwrites the hope that we can measure up. This Deuteronomic charter puts some hard realities in the place of such a phantom.

See, first, it says, that *it is a covenant-keeping God who makes you a people and gives meaning to your life.* "You are a people holy"—or "consecrated" (JB, AT)—"to the Lord" (vs. 6). Strictly speaking, it is *God* who is "holy," set apart, untouchable, unapproachable save as he himself opens the way. His people are "holy" only as they are "consecrated" by his choice of them as his servants. The New Testament parallels this by Jesus' words to the disciples: "You did not choose me, but I chose you" (John 15:16). Not the greatness of Israel, least among the peoples, but the goodness of God directed this choice (vs. 7). Unlike the world's gods, whose favors are for the good or the strong, the God of the Bible continually chooses the weak and unworthy (cf. I Cor. 1:26-31).

Voices from surprising quarters still see faith in such a God as the charter of our society. J. Wallace Hamilton noted two conspicuous enemies of Christianity and the democratic ideal who underscore the alliance of the two forces. Karl Marx declared that "the democratic concept of man is false. It holds that each man has value as a sovereign being. This is the dream, the illusion, the postulate of Christianity." And Adolf Hitler railed: "To the Christian doctrine of the significance of the human soul, I oppose with icy clarity the saving doctrine of the insignificance of the human soul." [22] Neopagans who would impose a different order know what makes us a people.

See, again, says this Deuteronomic charter, that *you cannot assume God's responsibilities.* He has reserved that prerogative to himself, and those who seek to usurp it pay a heavy price. "Know, therefore, that only the Lord your God is God, the steadfast God who keeps His gracious covenant to the thousandth generation of those who love Him and keep his commandments" (vs. 9 TMT). Whereas this promise is extended to the long line of the generations of the faithful, the condemnation is only to "those who hate him . . . ; he will not be slack with him who hates him, he will requite him to his face" (vs. 10), or "he makes him work out his punishment in person" (JB).

---

[21] Quoted in *The Christian Century,* Feb. 5, 1969, p. 176.

[22] J. Wallace Hamilton, *Serendipity* (Westwood, N.J.: Fleming H. Revell, 1965), p. 125.

The covenant gives identity to a people, but faces those who venture on their own with a load too heavy to bear.

This lone venturing troubles sensitive scientists in their new ethical dilemmas. "The means are at hand to manipulate the basic concepts of people, to impose values on them," says the report of a campus conference. Detailing techniques—brainwashing, lessons learned from animal conditioning, surgery, drugs, and other mind-altering devices—the story goes on: "The questions that must be faced, a noted scientist said today, are who is to decide the changes and what the changes are to be." In "programming" the values and behavior of a noted criminal, he asked, who shall decide the new values? The criminal? The psychiatrist? The criminal's parents? Who? Many who shared the discussion were convinced that we have no right to alter other people's values. "You have just voted to throw these children on society's scrap heap," he replied. "Without values they can't compete." [23] Such are the quandaries of those who assume godlike responsibility as they venture into the wild unknown.

See finally, the Deuteronomic charter concludes, that *you need guidance in facing the ethical dilemmas of confrontation with paganism.* "Therefore, observe faithfully the Instruction, the laws, and the norms, with which I charge you today" (vs. 11 TMT). No matter how free and permissive our situational ethics become, we still need "Instruction" and "norms."

Otherworldliness that Counts
II Corinthians 5:1-10

Twice in the preceding chapter Paul has rejoiced that "we do not lose heart" (4:1, 16). Now he tells the source of his courage: "For we know that if the earthly tent we live in is destroyed, we have a building from God, a house not made with hands, eternal in the heavens" (vs. 1).

Our current mood avoids life beyond this one—even in the translation of this passage. CPV attempts such a reading, assuming that by "the body" Paul means "the body of Christ" as a figure for the church. But much in the passage itself argues against this conception. Vss. 1-5 represent the bodily life by other figures—tent, clothing, and the like. How strange if Paul were to resort to such compounded enigmas, representing one figure by another—tent for body and body for church! The figure of a tent for our earthly body, which we leave for a permanent "building of God," aptly fits the straightforward sense of the passage. Whether we like it or not, Paul is dealing with Christian otherworldliness which makes a crucial difference in his life amid distressing circumstances *now.*

His faith in life with God, beyond death, is vivid. Note the contrast between the destruction of "the earthly *tent* we live in" and the permanence of our "*building* from God." The paired antitheses tumble over each other: tent—building; destroyed—eternal; earthly—in the heavens. The figure was already a familiar one:

For a perishable body presses down the soul,
and this tent of clay weighs down the teeming mind (Wisdom 9:15 JB).

[23] Leroy G. Augenstein, chairman of the Department of Biophysics, Michigan State University, as reported in the *St. Paul Dispatch,* Jan. 8, 1969.

Isaiah reports the lament of King Hezekiah after an illness:

> My dwelling is plucked up and removed from me
>   like a shepherd's tent;
> like a weaver I have rolled up my life;
>   he cuts me off from the loom;
> from day to night thou dost bring me to an end (Isa. 38:12).

What Paul brings new is the ringing assurance that the tent, discarded, is replaced by an indestructible "building from God." This, he says, makes a mighty difference.

It confronts us with responsibility. We need, even now, he says, "to put on our heavenly dwelling, so that by putting it on we may not be found naked" (vss. 2-3). Plato quotes Socrates as saying that mortal judgments are not well made because the judged "have their clothes on, for they are alive." But he adds that they will be more truly judged in the end, for "they shall be entirely stripped before they are judged, . . . and leave their brave attire strewn upon the earth." [24] Paul may not closely adhere to this body-soul anthropology, but he finds in it a convenient device to interpret something significant he has to say. One need not be left denuded, but can already put on the new attire of a heavenly quality of life.

Life beyond, awaiting us, demands opportunities now. "We must all appear in our true characters" (vs. 10 TCNT and AT); "we have all to appear without disguise" (MT); "all the truth about us will be brought out" (JB). Discarded, the body is not unimportant. Reward or punishment hinges on things "done in the body" (vs. 10). This truth corrects distortions that spring from an "over-graced" conception of salvation by faith. Though faith gives power to live responsibly, we *are accountable* for deeds "done in the body."

Paul's courage is rooted in this conviction that he is living already clothed for an eternity with God (vss. 6-7). "Yet I am confident, and I prefer to leave my home in the body and make my home with the Lord" (vs. 8 AT)—so he answers every adverse circumstance. In this conviction, the wife of a missionary killed in the line of duty was able to say: "Murray lives today in the Universal Mission of the World Church . . . . In this time of his new appointment I know we will continue with him in his work." In the strength of that faith she took new training and returned to the field where he had fallen, to carry on with the work he loved.[25] Otherworldly, to be sure; but it makes a difference *here*.

But I Will See You Again: John 16:16-22

Amid sorrows and dangers, Jesus promised his disciples inalienable confidence and joy. The reason? Death and reverses are real, *"but* I will see you again"* (vs. 22).

In typical Johannine fashion the key idea stands by means of statement,

[24] Plato, *Gorgias,* 523, Jowett translation.
[25] Lance Webb, *On the Edge of the Absurd* (Nashville: Abingdon Press, 1965), p. 151.

perplexed question, and Jesus' response—a threefold repetition. "A little while, and you will see me no more," Jesus says; "again a little while, and you will see me" (vss. 16-19). Thus he foreshadows his death and resurrection. John has already woven this theme into the Gospel (cf. 7:33; 14:19). The dawning gleams of the Resurrection shine through the darkening night of doubt, enmity, and threats of death.

Jesus assures the disciples that though they face sorrow in the midst of the world's happiness, it will end in rejoicing at the dawn of a new age (vss. 20-22). Worldly rejoicing over the crucifixion and the scattering or martyrdom of the disciples is illustrated by a dramatic scene in Revelation. Concerning two "witnesses" the seer writes that "those who dwell on the earth will rejoice over them and make merry and exchange presents, because these two prophets had been a torment to those who dwell on the earth" (Rev. 11:10). But a reversal is in store. For "after the three and a half days a breath of life from God entered them, and they stood up on their feet, and great fear fell on those who saw them" (Rev. 11:11). In such manner, the disciples' "sorrow will turn into joy" (vs. 20).

Idiomatic references associate this joy with the Messianic age. The metaphor of birth pangs (vs. 21) heralds a messianic dawn, as when the wars and sufferings of Matthew's apocalypse (Matt. 24:8) are referred to in the more literal translations of JB and NEB as "birth pangs," precursors of a new day. Isaiah describes the torment of the approaching "day of the Lord" as "agony like a woman in travail" (Isa. 13:6-8; 26:18, 21). Micah describes the sufferings of the "daughter of Zion" as "pangs . . . like a woman in travail," after which "the Lord will redeem you from the hand of your enemies" (Mic. 4:9-10). This passage, in biblical idiom, is a promise that beyond reverses God is preparing a new day.

Various possibilities for present-day interpretation suggest themselves. It could be a spelling out of reasons for the courage trumpeted in the summation of the chapter: "In the world you will have trouble. But courage! The victory is mine; I have conquered the world" (vs. 33 NEB). Personal danger, the massive threats of our time, the defeat of causes dear to us, wear our courage thin. But there are grounds for hope, not in circumstances but in the faith itself: (a) Christ goes into eclipse only to appear more fully. (b) An age of suffering and turmoil is God's way of clearing the ground for a new Age that is coming to birth. (c) We can live with indestructible joy because, though he passes from our sight, we do not pass from his.

Or there is food here for useful meditation on the struggles of a post-Christian age. The Christian community is a minority steadily slipping behind the population growth of a non-Christian world. Its life style is being inundated by pagan values. Within the Christian community itself, doubt is often deadlocked with faith. But (a) Christ's death in any age is a prelude to his resurrection; (b) a time of agonizing defeat has more than once been the precursor of a new age; (c) the new life can be a personal experience of the joy of his presence. Out of the gloom we see, with William Faulkner, that "a man can see so much further when he stands in the darkness than he does when, standing in the light, he tries to probe the darkness." [26]

[26] Quoted by Miller, *Man the Believer*, p. 136.

FIFTH SUNDAY AFTER EASTER

Living by Obedient Love
Deuteronomy 10:12-15, 20—11:1

Paul Ramsey holds that two realities sometimes severed are "precisely the same thing." "Total obedience to the demands of God's reign" is the first, and "perfect love for man" the other. "Obedience means no more than love and love fulfills every legitimate obedience." [27] Yet both terms need to be kept vitally active in ethical thinking and practice. Either without the other becomes a caricature. About the unified wholeness, *obedient love,* this passage from Deuteronomy points to three incisive truths.

It points first, to obedient love of God as *the core of the good life* (vss. 12-13). Powerful motivation rises from biblical tension between fear of God and love of God. The fear is not that cringing before a tyrant which paralyzes our higher powers. "To fear" (RSV) is "to revere" (TMT) or "to reverence" (MT). When religion loses this note, love of God becomes the easygoing familiarity of pampered children adrift from inviolable disciplines and stern necessities. Such religion loses the realism that holds the life of individuals and society together. But "the commandments and statutes of the Lord" structure our life for our good (vs. 13).

Yoked with love, obedience is not merely formal and external. The call "to serve the Lord" (vs. 12) derives less from his power than from inner responsiveness, suggested by the figure of the circumcized heart (vs. 16), of which John Wesley said:

Circumcision of heart implies humility, faith, hope, and charity. Humility, a right judgment of ourselves, cleanses our minds from those high conceits of our own perfections, from that undue opinion of our own abilities and attainments, which are the genuine fruit of a corrupted nature.[28]

A life-style that blesses us and our neighbors springs from such realism about ourselves and life's disciplined demands.

This passage points, second, to obedient love as *a response to God, whose awesomeness demands obedience, and whose love evokes our love.* He is the cosmic owner of "the heaven of heavens" (vs. 14)—vital reminder as man begins his mastery of space. God is "Lord of Lords" (vs. 17), "God supreme and Lord supreme" (TMT). Israel was reminded, in the face of surrounding polytheism, that his claims are first, highest, absolute; and in our pluralistic world, undivided loyalty to him can alone order our hierarchy of values. Our loyalty is tested at the point of our stewardship of an earth we use in trust; "to [him] belongs the earth with all that is in it" (vs. 14). In our "egocentric attitude" we treat nature as if we were no part of it, "as though there were neither past nor future." This is

[27] Paul Ramsey, *Basic Christian Ethics* (New York: Charles Scribner's Sons, 1950), p. 34.
[28] *The Works of John Wesley,* V, 203.

the thoughtless, extravagant, destructive attitude of modern man with regard to his natural environment, from which he has himself grown and on which his existence depends, his remorseless, greedy plundering of the treasures of this environment, his eagerness to defile it for ever with his industrial and human waste products, of which the by-products of atomic installations are only one among many, to defile them to such an extent that perhaps not even our own children, let alone future generations, will be able to live there.[29]

From such destructive violation of God's earth a proper sense of his ownership should long ago have delivered us.

This God who is sovereign owner of all things has "set his heart in love upon" a people chosen not for their worthiness but because of his freely offered goodness (vs. 15). "He executes justice" in behalf of helpless ones: "the fatherless and the widow" and the "sojourner" (vs. 18), "stranger" (TMT), or "resident alien" (AT). What does this say about *our* relation with minority peoples or the ghetto poor?

This passage points, finally, to obedient love as *the root of our identity, showing us who we are—a people called to serve.* Israel was reminded of its life in slavery, its puny strength, and how God chose this people for his purpose. Set against the foregoing chapters with their retracing of God's grace in the Exodus, this amounts to a vivid reminder that their very existence hung on their call to serve and witness (vss. 21-22). From its beginning the church has seen itself as called to be God's people, as Israel was called before it, not on account of our worthiness but by virtue of God's grace. Americans, given a vast unearned continent, richly stored, and, in its formative decades, free from the forces that had divided men and hampered liberty in older lands, speak of this as "God's country." Do we know that to be God's people is to be placed under special responsibility? Our identity born of grace, which makes us who we are and demands much of us, can be a revolutionary force transforming personal and national life.

What Is Authentic Christianity?
I John 5:1-5, 11

What is authentic Christianity? That question—still troubling the church—called forth the discussion that runs through these verses. Divisive factions known to history as Gnostics were claiming that only special knowledge of doctrines they held as a private preserve could produce the real Christian. Claiming superior Christianity, a special "spirituality," they held aloof from other men and from the practical dilemmas of the mundane world.

In our age this has its counterparts: attacks on the World Council of Churches and on other movements toward ecumenical unity, in the name of a superior orthodoxy; or divisiveness within the church on the ground of a superior knowledge of the Bible, a superior culture, a superior historical tradition. Whatever can guide us through the maze of these tests is vital to the church.

Individual Christians need some test of authenticity in their faith to

[29] G. Kennan, quoted by Gollwitzer, *The Demands of Freedom*, pp. 59-60.

guide them in the nurturing of a growing, responsible life before God. The doctrine of Assurance once gave Christians courage in times of crisis and danger. Whatever happened, they were in the hands of God; when they "fell on sleep," they would "awake in glory." Is there any equivalent assurance for us, in this age of sophistication? Here is one worth trying: "And this is the testimony, that God gave us eternal life, and this life is in his Son" (vs. 11).

Authentic Christianity is attested by a new dynamic of love and obedience, an "eternal life" already begun. It produces harmony in the church—not division. All those who believe "that Jesus is the Christ" are children of God (vs. 1). Loving God, we will love his children, even when their ideas and life-style differ from our own. Only in loving his children whom we see is there evidence that we love him whom we do not see. If this love is real it will issue in obedience (vss. 2-3). No "cheap grace" that short-cuts ethical imperatives can be harmonized with life in God. To those who love him and have the new life in him, "his commandments are not burdensome." As Jesus said, his way is an easy yoke and a light burden (Matt. 11:30); it fits our new nature, belongs to our new life; we do not chafe against it.

This authentic Christianity of love and obedience is not our achievement; it is God's gift. "God gave us eternal life, and this life is in his Son." "Born of God" (vs. 4), we can overcome the world. The "fightings and fears within, without" that constitute worldly life find resolution in trust in God. Faith knows this victory. To have it is to be very close to authentic Christianity.

Those who overcome the world are those who hold the central affirmation of the Church which, no elaborate ideological statement, simply affirms: "Jesus is the Son of God" (vs. 5). The explanatory statements of the creeds are little more than parentheses in this definitive affirmation of authentic Christian belief. Jesus—the Jesus of earthly life in Galilee, the Jesus of the Gospels—is the Son of God. He shows us what and who God is.

Assurance of sharing authentic Christianity lies in experiencing this love and obedience. God alone can give it. He "who believes that Jesus is the Christ is a child of God," and the test of belief is its fruitage in love and ethical living (vss. 1-5). Whoever is traveling this path has God's own testimony that he is one of God's children (vss. 6-10). It remains only to add that if we do not have these marks of God's action in our lives, we can receive them by turning from trust in ourselves to trust in Christ (vss. 4-5).

Dark Road to Glory: John 17:1-5

Fittingly this Gospel for the Sunday before Ascension Day deals with Jesus' prayer that the Father will "glorify" his Son. For Ascension Day dramatizes the faith that Jesus so obeyed God's loving and saving will that his humiliation on the Cross led to resurrection and "enthronement at God's right hand." All this declares the ultimate truth revealed in him, using the language of symbol to say what prosaic everyday speech cannot express. On the Sunday preceding the celebration of the Ascension, his prayer portrays the dark road that leads to his "glory."

What the church remembers as his "high priestly prayer" begins with what seems a strange petition for the humble Jesus: "Father, the hour has come; glorify thy Son" (vs. 1). In our idiom, for a man to say "This is my hour" is to say "This is my time of special opportunity, my moment to be honored." It is a phrase to be watched in the vocabulary of the Fourth Gospel. See its cumulative force: "My hour has not yet come" (2:4); "no one laid hands on him, because his hour had not yet come" (7:30); "no one arrested him, because his hour had not yet come" (8:20); "the hour has come for the Son of man to be glorified" (12:23); "and what shall I say, 'Father, save me from this hour'? No, for this purpose I have come to this hour. Father, glorify thy name." (12:27-28); "now before the feast of the Passover, when Jesus knew that his hour had come to depart out of this world . . ." (13:1). All references to "his hour" point to his crucifixion. Over that dark road he comes to "his hour" of glory.

The terms "glory" and "glorify" similarly connote crucifixion in the Johannine vocabulary. Following Judas' departure on his errand of betrayal, Jesus said, "Now is the Son of man glorified, and in him God is glorified; if God is glorified in him, God will also glorify him in himself, and glorify him at once" (13:31-32). Later, in the farewell discourse, he said, "The Spirit of truth . . . will glorify me, for he will take what is mine and declare it to you" (16:13-14). Thus, to "glorify" is to make the truth concerning Jesus, and through him concerning his Father, apparent; and this is generally in some way associated with his humiliation and crucifixion. "Glory", then connotes for John a complex whole consisting of humiliation-crucifixion-resurrection-exaltation. Jesus sought no glory for himself. "I do not receive glory from men" (5:41), he said. His was the glory he had with God "before the world was made" (vs. 5). It was his Father who glorified him (8:54). He gave himself to obedient love of the Father, traveling a dark road to glory.

The kind of "power" to which he refers in his prayer is worth noting. "Power over all flesh" (vs. 2) is power "over all mankind," (JB, TCNT, AT, NEB)—not power to get, but power to give. "For you gave him authority over all men, so that he might give eternal life to all those you gave him" (vs. 2 GNMM).

"Eternal life," in this prayer, is to know God (vs. 3), not by cognitive intellect but by intimate communion. This is the force of the word "know" as applied to our relation to God throughout the Bible. God makes himself known through his acts, as in the deliverance of his people from Egypt. But he is known even more surely by love's commitment, as in his tender word: "I will betroth you to me for ever; I will betroth you to me in righteousness and in justice, in steadfast love, and in mercy. I will betroth you to me in faithfulness; and you shall know the Lord" (Hos. 2:19-20). Sin blocks our knowledge of God, but a disciple's obedient trust in Jesus opens the way to saving knowledge: "Jesus then said to the Jews who had believed in him, 'If you continue in my word, you are truly my disciples, and you will know the truth, and the truth will make you free" (John 8:31-32). In intimate knowledge born of obedient love based on committed faith, we travel with him a disciplined road to glory.

ASCENSION SUNDAY

God's Triumph in the Humane
Daniel 7:9-10, 13-14

Only in the setting of the entire chapter can the two strophes of poetry which constitute this lection be read with full meaning. To interpret these poetic lines truly is to treat them as highlights of the closely knit chapter, which must be treated as a whole.

Relating Daniel's dream, the chapter exemplifies the meaning and purpose of this apocalyptic book of Daniel—a "tract for tough times," intended to strengthen the faithful in Israel against the attempt of Antiochus IV Epiphanes to Hellenize their life and paganize their faith. The vision of the four beasts (vss. 1-7) symbolizes the rise of four kingdoms, as vs. 17 delcares: the lion with eagle's wings, Babylon; the bear, the kingdom of the Medes; the leopard, the Persian empire; and the terrible fourth beast, Alexander and his successors—the ten horns being the cryptic way of speaking of the kings of the Seleucid dynasty. The new horn sprouting, which displaces three others (vs. 8) is Antiochus, who came to power only after crushing others whose claims to the throne rivaled his own. His "mouth speaking great things" (vs. 8), "proud words" (MT), "boasts" (JB), is further quoted in vs. 25:

> He shall speak words against the Most High,
>   and shall wear out the saints of the Most High,
>   and shall think to change the times and the law.

For approximately three and a half years—the "time, two times, and half a time" of vs. 25—Antiochus prolonged his persecutions. He attacked Jerusalem, razed its walls, and occupied the city. He forbade the Jewish rite of circumcision, prohibited observance of the Sabbath, destroyed the sacred books, sacrificed swine—ceremonially unclean to the Jews—upon the temple altar, reared pagan altars throughout the land, and inflicted untold suffering on the resisters who, under Judas Maccabeus, finally expelled him and his Hellenizing movement.

Asserting God's triumph over such usurpers of power, the hymns of this lection declare the divine sovereignty. In the face of the blasphemous boasts of Antiochus

> thrones were placed
>   and one that was ancient of days took his seat (vs. 9).

God, symbolized in this and the following lines, is secure on his throne despite these proud, cruel pagan monarchs. He sits in judgment (vss. 10, 26) and takes away the dominion of the seemingly invincible beast (vs. 26). The book is opened in which (12:1) the names of the faithful who will not be destroyed are recorded.

As the vision continues, the beast is killed and the other beasts are deprived of power. Sovereignty is transferred from these kingdoms, so savage that only fierce beasts can represent them, to a gentler, more humane power, "one like a son of man" (vs. 13). Just as the kingdoms of bestial power are represented by the beast metaphor, the humane successor is spoken of in the Aramaic idiom, "son of man"—that is, "a certain man," "a man." That the idiom is thus an expression of simple human identity becomes clear in the address to Daniel in the ensuing chapter: "Understand, O son of man, that the vision is for the time of the end" (8:17).

The contrast between the bestial kingdoms and the humane successor is epitomized in 7:17-18, where the beasts are identified as four kings, but their successor who "shall receive the kingdom . . . for ever and ever" is spoken of as "the saints of the Most High." Thus the figure sets Israel as a messianic people over against the pagan kingdoms of ferocious power.

Christians cannot read this chapter without recognizing its influence on Rev. 13, where the composite beast representing Rome, invested with the satanic power of the great dragon, has features of the four beasts of this chapter, echoing the blasphemous boasts of the last of their number. This beast, too, is defeated and deposed, the thrones of judgment are set up, and "the souls of those who had been beheaded for their testimony to Jesus and for the word of God . . . reigned with Christ a thousand years" (Rev. 20:4), the rule passing from the bestial to the faithfully humane "saints of the Most High," as in Daniel.

This triumph of the humane forces of God over the bestial forces of the earth finds expression in the Christian year through the symbol of the Ascension. Jesus supremely embodies "one like a son of man"—gentle, humane, the fulfillment of the best for which the messianic expectation stood. In the symbolism of his universality, his cosmic victory, the church declares that

> his dominion is an everlasting dominion,
> which shall not pass away (7:14).

For every age faith renews this conviction of God's victory. Whether amid the agonies of the rule of Antiochus, Nero's butcheries, the Napoleonic debacle, or Hitler's condemnation of millions to the gas chambers, this vision renews itself. One need not accept bizarre theories which read the ancient writers as soothsayers to realize that this truth spotlights *all* times. Whether in the crashing drama of war and nuclear holocaust or amid the prosaic treacheries of quieter days, this truth can sustain us. For it transcends times and places—as the truth of the Ascension and eternal victory of Christ transcends the world views and cosmologies in which differing ages express it. As D. T. Niles puts it:

Slavery is abolished, but the exploitation of man by man remains and takes many forms. Woman is liberated from the position of being a chattel, but man's respect for woman has still to maintain itself against the assaults of suggestive fashions, sophisticated social conventions, and the influence of cheap literature. Man wages eternal war against the forms of evil, while evil itself remains and takes on other forms.

Evil is man's predicament, a predicament from which God alone can deliver him.[30]

[30] D. T. Niles, *As Seeing the Invisible* (New York: Harper, 1961), pp. 155-56.

Yet deliver him God does, and "the saints of the Most High" struggle on in the dark times sustained by a faith that nothing on the horizon of carnage or corruption will overcome, a faith that God gives the victory to "one like a son of man."

How Vast the Resources
Ephesians 1:15-23

Much of the central meaning of Ascension Sunday is lodged in the prayer at the heart of this passage: "I pray that your inward eyes may be illumined, so that you may know what is the hope to which he calls you, what the wealth and glory of the share he offers you among his people in their heritage, and how vast the resources of his power open to us who trust in him" (vss. 18-19 NEB).

It would be inviting to pause over this prayer as a summing up of the Christian redemption. Tracey K. Jones, Jr., speaks aptly of three basic human needs: "Every man desires 'to be' someone, to be recognized as a person who has value . . . 'to belong' with those who will accept him as an equal . . . 'to do' something that will give purpose to his life." [31] He goes on to suggest that when the life, death, and resurrection of Christ are related to the meeting of these three needs, the whole man is redeemed. This prayer forges the links. The need "to be" someone is supplied by "vast resources" available through trust. "To belong" is to have a "share . . . among his people in their heritage." "To do" is to find purpose in a work "to which he calls you." See, then, what opens the way to this threefold fulfillment.

God makes it possible by the power that raised Christ from the dead and set him above all things (vss. 20-23). The same power that raised Christ from the dead has placed him "far above all rule and authority and power and dominion" (vs. 21). In the idiom of the first century, "rule," "authority," "dominion," "power," are names given to forces more than human, whether angelic (cf. Eph. 3:10; Col. 1:16; 2:10) or demonic (cf. Eph. 6:12; I Cor. 15:24; Col. 2:15) or both (cf. Rom. 8:38). In the thought of our time the nearest equivalent forces might be such psychological phenomena as complexes, obsessions, drives, manifestations of the *id*. Or they might be power structures in society, with their more than individually human capacity for good or evil. Or they could be such rampant forces as nationalism or racism. Christ, this passage declares, has been given power that transcends all such superhuman structures.

He is above "every name that is named, not only in this age but also in that which is to come." As in all biblical writing, the *name* stands for the *person*, Christ being above all. Hebraic thought divides time into "this age"—from creation to now—and "the age to come" when God will rule in his perfect kingdom. Christ is the supreme authority in both. We who live in this age can only bow to his authority, putting it to work in faith amid our contests of power—racial, international, and all others—employing his methods in the conflict, living by them as we hope to do in "the age to

[31] Jones, *Our Mission Today*, p. 69.

come," not waiting for that distant day before we begin to trust him to create our life-style.

His rule begins in the Church in order that it may be limitlessly extended beyond that embryonic fellowship (vss. 22-23). The church "is his body, the fulness of him who fills all in all." The *body* is clearly the instrument through which his mind and spirit work out his purpose in the world, but the *fulness* referred to is less obvious to interpret—as evidenced by the fact that NEB finds it necessary to offer three possible translations. Is the Church his fulness in the sense of a body needed to fulfill the intention of its head: "the completion of him who everywhere and in all things is complete" (KT)? Or is the church, as body, filled in all its parts with the life which is controlled by its head: "the Church is Christ's Body, and is filled by him who fills all things everywhere with his presence" (TCNT)? "Paul intends to shew how the great work of reconciliation has begun in the Church, in which all opposing elements have been brought together. What Christ has done in the Church he is to do for the whole universe." [32] Christ must have full control now, *within this body,* in order that ultimately his reign *in all things* may be acknowledged.

Why Celebrate Ascension? Luke 24:44-53

Since late in the fourth century the Church has celebrated the annual feast of the Ascension. Why? The *Apostolic Constitutions,* dating from that period, give one answer:

Count forty days, from the Lord's-day till the fifth day of the week, and celebrate the feast of the ascension of the Lord whereon He finished all his dispensation and constitution, and returned to that God and Father than sent Him, and sat down at the right hand of power, and remains there until His enemies are put under His feet; who also will come at the consummation of the world with power and great glory, to judge the quick and the dead, and to recompense to every one according to his works. [33]

Admittedly that is couched in the language of a world view we no longer hold. Ours is not the cozy universe presupposed here, in which our Lord might rise from a mountain into heaven. Why, then, should we continue to observe this festival in our calendar?

The dynamic movement of this lesson from Luke helps us to answer. In it Jesus reiterates the basic teaching of the New Testament proclamation: the prophecies are fulfilled in the coming of Christ, his death and rising, and the consequent call to repentance (vss. 44-47). The disciples are to be witnesses after they have received the promised power, for which they are enjoined to wait (vss. 48-49). After leading them as far as Bethany, Jesus blesses them and parts from them. They then return to Jerusalem with joy and continue to worship God in the temple (vss. 50-53).

In this parting from them we have the central symbol of the Ascension.

[32] E. F. Scott, *The Epistles of Paul* (New York: Harper, 1930), p. 159.
[33] Quoted in A. Allan McArthur, *The Evolution of the Christian Year* (London: SCM Press, 1953), p. 156.

Some later manuscripts add that he "was carried up into heaven," an idea which harmonizes the passage with Luke's continuing narrative in Acts 1. More important than the cosmology which provides the means of expression is the truth which it is meant to convey: Christ's complete lordship of heaven and earth, of time and eternity, of things human and divine. In a dramatic picture it puts what many words of prose could not say as memorably.

What does this mean in our violent world? Following the assassination of Martin Luther King, Jr., Carl Rowan wrote feelingly that the "gunman destroyed much of the slender barricade of reason and hope that has kept utter chaos away from our volatile urban area." In our violent society, he reminded his readers, many black people now believe they can secure justice only by force. Dr. King had been trying to prove to them "that there is an alternative to violence as a means of achieving justice," Rowan said, though "it now seems obvious that Dr. King could never prove this. Only white American society can." [34] This places on men of goodwill a heavy burden of leadership. We cannot shirk our responsibility, but Ascension Day supports confidence that since the Christ crucified by violence is universally victorious, his way holds the key to the future.

He was parted from them (vs. 51) in order that he might be forever present with them (vs. 49). John so reports Jesus' words on the eve of crucifixion: "It is to your advantage that I go away, for if I do not go away, the Counselor will not come" (John 16:7). Withdrawal is prelude to empowering Presence, for which the disciples are told to wait "until you are clothed with power from on high" (vs. 49).

Amid crucial issues, waiting is not easy. Elizabeth O'Connor reports sympathetically the urgency of some of her action-minded friends in the Church of the Saviour in Washington, D.C., who say: "The world is the arena of God's concern. The need is overpowering. Let's get on with it. This meditation, this silence business, taking a day for retreat—time to develop a quiet center, to ask questions—it's not for me. There's not that much time. The act is important." Others reply that the call to act does not mean "just any action. Action grows out of hearing the word of God. It is a particular action engaged in at a *kairos* moment—not action for action's sake." [35] Only such action born of obedient waiting is "clothed with power."

So the disciples, recognizing this parting with a visibly present Lord as an occasion for joy, not grief (vs. 52), celebrated it by praising God in the temple (vs. 53). Sharing with them, we see the dynamics of the Ascension as they emerge from this closely packed passage: Prophecy moves to fulfillment; what God begins he sees through to completion. Suffering moves to glory; life's pain, far from meaningless, can be redemptive. Experience moves to witness; we are given a life with him in order that we may share it. Waiting moves to empowerment; the life of vital usefulness cannot be hastily improvised. Parting moves to joyful presence; ascension means the local Christ has become universally and victoriously present.

[34] *Chicago Daily News*, April 5, 1968.
[35] O'Connor, *Journey Inward, Journey Outward*, p. 168.

PENTECOST SEASON

Pentecost Sunday celebrates, in a distinctively Christian sense, a festival which roots in the Old Testament. Originally an agricultural dedication, it became the commemoration of the giving of the Law at Sinai. Thus it expressed the completion of the relation to God as liberating redeemer of his people, celebrated at Passover. The Christian Pentecost, in like manner, celebrates completion of the events of the pascha—the Cross and Resurrection of our Lord—by the coming of the Holy Spirit. As the new Israel of God, the Church looks to Pentecost as the day of its birth.

Preaching at Rome in the fifth century, Leo the Great sets forth this identification of the two occasions in a Pentecost sermon:

For as of old, when the Hebrew nation were released from the Egyptians, on the fiftieth day after the sacrificing of the lamb the Law was given on Mount Sinai, so after the suffering of Christ, wherein the true Lamb of God was slain . . . the Holy Ghost came down . . . the second covenant was founded by the same Spirit that had instituted the first.[1]

[1] Quoted in McArthur, *The Evolution of the Christian Year*, p. 144.

With this festival, the Christian year enters its second half. The events which gave shape to the gospel are completed by the coming of the Spirit; the Church now goes forth to proclaim the good news. Hence two motifs run through the lections for this season: (1) the Church in mission, and (2) the Spirit recapitulating and making personal the lessons of the Christian revelation. In earlier seasons, the lections for a Sunday present dimensions of a common event or theme; Sundays after Pentecost, however, have only occasional flashes of thematic development. The Old Testament lessons for these Sundays make a little pilgrimage through great moments of the "salvation history"; Epistles for the first ten Sundays make a similar journey through the Acts; and the Gospels find focus in: (1) fuller exploration of Christ's lordship, (2) the life of the Church in mission, and (3) the growth of the new life born of the Spirit.

In numbering these Sundays after Pentecost, this lectionary follows the ancient practice of the Church, still adhered to by Roman Catholic practice. At a later date, the custom of numbering these Sundays after Trinity Sunday arose in northern Europe and has been followed in the Lutheran and Episcopal traditions. Since the Christian message is revealed more through *events* than generalized doctrines, there is good ground for this older practice of laying the stress of this long season on the Pentecost event and its implications. Trinity Sunday is always one week after Pentecost, but in this lectionary the lessons for that day are not Trinity lessons. The lectionary does offer Trinity scriptures, however, in its separate listing of Special Days. Observance of the day with these lections provides an important and needed occasion for the celebration of the experience and teaching of the doctrine of God in its fullest Christian development.

PENTECOST SUNDAY

New Covenant—New People
Jeremiah 31:31-34

In this landmark passage the New Testament reads the promise which Pentecost fulfilled. With the words, "the Holy Spirit also bears witness to us," the Letter to the Hebrews introduces an extended quotation from this passage (Heb. 10:15-17). Discovering in Christ the freedom that comes when the law is not an outer restraint but an inner assent, these early Christians remembered the assurance, "I will put my law within them, and I will write it upon their hearts" (vs. 33).

Nothing is so irksome as an *imposed* discipline, nothing so liberating as a discipline *espoused*. Many a man, desiring a happy marriage and a great home, chafes under the restraint it lays on his personal whims. Many a minister, eager to fulfill his calling, shrinks from the disciplined hours of study, the regularities in prayer, the demand for an exemplary life. Only when the covenant of marriage or a high calling is written on the heart does it become greatly liberating. Having found this blessed freedom in the new covenant, the men of Christianity's first age learned to think of themselves as a new, called people of God.

God's loving initiative, preceding our response, seeks us. Jeremiah had seen the waywardness of our wills, which cannot on their own initiative find grace to repent. "The sin of Judah is written with a pen of iron," he said; "with a point of diamond it is engraved on the tablet of their heart." (Jer. 17:1). The springs of motive corrupted, renewal can come only from forces planted equally deep within. What our sick wills cannot achieve, God can, as he writes his law on our hearts.

The New Testament declares he *has done so!* Sharing the wine of the last supper, Jesus said: "This cup is the new covenant in my blood" (I Cor. 11:25, Luke 22:20). Pointing to the source of apostolic service, Paul declared: "Our sufficiency is from God, who has qualified us to be ministers of a new covenant, not in a written code but in the Spirit; for the written code kills, but the Spirit gives life" (II Cor. 3:5-6). God has given us new motives by showing us his love in Christ and filling us with gratitude for sins forgiven. With the new motivation has come a new power to obey. Following our own impulses, we live amid warring fractions of ourselves; for every impulse represents the whim of a *moment* and the extension of *some part* of our nature. Only the law deeply espoused within, written on the heart, can make new men, for it alone makes us *whole*.

Responding, we are made part of a covenant *community.* As Jeremiah put it, as God's spokesman, "I will be their God, and they shall be my people" (vs. 33*b*). The Bible knows nothing of a religion limited to "what the individual does with his own solitariness." Out of the life of a community in covenant with God flows this great stream of cleansing, liberating faith. In the Old Testament, God is the God of Abraham, Isaac, and Jacob—the God of a covenant people. In the New Testament, God is known through the Church, and to be "in Christ" is to be in this community of the covenant. The relation to God is imbibed with the very life of the community; "they shall all know me, from the least of them to the greatest, says the Lord" (vs. 34). In periods when men are involved least in the espoused disciplines of a covenant community, they talk most of the "silence" of God.

Festival of Communication: Acts 2:1-8, 12-21

Multipling the *means* of communication, we have lost the *power* to communicate. We pour forth millions of words through increasingly sophisticated devices. Yet, across chasms of race, nation, industrial class, generation, and culture—even within the tender bonds of the family—we do not really hear and understand one another. Into this crisis Pentecost comes as a festival of communication.

The Bible so presents it. The phenomenon of glossolalia (vs. 4) is its surface manifestation. Experiencing a reversal of the curse of Babel (Genesis 11:1-9), men were drawn together into a shared understanding, so that they asked, "How is it that we hear, each of us in his own native language?" (vs. 8). The creative energy of motives awakened by the Good News gave power to the witness to leap the chasms that block communication. Within a generation, the message had crossed barriers of race and culture, to make its way to the remotest parts of Mediterranean civilization.

Through this classic New Testament model, Pentecost reminds us that we can speak the reconciling word, as beyond our clever proficiencies we expectantly seek the power of the Holy Spirit.

God's Spirit generates power to witness; so ran the promise: "You shall receive power when the Holy Spirit has come upon you; and you shall be my witnesses" (Acts 1:8). Having responded to God's leading in the words of Jesus, in prayer, and in acceptance of the missionary mandate, the apostles received this visitation of the Spirit as *power* to fulfill their calling.

The gift was not primarily that of "speaking in tongues." Possessing that gift, Paul wrote forcefully about its limitations (I Cor. 14:6-19). A seminary student put in a parable our proneness to speak in the "tongues" of technical jargon *about* God, with no authentic word *from* him. He wrote: "And Jesus said to them, 'Who do you say that I am?' And they replied, 'You are the eschatological manifestation of the ground of our being; the kerygma manifested in conflict and decision in the humanizing process.' And Jesus said, 'What?'" We need careful theological thinking, and men who think carefully in a common discipline must faciliate their work by a shared vocabulary; but we need, too, a new touch of the Spirit that will take theology beyond the academic to the deeply experienced. No less devoted to intellectual honesty, we must speak the truth in love.

Generating such power to witness, the Holy Spirit effects change, as portrayed in the metaphor of wind, a figure used by Jesus talking to Nicodemus about a complete change in his life (John 3:8). The sound "like the rush of a mighty wind" (vs. 2) is so vividly protrayed in the Greek that it can be read "a violent blast" (MT). Peter made its life-changing force explicit in his call to repent (vs. 38), which means literally to turn around, get a new mind.

Pentecost's power to produce change is seen in its sequel. Fearful men like Peter were made bold. The witnessing company was launched on ventures that changed everything, both within itself and in the communities it touched. To troubled situations it brought a word that was ultimately healing, but that first precipitated explosive controversies. Such power of holy daring combined with loving power to heal remains a perennial need of the church. In the midst of our crisis of communication we may well heed the call that made this festival of communication a reality: "Wait for the promise of the Father, . . . before many days you shall be baptized with the Holy Spirit" (Acts 1:4-5).

When Words Become Word
John 14:15-17, 25-27

Beyond words—whether of Jesus, the Bible, or Christian tradition —there is the Word addressed personally to us. Rich in words, we need the Word. Promising that the Holy Spirit "will teach you all things, and bring to your remembrance" all that our Lord has taught (vs. 26), Jesus assures us that this need can be met. A Word meant for us can bring challenge, change, renewal, the power of an abiding Presence.

When words thus become the Word, God's Spirit leads us into authentic understanding of Christ: He will "bring to your remembrance all that I have said to you" (vs. 26). Seeing and hearing much, the disciples had understood little. Witnessing Jesus' triumphal entry into Jerusalem, "they did not understand this at first; but when Jesus was glorified, then they remembered . . ." (John 12:16). Only in the Spirit's recollection could they comprehend. In the upper room, as he washed their feet, Jesus said, "What I am doing you do not know now, but afterward you will understand" (John 13:7). On the morning of the Resurrection they were incredulous, "for as yet they did not know the scripture, that he must rise from the dead" (John 20:9). Like us, they needed, more than to hear words and see sights, a touch of God's Spirit that would bring home a message peculiarly their own.

We need such a Word to bring us to life. For it is not so much true that "God is dead" as that *man* is dead. *Humanity* had died when the killers manned the Nazi death camps. *Man* was dead as nations supported the butchery, or stood idly by. Eating heartily and sleeping well while children are burned alive by napalm, we have joined the living death. Working at jobs we hate, sharing houses that—barren of companionship—have ceased to be homes, anesthetizing ourselves by the narcotic trivia of television, we die to what is most vitally human. Our tragic unconcern is summed up in a breezy phrase: "Man is dead—anybody got a cigarette?" [2]

When words become Word, they bring contagious creativity to our jaded, death-filled world. "The Counselor," Jesus said, "will teach you all things" (vs. 26). *Paracletos* ("Counselor") is too rich a word to lend itself to any single English equivalent, so that various translators read Comforter, Counselor, Helper, Advocate, Intercessor, Protector, Support, in their attempt to convey the truth that the reality that was in Jesus can be personally present to meet and renew us. When he does, we *understand* as we could not before, and creative new qualities are released in us. Lulled by the "peace of mind" cults, we easily miss the force of Jesus' promise of peace, "my own peace, such as the world cannot give" (vs. 27 NEB). No drugged escapism, his own peace was achieved, as the circumstances of that night testified, in the midst of an earth-changing struggle and in the shadow of a cross. "Peace," on his lips, has back of it all the vitality of the Hebrew *shalom,* a word vibrant with active, creative, abundant life.

All this, however, comes in advanced lessons in the school of Christ. Many of us never reach this graduate level, having failed to master the introductory lesson. New creativity through the Holy Spirit remains a futile hope until we take the first step: "If you love me, you will keep my commandments" (vs. 15). No easy word that! But in it everything begins.

FIRST SUNDAY AFTER PENTECOST

Seed of Disruption: Genesis 3:1-6, 22-23

The lectionary here begins a project which continues through the remaining half-year: retracing the highlights of the central proclamation of the good news of God under the Old Covenant. Sadly it must begin with the ac-

---

[2] This paragraph is suggested by the title sermon in Polish, *The Dead Cannot Praise God.*

count of the planting of the seed of disruption, from which human alienation and lostness spring. It reads the meaning of our life, not as the story of what happened to *one* man and *one* woman, once upon a time, but as the portrayal of what continually happens to *every* man and *every* woman. Understood as literal history, it issues primarily in the fruitless question, Did this happen? Read as interpretation of the human predicament, it leads to the stabbing realization, This is who I am!

In ancient Near Eastern mythology the serpent represented elemental evil locked in struggle with good. In Egypt, for instance, the god Ra was opposed by the demon Apophia, pictured as a serpent. The Genesis story, whatever it may have owed to this conception, has reworked it to be true to the biblical faith, in which God is supreme and there is no final dualism of good and evil. Here the serpent is a "creature that the Lord God had made," though "more subtle than any other wild creature"; "more cunning" (MT), "the most clever" (AT), "the shrewdest" (TMT). Significantly, he was shrewdest of the *wild* creatures God had made—which excepts man, who presumably had in him something akin to the diabolical shrewdness of this tempter. Temptations never spring from sources wholly external to ourselves.

The temptation begins with *an insinuating doubt*: "Did God really say . . . ?" (vs 1*b* JB and TMT). How do you *know* the commandment is true? Does it really apply *this* time? So persistent is the strategy that even Jesus was confronted by it: "If you are the Son of God . . . " (Matt. 4:3-6). It still confronts us: Are the commandments outmoded in this new age? Doesn't grace abolish law? Does the old ethic apply to this exceptional situation? Or to you as an exceptional person? Are not our ethics to be fabricated to fit situations?

Temptation appeals, second, to human ambition: our drive to be utterly autonomous, to make our own decisions apart from prior commitments, to run our own life in defiance of any supreme loyalty, to be the center of our own world. "You will be like God, knowing good and evil" (vs. 5). Of this overreaching, Ezekiel accused the king of Tyre, who said, "I am a god, I sit in the seat of the gods," supposing that his wealth and power were supreme—only to find that his pretensions brought the onslaughts of enemies who destroyed him (Ezek. 28:1-10). "You would not die at all," runs the temptation, "your eyes will be opened, and you will be like gods who know good from evil" (vs. 5 AT). So! You will learn to write your own commandments!

Disruption, not gratification, is the outcome. The verses omitted from the lection detail the rupture and twisting of relationships. The man and woman are set at odds with God, hiding from him and then accusing him of starting all he trouble: "The woman *You* put at my side—she gave me of the tree" (vs. 12 TMT, italics added). The shadow of this alibi also falls across their tender relationship with each other. They are made enemies of the serpent (vss. 14-15), the first enmity with the animal kingdom. Pain shadows their parenthood (vs. 16). The soil and their work with natural resources are afflicted with perverseness (vss. 17-19). Enmity arises between brothers (4:3-8). Even the basic bond of language is broken, so that words hide meaning instead of conveying it: "Am I my brother's keeper?" (4:9). For all this the summarizing symbol is ejection from Eden (3:23). Sin is here seen in its basic reality, not as isolated act but as utter alienation.

God's precaution against the man's taking "of the tree of life" to "eat, and live for ever" (vs. 22) takes issue with the ancient Near East myth. The Epic of Gilgamesh portrays the herb of life which men eat to become young again, which is lost through unfortunate circumstances. Not circumstance, responded the Genesis theologian, but the severing of a true relation with God, is the cause of the loss of man's happy condition. In the long sweep of the biblical struggle Christ so restores the relation that the Bible's opening in rebellion and fall is matched by its closing renewal of relation and restoration to abundant life: "Blessed are those who wash their robes, that they may have the right to the tree of life and that they may enter the city by the gates" (Rev. 22:14). As the Fall is not a story of far-off events buried in history's forgotten yesterdays, this promise of renewal is not deferred until some eschatological tomorrow. Fall and renewal are the story of *our life*.

Carriers of a Healing Word: Acts 3:1-7, 11-21

Hard on the heels of Pentecost, the Church began its twofold ministry of healing and preaching. The order is significant: first the healing power, then the public message. Faith in Christ, shared by witness in word and extended hand, enabled the lame man to walk (vss. 6-7). Called to the continuation of that ministry, we are here reminded that a muted, hesitant pulpit can find decisive influence only in the context of a church faithful to its healing ministry.

Healing was part and parcel of the new burst of power that came with Jesus. He himself saw it as an evidence of the invading power of the kingdom of God. "If it is by the finger of God that I cast out demons," he said, "then the kingdom of God has come upon you" (Luke 11:20). Disease was not God's intention for his creation; it was the work of forces at enmity with God. Integral to Jesus' work was the liberation of the victims of such evil. New Testament healing is not to be understood as the simple equivalent of modern faith healing or of psychiatry; yet healing then and healing now cast light upon each other. Suggestions of the place of healing in the life of the Church may be implied in this lection.

Healing is associated with the life of prayer. When they ministered to the lame man, "Peter and John were on their way up to the temple for the three o'clock hour of prayer" (vs. 1 AT). Praying not casually, now and then, they maintained a scheduled, disciplined life of prayer. In such a setting healing ministries occur.

Healing is preceded by change from impersonal handouts to personal encounter. "Both Peter and John looked straight at him and said, 'Look at us' " (vs. 4 JB). Expectant beggars and shamefaced passers-by glance evasively at each other! This scene changes that I-it evasion to I-Thou encounter.

Healing was given as a part of sharing whatever they had to give. The apostles did not disparage material aid. They did not say, "Silver and gold are unimportant"; they said, "I have no silver and gold, but I give you what I have" (vs. 6). In like mood, William Stringfellow advised a pastor who called to inquire how to help a woman about to be evicted for inability to pay her rent. Reforming lawyer that he is, Stringfellow did not respond with legal advice. Instead, he asked, "Does your church still have those expensive tapestries?" To the puzzled affirmative reply, he countered: "Then sell one of them and pay the rent." Affluent Christians have something direct to do about poverty and material need.

Healing comes "in the name" of Jesus Christ (vs. 6b). Of this Peter kept reminding the excited bystanders. "His name, by faith in his name, has made this man strong" (vs. 16). "By the name of Jesus Christ of Nazareth . . . this man is standing before you well" (4:10). Faith came not only by contagion from the faith of the apostles, but also by some knowledge of *Jesus*, either from prior contact or from the apostles' witness, in what must have been a more extended interview than this compressed account can detail.

Healing faith ventures personal involvement. "He took him by the right hand and raised him up" (vs. 7). The apostles threw themselves into the event with expectation. They put their faith on the line. They participated personally to the limit of their powers.

Healing supports proclamation. As an astonished crowd gathered (vs. 11), Peter seized the opportunity to preach the good news of God in Christ. What follows is an outline of the apostolic message, the strong core of the Christian gospel in any age: God has acted through "his servant Jesus" (vs. 13), who died at our hands, according to the scriptures (vss. 14, 15a, 18). We killed "the Author of life," its "source" (AT), "pioneer" (MT), "prince" (JB), "Guide" (TCNT), "him who has led the way to life" (NEB). "But God raised him from the dead" (vs. 15 TCNT). To this the apostles—the very Church itself—bear witness. By Christ's power the paralyzed man stands in new strength. The evidence of the Resurrection is the power it continues to release in tormented lives. Final victory is in store for the risen Christ (vs. 21); what God began in him he will ultimately bring to completion, to bless his children and all creation.

Peter's summary of the gospel closes with a note the Church must not lose: "Repent therefore, and turn again, that your sins may be blotted out, that times of refreshing may come from the presence of the Lord" (vs. 19). This is the final appeal in all of apostolic preaching. On any issue, it reminds us, we stand at odds with God, whose thoughts are not our thoughts. We must turn from our wrong direction if there is to be any real meeting. Underlying every other need is our need of "times of refreshing," the resotration of power that comes only from him.

Faith Renewed or Faith Abandoned
Matthew 11:2-6

A 1967 article in *Daedalus*, the Journal of the American Academy of Arts and Sciences, bore the title "Christianity: Renewed or Slowly Abandoned?" Truman B. Douglas remarks that we face the question in that form rather than in some such alternative as "Christianity vs. Communism," or "Christianity vs. Secularism," or any such simplified choice. The real question is whether we renew our faith or slowly let it die.

John faced such a choice. No rival teaching had challenged his faith in Christ. John's trouble was doubt that what Jesus was doing furnished adequate grounds for faith. He must renew belief or let it die. "Are you he who is to come, or shall we look for another?" (vs. 3). Paul Scherer once remarked that an adequate interpretation of this passage "begins by announcing that John in prison was bewildered, and so are we; it continues by pointing out that he took his trouble directly to Jesus, and so must we; and comes to its climax by reminding us that he got only an indirect answer, and so do we." [3] There could scarcely be a better outline.

John was bewildered. He had been confident that Jesus was "the coming one." In the days of his own popularity, when crowds gathered in the belief that John was the Messiah, he had pointed beyond himself to Jesus (John 1:20-23; 3:30; Matt. 3:14). Jesus had refused to be the kind of messianic liberator John expected. John looked for a leader who would cut down and burn the unproductive, act both by the Holy Spirit and with fire, thresh the grain of the people's life, and burn the chaff from it (Matt. 3:10-12). The figures point to the kind of violent messiah fostered in the popular mind by much of the literature of the period. "When John heard in prison about the deeds of the Christ" (vs. 2), it was clear that Jesus did not fit this picture.

We, too, are bewildered. Confusion about Christ's claims fills the air. Does he offer any final word about life's meaning? What is the nature of his authority? Noble ethical example? Wise ancient teacher? Some ultimate demand on our loyalty, obedience, and faith? If we do not expect him to validate his authority in ways as violent as John's figures suggest, are we nevertheless confused by expectations of dramatic external deeds that are at odds with his real intention?

John took his trouble directly to Jesus. To talk *about* one who is present, not *to* him, is an embarrassment and an insult. It belittles personality, reducing a person to an object. Yet this is often our way with Jesus. We talk *about* him, draw conclusions about him, drift away from him. We do not talk *to* him. Yet, if faith is not mere opinion but the ultimate dependence of our life, it is forged on the anvil of our own hard decisions in firsthand contact with him in whom we believe. Though the opinions of others can help us to clarify the issues, our final resort lies in direct contact with him. Dealing with what he does, we come to know who he is.

To John's inquiry, Jesus' reply stressed this need for personal decision: "Blessed is he who takes no offense at me" (vs. 6). The Greek here translated "offense" forms the root of our word "scandal." It can be variously translated, "finds no hindrance" (TCNT), "is repelled by nothing" (MT), "does not find me a stumbling-block" (NEB), "does not lose faith in me" (JB). Matthew's other uses of this verb throw light on its implication here. Summarizing the doubts of the Nazareth neighbors, Matthew writes that "they took offense at him" (13:57); knowing him face to face, they decided against him. At the last supper, Jesus said: "You will all fall away"—in Greek a form of the same verb—"because of me this night" (26:31). Peter asserted that "though they all fall away because of you, I will never fall away" (26:33). In a crisis of decision about final loyalties, the issue was whether they

[3] Paul Scherer, *The Word God Sent* (New York: Harper, 1965), p. 77.

would trust him (not theories about him) or find some other way than his. That is still our issue.

John got only an indirect answer. With no simple Yes or No, Jesus pointed to what he had been doing (vss. 4-5), the daily stuff of his ministry. Matthew had reported Jesus' work (8:1–9:34), and this recapitulates it in a little cameo drawing. John's knowledge of the Scriptures would find in this the suggestion of a conception of the Messiah at odds with the fiery conqueror he had expected. Isaiah painted such a picture as Jesus draws. "The blind receive their sight . . . , the deaf hear, . . . and the poor have good news preached to them" (vs. 5) almost exactly quotes Isa. 29:18-19. "The lame walk" recalls Isa. 35:6. "Lepers are cleansed . . . , and the dead are raised up" echoes Isa. 26:19. So, Jesus seems to have been saying, you will have to choose where the real values lie. Which kind of Messiah do you trust?

It is still our question. The Christ of the Gospels will not abandon the world. As James H. Cone observes, this is "a message about the ghetto, and all other injustices done in the name of democracy and religion to further the social, political, and economic interests of the oppressor. In Christ, God enters human affairs and takes sides with the oppressed. Their suffering becomes his; their despair, divine despair. Through Christ the poor man is offered freedom now to rebel against that which makes him other than human." [4] Meeting a Christ of such practical service, men are confirmed in faith.

Yet practical service cannot stand alone. Struggling to meet such real needs as better housing, the Church of the Saviour in Washington, D.C., discovered that people had to be changed by meeting something radically new. "That something 'new' had to be more than a house, essential as a house is. It had to be the Gospel breaking into a man's life. Jesus had not said, 'Go tell John, the poor have new houses.' He had said, 'Go tell John that the poor have good news preached to them.' " [5]

SECOND SUNDAY AFTER PENTECOST

Compact with Earth: Genesis 9:8-15

Earth, said the first astronauts to behold it from the perspective of a moon orbit, looked very special, the one precious spot of color in what seemed otherwise a black and white universe. Genesis, in similar mood, sees it as so "special" that God, knowing all its frustrations, made a compact with it. The story in Genesis 9 was written late in Israel's development. The reflections of Israel, in the long growth of its tradition, were here finally reported through a subtle theological mind.

The model of the covenant idea here employed was borrowed from the practice of imperial rulers who gave covenants to vassal kings. Despite mutuality of obligation, such covenants were not negotiated between equals; they were given by the free choice of the imperial power. Israel had found its sense of identity, and the cohesiveness of its life as a people, around such a

---

[4] Cone, *Black Theology and Black Power,* p. 36.
[5] O'Connor, *Journey Inward, Journey Outward,* p. 164.

pact with God, formed at Sinai. In the light of this vivid national experience they thought their way back to further self-understanding as interpreted by God's pact with Abraham. Unlike these covenants with a chosen people, the covenant with Noah was God's promise to all humanity, to the whole created world (vss. 8-10).

With its claim on all men, this covenant reflects a great truth: it is the nature of man to live under a claim. Mystery lays its claim on curiosity, and research develops. The needs of others lay their claim on conscience, and community develops. Duty lays its claim on moral choice, and character develops. Love lays its claim on responsible actions, and the most enriching experiences possible to men unfold. The Holy lays claim to our reverent awe, and all of life is brought under commitment that blesses while it confines. To spurn or neglect the claims upon us is to betray our humanity. To respond is to know that what most makes us human is our pact, not with some impersonal force, but with a Thou to whom we belong. In beautiful picture language, this old story represents the universality of this claim that makes us men.

God promises constancy in providing our earthly home (vs. 11). We often upset its ecology by our folly and avarice—plowing up a dust bowl, denuding the hills, exhausting the mineral resources, polluting air and water, and plunging headlong into nuclear competition which may attack creation itself. But God and his earth abide faithful. We inherit this stable earth-home under a covenant that calls for stewardship of its resources.

Even beyond the changes of outward environment, however, God himself keeps covenant love unbroken. It was so that the prophet understood this passage when, in the depths of the Exile, he remembered God's constancy. It is "like the days of Noah," the prophet declared. As God swore then that the waters "should no more go over the earth," he has sworn steadfastness in his dealings with his burdened people (Isa. 54:9).

> For the mountains may depart
>   and the hills be removed,
> but my steadfast love shall not depart
>   from you (Isa. 54:10).

A part of the covenant-making process is some outward sign by which the pact is continually renewed. The covenant with Abraham is signed by circumcision, the Sinai covenant by Passover, the new covenant with Christ by the Lord's Supper. Fittingly this covenant with the whole earth has a cosmic sign, the bow set in the clouds, which stands as a perpetual call to worship and covenant faithfulness.

> See the rainbow and praise its maker,
>   so superbly beautiful in its splendour.
> Across the sky it forms a glorious arc
>   drawn by the hands of the Most High
>   (Ecclesiasticus 43:11-13 JB).

Such a call to praise we can understand. The biblical writer sees it as more, however; it is God's everlasting reminder *to himself* that he has promised such love that nothing "in all creation will be able to separate us from the love of God in Christ Jesus our Lord" (Rom. 8:39).

Jesus Versus Official Religion
Acts 4:8, 10-13, 18-20

Conflict between official religion and the living Spirit of Jesus Christ, running through this passage, is dramatically concentrated in one telltale sentence. Its subject, "they," refers to the "rulers of the people and elders" (vs. 8)—the reigning hierarchy of official religion—whom Peter was addressing. "Now as they observed the boldness of Peter and John, and noted that they were untrained laymen, they began to wonder, then recognized them as former companions of Jesus" (vs. 13 NEB). There we have the elements of the struggle: respectable official religion confronted by "uneducated, common men" (RSV), "untrained laymen" who have been "companions of Jesus." This sets no premium on ignorance. It warrants no hasty assumption that "untrained laymen" are always saints, or ecclesiastics always devils. It does sound warning that the institutionalizing process creates tension with the living Spirit of Christ.

Peter and John made the issue painfully clear. "Whether it is right in the sight of God to listen to you rather than to God, you must judge; for we cannot but speak of what we have seen and heard" (vss. 19-20). "The irony, sarcasm, and boldness of this reply, addressed to a religious group, the religious rulers of the nation, cannot be exaggerated." [6] Interpreting God's will was their profession! How could these "untrained laymen" dare to challenge them at this central point?

Yet the issue keeps emerging. When a minister lent religious sanction to proposals of hotheaded action in the *Pueblo* incident, it was an untrained layman, newspaper columnist Mike Royko, who made the apt response:

If I understood him correctly, he said God wanted us to get into a war with North Korea to free the Pueblo crew, an act that surely would have resulted in the entire Pueblo crew being killed, leaving us with dead crewmen and a big war in which a lot more people would be getting killed. Maybe Mr. Lindstrom is correct about what God wanted. But if he is, I'm sure happy that God tells these things to Mr. Lindstrom, and not to the Pentagon. [7]

That was a prophetic word from a lay quarter, full of the apostles' scorn of sail-trimming relativities. "We cannot but speak of what we have seen and heard."

If you cannot refute the gospel, silence it! (vs. 18). This is still the strategy of those who would end the proclamation of social implications of God's love for *all* his children. Such voices of "official religion" frequently rise from the more comfortably upholstered pews, pressing the old demand that ministers or church body preach a "spiritual" gospel and let the "political" issues of economic affairs and human rights alone.

Peter and John denied the truth of such a distinction. "Jesus Christ of Nazareth, whom *you* crucified, whom *God* raised from the dead, by him *this*

---

[6] Grant, *Nelson's Bible Commentary*, VI, 431.
[7] *Chicago Daily News,* Jan. 1, 1969.

man is standing before you well" (vs. 10, italics added). "You crucified," "God raised," "this man standing"—faith's triangle makes the spiritual continuous with the practical. Jesus was crucified in no small part because he seemed to be a political threat: "If you release this man, you are not Caesar's friend" (John 19:12). His attitude toward power on the one hand and law on the other made him the victim of a political conflict between the Pharisees and Zealots. If he had peached a comfortably remote "spiritual" gospel, there would have been no crucifixion. But God raised him, and his continuing life got the apostles into trouble about such human rights as the healing of an obscure man and freedom of speech tested by an unpopular message.

"There is no other name under heaven given among men by which we must be saved" (vs. 12*b*), the apostles declared. In their culture, *name* was all but equivalent to *person*. To declare the man cured "by the name of Jesus" (vs. 10) was to pronounce him well "through the power of Jesus" (AT). "There is salvation in no one else" (vs. 12*a*) takes added meaning by noting that the Greek uses the definite article. "The salvation" thus refers to the anticipated well-being of a new messianic age, to which he leads us forward. Official religion cherishes settled answers that fit yesterday. Those who find "the salvation" in him are constantly plunged into new issues where, exposed to the dangers of their own fallibility, they must find new answers in obedient action under his guidance.

Christ's Commando Mission: Luke 10:1-11

"Carry no purse, no bag, no sandals," ran the orders, "and salute no one on the road" (vs. 4). Sent on a dangerous mission into hostile territory (vs. 3), they must not be cumbered with baggage. There was no time for the elaborate social amenities of the oriental "salute" on the road. They were to take potluck wherever they might be, with no pleasant "visiting around" to receive the favors of many hosts. Commandos behind enemy lines, they were to travel light and "eat off the country" (vss. 7-8).

The orders were given to "seventy others"—seventy-two, according to some early manuscripts—beyond the immediate circle of the twelve (vs. 1). Luke seems to see in the story an indication of the church's world mission. The traditional seventy-two nations of the world (Gen. 10) or the seventy elders who assisted Moses (Exod. 24:1; Num. 11:16-29) suggest a symbolic association that may have been in his mind, pointing to the wider structure of the Church reaching out to all nations.

Jesus sent them "into every town and place where he himself was about to come" (vs. 1). His messangers do not take Christ to the world; they prepare men to respond to the Christ who, of his own volition and power, comes among them. We who believe that Christ brings the fullest life are under continuing imperative to share in preparing men for his coming. What we need, others need. To withhold it is either to confess that he brings us no indispensable blessing that other men might need, or to refuse obedience to his command. As James Denney once said, "Some people do not believe in missions. They have no right to believe in missions: they do not believe in Christ." [8]

[8] Jones, *Our Mission Today*, p. 42.

"The harvest . . . plentiful, the laborers . . . few," we are called to pray that God will "send out laborers" (vs. 2). Reference to abundant harvest reflected no passing euphoria on a day of transient success. Jesus applied the term to crowds "harassed and helpless, like sheep without a shepherd" (Matt. 9:36). He spoke it of the response made by a Samaritan village (John 4:35). Not passing popularity, but urgent need, called forth these words. Jesus declares that God is at work, his kingdom near both to those who respond and to those who do not (vss. 9-11). Responsive men are needed to work in the harvest.

They carry a salutation of peace. "Peace be to this house!" (vs. 5) was a traditional salutation (Judges 19:20). Peace *(shalom)*, meaning harmony, order, welfare, health, was a primary characteristic of the expected messianic kingdom. Yet Jesus foresaw that men might reject it. In that case, he said, "it shall return to you." Not losing our peace when others trample upon it, we are to take it back into ourselves.

To heal the sick and proclaim the kingdom are, according to these orders, parts of the same act (vs. 9). Unless we *do* for men's ills all that we can, there is no valid message of good will to *proclaim*. But unless we *proclaim* the message, men will not understand what we *do*. The Church is called to plant hospitals and medical ministries, keep health and healing related to its prayer, and concern itself with such sicknesses of society as contemporary anger, anomie, and alienation.

Men are defeated by the specialties and mechanizations of technological society.

Engulfed in impersonal masses, many rendered superfluous, they feel angry as they sense a twofold loss of utility (i.e., of functional neededness and ability) and identity (i.e., of the self-recognition that dies without social recognition) . . . . Next comes anomie—apathy, listlessness, indifference—in which value interests or concerns are dropped as false and futile hopes . . . . Apathy follows anger because anger is too intense to tolerate very long . . . . They often end in actual alienation. Consciously or unconsciously, the victims of technology and magnitude go on to *withdrawal.*[9]

Such maladies underlie much of the social upheaval of our time. As Christians we are called to the struggle to heal.

There is a parting word. Even when the message is rejected we can say, "Nevertheless . . . the kingdom of God has come near" (vs. 11). It depends on no man's subjective evaluation. The God of the kingdom *rules;* he does not supplicate an electorate for votes.

THIRD SUNDAY AFTER PENTECOST

Hound of Heaven: Genesis 28:10-22

"Surely the Lord is in this place; and I did not know it" (vs. 16). In this exclamation, following the vision in his dream, Jacob told the story of his life.

---

[9] Joseph Fletcher, *Moral Responsibility* (Philadelphia: Westminster Press, 1967), pp. 225-26.

God was at work at every major turning point, not because of Jacob's cooperation but in spite of his resistance. Like Francis Thompson's "Hound of Heaven," he pursued him into all hiding places with the relentless tread of a disturbed conscience or with the haunting impact of plans rerouted over unexpected detours, only in the end to reveal himself as Jacob's one true Friend.

Perhaps it is the story of our life, too. The accounts of the patriarchs in Genesis were not set down simply as entertaining or edifying stories. They were not recorded as history for history's sake. They were a part of Israel's attempt to understand her own life. These are our forebears, the tradition was saying. This is the rock from which we were hewn. These are the kind of people and experiences from which we sprang. This is who we are. Jacob's record affirms: we have known God not because we were good people in quest of him, but despite the fact that we were shrewd, evasive people avoiding him. Over and over again our record, too, has been gathered up in Jacob's exclamation, "Surely the Lord is in this place; and I did not know it."

When "Jacob left Beer-sheba, and went toward Haran" (vs. 10), he was a fugitive from his brother's wrath evoked by his own scheming fraud. Esau's birthright and patriarchal blessing had fallen to Jacob's grasping dishonesty. Before the story closes, in another game of wits, Jacob will have outschemed the crafty Laban. His hand against his brother men, his heart at odds with God, he is not, however, beyond God's reach. The Lord of history can work even through unworthy persons and unsavory situations, turning outcomes to his own purposes. "God's guiding hand, though half-hidden, is nonetheless present." [10]

When "he dreamed that there was a ladder set up on the earth, and the top of it reached to heaven; and behold, the angels of God were ascending and descending on it" (vs. 12), God was reaching him through the voice of the suppressed good. In a memorable sermon based on this passage, Lynn Harold Hough asked,

have not the Freudians told us that dreams are the ghosts of inhibited desires; that the indulgence for which we crave, but to which we will not surrender, like the ghost of Hamlet's father, will not rest, but comes marching into our dreams, and prepares from the fortress of the subconscious to storm our lines of resistance and to beat them down at last? . . . That is only half the story. An inhibited desire for goodness will behave in just the same way. The goodness we have desired but have not admitted to a place of command in our lives will come back to haunt us in imperishable dreams. [11]

Picturing the rearing which planted in Jacob visions of something better than his crafty duplicity, despite which he went his own self-aggrandizing way, Hough continued: "At last Jacob finds himself alone, away from the temptation to selfish double-dealing, and in the silence and loneliness of the night in the wilderness, the idealism which he has so long ignored, the piety which he has so long inhibited, breaks out to haunt his very dreams." Though the an-

[10] L. Hicks, article on "Jacob," *Interpreter's Dictionary of the Bible*, II, 786.
[11] Lynn Harold Hough, *Imperishable Dreams* (Nashville: Abingdon Press, 1929), pp. 14, 15.

cient writer probably had in mind no such psychological analysis, it does help us to understand one of God's ways of reaching us despite our evasion and flight.

Vowing fealty in exchange for God's favors (vss. 20-22), Jacob had to deal ultimately with God's intention to do unexpected things with him. God plays no favorites. For only one purpose would he call the people who were to descend from Jacob: that "by you and your descendants shall all the families of the earth bless themselves" (vs. 14). Thus to the self-seeking Jacob, God renewed the covenant he had made with Abraham. He would make of this family a people whom he would use for a witness to all mankind. Not until Jacob was so broken that he limped and so changed that Jacob "the Supplanter" (Gen. 27:36) became Israel who "persevered with God" (Gen. 32), could the promise be fulfilled. To Jacob, as to us, it happened not because he was good, but because God's grace prevailed in the tangled but strangely guided web of events.

So the Church Had Peace: Acts 9:22, 26-31

"So the church throughout all Judea and Galilee and Samaria had peace and was built up" (vs. 31a). Strange peace! The Hellenists plotting the death of Paul (vss. 28-30) hope to silence him as they have silenced the troublesome Stephen. This announcement of "peace" concluded the first major section of the Acts. What has gone before? A tale of leaders preaching under threat of death, of the duplicity and discipline of Ananias and Sapphira, of the martyrdom of Stephen, of Paul's stormy conversion and early ministry, and of the plot against him. Such peace offers no such safety and freedom from controversy as we fondly long for. The church prospered under hurricane conditions. "So the church had peace . . . and was built up." Strange logic! Trouble everywhere; so the church had peace! What guidelines does this offer for the church in our time?

For one thing, the harassed church stood resolutely on its faith and message "that Jesus was the Christ" (vs. 22). This phrase or its near equivalent is a recurring summary of the message of these early preachers (Acts 2:36; 18:5, 28). It sets a vital view of the Incarnation in corrective contrast with all vague incarnationism that talks vapidly of God's emptying himself into humanity. Jesus, historic personality whose mind, teaching, life, death, resurrection, and continuing influence give sharp definition to his meaning, is the locus of the Incarnation. The Christ is no undefined generality, no mystical spirit; he is a presence and a standard: "*Jesus* is the Christ." This was Peter's message at Pentecost. It was Paul's message. It is the continuing message of the Church wherever it has vitality.

As a second factor in the Church's strange ability to have peace in the midst of storm, to be built up under attack, consider the great brotherhood exemplified by Barnabas. The little Christian community had ample reason to fear Saul (vs. 26). Barnabas, however, laid his own influence on the line, taking the terrifying convert in hand and vouching for his new life and usefulness in Christ (vs. 27). Barnabas lived up to the meaning of his name, "Son of Consolation" (KJV) or, in the RSV translation, "Son of encouragement" (4:36-37). It was he who began the practice of putting one's material resources at the disposal of the community (4:37), he who became a trusted emissary of the church (11:22-24), he whose leadership in the congregation at Antioch gave his name first place in the roster of its prophets and teachers (13:1). Not content to leave Saul unshepherded in Tarsus, Barnabas went to look for him and took him to share his home and his work in Antioch (11: 22-26).

When relief was to be sent to the impoverished Christians at Jerusalem, it was Barnabas and Saul whom the Christians of Antioch trusted for the mission. Leader of the early missionary undertakings, Barnabas is named first in the "Barnabas and Saul" team. When John Mark failed on the first mission, it was Barnabas who gave him another chance (15:39). "Son of encouragement," he is the patron saint of those who find and advance others who later outshine them and who, in the process, immeasurably advance the cause of good and of God in the world. It was this man who took Saul "by the hand" (vs. 27 NEB, TCNT, and PT) and won for him a hearing. A church shepherded by such great souls who spread brotherhood around them can have peace even amid storms.

Given these factors, a third follows—courageous faith that takes the tests in stride, "walking in the fear of the Lord and in the comfort the Holy Spirit" (vs. 31). That a period of several years can be summarized in these stark items testifies to the centrality of this courageous faith that rode out the storm.

When High Religion Fails: John 3:4-17

Nicodemus exemplifies high religion. He had come for serious religious talk, addressing Jesus with great respect, confident that he had displayed supernatural powers (vss. 1-2). Almost shockingly Jesus replied with a demand for a completely new life (vs. 3), as if to say: Good as your high religion may be, we need to cut through all this to something far more central. Religion is something *you do*; what you need is a new birth which *God gives*. "Unless one is born anew, he cannot see the kingdom of God" (vs. 3).

John's Gospel carries much of its message through conversations between Jesus and people selected as representative types. Nicodemus is one. High-minded, disciplined, deeply religious, he represents the Judaism of Jesus' day at its best. It is quite possible that the first century brought forth many such half-converts. What makes Nicodemus interesting to us now, however, is that his type of self-sufficient good man, trusting some code as sufficient guide for life, is still with us. Seeing in Jesus an admirable teacher, he is astonished at any suggestion that a little more enlightenment is not enough.

Jesus declares it is new birth that admits a man to authenticity of personal being. The "kingdom" or rule of God, comes to those "born of water and the Spirit" (vs. 5). "A teacher of Israel" (vs. 10), at home in the Old Testament, would understand this, remembering such words as, "I will sprinkle clean water upon you, and you shall be clean from all your uncleanness, and from all your idols I will cleanse you" (Ezek. 36:25). The break with a defiled past is God's act of grace, not our achievement. New life in

Christ turns us from striving "to be somebody" by our own acts, to the simplicity of God's children living in humble gratitude for his love.

With a pun on the word *pneuma* (Greek for both *wind* and *spirit*) Jesus suggests that the new life is born of the Spirit as mysteriously as the blowing of the wind. It is no doing of our own. Trained in the Old Testament, Nicodemus would find rich associations to add depth to the play on words. He might have recalled: "As you do not know how the spirit comes to the bones in the womb of a woman with child, so you do not know the work of God who makes everything" (Eccles. 11:5). What this suggests concerning the mystery of our creation, Jesus now applies to the new creation which God works in those who live by faith.

When Nicodemus continues to press the question, "How?" (vs. 9), Jesus replies in the plural, "You all reject our testimony" (NEB). How do we receive the new birth? By humble acceptance of God's gift (a) as reported from experience (vss. 11-12) and (b) as presented in the lifting up of Christ (vss. 13-15). "We"—the plural suggests not only Jesus but all who have found the new life through faith—"bear witness to what we have seen." No armchair theory, this rebirth is the experience of many who have been given "the new being" in Christ. It comes when Christ is "lifted up"—as on the cross.

Wilderness legend told of Moses setting up a bronze serpent to which the people looked and were delivered from the venomous snakes which infested the area, their lives being thus saved (Num. 21:9). The Wisdom of Solomon (16:5-7), recounting the incident, emphasizes that this should not be seen as primitive magic but as God's act of grace to those who have faith. "For," it concludes, "he that turned toward it was not saved because of that which was beheld, but because of thee, the Saviour of all" (KJV). Jesus, John is saying, is similarly lifted up on the cross, as the revealing sign of God's saving love.

The passage concludes with John's own meditation on the meaning of all this: To those who respond in faith to God's love he gives new, authentic being, possessing the quality of the eternal (vss. 16-17). God "*loved* the world"; the verb is in the aorist tense, signifying an *act* of love done once for all in the gift of his "only Son," who belonged to him with closeness no other could share. The whole world is included in this love. Three times in one sentence (vs. 17) "the world" is named. God loved it, gave his Son for it, saved it. It is precious, not in its own right, but as the object of God's love and the field of his creative and redeeming action. Salvation is his gift of new being in Christ.

FOURTH SUNDAY AFTER PENTECOST

Does God Act in History? Genesis 45:4-11

This dramatic climax of the Joseph saga throws light on one of our most pressing questions. Does God work in history? Amid the horrors of our time the query grows insistent. If God moves in events, when they contradict all that he stands for, what can he be doing?

Many dismiss the question as a diversion of energy from necessary struggle against evil. Studs Terkel interviewed one such man, a Chicago laborer, who said:

Give Christianity a rest and God a rest and teach man he's living in a world that belongs to him, and he's only going to get out of the world what he puts into it. Teach man that in order to stand he's got to stand on the two feet the good Lord gave him and not use the Lord as a third foot or a third hand: "What I can't do, oh Lord, you will do for me. Or help me do." [12]

The question cannot be so easily dismissed. For it is in essence the necessary question whether life has meaning. Is there purpose in life? Is there hope that our struggles can come to some ultimate good? Such inquiry does not evade effort; it sustains it.

Joseph's brothers had sold him into slavery. A slave, he had suffered hot temptation and cold vindictiveness, had been unjustly imprisoned, and at last had come to amazing eminence. Finally confronting his brothers again, he offered magnanimous forgiveness. "Do not be distressed, or angry with yourselves, because you sold me here," he said; "for God sent me before you to preserve life . . . . So it was not you who sent me here, but God" (vss. 5, 8). Thus he declared his faith as he looked back on the dark journey. It had not always been easy to see what God was doing. Yet in retrospect, what he had sturdily trusted by faith became a certainty. God does work in the mysterious interplay between his divine will and rebellious human acts. We have our part to play, but we are never deserted by him who works in unseen ways.

In ways surprising to us, he weaves his will into our affairs. Providence is not a process of miraculous exemption from the human struggle. That would make prayer the travesty which Reinhold Niebuhr once branded as lobbying for special favors in the courts of the Almighty. Providence works through dependable regularities in an orderly universe. Faith responds in disciplined obedience.

In Joseph's pilgimage, God wove his design in interaction with human acts. There were dark motives and darker deeds: Joseph's adolescent arrogance, his brothers' jealousy and crafty revenge, the attempts of Potiphar's wife to seduce him, his response in integrity, her sordid accusations, the ensuing miscarriage of justice. Who can believe that God intended such evil? Yet in it all Joseph found opportunities to obey. From it all came the call to crucial national responsibility. Looking back in faith, Joseph could say: "So it was not you who you who sent me here, but God." In a final dramatic scene, Joseph sums up the interaction: "You meant evil against me; but God meant it for good, to bring it about that many people should be kept alive" (50:20).

Interacting thus, God called a servant people through whom he advanced his purpose for the world. As the stories of the patriarchs reflect Israel's search for self-understanding, Joseph's saga provides a vital link. "God sent me before you to preserve life"—here is the key truth that God

[12] Studs Terkel, *Division Street: America* (New York: Random House, 1967), p. 126.

calls men not to privilege but to responsibility. He called Israel as a people set apart for costly witness, through whom all the peoples of the earth would be blessed. The martyred Bonhoeffer testified, "When God calls a man, he bids him come and die." No call to forsake the world in churchly separation, Joseph's call demanded that he help to save an agrarian economy and avert a famine. God calls us, not out of the world's daily work but into it.

God works in history through persons. Through Joseph he worked in a slave who sought his master's welfare; in a youth who held faith firmly in pagan surroundings; in a man who, when wronged, protected the good name of his temptress, when imprisoned helped his fellow prisoners, and when elevated relieved the suffering of his society. God moved amid the confusion as guide and in the suffering as One who shared the pain and knew how to use it.

What this story begins, Christ completes. "Do not be distressed, or angry with yourselves, because you sent me here," said Joseph. Christ completes that: "Father, forgive them; for they know not what they do" (Luke 23:34). "God sent me before you to preserve life," Joseph declared. Christ completes that: "God sent the Son into the world, . . . that the world might be saved through him" (John 3:17).

God Unbound by Custom: Acts 15:1, 6-11

Hinging on the issue joined between "the custom of Moses" and the Holy Spirit breaking new ground, this passage portrays the God whom custom cannot bind.

Noting that the issue arose when "some men came down from Judea and were teaching the brethren" (vs. 1), Halford E. Luccock observed that

This conflict between the strict Jewish party at Jerusalem and in Judea and the more liberal and adventurous church at Antioch illustrates the eternal tension between the crowd at headquarters and the people in the field. . . . There was the inevitable struggle between rigid traditionalists and experimentalists. There was the clash between the Jewish and the Greek factions. But there was also the difference in point of view between the home base and the front line.[13]

Luccock cited instances of this tension in a variety of fields. It applies to the military: "An American journalist once said that the British generals tried hard for four years to lose the war but were frustrated by the common soldiers."[14] It applies to education: "The whole tendency of American institutions is to breed ten administrators to one real teacher."[15] It applies to churchmen:

We get a glimpse of another danger in the exclamation of Mandell Creighton on accepting the office of bishop of London: "I shall never have time to learn anything more." Bishop Creighton learned a lot more after becoming a bishop; so have many other bishops. But the foreboding he expressed does envisage clearly the liability of ecclesiastical headquarters.[16]

[13] Halford E. Luccock, *The Acts of the Apostles in Present-Day Preaching* (Chicago: Willett, Clark, 1939), II, 100.
[14] *Ibid.*, p. 101.
[15] *Ibid.*
[16] *Ibid.*, p. 102.

One need not join the headquarters elite to be trapped by "the headquarters mind." "The Organization Man" may be the merest dot at the bottom of the organization chart, but his yen to rise in the system hampers new outbreaks of the Spirit by the drag of "the custom of Moses." Peter's word here is addressed to us all.

In the crisis Peter continued his role at Pentecost, when the Spirit did a new thing. There he had been used as the conveyer of the Good News to pagans. By his vision at Joppa he had been led again to share the message with people once rejected as outsiders (Acts 10:1-48). On both occasions, the Spirit's presence had been evident in the ecstatic utterance of the Gentile believers, and in their new life. Of this, Peter reminded those who pitted old customs against the newly outbreaking Spirit (vss. 6-8).

"Why do you make trial of God?" he asked. The old customs—represented in a law with 365 "Thou shalt nots" and 248 "Thou shalts"—had been a yoke too heavy to bear. It was their stress on this law that Jesus denounced in the Pharisees: "They bind heavy burdens, hard to bear, and lay them on men's shoulders" (Matt. 23:4). Paul underscored it to the Galatians struggling with the same issue: "Do not submit again to a yoke of slavery" (Gal. 5:1). There is a better way: "We shall be saved through the grace of the Lord Jesus" (vs. 11).

The issue keeps recurring in new types of missionary adventure, in issues churned up by social turmoil, in each generation's "new theology," in explosive encounters of old customs with "new morality." As a distinguished British layman lamented at the World Conference on Church and Society, "We want to know from the theologians where is God at work in these dynamic forces and where is the devil at work?" Even the theologians are often puzzled! Nothing wears a halo of divine presence merely because it is new; yet investigation should begin with a clear perception that we deal with a God unbound by custom.

What Makes a Church? Matthew 16:13-19

"On this rock I will build my church" (vs. 18). What rock? The question has been debated long. Its significance is hard to overstate. For in the struggles to renew the Church we are lost without some clear answer to the question, "What *makes* a church?" When is the church true to its Lord's intention?

Climaxing the ministry in Galilee, pointing to the Jerusalem crisis and the Cross, this pivotal incident is the turning point of the gospel story. Much in Matthew's telling of it gives evidence of late theological elaboration of the earlier accounts (Mark 8:27-30; Luke 9:18-20). Mark and Luke refer neither to Peter and the keys of the kingdom, nor to Peter as the rock on which Christ would build his church. In them, Peter does not elaborate his simple statement, "You are the Christ," by adding "the Son of the living God." It is hard to believe that if Matthew's account had represented the earlier tradition, Mark and Luke would have suppressed sayings so sententious. Matthew rather elaborates the simpler early accounts.

It is significant that only with Matthew's ascription, "the Son of the living God," do we read, "on this rock I will build my church" (vs. 18). Where this faith is present the church exists; where it is wanting, we have an ethical, cultural, or religious society—something less than the Church of the Lord Jesus Christ.

This definitive faith is no inference from observed wonders. The disciples had been reporting popular impressions concerning Jesus (vs. 14), but these current "flesh and blood" rumors were not the basis of Peter's confession. To know God is to be encountered directly by the Father (vs. 17). To know any person hinges on admission to a personal I-Thou relation. To know God through Jesus is to be admitted to this direct insight.

Jesus' reply—"You are Peter, and on this rock I will build my church . . . . I will give you the keys of the kingdom of heaven" (vss. 18-19)—needs careful attention. Peter's name *meant* "rock," and Jesus' words play upon this double meaning. The debate as to whether the rock is *Peter* or Peter's *confession* is fruitless. Marvin R. Vincent's comment that "the church is built, not on *confessions*, but on *confessors*—living men," is true. Yet the either-or is too neat; the church is built on *both*. Peter is important, yet to build a hierarchical structure on this text is to read into it too much. One needs also to read other New Testament declarations: "For no other foundation can anyone lay than that which is laid, which is Jesus Christ" (I Cor. 3:11); "built upon the foundation of the apostles and prophets, Christ Jesus himself being the chief cornerstone" (Eph. 2:20).

"Whatever you prohibit on earth will be prohibited in heaven, and whatever you permit on earth will be permitted in heaven" (vs. 19 MT) is a reading closely paralleled by nearly all current translators. In Roman Catholic exegesis, the powers of "binding and loosing" include both discipline and doctrinal decision. In these, Peter's verdicts "and the pronouncements he makes will be ratified by God in heaven . . . ; these enduring promises hold good not only for Peter himself but also for Peter's successors" (JB note). Non-Roman exegesis, on the other hand, sees this as applying to Peter first in point of time, but passing to the collective authority of the apostles and the church. According to John 20:22-23, the resurrected Christ conferred this power on the assembled disciples. Concerning internal differences, Jesus made "the church," the assembled congregation, the ultimate arbiter (Matt. 18:17). In this connection he speaks the words concerning "binding and loosing" to the disciples (18:1-18). It is the glorified Christ himself who is finally represented as saying, "I died, and behold I am alive for evermore, and I have the keys of Death and Hades" (Rev. 1:18).

In the light of all this, what makes a church? Is it not faith's perception that Jesus is "the Christ, the Son of the living God," which issues in a forgiving fellowhip in which men accept the discipline and guidance of the Spirit-filled company? Defining its basis of membership, the World Council of Churches makes this the principle:

The World Council of Churches is a fellowship of Churches which confess the Lord Jesus Christ as God and Saviour according to the Scriptures and therefore seek to fulfil together their common calling to the glory of one God, Father, Son and Holy Spirit.[17]

[17] *The New Delhi Report,* pp. 37 ff.

FIFTH SUNDAY AFTER PENTECOST

Grace—and Guidelines: Exodus 20:1-20

Is there still authority in the Ten Commandments? Many minds are convinced that commands are now replaced by the principle that "What acts are right may depend on circumstances." Admitting the pull of circumstance on conscience, William Temple went on to say: "But there is an absolute obligation to will whatever may on each occasion be right." [18] Moreover, we are neither such geniuses of moral imagination nor such paragons of personal self-effacement, that—assaulted by the urgency of the situation and blinded by self-interest—we can improvise the "right." Contextual decisions still need guidelines.

In the Commandments, guidelines are given by grace. Scholars point out that these verses do not come from the usual strands of source material of the Pentateuch but are inserted here under the influence of the prophetic movement of the eighth century B.C. Prophetic, not legalistic, they embody insight into the nature of our relation to God. Their first word is a reminder of God's grace, "I am the Lord your God, who brought you out of the land of Egypt, out of the house of bondage" (vs. 2). As the story continues after the commandments, the people stand in trembling awe of God's mysterious holiness, and Moses reassures them, "Do not fear; for God has come to prove you, and that the fear of him may be before your eyes, that you may not sin" (vss. 18-20). There is an awesome demand in the divine dimension of life seen in the basic relationships to which the Commandments give structure. In them, however, God confronts us with grace, shown by his deliverance and call of his people. This grace is the basis of all right relation. It is never vague or amorphous. Leo Baeck, Jewish leader in Berlin during the Nazi terror, has a wise word for us:

There are two experiences of the human soul in which the meaning of life takes on for a man a vital significance: the experience of mystery, and the experience of commandment; or, as we may also put it, the knowledge of what is real and the knowledge of what is to be realized.

It is this experience of "mystery and commandment," he says, that preserves both our individual uniqueness and our relation to the world. "Whoever knows only mystery becomes merely unique and knows only the days of silence. Whoever knows only the tasks is only among men and knows only the days of work and the times of recess." [19] It is our sense of *both commandments and the awesome grace from which they come* that makes us fully formed persons with a valid relation to the world of men.

The first four commandments contain the basic guidelines for our relation to God (vss. 3-12). He lays upon his people the claim of his covenant that will admit no rival loyalty (vs. 3). All order proceeds from God. Laws that structure life show him in action. He is not to be worshiped in "graven

[18] Quoted by Fletcher, *Moral Responsibilty*, p. 76.
[19] Leo Baeck as quoted by Henry E. Horn, *The Christian in Modern Style* (Philadelphia: Fortress Press, 1968), p. 73.

images"—nor in systems or creeds or anything we have made as the guarantee that we can manipulate our own destinies or control his will (vss. 4-6). This extends to the Bible's horror of the deified state as the most terrible of idolatries, and to Jesus' warning that we cannot serve God and mammon (Matt. 6:24). Since the use of God's name implies a personal relation with him, we are forbidden to use it in cursing, or the reinforcing of our personal word, or in any other way in which we bring the Highest down to serve our own ends under our intended control (vs. 7). The sabbath is to be kept as a day of holy rest for reasons both theological (vs. 11) and socio-humanitarian (Deut. 5:14-15). Unrivaled commitment, refusal to let any earthly creation represent him, reverence for his name, and the keeping of a day for communion with him, serve as guidelines to right relation to God.

Between these four commandments and the five that structure human relations, the mandate to honor our parents provides a bridge (vs. 12).

The promise contained in the commandment indicates that the maintenance of the family is understood to relate to the promise of God: Israel is to be a holy people, faithful to the covenant, through whom God's purpose for mankind is to find fulfilment. Dishonoring of parents thus implies contempt for God's people and for his purpose through this people.[20]

Honor for tradition, as represented in the family and what is precious to it, keeps adventure into new times and experiences from degenerating into anarchy and aimlessness.

Human relations have their first guideline in reverence for life (vs. 13). Not only murder, but all killing is forbidden—a necessary reminder in a day of wholesale death by accident, mislabeling, and bad housing. The marriage relation is declared inviolable (vs. 14) inasmuch as God has purposed the unity of man and woman in marriage (Gen. 1:27; 2:18, 21, 24; I Cor. 6:15-17). Property rights are not to be transgressed (vs. 15), for a man's possessions are so truly an extension of himself that to steal what he owns is to violate his person. False testimony against any other with whom one deals is forbidden (vs. 16) as an offense against the unity of the community and the honor of the God of truth. Even to desire what belongs to another is proscribed (vs. 17) as divisive and shatters community solidarity by jealousy, and inner integrity by conflict between duty and desire.

Here, then, are clear, indispensable guidelines for life under grace.

Concluding that God Had Called
Acts 16:1-10

"Immediately we sought to go on into Macedonia, concluding that God had called us to preach the gospel to them" (vs. 10). Strange outcome from a series of baffling frustrations! At one point "forbidden by the Holy Spirit," at another "the Spirit of Jesus did not allow them" (vss. 6, 7); then, where it was least expected, "concluding that God had called." Would this be our response to like situations?

There was a more immediate explanation of the obstructions. The way

[20] W. J. Harrelson, article on "Ten Commandments," *Interpreter's Dictionary of the Bible*, IV, 571.

into Phrygia, Galatia, and Bithynia may have been blocked by the Jewish opposition these missionaries had earlier encountered in Galatia. Asia (vs. 6), thus closed to Paul, was a land of wealth and teeming populations, holding an important place at the western extremity of Asia Minor. Paul's heart seems to have been set on planting the gospel there. Yet, when factionalism barred the gates, he could so face it that his companion, Luke, wrote: "forbidden by the Holy Spirit . . . the Spirit of Jesus did not allow." Are even frustrating obstacles sometimes pointers to God's will?

After the series of frustrations of his purpose to "speak the word in Asia," Paul had a dream of a man from Macedonia inviting him. Suddenly all the perplexities of preceding days were crystallized. We might explain it as the subconscious breaking through after long pondering on a problem. Not so naïve as to quibble with our explanation of the *mechanism*, Paul would point beyond it to its *Source*, "concluding that God had called us." There is light here for our vexed question as to *how*, or *whether*, God calls.

The first paragraph of this lection (vss. 1-5) shows the care with which these God-guided men worked their way through tangled religious and ethical problems. Paul's circumcision of Timothy evokes varied responses from commentators. Some dismiss it as "a piece of garbled tradition," so at odds with Paul's known position as to be incredible in its present form. He did not require the circumcision of Titus the Greek (Gal. 2:3), and he sternly denounced the preaching of circumcision (Gal. 5:1-12). Others, noting these facts, suggest that although Paul would not sanction circumcision of converts from paganism, Timothy had a Jewish mother and was in the eyes of the law an Israelite.

Reared in the Jewish tradition (II Tim. 3:15), he had not yet fulfilled a demand of his earlier life. Though the gospel did not require circumcision, the rite was a part of his reconciliation with the past from which he had come. Still others see in this act a preparation of Timothy for the missionary work on which he was embarking. Working chiefly in the synagogues as a base of operation, a son of Jewish parentage would get no hearing there unless he had fulfilled this elementary demand of the law.

Is this a specific example of Paul's Christian self-discipline? Free to "love God and then do as he pleases," he was not free to offend the tender conscience of any whose scruples would be violated. They would see in his conduct a witness to anarchy, not true freedom. As these missionaries traveled, "they delivered to them for observance the decisions which had been reached by the apostles and elders who were at Jerusalem" (vs. 4). One decision (Acts 15) had to do with this question of circumcision. The council had concluded that they should "lay upon you no greater burden than these necessary things: that you abstain from what has been sacrificed to idols and from blood and from what is strangled and from unchastity" (15:28-29). Thus the principle seems to have been that, in the case of a man of Jewish background going among Jews, they would not assert their freedom at the cost of others' consciences; but that in the confrontation with paganism there could be no compromise with irreverence or impurity. Respectful toward conscience, adamant before pagan practices, this is a long way from standardless religion-in-general.

Out of Badness: Luke 19:1-10

Willie Stark, the political boss in Robert Penn Warren's *All the King's Men,* makes an astute observation about another of the characters. The man had inherited a fortune. But, Stark said, he wanted something nobody can inherit:

"Goodness. Yeah, just plain, simple goodness. Well you can't inherit that from anybody. You got to make it, Doc. If you want it. And you got to make it out of badness. Badness. And you know why, Doc? . . . Because there isn't anything else to make it out of." [21]

In another conversation, Stark declares that although he has built his career on political blackmail, he has never framed anybody. "Because," he explains, "it ain't ever necessary. You don't ever have to frame anybody, because the truth is always sufficient." Accused of taking too low a view of human nature, he responds, "I went to a Presbyterian Sunday school back in the days when they still had some theology, and that much of it stuck. And . . . I have found it very valuable." [22]
Willie Stark's tragedy was not that what he learned and valued was false. Rather he had absorbed the theological *problem* without glimpsing the *solution.* There *is* nothing but "badness" to make goodness of. There *is* enough dark truth about any man to undo him. Zacchaeus, in this brief passage, fits that description of our predicament. Not until something from outside himself happens to Zacchaeus can he make goodness "out of badness." There was hope for Zacchaeus—there might have been hope for Willie Stark—in the great good news that "the Son of man came to seek and to save the lost" (vs. 10).
Jesus' mission was to the lost—to those who had nothing but badness as raw material (Matt. 10:6; 15:24; 18:12-14; Luke 15:3-10). Salvation for sinners rather than for those who were conspicuously "righteous" was the most distinctive thing about his ministry. When he said, "Your faith has saved you," it was equivalent to saying, "Your sins are forgiven" (Luke 7:48-50). Repentance and amendment of one's ways were essential, but they came not as the *price* which *purchased* forgiveness; they evidenced *acceptance* of forgiveness already given.
Zacchaeus the rich tax collector was obviously wrong. He profited, as do we, from the injustice of the system to which he belonged. But he had other hungers. "He sought to see who Jesus was" (vs. 3), "what Jesus was like" (TCNT), "what kind of man Jesus was" (JB). He wanted to know Jesus. Amid our complicity in wrong, we can share that concern.
Though Zacchaeus did not know Jesus, Jesus knew *him*—even as he "finds" us, "speaks to our condition." Concerned with people, perhaps knowing Zacchaeus' reputation, Jesus quickly recognized him and entered his life with loving acceptance (vss. 4-6). Zacchaeus "received him joyfully." In Paul Tillich's meaningful term he accepted the fact that he was accepted.

[21] Robert Penn Warren, *All the King's Men* (New York: The Modern Library), p. 272.
[22] *Ibid.,* p. 358.

In contrast to the religion of the time, Jesus presented salvation as the gift of God. Pharisaic religion, and much other teaching of the period—as, for instance, that of the community of Qumran—insisted that we must first be righteous and so *earn* our salvation. This, however, was a perversion of the high insight of the Old Testament that Israel was saved because God is righteous, not because Israel was (Deut. 9:4-6). Salvation "is not something that is deduced from the character of God as this has been philosophically discerned; it is the fact from which the people of God deduce his character of love." [23] For those saved from Egyptian bondage and for all subsequent generations, the experience of God's saving love came first. Liberation from false standards and outlooks that tangle us in a meaningless existence always precedes the theology that explains it. God accepts us as we are. Responding, we accept the fact that we are accepted. The result, for us as for Zacchaeus, can be a new life that now makes goodness out of badness (vss. 8-10).

SIXTH SUNDAY AFTER PENTECOST

Transfer of Power
Numbers 27:12-14a, 15-20, 22-23

This account of the orderly transfer of power and leadership from Moses to Joshua speaks of three significant and perennial realities.

The first is the cost of human self-vindication, even in God-given leaders. God had decreed (Deut. 1:37) that none of the disobedient wilderness generation, including Moses, should inherit the good land promised to the fathers. The explanation offered by this source deals with the incident (Exod. 17:1-7, Num. 20:2-13) in which the wandering Israelites rebelled against Moses, and by implication against the Lord whose guidance Moses expressed. As they traveled through waterless desert, Moses, at God's command, struck the rock with his staff and a spring gushed forth. But, according to the Numbers account, he acted in self-vindication and anger against the people. Not interpreting the event as a gift of the Lord, he received God's judgment that he should not complete the mission to the promised land. Legendary as this material may be, it interprets one tragic strand of the human predicament: our defensiveness, determined to vindicate ourselves, blocks the fulfillment of our best.

The account speaks, again, of the delay of God's intentions by the rebellion and doubt of his people. What appears to be a bit of geographical detail (vs. 14b) in the parenthetic sentence omitted from the lection may carry deeper implications. In Hebrew, Meribah means "to strive or contend," or it may mean "Waters of Quarrel" (Numbers 20:13, TMT note). In another reference, TMT translates: "The place was called Massah (i.e. 'Trial') and Meribah (i.e. 'Quarrel'), because the Israelites quarreled and because they tried the Lord, saying, 'Is the Lord present among us or not?'" (Exod. 17:7 TMT). Legendary though the tradition may be, it reflects our

[23] Alan Richardson, article on "Salvation," *Interpreter's Dictionary of the Bible*, IV, 172.

persistent experience of great movements delayed by quarreling and doubt. How often quarrels within the church have wounded faith and blocked the advance of the gospel in ways more deadly than attacks from without could ever be!

The account speaks, finally, of the persistence of God in effecting his purpose through the continuity by which he leads his people. Moses prayed that a leader might be given "who shall conduct all their affairs for them and who shall lead them in all matters and whom they shall follow in all matters" (vs. 17 TMT note). Joshua was singled out as "a man in whom is the spirit" (vs. 18), "an inspired man" (TMT), and invested with some of the "authority" of Moses, after being commissioned by Moses in the presence of the priest and the assembled community. (See Deut. 31:1-8, 23 for the Deuteronomist's interpretation of this commissioning speech.) Thus, by God's command, the orderly transfer of leadership of the people was effected, meeting a necessity permanently embedded in the realities of social and ecclesiastical affairs. God's concern, not limited to lofty "spiritual" considerations, continually touches such mundane affairs of our earthbound life.

This scene presents the needed leader as a shepherd of his people. Long afterward, Jesus would see the people as Moses here feared they might be, "harassed and helpless, like sheep without a shepherd" (Matt. 9:36). Their need laid a call upon him: seeing them shepherdless, he spoke of the waiting "harvest." For he comes to meet this need, the one leader who accepts a cross without defensive efforts at self-vindication; whose sacrificial love heals our rebellious quarrels; who, as our eternal contemporary, anticipates the issues and problems of every age and amid all changes of leadership remains our dependable "shepherd."

Faith Open to the Moment
Acts 18:24–19:6

Thomas J. J. Altizer has spoken helpfully of our need of "faith open to the moment." We must "either speak to the moment," he urges, "or exist in silence." In this scene from the Acts of the Apostles we see the Christian faith, at a pivotal turning point, making exactly this decision. "When Paul had laid his hands upon them, the Holy Spirit came on them; and they spoke with tongues and prophesied" (19:6). The ecstatic joy—"they spoke with tongues"—erupted from the sense of complete fulfillment of all that they had yearned to be, the fresh insight into the meaning of their tangled lives, the release from the old frustrations born of trying to save themselves by moral resolution, the fresh access of power to face the living moment. Christian faith has known these gifts as the experience of the Holy Spirit. Such a paradigm of authentic Christian experience is this that the faith is never true to itself unless it is living thus "open to the moment."

This truth is highlighted against the background of another approach to the religious life. Apollos, in this story, "knew only the baptism of John" (18:25; 19:3). That, as Paul reminded them, was a "baptism of repentance" (19:4)—good as far as it went, but dealing only with *things they did,* unaware of *what God could do for them.* To see themselves with the realism evoked by John's moral scrutiny was necessary. But, Paul reminded them, something else was equally vital. They must bring their faith to bear on the living moment. They must realize that the long expected is about to happen *now*. They must expect that at any moment God will do mighty things. Such immediacy was implicit in John's "telling the people to believe in the one who was to come after him, that is, Jesus" (19:4).

Such immediacy characterizes any vital use of the Bible. To precipitate a living faith, it must be allowed to step out of the historic past into the throbbing present. We must see in its episodes "the isness of the was." When we read it thus, the Pharisee holds the mirror to our self-righteousness, the paralytic portrays our own guilt as it cripples the person we might have been, the blind whom Jesus gave their sight are part and parcel of our unseeing ways, sinners reflect our brokenness and alienation. Reading thus, we say, "This is who I am." But Jesus enters the picture, and wondering, we add: "This is who I was meant to be. This is who, by God's grace, I can yet be."

We need more than the *example* of Jesus. We need his *Lordship*. In this story, Apollos is first found teaching "accurately the things concerning Jesus, though he knew only the baptism of John" (18:25). That is, he had the story of the doings of the man Jesus, but no message that through him a new life begins. When Priscilla and Aquila had instructed him more fully, he began "showing by the scriptures that the Christ was Jesus" (18:28); i.e., in Jesus, whose story Apollos could tell eloquently (18:24), they met the present experience of him who brings the new Age.

New life breaks out in him. God's presence is no vague mystical experience. It is encountered through Jesus, whose known deeds portray God's visible and definable character. God is incarnated in *him*, not—as some careless popular theology would have it—in humanity. Incarnation in humanity leaves us with only our subjective intuitions as guides to the divine presence. The tragedy of the so-called "German Christians," the branch of the church which endorsed Nazi ideology, reveals how non-biblical intuitionism can betray us. A faith open to the moment, not content with generalized tributes to Jesus, keeps meeting him as the Christ who brings God's transforming touch.

Subjecting ourselves to the Lordship of Jesus, we are given fresh joy and insight, New Testament signs of the Holy Spirit's presence. Paul led the people beyond John's baptism of moral improvement to Jesus' baptism, in which we die with Christ and with him rise to new life (Rom. 6:1-10). "When Paul had laid his hands upon them, the Holy Spirit came on them" (19:6). They faced the living moment with ecstatic joy and released powers. The old self off their hands, their faith opening them to the new life God gives through Christ, they found clarity and fulfillment. Their story unfolds not a quaint glimpse of antiquity, but the living model of faith open to each new moment in which we live.

Life to the Full: John 10:1-10

"I have come that they may have life and have it to the full" (vs. 10 MT). Jesus offers the gift of a new quality of existence. For the Synoptic Gospels it is "the kingdom of God"; for Paul, "salvation"; for Tillich, "the new being"; for Bultmann, "authentic existence." For John, it is "life," "eternal life," "life to the full." What specifics does this passage offer regarding that gift?

As these parables portray the shepherd, we shall miss the key if we base our interpretation on the romanticized figure of the Palestinian shepherd fondling woolly lambs. Jesus did not invent the figure, though he turned it to his own important use. Since it was already familiar in his day, we shall need to see the connotations it carried in his time. Those who heard it first would remember Ezekiel's contrast between false and true shepherds. The self-aggrandizing political leaders of his time he branded false shepherds. The coming messianic king would be the true shepherd (Ezek. 34:23-29; cf. comment on the Old Testament lesson for the Third Sunday after Easter). That Jesus' figure recalled such associations is suggested by the fact that immediately on the heels of these shepherd sayings, the people demanded, "If you are the Christ, tell us plainly" (vs. 24).

"All who came before me are thieves and robbers" (vs. 8). Who are these repudiated ones? It will not do to answer, as some have: "Such leaders as Confucius or the Buddha." No such contrast could have occurred to the first hearers of these words. Marcion was probably wrong in identifying the "thieves and robbers" with Pharisees, Moses, and John the Baptist. Such identification contradicts Jesus' attitudes toward Moses and John.

The Fourth Gospel may well reflect the abortive messianic uprisings under such aspiring "saviors" as Theudas and Judas the Galilean, recalled by Gamaliel in his famous speech to the council (Acts 5:33-39). Even before Jesus' time, such leaders had plunged the country into bloody revolt. In contrast with these whose political ambitions and martial methods brought death, Jesus and his movement of the Spirit brought abundant life. They were the "thieves and robbers," he the "good shepherd."

The Pharisees may have been included in the criticism. "Truly, truly, I say to you," the words with which this passage opens, are usually a way of emphasizing a strong point in a discussion already under way. Jesus has been in controversy with the Pharisees over the blind man restored to sight. To that discussion the conversation reverts following the shepherd parables (vs. 21). The Synoptics remember Jesus moved by the crowds who gathered around him like shepherdless sheep (Mark 6:34; Matt. 9:36), and the Pharisees with little care for the outcasts (Luke 15:1-2). To their callousness he responded with a shepherd parable (Luke 15:3-7). John, likewise, shows him responding to the Pharisees' insensitivity to the need of the recovered blind man, and their boast that *they* could see. In contrast with these, whose religion was more concerned with doctrines and rules than with needs of persons, Jesus and his movement of loving concern brought abundant life. They were "thieves and robbers," he the "good shepherd."

Three parables are packed into these few lines. The first (vss. 1-3a) shows that there is only one way to enter the sheepfold—the way of the true shepherd for whom the gate is opened. These violent messianic pretenders and rule-bound religious leaders have tried other ways with disastrous results. The second (vss. 3b-5) is reminiscent of Joshua. Like the shepherd, he "led them out." He was commissioned as one who "shall lead them out and bring them in; that the congregation of the Lord may not be as sheep which have no shepherd" (Num. 27:17). Jesus thought of his ministry in these terms

(Mark 6:34; Matt. 9:36). In his shepherd parables he spoke of the kind of close relation to individual need which he evidenced in his personal follow-up of the blind man (John 9:35-39). The third parable is his "I am the door" saying (vs. 9), of which F. C. Grant remarks that seeing the shepherd himself as lying across the gateless opening in the sheepfold wall, making his body the protector of the sheep, "is a modern exegetical fancy with little foundation." [24] The one point of the saying is that the door leads to salvation, found by passing "through" Jesus. Led in and out "through" him and his ways, we find life to the full.

SEVENTH SUNDAY AFTER PENTECOST

Grace Through Routine
Joshua 24:1-15, 24

Joshua's address hurls a vigorous challenge "to those who would like to keep grace uncontaminated with the ordinary routine of nature and history." [25] The Bible will stand for no such sterile separation, and of this Joshua's whole argument provides vivid evidence. Sermons and lessons on this passage almost inevitably zero in on Joshua's stirring challenge: "Choose this day whom you will serve . . . ; but as for me and my house, we will serve the Lord" (vs. 15). This thrilling rhetoric is all but meaningless, however, apart from the summary of God's action which precedes it. The strong *imperatives* of the summons to a verdict rest on the mighty *indicatives* of the historical argument of vss. 1-13. This is "recital theology" which sees God's hand in the choice, development, deliverance, and unfolding life of Israel. It epitomizes the core proclamation of the Old Testament seen in parallel professions of faith in Deut. 6:21-24; 26:5-9. As such, it brings the Hexateuch to a climactic conclusion.

Joshua made no such mistake as sometimes mires our evangelism in a bog of vague appeals to "choose the Lord" without saying *what* Lord we mean or what follows from the choice. He may well have been offering a share in the covenant to peoples who had not experienced the marvels of the Exodus or the trials of the desert. In doing so, he showed them the nature of the covenant relation to God by telling the story of events in which Israel had met grace through "ordinary routine" events "of nature and history."

He recalls, first, the beginnings of Israel's life in God's choice of Abraham and his gift of Isaac, and to Isaac, Jacob and Esau (vss. 1-4). How do we view the coming of pivotal leaders? The existentialist slogan, "Man makes himself," is a piece of human presumption. For the creative choices of which it boasts are rendered within the framework of life given by the evolutionary process, by biological inheritance, and by a multitude of influences that have played upon us. No man makes his decisions in free-wheeling isolation from these conditioning factors. The biblical pattern of call and response is far nearer the truth than the myth of self-made man ever can

[24] Grant, *Nelson's Bible Commentary, ad loc.*
[25] The phrase is borrowed from Miller, *Man the Believer,* p. 112.

be. The God we are called to choose is the God who works through these formative forces that made us.

Joshua recounts, second, the epic of liberation from Egyptian slavery (vss. 5-7). In this story the providential is still more evident. There need be no contradiction between such reading of events and our modern approach to phenomena as following canons of causality in a dependable order of nature. The coming of Moses, born of his racial genes, educated in the family of the Pharaoh, trained in the lore of the desert, summoned by a concerned conscience, motivated by courageous and creative faith, can be told as the saga of a man molded by the forces of "the ordinary routine of nature and history." This does not deny a simultaneous understanding of it as directed by the God of creation, redemption, and growth.

The deliverance at the Red Sea presents no conflict between the law-abiding and the providential. It is, rather, the action of providence through the orderly forces of nature. The Red Sea of this passage, historians are agreed, was more properly the Sea of Reeds (cf. JB, MT). Its exact location cannot be pinpointed, but all studies indicate one or another of the reedy lakes, Menzaleh, Timsah, or Sirbonis, in the general region of the present Gulf of Suez. The Israelites, helped by a strong east wind, could have crossed such a region on foot, but their pursuers' heavy chariots would have been bogged down in the soft mud and finally engulfed by the returning waters. This natural explanation does not diminish the historical creativity of the experience, which permitted the people to establish an independent life. Nothing about the natural event compels the acceptance of faith's interpretation, but neither does it make the faith-reading impossible. To quote Samuel H. Miller:

> In the Bible, God is revealed not through the sacred ceremony, but through the secular event. From Sinai to Capernaum, the grace of God moves through the world, not in spite of it. The doctrine of the Incarnation makes no sense if the sacred is separated from the secular. "The Word made flesh" is an offensive declaration to those who would like to keep grace uncontaminated with the ordinary routine of nature and history. In short, one may well declare, "I believe in the secular as the potential ground of the sacred." [26]

The God we are called to choose is the God who thus works through daily forces which we must use as faithful stewards because they are his.

Joshua reviews, finally, a condensed summary of the conquest of Canaan (vss. 8-13). As the biblical records continually point out, these victories were not the result of the numbers or prowess of the Israelites. This people was "the fewest of all the peoples" (Deut. 7:7). By what we might call "fortunate circumstances" Israel triumphed. Could it not also be true that through the circumstances God was at work to shape the future and to forge them into a people through whom he could reveal his ways of working?

The historian Arnold Toynbee has developed his view of such movements of history under the figures of challenge and response and the strengthening of an oppressed proletariat as the creative forces in the making of civilizations. Is this not a more reserved statement of what Israel saw in the

[26] *Ibid.*

imagery of faith: that, beyond this people's efforts, great things *had been done for* them? Is this not essential to any reading of history that does not lead either to the fatalistic undoing of the oppressed or to the self-destructive pride of the fortunate?

Joshua's covenant ceremony lays its permanent claim on faith. His call comes afresh to us. Its vital meaning, however, rests on the clarity with which we see the nature of God, who comes to us amid the secular demands of our life, bringing the gift of his grace.

Jesus and the Resurrection: Acts 17:21-31

The Athenian philosophers heard Paul preach on "Jesus and the resurrection"—and thought these were two foreign deities! (vss. 16-20). Some commentators belittle this speech on the ground that it appeals too much to the current Greek philosophies. They note that going from Athens to Corinth, Paul "decided to know nothing among you except Jesus Christ and him crucified" (I Cor. 2:2). As if that were a new idea when he went to Corinth! To argue thus is to be insensitive to the sweep of Paul's message at Athens, with its strong word on the Resurrection.

The Athens appeal was not the fiasco that such critics assume. It had its victories. Dionysius, Damaris, and others "joined him and believed" (vs. 34). Winning converts among the town fathers, philosophers, and intelligentsia of Athens was no small achievement! Paul's appeal, here as elsewhere, is the heart of the gospel: God has acted through Jesus who died and lives again; God continues to act through him, as he confronts us now. It was a message in head-on collision with their axiom, and ours:

> That no life lives forever;
> That dead men rise up never.[27]

But Christian witness builds on the reality of the living Lord and our encounter with him. Unless we are sure of that, we fumble with all other aspects of the Christian life.

Christ comes to us in our dealing with the new. The Athenians "spent their time in nothing except telling or hearing something new" (vs. 21), and so do we. Research is the air we breathe, new theories accompany every sunrise, new theologies appear as regularly as new car models. We need not decry the new. God's Word comes to us out of continuing conversation between inherited tradition and the mind of the age. He speaks to us at the moving front of experience.

Christ comes to us, as he did at Athens, in our quest of the unknown. They had erected an altar "to an unknown god," and Paul turned this wistful paganism to the service of the gospel, introducing Christ to them through the unknown (vs. 23). A new historical caution has convinced many of us that our sources concerning Jesus are so fully couched in the language of faith that it is now impossible to recover "the historical Jesus." Yet the living Christ is savingly real when we meet him as he is defined by the Jesus of the

[27] Algernon Charles Swinburne, "The Garden of Proserpine," from stanza 11.

gospels. That is not such a picture as scientific historians would create, but a Christ no less real, who made a vital difference in the lives of men who recorded the experiences that had been most crucial to them. The Christ who matters most is not a figure reconstructed *from* history; he is one who has made a telling impact *upon* history. That Christ we can know. From the gospel accounts we proceed to the question which must be faced in the midst of contested issues: What does he mean for my conduct *now, here?* In the midst of such unknowns he reveals himself to us.

Christ comes to us, as he did at Athens, in the reality of repentance. "The times of ignorance God overlooked," Paul declared, not condemning a paganism that had not heard the Gospel, "but now he commands all men everywhere to repent" (vs. 30). Some years ago an anthology of preaching appeared under the title, *Sermons to Intellectuals.* But there is no separate gospel for "intellectuals," there is only a gospel for *humans.* Paul was preaching a "sermon to intellectuals" at Athens. He tailored his *introduction* to their peculiar interests, but he aimed his *message* straight at the common human need: "God . . . commands all men everywhere to repent."

On Learning to Listen: Luke 8:4-15

"As he said this, he called out, 'He who has ears to hear, let him hear.' " (vs. 8*b*). It was his characteristic way, repeated often in the gospels, of calling attention to something of special importance (Matt. 11:15; 13:9; Mark 4:9, 23: 7:16; Luke 8:8; 14:35). We modern activists hurry quickly over the *listening*, that we may come more directly to the *doing.*

With all his concern about what we *do*, Jesus was sure it is important first to *hear.* This parable likens seed fallen on the hard soil of a path, or the thin soil over rock, or among thorns, or on good ground, to different kinds of hearing. Urgently Jesus presses us to hear, supporting the injunction with a principle: "Take heed then how you hear; for to him who has will more be given, and from him who has not, even what he thinks that he has will be taken away" (vs. 18). On the basis of what we have really heard we can understand more, and what we have failed to hear will leave our little stock of understanding to atrophy and diminish. Who can obey an order he has not heard? Or act on wisdom he has not learned? Or respond to a gospel he has not received?

In this passage we have a pattern found nowhere else in Jesus' teaching—a parable followed by an explanation which builds an allegory around the original story. Most scholarly opinion holds that the parable (vss. 4-8) comes directly from Jesus, while the allegory (vss. 9-15) embodies the substance of a sermon in the first-century church, using the parable as its text. Both speak significantly to us, but let us look first at the parable.

Without the allegory that follows, this little vignette would scarcely suggest a kind of hearing for every kind of soil. It is a basic principle of interpretation that we must seek the one unified point made by a parable, and in this one we would see a farmer working with all the difficulties of planting—yet reaping a harvest in spite of everything. This may have been the point Jesus originally made.

He was planting amid hazards. Doubts surrounded him. Powerful leaders opposed him. Many of those who had once followed fell away. Nevertheless, he declared, God would reap his harvest. Like a farmer who lost some seed one way and some another, he would not be defeated. In the speech of his day, harvest was a familiar metaphor for God's kingdom and judgment. The parable said that, no matter what got in the way, judgment and the kingdom were coming. God will act; men had better be ready! "He who has ears to hear, let him hear."

The early church homily applied the principle in the situation faced by embattled Christians. Despite all the seeming impossibilites of spreading the Word in that hostile world, it was saying, we witnesses are not responsible for what men do with the message. It is our task to *sow*; we can leave the harvest in the hands of God.

Along with this assurance, the homily gave warning: *hearing* the word is our business! But some of us are like the beaten path; much coming and going about a host of hurrying concerns makes it hard for the seed to sink in. Some of us are like rocky soil; we respond with a lush growth at first but give our Lord's leading no real root in our lives. Some of us are like thorny soil; "the cares and riches and pleasures of life" (vs. 14) choke out our discipleship. Which kind of hearing we offer him is crucial, for the hearvest is God's judgment. It is worth all it costs so to cultivate our receiving of the gospel that we become like the good soil, "those who, hearing the word, hold it fast in an honest and good heart, and bring forth fruit with patience" (vs. 15).

To our time the passage speaks with a ringing call. We are activists, and it reminds us that nothing we can *do* is of much importance unless in worship and prayer we take great pains to *hear*. We are discouraged in our witness by a "post-Christian" world that seems to be turning away from the gospel, and it reminds us we have only one task: to go on with our witness, leaving the outcome in the hands of God. We are absorbed by the preoccupations of the glittering secularism around us, and it reminds us that all this must not be allowed to turn us aside from a quiet and faithful receiving of God's good news.[28]

EIGHTH SUNDAY AFTER PENTECOST

Too Many for Victory
Judges 7:2-7, 19-22

"The Lord said to Gideon, 'The people with you are too many for me to give the Midianites into their hand, lest Israel vaunt themselves against me, saying, "My own hand has delivered me" ' " (vs. 2). Too many! To us strange, it was to Isreal the normal language of faith. Some victories can be won by numbers, but not the important, lasting ones. *They* are won by quiet forces through which the hand of God is at work. Beneath the strange amalgam of shrewdness and faith which constitutes this glimpse of Israel's remembered past, that truth lies embedded.

[28] Portions of this comment are adapted from a church school lesson contributed by the author in *The Adult Student*.

Annual Bedouin raids at harvest time had been depriving Israelite farmers of the fruit of their toil. Against these, at God's call, Gideon led his people in a war of defense, of which this lection tells the decisive battle.

The narrative combines two intertwined sources which tell of the reduction of the size of Gideon's army and of the strategically planned and tellingly executed attack. Thirty-two thousand men were too many, "lest Israel vaunt themselves" on their own prowess (vs. 2). At God's direction, Gideon released all the fainthearted who wished to turn back, twenty-two thousand in all (vs. 3). But the remaining ten thousand were still too many. God then directed a second test, by which all the men who knelt to drink at the brook were eliminated, and only those who scooped up water, to drink from their hands while they remained on their feet, were retained (vss. 4-7). Presumably the quality here prized was that of alert battle-readiness, though the story is less concerned with human qualities than with such reduction of numbers that it might be clear that the victory was of divine origin. After this second test, only three hundred men remained. With them the victory was won (vs. 8).

Creeping into the enemy camp by night and hearing the fearful talk of some of the warriors, Gideon devised a plan to exploit their potential panic. Dividing his remnant army into three companies posted around the enemy camp, he equipped his men with torches inside shielding jars, and with trumpets (vss. 9-18). On his signal, in the dead of night they sounded the trumpets and broke the jars. The sudden blare and clash were accompained by the flash of light as of a surrounding host, shouting, "A sword for the Lord and for Gideon!" (vss. 19-20). In frightened confusion, "every man's sword against his fellow," the enemy was put to rout (vss. 21-22).

The theme, too many for victory, is a central element in the Old Testament's "salvation history." Jeremiah made it explicit in his injunction:

Thus says the Lord: "Let not the wise man glory in his wisdom, let not the mighty man glory in his might, let not the rich man glory in his riches; but let him who glories glory in this, that he understands and knows me, that I am the Lord who practice kindness, justice, and righteousness in the earth; for in these things I delight, says the Lord" (Jer. 9:23-24).

Hezekiah appealed to it when he assured his people, cringing before the approach of Sennacherib, "With him is an arm of flesh; but with us is the Lord our God" (II Chron. 32:1-8). It was dramatized in the choice of David for kingship despite the impressiveness of his elder brothers who overshadowed him (I Sam. 16:1-13). The seemingly helpless shepherd boy then slew the giant champion of the enemy host (I Sam. 17:19-49).

It is a timeless theme. Martin Luther King's Freedom Movement was built upon it. Obscure people can find meaning in a purposeful struggle by means of it. The march from Selma to Montgomery in 1965 affords a memorable glimpse of such people:

One 65-year-old man, asked on the third day if he was hurting, replied, "I been hurtin' for sixty-five years. I can hurt one day more." A one-legged white man who could cover ground with his two crutches at a surprising speed, had a stock reply to those who questioned him about his condition. "I'm fine," he would reply, "but you look kinda tired!" Many local Negroes on the march wore shoes that were "hand-me-downs" and poorly fitting, or too cheaply built for a march of this sort. One 16-year-old girl finally had to carry her shoes in her hand. The miles of rough asphalt occasionally brought tears of pain trickling down her cheeks, but she went doggedly on.[29]

Such people exemplify Gideon's band in a new time. Their lives are dignified by the sense of participating in a struggle to which they make an important contribution but in which the final victory depends on the Lord.

Underscoring this theme, Paul wrote: "God chose what is foolish in the world to shame the wise, God chose what is weak in the world to shame the strong" (I Cor. 1:27).

Marching Orders for Mission
Acts 20:17-28, 32

"Take heed to yourselves and to all the flock, in which the Holy Spirit has made you guardians, to feed the church of the Lord which he obtained with his own blood" (vs. 28). The first missionary is finishing one of his most important addresses. Having learned how Paul preached to a Jewish audience (Acts 13) and to pagans (Acts 17), we now hear him speaking in the inner circle of the Church.

The setting lends impressiveness to the utterance. Racing against time to reach Jerusalem by Pentecost, Paul sailed down the coast of Asia Minor. He bypassed Ephesus, because to go there would be to risk delay by involvement with a beloved congregation. His bond of comradeship would put him under necessity of a stay he could ill afford. So he sent for the elders of the Ephesian church to meet him at the nearby port of Miletus. There, in terms similar to those of the letters to Timothy and Titus, he laid upon them the urgency of their pastoral responsibility, giving them their marching orders for mission.

Because the church has lived in perplexity about such problems as he deals with, his words are important to us. The Roman Catholic scholar, Pierre Charles, has described the changes in Protestant motivation for mission over a period of a century and a half. Near the end of the eighteenth century, he says, missionary endeavor was driven by the *fear of God*; because God is a righteous judge, and because non-Christian lands needed cleansing, mission was an inescapable demand. Half a century later, the motive had become that of the *love of God*, of which all men must be told. In the period of World War I, still another change sent missionaries out because of the *love of man*, to bind a fragmented world into one community. In the Cold War era, a fourth motive has appeared—the *fear of man*, which makes mission a bulwark against Communism in a world of potential revolution. A current missionary strategist observes that whether this analysis is fair or not, "it is a reminder that in every generation Christians must get their bearings as to where they are and what the Scripture says to them about the gospel." [30] Paul's marching orders can help to meet this need.

[29] From the firsthand account by Rodney Shaw published in *Concern*, April 15, 1965.

[30] Tracey K. Jones, Jr., *Our Mission Today*, p. 59.

He guides us to "feed the church of the Lord" (vs. 28) under the pressure of spiritual urgency. His own example lends power to his words. "And now, behold, I am going to Jerusalem, bound in the Spirit, not knowing what shall befall me there" (vs. 22). He is "under the constraint of the Spirit" (NEB), "under the binding force of the Spirit" (MT), "the Spirit compels" (AT). In these strong terms Paul depicts the quality of conviction and the sense of divine guidance which impel him on the long journey he is now hurrying to complete. Out of conviction so shaped and resolutely held, this speech gathers up Paul's earlier ministry and looks to the ventures and tests that lie ahead.

He guides us, second, to undertake our mission with the disciplined dedication he has exemplified. Since it was among these Ephesian leaders that Paul formed the conviction in which he has acted "under the binding force of the Spirit," his life, as they have known it, gives weight to his persistent response to God's leading. To that life he calls attention (vss. 18-21). He has served the Lord "with all humility and with tears and with trials which befell me through the plots of the Jews" (vs. 19). Here we catch the demeanor of the man: *humility,* though he is one of the uniquely creative figures of all time; *tears* and *trials,* as he gives himself with unstinting abandon to the demanding work of his calling; the endurance of *plots,* as he carries through his convictions against cruel opposition.

In such a setting and demeanor he shows us his third counsel for feeding the Church. It is a methodology of (a) pastoral care—"I never shrank from telling you anything that was for your good" (vs. 20 AT); (b) instruction—"I taught you, in public and in your homes" (vs. 20 NEB); (c) evangelism—"urging both Jews and Greeks to turn to God and to believe in our Lord Jesus" (vs. 21 JB). He does not regard his life "a thing to waste words on" (vs. 24 JB), if only he can carry out the mission his Lord has given him—"to bear witness to the Good News of God's grace." The power of the Church still resides in ministries so performed.

He closes with a fourth counsel, to work with confidence that God and "the word of his grace" can build us up and give us an "inheritance among all those who are sanctified" (vs. 32), or "among all who are dedicated to him" (NEB). Dedication supplies its own motive: to share a heritage among the dedicated. Life in such great company is incentive enough.

Called to the Authentic
Matthew 10:16-33

We live torn between hunger to be real and the drive to be comfortable. Sickened by his professional agreeability, a salesman wonders, "Will I allow myself to have an opinion, or is the sale more important to me?" [31] Many of us live among such threats to our authentic personhood.

Jesus spoke to our quandary. "I send you out as sheep in the midst of wolves; so be wise as serpents and innocent as doves" (vs. 16). Sent among hostile unbelievers, the disciples must of necessity be "wise," i.e., wary; they were also to be "innocent"—the Greek at this point is literally *unmixed,*

[31] Terkel, *Division Street: America,* p. 305.

unadulterated, guileless. In the face of fierce opposition, he was saying, dare to be who you are. In a secularized approximation of this simple authenticity, Frank Lloyd Wright justified his adamant stand for artistic integrity. He had to choose, he said, "between being self-confidently arrogant and hypocritically humble." A third choice might be the humility of penitence combined with the assertiveness of grateful loyalty to the real. In any case, authenticity is our crying need.

You can be an authentic person, Jesus seems to say, confident *that God sustains those who genuinely stand for something.* He calls his disciples "to bear testimony" (vs. 18) among fearful hazards. "Have no fear of them; for nothing is covered that will not be revealed, or hidden that will not be known" (vs. 26). Your testimony may be stifled or twisted, but the truth will vindicate itself; the future belongs to it. You can take your stand on that. "He who endures to the end"—who holds his course, who is all one thing, who continues to be who he is—"will be saved" (vs. 22*b*); God supports his authentic life.

One of the marks of competent authority is sensitive concern for the minute. The keen engineer spots the small malfunctioning part in the vast machine; the master conductor detects the one note off key in the great orchestra; God cares for individuals in an engulfing universe, marking the sparrow's fall and numbering the hairs of our heads (vss. 29-30). He does not coddle his witnesses. Persecutors may "kill the body"; they "cannot kill the soul" (vs. 28).

You can be an authentic person, Jesus seems to say, *taking your stand on real issues.* Men may go to great lengths to oppose you—"deliver you up to councils, and flog you in their synagogues" (vs. 17). That became stark fact; it happened to Paul five times (II Cor. 11:24). Such standing on issues is a part of Christian authenticity, whether the contested matter is a social issue such as civil rights or nuclear escalation, or a personal issue such as sexual purity or abstinence from alcoholic beverages in a permissive society.

To many a modern the Church's witness to its convictions has a hollow ring. "The average white person," a workingman reflected,

you ask him about integration, is the Negro equal? He wants to scream NO. But he thinks back and he's a Christian. Now he knows in his heart that he doesn't believe he's equal, but all this Christian training almost forces him to say yes. He's saying yes to a lie, but he has to come face-to-face with the truth someday.[32]

Have we taught men to see us that way? Our Lord calls us to authentic stands that will clear the air of such notions of insincere witness.

You can be an authentic person, Jesus seems to say, *sustained by loyalty to your Lord.* One of the weaknesses making for equivocal witness and inauthentic discipleship is our fear of divisiveness within the Christian fellowship. Men counsel silence on troublesome issues, lest by being controversial we hurt the Church. In the end, only one division is hurtful—our separation from our Lord. "Whoever denies me before men," he says, "I also will deny before my Father who is in heaven" (vs. 33). We cannot have it

[32] *Ibid.,* p. 126.

both ways. Either we trim conviction to avoid controversy, and lose touch with him; or we stand with him on real convictions, at risk of controversy. A church which forgets this is already divided at the most fatal point. As Bernard Shaw said of William Ernest Henley, we then have "great powers of expression—and nothing significant to say."

NINTH SUNDAY AFTER PENTECOST

Choosing Faith's Stance
Ruth 1:1, 4-9, 16, 19a

When you pick up one end of a stick you pick up the other. And when you choose an environment you open yourself to the outlook and loyalties it represents. To opt for isolated individualism is to cut off the nourishment of a covenant community. To throw in one's lot with a people is to be profoundly influenced by all that gives their life its meaning.

Ruth made this choice. "Your people shall be my people, and your God my God" (vs. 16). This climactic line interprets the book of Ruth, well called the most perfect short story in all literature. Liturgical use demands a cutting, and today's lection is as good as any. One can find meaning in the lection, however, only as it represents the classic gem of the whole story of Ruth.

Naomi, whose husband and two sons have died in the land of Moab, starts home to her own people, Israel, with her widowed daughters-in-law. At her urging, Orpah turns back, but Ruth insists that Naomi's people and future are her own. Gleaning in the harvest according to the law which provides that privilege for the poor, Ruth is kindly treated in the fields of the wealthy Boaz. As a kinsman of Naomi's deceased husband, Boaz accepts the responsibility of a Levirate marriage with Ruth, to raise up an heir to continue the family line of the dead. To this union is born a son, Obed "the father of Jesse, the father of David" (4:17). Since Ruth belonged to pagan Moab, the entire story hinges on her momentous choice declared in the classic lines: "Where you go I will go, and where you lodge I will lodge; your people shall be my people, and your God my God" (vs. 16).

Readings from Ruth are still central to the synagogue service on the festival of Shavuoth (Pentecost), the occasion of confirmation of Jewish youth who have completed their religious instruction. With its declaration of fealty to the people of God, based on an irrevocable choice, the text is peculiarly fitting for such an occasion. Note its strong pointers to the reality of faith, for Christians as well as Jews.

Faith stands on a momentous and deliberate choice. For Ruth it was bound in one bundle with her acceptance of the uncertain future of Naomi, a choice based on loyal love. It entailed a break with her old life and an acceptance of "your people" as "my people." The choice of a new people meant the acceptance of a change of ultimate ground of dependence and final loyalties: "And your God my God." Faith thus chooses a new stance from which one interprets all of experience and determines all other choices.

Near the end of the nineteenth century, William James declared this in *The Will to Believe.* "Emphasizing the role of the nature of the knower in the character and validity of knowledge, he insisted that any view of the world is

a compromise between the objectively given and the personally desired." [33]
Since most of our basic human choices must be made before all the facts
have become available, we have not only a right but an obligation to choose a
way that makes sense of both the present and foreseeable future. In our time,
the existentialists have pointed out how the viewpoint of the observer determines his purportedly "objective" report of the world outside himself. A life
stance must be chosen as responsibly and intelligently as one can manage.

Faith matures through fealty to the people of God and their ways. Accepting Naomi's lot as her own, Ruth gave herself in loyal obedience to the
ways of Israel. Her gleaning and her association with Boaz show Israel's
religious laws of social welfare in action. Boaz is zealously faithful to the
same laws: (a) in his careful provisions for the protection of Ruth, whose
foreignness might have been exploited by the harvesters, and (b) in his
devotion to the spirit and letter of the law of Levirate marriage. He could
have avoided the responsibility, since he was not the nearest kin. Instead, he
precipitated the issue and accepted the role which the nearer kinsman
declined. Thereby he accepted a real cost, since any heir of this marriage
would assume the name and continue the line of Ruth's deceased first husband, thus dividing the heritage of other heirs. This story of faith portrays
fealty to the people of God and their ways.

Life in the Church is no incidental accompaniment of faith; it is faith's
essence. Entailed in the Church's mission to the secular world is the obligation not to become secularized. A church lost in the world is no longer on
mission. Only those who keep close association with the people of God will
long have anything to share with the world to which they are sent.

Faith reaches "outsiders" through the loving concern of human agents.
Through its whole fabric this story weaves Ruth's foreignness (cf. 1:4, 22;
2:2, 6, 10-13, 21; 4:5, 10). Against the Moabites, to whom she belonged, the
law of exclusion was specific: "No Ammonite or Moabite shall enter the
assembly of the Lord; even to the tenth generation none belonging to them
shall ever enter the assembly of the Lord" (Deut. 23:3). Yet Naomi and
Boaz took Ruth into the most tender relations. Ruth became the great-
grandmother of Israel's greatest king, David; and from the line of her descendants came Israel's greatest Son, Jesus.

In the face of all exclusiveness—postexilic Judaism, Christian
parochialism, anti-Semitic bigotry, contemporary racism—this story cries out
that God works through the "foreigner" to achieve his ends, and that the
"outsider" is brought into the household of faith through the humane inclusiveness of men and women like Boaz and Naomi, who do their mission work
by unexpected kindness to the most glaringly *different* person nearest at
hand.

Chained for Hope
Acts 28:16-20, 23-24, 30-31

"It is because of the hope of Israel that I am bound with this chain" (vs.
20). Hope never has easy going. *Cynicism* is against it, *doubt* is against it,

[33] William Rose Benet, *The Reader's Encyclopedia* (New York: Thomas Y.
Crowell, 2nd ed., 1965), article on William James.

often the most obvious *facts* are against it. Yet hope became the pivotal issue in Paul's last imprisonment. Preaching to his fellow Jews in Rome, his theme is "the hope of Israel." That hope, Paul says, is *Jesus as the fulfillment of the hope of the Resurrection and the initiator of the kingdom of God.*

As the thread of Acts makes clear, this hope is no generalized messianic expectation. *It is the hope of resurrection* cherished by the Pharisaic party, to which Paul belonged. "Brethren," he had cried before the council, "I am a Pharisee, a son of Pharisees; with respect to the hope and the resurrection of the dead I am on trial" (Acts 23:6). Before the governor he had presented his case as a follower of "the Way," faithful to the prophetic religion of Israel, "having a hope in God . . . that there will be a resurrection of both the just and the unjust" (24:14-15). This hope was a point of contention between Pharisees and Sadducees, the latter "annoyed because they were . . . proclaiming in Jesus the resurrection from the dead" (4:2). For this message focused on the Resurrection, Paul paid the price of the scoffings of sophisticated Greeks at Athens, persecutions by Sadducean Jews, and final imprisonment at the hands of the Romans. Of the eight uses of the word "hope" in Luke-Acts, four (*all* that occur in speeches of Peter and Paul) show the Resurrection as the content of the hope. For a Christian, to preach or teach about hope is to deal with the Resurrection.

The kingdom of God, initiated by Jesus, stands on the Resurrection. If crucifixion was the end, there was no victory and no kingdom. The historic fact of the Resurrection vindicates the kingdom hope. Linked with the Resurrection in Paul's preaching, the kingdom provides another focal point in this culminating scene of his ministry. From morning to night he is seen "testifying to the kingdom of God and trying to convince them about Jesus" (vs. 23). This theme, too, has been woven through Acts. The prefatory paragraph announced it, recalling the forty days in which Jesus appeared to the disciples, "speaking of the kingdom of God" (1:3). For three months at Ephesus, Paul "spoke boldly, arguing and pleading about the kingdom of God" (19:8). Philip "preached . . . the kingdom of God" (8:12). In his farewell to the Ephesus elders, Paul summarized, "I have gone about preaching the kingdom" (20:25). It is appropriate, then, that he closes his recorded ministry, in this passage, still "preaching the kingdom of God and teaching about the Lord Jesus Christ" (vs. 31).

Jesus, hope, resurrection, kingdom—their unity is so organic in the Christian message that to deal with one is to deal with all.

Church's Model, Sinner's Hope
Luke 15:1-10

Luke's fifteenth chapter underscores one proposition: Jesus' care for despised sinners reveals God's saving concern for the lost. The parable of the prodigal, which closes the chapter, receives separate notice on the Ninth Sunday of Kingdomtide: here we face the first two parables, a matching pair. Joachim Jeremias characterizes them as "Jesus' defence of the gospel: 'since God's mercy is so infinite that his supreme joy is in forgiving, my mission as Saviour is to wrest his prey from Satan and to bring home the lost.' " [34]

[34] Jeremias, *The Parables of Jesus*, p. 136.

"So he told them this parable" (vs. 3) introduces the collection on the lost and found, making them clearly our Lord's reply to heartless religionists who neither cared for sinful "outsiders" themselves nor approved Jesus' doing so. Strongly attracted, "the tax collectors and sinners were all drawing near to hear him" (vs. 1). We might call the tax collectors, as agents of Roman occupation, "dirty politicians." Not all notorious wrongdoers, the "sinners" included "the careless and unconcerned about religious proprieties, whom the sanctimonious looked down upon as an uncovenanted lower class." [35] Such people found in Jesus a reality which spoke to neglected but uneasy consciences. Forgiveness of sinners was not new in the religion of the time; resolute *search* for them. It is the *search* that these parables underscore. In this they articulate what Jesus *was* and *did*. In these parables he explained his ministry.

The contrast between him and the religious establishment lays a constant call on the Church. Meant to be his body, it is tempted to lapse into the ways of the scribes and Pharisees (vs. 2) who grumbled (NEB) not because men were lost, but because a religious teacher wasted time and risked contamination with such people. As the Jewish scholar Montefiore observes, Jesus did not "make light of sin, but . . . gave comfort to the sinners." For the Church, that is the model of life as his Body.

Despite their differences, two parables converge on one dominant point. The first deals with a man, the second with a woman. One speaks of a sheep which strayed by its own action, the other of a coin lost by careless handling. One portrays a moderately well-to-do shepherd, who had a hundred sheep in a region where flocks varied from twenty to two hundred; the other shows a poor woman who turned the house upside down to find a coin worth about sixteen cents. All this sets the stage for one figure—the concerned owner who is not content with the safe majority of his holdings as long as one prized possession is missing. That, said Jesus, is how it is with God. "Joy in heaven" (vs. 7) and "joy before the angels of God" (vs. 10) depend on the recovery of one lost sinner.

Jesus gave controlling prominence to a concern that had run through familiar teaching. God revealed himself to Moses as "merciful and gracious, slow to anger, and abounding in steadfast love and faithfulness" (Exod. 34:6). Hosea reported God's cry to straying, wayward people: "How can I give you up, O Ephraim!" (Hos. 11:8-9). The psalmist dared pray, "I have gone astray like a lost sheep; seek thy servant" (Ps. 119:176). Ezekiel could ask, "Have I any pleasure in the death of the wicked, says the Lord God, and not rather that he should turn from his way and live?" (Ezek. 18:23; 33:11). It remained for Jesus to make *dominant* the passionate *search* for the lost.

Like the shepherd, he will not forsake "the one which is lost, until he finds it" (vs. 4). Like the woman, he attaches to the lost value which far exceeds its market price. The ten coins (vs. 8) "will remind every one who is familiar with Arab Palestine of the woman's head-dress bedecked with coins which is part of her dowry, and may not be laid aside, even in sleep." [36]

[35] Walter Russell Bowie, *The Compassionate Christ* (Nashville: Abingdon Press, 1965), p. 202.

[36] Jeremias, *The Parables of Jesus*, p. 134.

That her dowry consisted of such poor coins, not the hundreds of gold and silver pieces others might have, simply emphasizes that for this poor woman it was not market value that was involved, but *worth to her* in terms of personal involvement. Just so, Jesus said, God cares for sinners; that is why I search for them.

The search did not stop short of the Cross. Even there, a bond was set up between him and the repentant criminal to whom he gave absolution: "To day you will be with me in Paradise" (Luke 23:39-43). That, the assurance by which alone each of us can live, is the commission laid upon us who belong to his Body.

TENTH SUNDAY AFTER PENTECOST

Faith's Stake in Government
I Samuel 9:15-17; 10:1

Separation of church and state need not become divorce of faith from government. To this truth the Bible bears perpetual witness, as in this reading from I Samuel, which interweaves two accounts of the choice of Saul as Israel's first king. The earlier source dealt chiefly with *events,* the later with Samuel's *motives* as they were remembered in the tradition transmitted through the fellowship of the prophets.

The late source (I Sam. 8:10-18) details Samuel's opposition to the establishment of a monarchy. A king would take young men for military service and maidens as palace domestics. He would enrich his coffers at the expense of the people's lands and tithes of their produce. He would exhaust productivity by demanding the best servants and draft animals. Although details of these warnings may have been colored by later experience, there is no reason to suppose the main issues were not foreseen by Samuel. To popular insistence, however, he yielded grudging compliance.

Chapter 9 plunges into a story from the earlier account. Saul is introduced again as we are told of his search for his father's stray asses. Unable to find them, he resorted to Samuel as a reputed seer who might direct the search. The prophet recognized in Saul the man who would fulfill God's promise concerning one "who shall rule over my people" (9:17). After first sharing publicly with Saul in a religious festival, Samuel anointed him (10:1) but did so privately (9:27). This participation by the prophet in the affairs of state suggests important relations of faith to government.

For one thing, the problem of government stems from its involvement in and tainting by human sinfulness. Both figure prominently in this record. The problem led the fathers of the American Constitution to believe that man as a child of God must be trusted with a determining voice in the government under which he lives, but because he is sinful his leaders must be restrained by a system of checks and balances among constitutionally divided powers.

For another, sovereignty derives both from the people and from God. In response to Saul's charismatic leadership the people acclaimed him king (10:20-24), but even before that, he was anointed in the name of God (10:1). Democracy preserves the theory that sovereignty rests with the people, who delegate authority to various units of government. World Federalists reason that, just as we delegate parts of our sovereign power to local, state, and federal government, we can delegate other powers to a world government. Democratic theory needs the check of a constant return to the other derivation of sovereignty, not from the people but from God. Questions not merely pragmatic but ultimate—truth, justice, mercy, humility before God, and charity to man—must be consulted if we are to be rightly governed in a durable society.

One alone is King of kings and Lord of lords. Saul proved a disappointing monarch who only partially established his rule in the land. It remained for David to enlarge the kingdom and to achieve a working harmony between the king's religious and civil functions. After a brief golden age, such welfare was never again known in Israel. The people looked for a messianic Son of David who would bring restoration. The fulfillment in Jesus differed from the expectation; in the difference lay its universal validity. He has come; knowing his teaching and spirit, we can apply them to our common life as test and mandate. In a fuller sense, he is still to come. We strive to conform the present to his ways as key to the future, which is his.

Meaning of Salvation: Romans 8:14-39

No brief comment can do justice to this passage, the longest in the lectionary and one of the most closely packed. Bypassing words and phrases that invite extended meditation, single sentences that unlock whole theologies, we must seek out its central theme. It shows God at work for the salvation of our whole nature through the present action of his Spirit.

Paul has etched the dilemma of our warped nature (chap. 7). Christ, he declares, has resolved the dilemma by taking our nature upon himself and winning the decisive victory over it (8:1-3). It remains for God's Spirit to apply this general victory in each of us. "He did this in order that the Law's just demands might be satisfied in us, who behave not as our unspiritual nature but as the Spirit dictates" (vs. 4 JB). Step by step, the remainder of the chapter works out the implications of this truth. Although our leaderless insistence on our own freedom has "futility" written all over it, "the Spirit of him who raised Jesus from the dead" is at work to win victory by an inward transformation (vss. 5-13). Not only has God worked the wonder of the Resurrection, he is still at work. Today's lection shows what this means.

It shows us first (vss. 14-17) that *God has made us his sons*, with a twofold consequence: We are set free from fear, and we are able to pray with confidence. Our cry is to our Father, "Abba," the child's cry to his loved father within the intimacy of the family circle. It is the language of liturgy, recalling the opening words of the Lord's Prayer. It is the opening phrase of Jesus' prayer in Gethsemane (Mark 14:36) and should be invested with overtones of that prayer. The cry is evidence that "the Spirit himself and our spirit bear united witness that we are children of God" (vs. 16 JB). Co-heirs with Christ, we share his sufferings, but also his victory.

Returning to this theme (vss. 26-27) Paul testifies that our prayers, both personal and liturgical, have the support and guidance of the Spirit. The church echoes this insight in a classic collect which begins: "Almighty God, from whom every good prayer cometh, and who pourest out, on all who desire it, the spirit of grace and supplication." "*From* whom"! Prayers are not only *addressed to* God, but have their *origin in* him; only as he first moves within us have we the wit to pray.

Further, God opens the *future before us* (vss. 18-25). In our sin, nature itself is "subjected to futility" and "bondage to decay" (vss. 20-21). This "decadence" (JB) is interpreted by the Genesis insight that in man's fall, a blight fell on the whole created world (Gen. 3:14-19). Experience verifies the tragedy. Disease, death, natural calamities are ever with us. Greed and conflict produce dust bowls, atomic fallout, industrial wastes polluting air and water, pesticides upsetting the ecological balance. Are we about to transplant earth's apocalyptic horrors to the moon? Yet God underwrites a future. "From the beginning till now the entire creation, as we know, has been groaning in one great act of giving birth" (vs. 22 JB). We too (vss. 15-17) already experience a relation to God that must be seen as "firstfruits of the harvest to come" (vs. 23 NEB). The fact that we do not yet see all this fully realized does not invalidate its promise. For we are saved through hope. If we already possessed all this, we should need no salvation. But "we must hope to be saved since we are not saved yet—it is something we must wait for with patience" (vs. 25 JB). Our present experience of sonship which makes it possible to share Jesus' prayer, foreshadows fuller experience still to come.

We need not wait for a distant future. *God now shares his people's struggles* (vss. 28-30). "We know also that those who love God, those who have been called in terms of his purpose, have his aid and interest in everything" (vs. 28 MT). "We know that in everything God works with those who love him, . . . to bring about what is good" (AT). This does not hint that only good happens to God's chosen. Discipleship is a life and death affair (vs. 13); we have to kill off the impulses of our human nature! Elsewhere (II Cor. 11:24-29) Paul tells us the hazards to which the love of God subjected him. Nevertheless, he says, God is at our side in the struggle. God calls, as once he called his people Israel. Note the social, corporate dimension of that call. He works to make the called into the predestined image of his Son. Emil Brunner's word on "predestined" brings needed clarification.

God's thought, God's will is the absolute priority. That God has "chosen" a creation is the reason why created things exist; that God has chosen us men as his creaturely image is the ground of our existence as men; that God has loved us from eternity in Jesus Christ is the ground of our salvation.[37]

Thus chosen, we are "called," "justified," "glorified"—a soaring crescendo. "And so God called those whom he had set apart; not only did he call them, but he also put them right with himself; not only did he put them right with himself, but he also shared his glory with them" (vs. 30 GNMM).

Thus our whole salvation is God's doing. Therefore it cannot fail (vss. 31-39). With him on our side, who can stand against us? Surely not Christ!

[37] Emil Brunner, *The Letter to the Romans* (Philadelphia: Westminster Press, 1959), p. 77.

Christ gave himself for us, and his sacrifice stands as a constant plea in our behalf! Nothing in this world or out of it, in time or eternity, nothing in all creation can separate us from God's love as we know it in Christ. This is what it means to be saved by God's action in Christ and his Spirit at work in us.

When the Impossible Blocks Our Way
Luke 18:18-30

How deal with the impossible? Impasses pose the question—pain, wild impulses, family love betrayed, tasks beyond our strength, a church at odds with its mission. Brash sufficiency has a false ring: "The difficult we do immediately; the impossible takes a little longer." Men shout such boasts in the face of physical hazards. But when any life worth living confronts the impossible, what then?

"What is impossible with men is possible with God" (vs. 27). Like us, Jesus' questioner was searching for fulfillment: "What shall I do to inherit eternal life?" (vs. 18) Life of the quality of the Age to come? Life adequate? Life lasting? One of Arthur Miller's characters, a wise old furniture dealer, sick of shoddy goods built for quick obsolescence, has a word for our ways. "What is the key word today?" he asks. "Disposable. The more you can throw it away the more it's beautiful. The car, the furniture, the wife, the children—everything has to be disposable." [38] How find life that is *not* disposable, life that lasts? Full, lasting life which meets the challenge of the impossible is God's gift to those who serve him with obedient and loving abandon.

Fullest life begins in obedience: "You know the commandments" (vs. 20). No shortcuts can bypass that—no "Good Teacher" (vs. 18), no new secret, no mystical experience, no sophisticated philosophy. "No one is good but God alone" (vs. 19b). That being so, it follows that there is just one place to start: "You know the commandments." This is no call to legalism that despoils real goodness. It is a reminder that situation ethics need guidelines to hold us against temptation and our endless capacity to rationalize our desires. Life without obedience ends in emptiness. Marcia Davenport leaves a sophisticated, glamorous character, home from Europe, hollow and lonely after an illicit affair, saying to her mirrored reflection: "Who is this, standing alone in an empty apartment in Fifth Avenue, the owner of it and of everything it contains and of a good deal else . . . but not the owner of a self? [39] "You know the commandments"; full life cannot bypass that.

But commandments alone cannot deliver full life. Thinking we have fully kept them, we reflect how little we understand. Truly understanding them, we cannot face ourselves in our failure. Commandments had left the moral man in this story unsatisfied; otherwise he would not have asked his question.

Jesus pointed beyond obedience to dedication: "Sell all that you have and distribute to the poor, and you will have treasure in heaven; and come, follow me" (vs. 22). The man needed something to call him out of himself,

[38] Arthur Miller, *The Price* (New York: Viking Press, 1968), pp. 40-41.

[39] Marcia Davenport, *The Constant Image* (New York: Scribner's, 1960), p. 224.

such as Dr. Wilfred T. Grenfell found when he left the promise of wealth and recognition to invest a life of hardship in the welfare of fisherfolk in Laborador. "Christ," he said in the midst of the toil, "is giving me in this world ten times, nay, the proverbial hundred fold, as good times as I could enjoy in any other way." [40] There is full life in such investment; full life in risking for a conviction; full life in a home where the cry, "What do I get out of it?" yields to love with abandon.

We cannot satisfy so strong a challenge. The man "became sad, for he was very rich" (vs. 23). The cost was too high. "It is easier," said Jesus, "for a camel to go through the eye of a needle than for a rich man to enter the kingdom of God" (vs. 25). Speculations about the metaphor are beside the point. Jesus is stressing the terrible difficulty. The man was intelligent, asking one of the world's best questions. He was moral, having kept the commandments from his youth. He was rich. None of these things could give him the full life he craved. In wonder the disciples asked, "Then who can be saved?" (vs. 26). The difficulty seemed insurmountable.

Full life, Jesus replied, rests on trust: "What is impossible with men is possible with God." A psychiatrist said of a patient, "These people say they *can* not, their friends say they *will* not, we doctors know they *cannot will.*" That is often our case. But what our diseased wills cannot bring off, God can accomplish in us by the liberating, empowering impact of his grace.

Peter concluded the interview: "We have left our homes" (vs. 28). So much we have done, even if this man could not leave what he had! We have been obedient, gone beyond obedience to dedication, trusted God. What do we get? Jesus replies: "Manifold more in this time"—adventure, creativity, fulfillment, fellowship—"and in the age to come eternal life" (vs. 30). When the impossible blocks our path, full life is possible with God.

ELEVENTH SUNDAY AFTER PENTECOST

In Whom History Turns a Corner
I Samuel 16:1-13

Here we witness a formative moment in the life of one of the little handful of men in whom history has turned major corners. David gave Israel its golden era and played a pivotal part in the religious tradition through which this people made creative impact on the life of the world. The messianic hope, fulfilled and transformed in Christ, found its model in David's kingship. Other accounts depict David's elevation to power as he won popular acclaim (II Sam. 2:4; 5:3); this lection focuses on the inner meaning of his selection. It suggests God's ways of acting in decisive hours.

God acts through a man of deep feeling and daring conviction. As the story opens, Samuel grieves over Saul whom the Lord has rejected. In light of the circumstances his sorrow is doubly touching. For Samuel had first resisted the popular demand for a king and then reluctantly anointed Saul. Once

---

[40] Wilfred Thomas Grenfell, *What Christ Means to Me* (Boston: Houghton Mifflin, 1927), p. 40.

committed, Samuel so identified himself with the infant monarchy that the king's failure deeply afflicted him. Samuel, commissioned of the Lord to denounce Saul for failure to carry out the ban against the Amalekites, poured out his anger against the Lord in a whole night of intercessory prayer (15:10). Yet when day came, he confronted Saul in the stormy interview.

After this encounter he had reason to fear death at Saul's hands for anointing a new king (vs. 2). Yet, once convinced it was right, he resolutely carried out the assignment. A man of such unflinching conviction won the "trembling" respect of the people. With some reason they asked, "Do you come peaceably?" (vs. 4). Leadership so intensely human, yet so devoted to God's will, wields power. Through such men God acts. Their ministry may touch the most pivotal characters.

God acts too, in searching the inner purposes of men. Impressive appearance and mighty physique constitute no credentials before him (vss. 6-8). Did this insight come to Samuel through the collapse of Saul's career? Handsome appearance, head and shoulders above his fellows, first commended Saul (9:2; 10:23). "Man looks on the outward appearance, but the Lord looks on the heart" (vs. 7), said the inner voice. Jesus went further, to proclaim inward purity the key to communion: "Blessed are the pure in heart, for they shall see God" (Matt. 5:8).

God acts further, through those in whom power is least expected. Youngest of Jesse's eight sons, David seemed too unimportant to call in for Samuel's scrutiny. He was "keeping the sheep" (vs. 11). "Those few sheep in the wilderness" (17:28), according to Eliab's sneer when David came to visit his soldier brothers. Yet this man was to become Israel's most memorable king—save one, a Carpenter whose kingly acclaim was placarded on the Cross (Matt. 27:37).

Arnold Toynbee writes of the rejected proletariat who once and again hold the key to the future. Israel's story keeps returning to that theme. Gideon was called to deliver his harassed people despite the plea, "My clan is the weakest in Manasseh, and I am the least in my family" (Judg. 6:15). Israel lived under prophetic reminder that God chose to act through them not because of their might, but in spite of their minuteness (Deut. 7:7). Jeremiah warned that the great of the earth could not glory in their wisdom, riches, or power, but only in obedient knowledge of the Lord (Jer. 9:23-24). The warning is timely for "the affluent society" in the nation that boasts power beyond any in previous history. God has repeatedly turned from such peoples to build the future through the rejected and the seemingly powerless. At history's pivot points contests of might have low priority.

Reflecting the Splendor
II Corinthians 3:4-11, 17-18

All of us, reflecting the splendor of the Lord in our unveiled faces, are being changed into likeness to him, from one degree of splendor to another, for this comes from the Lord who is the Spirit (vs. 18 AT).

How strange it all sounds! "Reflecting the splendor of the Lord" can we mirror Christ? Amid the tinsel and tawdriness of our society? Torn by our inner conflicts? Admiring him, yet doubting with all the force of our self-sufficient humanism? Reflect him or not, we are drawn to him. He haunts us, calling us to be more than we are—as, in this memorable declaration, Paul asserts that we can be. Twenty centuries of experience underscore the assertion.

"Reflecting the splendor" is not of our doing. It is God at work in us. We "are *being changed.*" It does not happen all at once. Some years ago there was a furor over a group of "Drug Addicts for Jesus" who rented an abandoned farm on which to work out a new life for themselves. Neighbors feared and resented them. Part of the objection converged on allegedly foul language overheard on the rural party line. A wise counselor reminded objectors that with deeply ingrained language habits there is bound to be a lag. But, he pointed out, what was vital was that in so many areas of their life they were being changed under the impact of Christ. Change can come to us too, by a power from beyond us that lifts by degrees—"from one degree of splendor to another."

Adverse environment need not deter. More than external conditioning or our own resolute spirit is combatting the forces that would degrade and wear us down. "Our sufficiency is from God, who has qualified us to be ministers of a new covenant, . . . The written code"—human maxims and philosophy— "kills, but the Spirit gives life" (vss. 5-6). Not a more adamant will is our need, but more trustful exposure to him.

God changes us by exposure to the Christ we "reflect." Our generation is painfully aware of the impossibility of knowing Jesus with historical completeness. The documents through which we meet him are vivid expressions of faith, not historians' memoirs. This insight gained currency through Albert Schweitzer's research in *The Quest of the Historical Jesus.* Yet beyond his historical skepticism Schweitzer saw a life-changing reality.

He comes to us as One unknown, without a name, as of old, by the lake-side, He came to those men who knew Him not. He speaks to us the same word: "Follow thou me!" and sets us to the tasks which He has to fulfil for our time. He commands. And to those who obey Him, whether they be wise or simple, He will reveal Himself in the toils, the conflicts, the sufferings which they shall pass through in His fellowship, and, as an ineffable mystery, they shall learn in their own experience Who He is.[41]

What God has begun in us through Jesus, he will complete in us through the presence and power of his Spirit. As Paul says, "this comes from the Lord who is the Spirit" (vs. 18). We are absurdly boastful creatures! In a newspaper interview, a violent white objector to racial integration on Chicago's West Side declared: "Whites are better because they made themselves that way." Unschooled, the woman might be forgiven for such monumental ignorance of history and sociological forces as this swaggering line suggests. But for a self-styled Christian to talk so, without realizing the blasphemy, is incredible. A moral chasm of Grand Canyon proportions yawns between such boasts by violent oppressors and the words of a Negro girl they injured: "Every night when we leave the church to begin our march, we are

[41] Albert Schweitzer, *The Quest of the Historical Jesus* (New York: Macmillan, 1926), p. 401.

prepared to die. Last night I thought my time had come." Underlying the moral difference is the spiritual reality that we do not *make ourselves*. God made us. We have spoiled his image, but he does not give up. In trustful exposure to him there is still the possibility of "reflecting the splendor."

Prayer and the Secular Christian
Luke 11:1-4, 9-13

Between Bonhoeffer's "religionless Christianity" and the prayerless secularity sometimes made of it there looms a world of difference. Bonhoeffer scorned religious escapism that would substitute pious exercises for real sharing in the world's struggle. From the days of his early concern with the life of the Bruderhaus to the last of his prison letters, however, his disciplined prayer life is a constantly crucial aspect of his spiritual pilgrimage. Jesus' lesson on prayer speaks cogently to our need as secular Christians.

When "he was praying in a certain place," the disciples asked for his secret (vs. 1). Well they might! According to Luke's report, prayer was pivotal to his key experiences. During prayer following his baptism "the Holy Spirit descended upon him" (Luke 3:21-22). When the crowds pressed him for teaching and healing, "he withdrew to the wilderness and prayed" (5:15-16). His call of the disciples followed a whole night of prayer (6:12). Peter first confessed him as Christ in the atmosphere of a prayer retreat (9:18-20). The transfiguration occurred "as he was praying" on a mountain (9:28-29). On the night of his arrest, he found clarity and strength in prayer on the Mount of Olives (22:39-44). Only the disciples—"practical" men who prepared for strain by sleep—failed when the stress came (22:45-46). To try to follow Jesus in ethical idealism without disciplined prayer is to reduce the gospel to shreds and tatters.

We are "challenged to participate in the sufferings of God at the hands of a godless world," [42] Bonhoeffer reminds us. In relation to this call, he says we are asked: "Could you not watch with me one hour?" (Matt. 26:40). This challenge to allow our prayer to lead us into costly sharing in God's struggle, not turning from prayer to a merely bustling plunge into the world, constitutes the true meaning of "religionless Christianity." Note how our Lord's Prayer points up the issues.

"Father, hallowed be thy name" (vs. 2a). Prayer remembers that any healing wholeness we bring to secular life must rest on some area kept holy. Prayer is more than monologue. It is dialogue with One who transcends us. Unless reverence for his nature makes the love, justice, and truth that flow from him inviolably holy, our entrance into the secular world will not end in helpful ministry; it will level us down to a common denominator of depletion and defilement.

"Thy kingdom come" (vs. 2b) sets the goal of service as nothing less than God's reign. John Updike depicts Connor, Superintendent in *The Poorhouse Fair*, as a man "devout in the service of humanity." Yet Connor never really understands or shares in a truly human relationship with another

[42] Dietrich Bonhoeffer, *Letters and Papers from Prison*, p. 222.

person. In the end he does not so much serve human need as complicate it. As Updike describes him, Connor has no place in his thought or feeling for anything transcendent.

The theatre of his deeds was filled with people he would never meet—the administrators, the report-readers—and beyond these black blank heads hung the white walls of the universe, the listless, permissive mother for whom Connor felt not a shred of awe, though, orthodox in the way of popular humanist orators, he claimed he did. . . . Ideally, his dedication wore blinders, but he was too weak not to glance to the side for signs of approval. The sculptor has his rock and the saint the silence of his Lord, but a man like Connor who has vowed to bring order and beauty out of human substance has no third factor; he is a slave, at first, to gratitude. In time, he knew, this tender place grows callous; he had heard the older men whose disciple he was discuss, not entirely in joking, mass murder as the ultimate kindness the enlightened could perform for the others.[43]

Thus a perceptive novelist, setting out to draw "a caricature of contemporary decadence," [44] locates one of its sources of infection in "devout service of humanity." "Thy kingdom come"—if that prayer is not our guide, it becomes our judge.

"Give us each day our daily bread" (vs. 3) confesses our need of help from beyond ourselves. God is no *deus ex machina* who fills the gaps in our self-sufficiency. His providence is not a special favor granted here and there in some eleventh-hour need. He is present in the regularities of the world. We despoil the world if we deal with it as exploiters of meaningless material, not stewards of God's creation dependent on him for our daily bread.

"Forgive us our sins" (vs. 4) reflects the forgotten need of an optimistic secular world. Self-righteous cruelty and unhealed guilt haunt us as twin evils. Losing our sense of sinfulness, we make excessive demands upon our neighbors and level too severe accusations against them. Trying to deal with guilt *feelings* apart from forgiveness, we are left in crippling anxiety. G. K. Chesterton was right; the good news of the gospel is just the good news of original sin, that what we are is not what we were meant to be. So we need not stay the way we are.

"And lead us not into temptation" (vs. 4b) concludes the prayer. Our plunge into the secular world has hazards which the wise will not incur with bold bravado. "Do not put us to the test" (JB), for we have little strength to face it. Even Jesus came to the cross from a prayer vigil in which he searched for some alternative to the "cup" he was about to drink. We, whose strength is less, sharing the world's need as good disciples, will pray to be spared temptation where we may.

The lection closes with assurance that God does respond to the persistent prayer that asks, seeks, knocks. Even more than a father gives good gifts to a pleading son, God gives the supreme gift—the Holy Spirit—to those who ask him (vss. 9-13).

[43] Updike, *The Poorhouse Fair*, pp. 12-14.
[44] *Ibid.*, Foreword to the Modern Library edition.

TWELFTH SUNDAY AFTER PENTECOST

From Condemnation to Confession
II Samuel 12:1-10, 13a

From *"he* deserves to die" to *"I* have sinned" is one of the world's longest journeys. In a society torn to shreds by recrimination it is one of the most needed. Our infinite capacity to rationalize our personal comfort makes it one of the rarest. In the brief span of an interview, the powerful King David was led to cover this vast distance. Three elements in the story stand out.

One is the ministry of Nathan. He used *skill* in getting through David's defenses with one of the most memorable parables in all literature (vss. 1-4). He had passionate *initiative* in going to the king with his message, rather than waiting for a favorable opening that might never come (vs. 1). And he had the *courage* of an uncomfortable and dangerous forthrightness: "You are the man" (vs. 7).

These qualities in Nathan's ministry led David to his first response, moral indignation and kingly condemnation. It was a good beginning. As royal judge, David answered strictly according to the law: "He shall restore the lamb fourfold" (vs. 6). For the statute in the matter read, "If a man steals . . . a sheep, and kills it or sells it, he shall pay . . . four sheep" (Exod. 22:1). In the Septuagint translation, David demands sevenfold restitution, and some scholars believe the Hebrew text has been toned down to harmonize his judgment with the law; at any rate, he began on this level of legality which restrained his passionate indignation—"The man . . . *deserves* to die; and he *shall* restore . . ." He is getting off too easy, David seems to say; but I must judge him according to law. Nathan's ministry stands out in the story, as it leads to David's judgment of himself.

Personal accountability that knows no exceptions, even for a king, also stands out. Nathan reminds David that he has sinned against God, not merely against law or against Uriah. He holds his kingly power under God. In violating the trust he has "despised the word of the Lord, to do what is evil in his sight" (vss. 7-9). The prophet detailed the indictment: David had violated the rights of Uriah—rights inviolable even by king against commoner; he had committed adultery in taking Uriah's wife, violating the sanctity of marriage and the family, threatening the foundations of the society it was his kingly duty to defend; and he had slain Uriah "with the sword of the Ammonites" (vs. 9). No sophistry could make anything but murder of David's order which intentionally exposed Bathsheba's husband to mortal danger. David was led to see the dimensions of a wrong he had carefully concealed from his own accusing conscience.

Hope that lies in confession of sin stands out. David's deed was no mere mistake. It was more than moral lapse. It violated a bond with God; David had "utterly scorned the Lord" (vs. 14). He was not dealing with impersonal moral law, blind fate, pursuing nemesis; he was dealing with God, who would not set moral accountability aside, but would have mercy (vss. 13b-14). "I have sinned against the Lord" (vs. 13a), confessed the king. Quite apart from Davidic authorship, there is a depth of insight into the mood and meaning of David's confession in the penitential psalm:

> I acknowledged my sin to thee,
>> and I did not hide my iniquity;
> I said, "I will confess my transgressions to the Lord";
>> then thou didst forgive the guilt of my sin (Ps. 32:5).

"Thou didst forgive"—that is the blessed discovery of those who make the journey from "*he* deserves to die" to "*I* have sinned."

Glory in the Church: Ephesians 3:13-21

Now to him who by the power at work within us is able to do far more abundantly than all that we ask or think, to him be glory in the church and in Christ Jesus to all generations, for ever and ever. Amen (vss. 20-21).

This doxology, which gathers up the threads of the first major section of the Letter to the Ephesians, daringly associates "glory" and "church"—terms the temper of our time sets poles apart. This is the day of "the humiliation of the church"; for "the restless church" has discovered that we are "God's frozen people" resting in "the comfortable pew," vainly expecting to hear God's Word from "the empty pulpit," although we are lost in "the suburban captivity of the church."[45] Caught in that morass, we hear this heartening word: "To him be *glory* in the church!"

The Church has one business: to give God glory. This thread runs through the whole Ephesian letter. Forged from diverse backgrounds of Jewish and Gentile Christians, it is called, redeemed, empowered for the sole purpose "that the universe, all in heaven and on earth, might be brought into a unity in Christ" (1:3-10 NEB).

This is still the task. A journalist, typical of many, points to it: "I was not one of the ninety-nine sheep safely in the fold. I was the hundredth sheep clinging to a cliff overhanging the abyss in the dark night."[46] These "hundredth sheep" do not eagerly welcome the message of God's love. They hide from it behind many masks—fortify themselves against it with status symbols. The Church glorifies God by its concerned wooing of such thorny outsiders, "that . . . all in heaven and on earth might be brought into a unity in Christ."

The Church glorifies God by fearlessly facing explosive issues in the world he loves—race, war, urban blight, and other vexing problems. Amid the troubles of the mid-sixties, a half-intoxicated Cuban was ejected from an airport restaurant because he insisted on shouting his country's need for American attention. Before calling the police, a waitress told him: "This is a business establishment. We don't want no trouble." After he was gone, a sailor who had sat quietly at the lunch counter said to her, "Look, he wasn't

---

[45] The phrases in quotation marks are, of course, book titles from the 1960s representing only a sampling of widely read works sharply critical of the church.

[46] William Kilbourn, ed., *The Restless Church* (Philadelphia: Lippincott, 1966), p. 4. The quotation is from Elizabeth Kilbourn.

trying to make you no trouble. He was trying to tell you you *got* trouble."
Pressing uncomfortable issues, the Church does not seek to "make trouble"; it
reminds us we "*got* trouble." Only when thorny issues are openly faced can
we find the reconciliation that gives God glory.

The Church has one power: God at work in it—"Now to him who by
the power at work within us . . ." (vs. 20). The epistle reminds us that we
may know "how vast the resources of his power open to us who trust in him"
(1:19 NEB). The Church can express this power by its preaching witness to
his acts in history, by its personal witness to power that has made a difference
in the lives of its people, and by its corporate witness to his mandate which
thrusts us into the struggle to meet human need.

The Church has one Lord: "who is able to do far more abundantly than
all that we ask or think." He won into the fold Gentiles whose "world was
without hope and without God" (2:12 NEB). Christians whose ancestors
were savages in the forests of Europe when Paul set out on his missionary
journeys may be profoundly grateful! Christians, of whatever ethnic stock,
have been won out of only one background, paganism—with its fears and
deep enmities—into "a single new humanity . . . through the cross" (2:15-
16 NEB). Pray that in the one Lord such victories may continue! This is
"glory in the church."

A Secret for the Restless: Matthew 11:25-30

These brief poetic lines state the secret which, throughout a whole section of the Matthean Gospel, men consistently miss. (Cf. 11:2–13:50.)
Dealing with "the hidden revelation," the section has reported John's
mystified question from prison; the incomprehension of a public which, for
opposite reasons, has rejected both John and Jesus; and the deafness of
Galilean cities that could not hear Christ's message. The section which
follows this passage reports the blindness of religious leaders who placed sabbath ceremonial above God's new revelation, the imperviousness of those who
thought the healing of broken men to be the work of the prince of demons,
and the parables by which Jesus tried to stab men awake to the open secret
of the kingdom. This passage itself states the secret in concise thematic
fashion: In his own "hidden" teaching and in the kingdom he personifies,
Jesus offers a new obedience which ends the restlessness caused by our
disobedience. There are two strong assertions.

First, that the gospel—hidden from the "wise" whose sophistication
inhibits simple faith—is revealed to "babes" who accept what God gives
them through his Son (vss. 25-27). This truth struck Paul with force. From
Isaiah he quoted:

> I will destroy the wisdom of the wise,
> and the cleverness of the clever I will thwart (I Cor. 1:19),

commenting that "God chose what is foolish in the world to shame the wise"
(I Cor. 1:27). Among those whom he called, not many "were wise according
to worldly standards, not many were powerful, not many were of noble birth"
(I Cor. 1:26). The gospel is not *anti*-intellectual, but it is not *achieved* by in-

tellect. It must be accepted as a personal response to a Person, a "transforming friendship."[47] It then finds expression in loyal obedience in the midst of
human affairs.

With this obedience the second assertion of the passage deals. The gospel
brings freedom under Christ's new inner law, for he is the true Wisdom
which fits our nature and for which we were intended (vss. 28-30). This
brief, hymnlike statement bears striking resemblances to the song of
personified Wisdom, in Ecclesiasticus.

> Draw near unto me, ye unlearned,
> And lodge in the house of instruction.
> Say, wherefore are ye lacking in these things,
> And your souls are very thirsty? . . .
> Put your neck under the yoke,
> And let your soul receive instruction:
> She is hard at hand to find.
> Behold with your eyes,
> How that I laboured but a little,
> And found for myself much rest (Ecclus. 51:23-24, 26-27).

Like Wisdom, Jesus as God's agent offers fullness of life.

Invited to take his "yoke," we are called to the new Law incarnate in
him. "Yoke" is a biblical idiom for God's law to his covenant people. Jeremiah
rebukes apostate Israel:

> For long ago you broke your yoke
>   and burst your bonds;
>   and you said, "I will not serve" (Jer. 2:20).

> "For they know the way of the Lord,
>   the law of their God."
> But they all alike had broken the yoke,
>   they had burst the bonds (Jer. 5:5).

The prophet declares that, rejecting obedience, Israel has rejected the way to
"rest for your souls" (Jer. 6:16). Those who first heard Jesus' invitation to
rest under his yoke, steeped as they were in Old Testament lore, must have
heard it in the light of such lines as these.

"All who labor" (vs. 28) may refer to those who "are heavy laden" by
scribal legalism. Peter suggests this: "Why do you make trial of God by putting a yoke upon the neck of the disciples which neither our fathers nor we
have been able to bear?" (Acts 15:10). Matthew shows how the yoke of the
old law has burdened men, and how Jesus offered a yoke of a better sort
(Chapter 12). But the invitation extends beyond freedom from legalism.
"Since no man can be free from *yoke and burden*, since he must *learn* from
someone, Jesus offers himself and his control, for that men will find the most
bearable of all."[48] Here, then, is a secret for the restless: in obedience to the

---

[47] The phrase is both the title of one of Leslie Weatherhead's books and a
recurring theme of his notable ministry.

[48] Theodore H. Robinson, *The Gospel of Matthew*, Moffatt New Testament
Commentary series (New York: Harper, 1927), p. 106.

new law and wisdom personified in Jesus we are assured the life that fits and fulfills our nature.

THIRTEENTH SUNDAY AFTER PENTECOST

Prophetic Religion Versus Edifice Complex
I Chronicles 28:1-3, 5-10

One of the oldest spiritual battle lines is drawn between prophetic religion and what has been called the church's edifice complex. Does "building the house of God" serve the real purpose of the body of Christ? Debate within one of America's largest congregations proposing to build a five-million-dollar house of worship repeated the ancient pros and cons.

On one side, it was said that "a new sanctuary was needed if the five constituents of meaningful worship—preaching, prayer, sacraments, fellowship and mission—were to be honored as they should be." The proposed building would herald a "renewal of faith in a time of great indecision in the world. . . . The church leaders agree that the building program is the spark of revitalization we need to take a strong stand." On the other side it was said that the church's image was better "just the way it is when we are helping others and not just ourselves." At the time, the church was contributing nearly a third of a million dollars a year—almost half its budget—to benevolences. It was argued that the new building would reduce that stewardship. Thus continues a controversy centuries long. Within it this glimpse of the valedictory stage of David's reign speaks its vivid word.

The story recalls the service of the Temple to the faith of Israel. For the temple gave uniformity and a norm of criticism to what was otherwise a widely dispersed cluster of religious practices at local shrines. Thus it helped to fortify Israel against the pressure of surrounding pagan rites. Apart from its ministry, an acculturated Israel might have conformed to Canaanite practices and beliefs.

Organized religion, including the much scorned "institutional church," serves that purpose in each new age. As the later history of Israel attested, it may freeze into immobility and stifle the spirit. This functional disease does not so much define as pervert its true role. George Fox prophetically protested against a hardened, formalized church and its "steeple houses" in his day; and the Society of Friends has remained a permanent witness for a more flexible, mystically perceptive, socially pioneering expression of Christian faith. While such protest movements provide important *correctives*, they would be inadequate *carriers* of the faith. The institutional church, with its articulate worship, preaching, and teaching, is the necessary body within which these corpuscles do their cleansing work.

Yet it was not the temple which gave the faith its creative forward thrusts. Nathan had forcibly reminded David of this truth (I Chron. 17:3-6) in sternly forbidding the building of the temple at an earlier stage. When the Exile removed Israel from access to the temple at Jerusalem, the faith entered one of its most spiritually creative periods.

David's charge to Solomon (vss. 9-10), full of moral and spiritual counsel, is followed (vss. 11-19) by details of furnishings and architecture. We do well to remember that rubrics and structure take meaning from their service to the spirit. Legal prescriptions for temple rituals should be read in the light of the Psalms. The descriptions of the rituals seem cold and formal, the Psalms warmly spiritual. Yet the Psalms accompanied the rituals. They report the words, songs, and emotions of those who performed the temple rites. We need both the inner spirituality and the liturgical body that carries it. To separate prophetic religion from its "edifice complex" is to corrupt both.

Remain Victors on the Field: Ephesians 6:10-20

Real victory is not determined by a "body count"—to use the barbaric phrase of military releases from Vietnam; the real victor owns the contested ground when the fighting ends. So says this Epistle: "having done all, to stand" (vs. 13) or "having fought to the end, to remain victors on the field" (Weymouth). This concluding passage in the Ephesian letter summarizing important themes of that document, speaks forcefully to Christians today.

First, it declares, *we are in a real fight, not against persons but against whole systems of life possessed of demonic power* (vss. 10-12). Our fight against "principalities," "powers," "world rulers of darkness," "spiritual hosts of wickedness in the heavenly places," is described in the astrological imagery of the ancient Near East. Modern translations help us to identify them in terms of our own world view. "We are not fighting against human beings, but against the wicked spiritual forces in the heavenly world, the rulers, authorities, and cosmic powers of this dark age" (vs. 12 GNMM); against "the Sovereignties and the Powers who originate the darkness in this world, the spiritual army of evil in the heavens" (JB); "against the leaders, politicians and heads of state of this dark world, against spiritual wickedness in high places" (CPV). The more-than-human dimension of this passage is better seen as structures, modes of organizing power, than as individuals, save as persons express and incarnate the structures. The demonic is a finite reality which makes infinite claims for itself and infinite demands on the loyalties of others. It is against this, the letter says, that we fight.

To take but one example, think of the way in which East and West today arrogate infinite claims and demands to Communism, on the one hand, and democracy on the other.

Some Americans seem to believe that it is possible to be a Christian only in a democratic, capitalistic society. This is simply not true. Jesus did not live in such a society. Neither did Augustine, Francis of Assisi, or Martin Luther. The Church can survive and be effective in every kind of social system. This does not suggest that it can be equally effective in any system. It is obvious that in a free society it will have much more opportunity. Yet the Church can survive and witness in every society. Almost all the younger churches are living in socialist welfare states.[49]

---

[49] Jones, *Our Mission Today*, p. 131.

That sets the picture. Our fight is against systems that make idolatrous claims for themselves, whether they be nations, corporations, social systems, racist ideologies, or whatever.

Second, *for this fight we need "the whole armor of God"* (vs. 11). The stress is on the *whole* armor; no fragmented gospel assembled from our preferences will do. It is all put together "with truth as your belt" (vs. 14 PT). No generalized truth but the truth in Jesus—the only truth this letter recognizes—unifies all: "You also, who have heard the word of truth, the gospel of your salvation" (1:13). "No longer be children, tossed to and fro and carried about by every wind of doctrine. . . . Rather, speaking the truth in love, we are to grow up in every way into him . . . into Christ" (4:14-15). "Assuming that you have heard about him and were taught in him, as the truth is in Jesus" (4:21).

All parts of the armor should be interpreted according to parallel uses of the key words elsewhere in Ephesians. "The breastplate of righteousness" (vs. 14) combines ethical goodness and salvation itself (4:24). Christian ethical conduct grows out of Christian salvation. "The gospel of peace" (vs. 15) is God's gift (1:2) reconciling warring parties in "one new man" through Christ (2:13-18) in the unity the spirit creates (4:3). With this we must be "shod."

It has been said that the secret of the Roman conquests was the attention bestowed on the soldier's boots. . . . Paul is evidently thinking, however, of the prophetic message about "the feet of him that brings good tidings" (Isa. 52:7), and his words may thus be taken to refer to the missionary spirit, the preparedness or readiness to carry the gospel everywhere. As the soldier had to be fit to march instantly at the word of command, so the Christian must be prepared, at all times, to answer the call of Christ.[50]

It is a useful subject of meditation thus to go through the items of "the *whole* armor of God," seeing their meaning in the light of the use of the terms elsewhere in the letter. This summarizing passage asserts that no partial gospel will do.

Third, *thus armed for the fight,* we need a life of prayer. "Do all this in prayer, asking for God's help" (vs. 18 GNMM). Prayer keeps the armor in good condition; it can hardly be kept ready and useful in any other way. We are to "pray on every occasion, as the Spirit leads." For this reason we are to "keep alert and never give up" (GNMM). No isolated individual meditation, prayer binds us to the community of faith by intercession, "always interceding for all God's people" (vs. 19 NEB). The writer closes the section by requesting prayers for his own preaching ministry, "that I may be granted the right words when I open my mouth, and may boldly and freely make known his hidden purpose, for which I am an ambassador—in chains" (vss. 19-20 NEB). Arming for Christian warfare is thus seen as one integrated concern, the Christian person, the Christian community, and the Christian messenger all alike dependent on one another and bound together in the life of prayer.

[50] Scott, *The Epistle to the Ephesians,* Moffatt New Testament Commentary series, pp. 252-53.

His Life as Ransom: Matthew 20:20-28

"The Son of man came not to be served but to serve, and to give his life as a ransom for many" (vs. 28).

The idea of Christ as ransom has received such stress in Christian thought that we do well to examine its biblical setting. Popular musings on the figure itself can stray far from the biblical passages that gave it currency. See our Lord's life as ransom, as this Gospel passage illuminates it.

The "ransom" saying climaxes Jesus' teaching about greatness through service—a teaching so recurringly woven into the gospel records (cf. Luke 22:24-26; Matt. 23:11; Mark 9:33-37) that it inevitably stands out as one of Jesus' principal emphases in dealing with his disciples. No matter how much the narrative settings differ, the *teaching* remains the same. The narratives throw light on the teaching, however, as occurs in today's lection.

It all begins with the request for special preferment that came from "the mother of the sons of Zebedee" (vs. 20). "Are you able to drink the cup that I am to drink?" Jesus asked, and they glibly replied, "We are able" (vs. 22). How little they understood! The silly shallowness of their reply becomes clear when Jesus, in Gethsemane, prays repeatedly that his cup may pass, adding his divine "nevertheless" (Matt. 26:39). "Drinking his cup" was to be avoided, if possible, or in any case undertaken only after utmost preparation in prayer. Like us, they approached it lightly as an honor to be grasped. Jesus replied that, though they might indeed share his cup of suffering, it was his role not to apportion honors but only to give himself "as a ransom for many." God alone could determine to whom the honors were due.

The indignation of the other disciples (vs. 24) shows how they shared the ignominious grasping of James and John. With no sorrow that two of their number so misunderstood the ways of the kingdom, the others jealously contended for the same preferment! That grasping holds the mirror to every man who reads it. We dare approach it only in self-examination.

Such ambitions, Jesus said, characterize not true disciples, but "the rulers of the Gentiles" (vs. 25). No ethnic, Jew-Gentile, contrast is implied, but a distinction between the faithful and the outside world: "You know that in the world, rulers lord it over their subjects" (NEB). Among disciples greatness is measured by servitude. He who has first place must be slave to the others (vss. 26-27).

Only within such a setting in human relations does the "ransom" saying speak with biblical reality. It is the ultimate example of greatness through service. He gave "his life as a ransom for many." The giving of his life (*psuche*) implies not so much the act of laying it down in death as the pouring it out from beginning to end in self-giving. The Greek *psuche*, used here, implies life on earth in its external, physical aspects. The soul, feelings, emotions are so interwoven that no sharp distinctions can be drawn among them. Ransom theology drawn from this passage must not isolate "ransom" in his death; Jesus, "the Man for others," gave his life (*psuche*) from the beginning.

As T. H. Robinson has pointed out, the Hebrew idea of ransom could mean money paid for the release of a person or animal from serious jeopardy. It never was used to speak of the sacrificial slaying of animals "or for the substitution of the sin-victim for the sinner." Thus, to identify ransom chiefly with the Cross is to tear it from its roots in the culture that gave us the figure. The New Testament does not make that mistake, either here or in such other references as: "the man Christ Jesus, who gave himself as a ransom for all" (I Tim. 2:5-6), or "Jesus Christ, who gave himself for us to redeem us from all iniquity" (Titus 2:13-14). Winston Churchill's famous tribute to the men of the RAF in World War II—"Never in the field of human conflict was so much owed by so many to so few"—makes something of an approach to what is intended here. Though many gallant fliers died, we are indebted not for their death only. Their "ransom" was their life of service, to which death was a climactic episode.

We look to Christ's whole life as ransom; not least as ransom from over-weening ambition and glib self-assurance that says, without looking for resources beyond ourselves, "we are able."

FOURTEENTH SUNDAY AFTER PENTECOST

Dimensions of Worship
II Chronicles 6:1, 18-21

One-dimensional worship is dull. Equate it with "the celebration of life," and you reduce it to the horizontal enjoyment of the world here and now. Center it in "the gathered community," and you have a cozy in-group affair. From all single-dimension approaches we need to be delivered. There is awe, joy, and power in the three-dimensional view expressed in the lofty prayer which the Chronicler places on the lips of Solomon at the dedication of the temple.

This worship has *a commanding sense of height*: "Behold, heaven and the highest heaven cannot contain thee; how much less this house which I have built!" (vs. 18). Solomon could conceive no space-age immensities in his limited cosmic picture. Nevertheless, the prayers of devout astronauts, who see earth in a startlingly new perspective, not inappropriately come to our minds as we read these words. God dwells in the "thick darkness" (vs. 1) of mysteries we cannot penetrate and of transcendence our space probes cannot explore. Worship which confies itself to the celebration of known experience or which rationalizes our life in philosophers' language, will always be anemic. The psalmist knew better.

Whither shall I go from thy Spirit?
Or whither shall I flee from thy presence? (Ps. 139:7).

It is fruitless to flee to the heavens, to the place of the dead, "the uttermost parts of the sea," or the deepest darkness; for wherever we go, the verdict is the same,

even there thy hand shall lead me,
and thy right hand shall hold me. (Ps. 139:10).

Vital worship must always have this dimension of transcendent height.

It needs also a *vast sense of breadth*: "hearken thou to the supplications of thy servant and of thy people Israel, when they pray toward this place" (vs. 21*a*). Even private prayer springs from the life of a covenant people. No one of us is able to invent the prayer idea, or use it creatively, alone. Each man inhabits a little world of introspection and personal anxiety, so long as his prayer is only *his* prayer. Personal devotions breathe vitality when they extend the devotions of a covenant people.

Beyond the brief cutting in this lection, Solomon's prayer includes the "foreigner, who is not of thy people Israel" who may come and pray "toward this house" (vss. 32-33). Beyond Solomon's expectation that was answered in the new covenant people from many nations who pray to the Father as he is known through his Son, Jesus Christ. The New Testament sees in Jesus the temple not made with hands, destroyed and raised again as the Resurrection brings a new Israel into being (cf. Matt. 26:61; John 2:13-25). We are called, to be built as "living stones . . . into a spiritual house" (I Peter 2:5) vast in its breadth. Vital worship draws us into this dimension of participation in the life of the people of God.

Beyond the height of divine transcendence and the breadth of participation in a covenant people, vital worship is characterized by a *probing sense of inwardness*: "and when thou hearest, forgive" (vs. 21*b*). The "gone-wrongness" of our human predicament always confronts us in worship. We worship to do something about our sins! To come to worship unaware that we are at odds with life and with God is to be too blind to do anything significant. We can do more than confess our sins *after* we have confessed; we cannot do more than confess them *until* we have confessed. Self-righteous persons, wanting to reform others; self-righteous nations, barricaded behind the doctrine of national sovereignty that must always find wrong in others, never in ourselves—we need to begin a new life with the realism of genuine confession: "and when thou hearest, forgive."

Unity: Achieved and Given: Ephesians 4:1-8

"There never were two compatible people!" So Gilbert K. Chesterton dismissed the notion of incompatibility as grounds for divorce. Lasting unity is achieved by mature and patient love. True of marriage, this is the story of that other loving but trying union, the Christian Church. One book of the New Testament—the Letter to the Ephesians—devotes its chief attention to this abiding need. How do Christians from widely diverse backgrounds live together in unity? Churches and families, alike, need a dependable answer to that question. This lection offers two answers: (1) Unity must be *achieved*. (2) Unity can be achieved because its foundations are *given*.

We start with the *struggle to achieve*, since the barriers to unity are in us. Only as we work at the essential changes in ourselves can anything else we do take us far. "The task is always to change ourselves—to deal with that in us which prevents our going forth to meet the other," writes Elizabeth O'Connor. Short of that, she says,

We will rationalize that it is unprofitable to stick with this particular grouping when there are more congenial people and more congenial circumstances in other places—"people who think the way I think and feel like I feel"—all of which, when you reflect on it, is rather dull, and in the second place probably a fiction, since a sure fact about the next group one joins is that one person there is certain to be the same—saying the same things, doing the same things, and evoking the same kind of response. But of course, we can always move on again when we have settled in enough for the rough edges of another person to rub against our own rough edges.[51]

The New Testament has little traffic with an invisible "Body of Christ." It is always up against the hard realities of living among differences within the *visible* Body. This Epistle says some significant things about our own behavior as the route over which unity is attained: such as living "with all lowliness and meekness" (vs. 2), "with perfect modesty and gentleness" (MT). As if that were not demanding enough, it adds "with patience," using a Greek word for long endurance under test, disciplined refusal to yield to passion, especially to anger. To drive the point home, it explains further: "forbearing one another in love," or "bearing with one another lovingly" (AT). We must work at it! "Spare no effort to make fast with bonds of peace the unity which the Spirit gives" (vs. 3 NEB).

So we come to the *gift!* How could we *achieve* so much were not foundations *given?* Prior to our act there exists a given unity: "There is one body" (vs. 4), of which the Ephesian letter has spoken from the beginning: "the church, which is his body, the fulness of him who fills all in all" (1:22-23). And there is "one Spirit," for as the writer has already explained, through Christ both Jew and Gentile "have access in one Spirit to the Father" (2:18). We are "called to the one hope that belongs to your call" (vs. 4). We have "one Lord" and "one faith" (vs. 5), despite variant creeds or theological formulations—one common dependence, one ultimate trust. We have "one baptism," all entering the faith by the one entrance of sharing in the grace represented by baptism into Christ. So there is "one God and Father of us all." With such unifying foundations *given*, we confidently work toward the *achievement* of unity.

This given foundation becomes personal in the gift each has received from Christ (vss. 7-8). "Grace was given to each of us according to the measure of Christ's gift," or "Each one of us has been given a special gift, in proportion to what Christ has given" (GNMM). With a poetic finish, freely quoting Psalm 18, the passage reminds us of Christ's final victory over all obstacles, even death itself, as a hint of how utterly changing his gifts can be. We can *achieve* unity because its foundations have been *given*.

Verifying a Miracle: John 2:1-11

"This, the first of his signs, Jesus did at Cana in Galilee" (vs. 11). Thus concluding this narrative, John introduces his "Book of Signs." Chapters 2–11 are replete with such material. In each case there is a wonderful event, which leads to a clarifying conversation, upon which the writer then offers some reflections. The physical event is reported primarily to precipitate the conversation and the reflection.

[51] O'Connor, *Journey Inward, Journey Outward*, pp. 26-27.

In this case water becomes wine, though it is immediately apparent that the real interest is not in what happened inside the water jars. John is more concerned with miracles that happen in the lives of people. For miracles are needed. Dull, possible things, like an alcoholic resolving to drink no more, cannot save us. On our way to death, W. H. Auden cried, we need a miracle! When an alcoholic—or any other mortal—is up against life's hardest fight, something more than such "possible" things as resolutions becomes a necessity. What happens in water jars is marginal; what happens in men is crucial. This story is chiefly about a miracle we can verify because it can happen in us.

"They have no wine" (vs. 3), Jesus' mother reported. It was a way of saying, "They have no joy." The psalmist, recounting God's good gifts, includes "wine to gladden the heart of man" (Ps. 104:15), and there seems to have been a common saying of the time, "Where there is no wine, there is no joy." But Jesus brought it in abundance! The water-become-wine filled, "up to the brim," six stone jars . . . each holding twenty or thirty gallons" (vss. 6-7)—120 to 180 gallons of wine! Does this focus on a beverage? Or on joy that knows no limit? Christ keeps performing the miracle of creating irrepressible joy where circumstances would least lead us to expect it.

Paul, for example, tells us of a life of almost unparalleled hardship (II Cor. 11:23-29), yet from his last imprisonment he wrote a letter so full of rejoicing that when, near the end, he repeated the word, it was almost with apology: "*Again* I will say, Rejoice." Within a few sentences he reveals the source of the rejoicing: "I can do all things in him who strengthens me" (Phil. 4:4, 13). In our time, Kagawa, "the St. Francis of Japan," poor, diseased, almost blind, repeatedly imprisoned for his convictions, but radiating joy, exclaimed, "God threw in everything when he gave me Christ!" These are miracles that matter, and they can happen again in us.

Jesus gives joy by purifying our lives. The six stone jars were "for the Jewish rites of purification" (vs. 6). In the Synoptic Gospels Jesus likens his teaching to new wine in old wineskins (Mark 2:22); John puts it into an acted parable. Because old rites of purification have not given joy and new life, Jesus "fills" the old emptiness "up to the brim." Men are left saying, "You have kept the good wine until now" (vs. 10).

How does he bring this new wine of joy in life set right? Not by the old purifications, which involved repeated ceremonial washings, but by his own self-giving. His strange saying to his mother, "My hour has not yet come" (vs. 4) is John's way of pointing to the Cross. In this Gospel Jesus speaks repeatedly of "his hour," each time referring to the final offering of his life. What the old rites could not give, his love and forgiveness can. This miracle, utterly changing, is open to endless verification as it happens again and again in the lives of men and women who accept his gift.

Acceptance is necessary, as the last words of this lection remind us. "His disciples believed in him" (vs. 11). Belief, in John's vocabulary, is never merely the intellectual acceptance of an idea. It is a personal relation. To believe in Jesus is to be his friend, to trust him, to keep faith with him, to depend on what he offers. "His disciples believed in him"; for this is what it means to *be* a disciple! In this relation with a transforming Lord everything is changed. No *possible* thing can save us, but with Christ the *impossible* keeps happening.

FIFTEENTH SUNDAY AFTER PENTECOST

This Vile World a Friend?
II Kings 17:5-14, 18-23

A world-affirming generation can find no depth of meaning in such lines as spoke to another age:

> Is this vile world a friend to grace,
> To help me on to God? [52]

Troubled, in need of help, the world as we now view it is not a vile enemy of goodness. Yet the integrity of biblical faith stands in perpetual tension with the culture of each successive age. Out of such struggle this segment of Israel's history speaks.

The Northern Kingdom had broken up, and the experience came as a shock to the people's faith. How could God have allowed his chosen to suffer defeat? Was he less than the gods of the surrounding peoples? Prophetic faith saw the people's apostasy as the answer. In violation of God's command, they had worshiped the local deities of their neighbors (vss. 7-8).

To the Canaanite peoples these deities stood as guarantors of fertility for field and herd. Moving into the area, Israel felt a strong impulse to adopt these religious practices as a part of the transition from their former nomadic life to that of settled farmers. The struggle gave rise to stern commands to "destroy all the places where the nations whom you shall dispossess served their gods, upon the high mountains and upon the hills and under every green tree" (Deut. 12:2-3). If this offends our sense of tolerance and ecumenicity, we do well to recall what the worship of these gods entailed.

For the Baal gods and their consorts, the Asherim, patrons of fertility, were worshiped in licentious rites, including temple prostitution, which by "sympathetic magic" were intended to assure productive agriculture. This passage describes the people's departure from their own faith, tolerating and imitating these cults (vss. 9-12). The prophets had denounced these practices and called Israel back from them, but the people refused to listen (vss. 13-14). Worshiping golden calves, Asherah and Baal, they resorted to divination, sorcery, and the sacrifice of their sons and daughters as burnt offerings (vss. 15-17).

Therefore, this recall to faith declares, God has rejected Israel and delivered his people into the hands of marauders (vss. 18-20). King Jeroboam has exerted a wicked influence by the adoption of these Canaanite cults, and the consequence has been the deportation of the people to Assyria (vss. 21-23). Amid changing details the contest continues. Baal and Asherah in Canaanite form no longer tempt us. Yet we live in what Vance Packard

---

[52] From the third stanza of Isaac Watts' hymn, "Am I a Soldier of the Cross?"

has aptly named "the sexual wilderness" where multitudes are troubled not so much by a sense of the *violation* of standards as by a *lack* of any standards that might guide them.

Dr. Graham B. Blaine, Jr., chief of psychiatry at Harvard University Health Services, told a recent meeting of the Academy of Religion and Mental Health that young people need and secretly want "clearly defined guidelines." But what they often get—from churches as well as parents—is a lot of vague talk about morality being dependent upon circumstances. Theologians who strive for modernity, he said, may believe that they are appealing to young people when they assure them the only absolute requirement of Christian morality is to love God. But in fact, they are "failing to provide the firm guidance that young people need and inwardly seek." [53]

In many forms we still face the contest of true faith with popular religions of the land; in the sanctions of success materially measured, in racism pervading both secular community and many areas of the church's life, in the popular paganisms of astrology and other fatalisms. Like this prophetic protest overheard from Israel's historic yesterdays, we need to sharpen the issue.

My God Will Supply: Philippians 4:4-9, 19-20

"My God will supply every need of yours according to his riches in glory in Christ Jesus" (vs. 19). No cheap optimism, this is the hard-bought faith of a prisoner with probable execution staring him in the face. He is God's happy warrior. "Rejoice," recurring word in his letter, comes finally in the ejaculation, "Yes, I'll say it again—Rejoice" (vs. 4).

The word has already occurred no less than six times in three short chapters. Each occasion of rejoicing is significant. Partisanship has prompted the preaching of some who have seized the opportunity of Paul's imprisonment to press their slanted version of the gospel. Yet "in every way, whether in pretense or in truth, Christ is proclaimed; and in that I rejoice" (1:18). Facing the possibility that death will terminate his imprisonment, he writes, "Even if I am to be poured out as a libation upon the sacrificial offering of your faith, I am glad and rejoice with you all" (2:17). Such joy should be shared: "Likewise you also should be glad and rejoice with me" (2:18). Though his faithful "fellow worker and fellow soldier" Epaphroditus has been ill to the brink of death, Paul is now sending him to Philippi, that the friends there may see how good God has been to grant his recovery, "that you may rejoice at seeing him again" (2:28). "Finally, my brethren," the concluding section of the letter begins, "rejoice in the Lord" (3:1).

This rejoicing is the product of God's sufficiency "to supply every need"—through dedication, through the wonder of the preaching of the gospel from whatever motive, through his acceptance of the disciple's sacrifice as a fulfillment of life, through his care in illness—"according to his riches . . . in Christ Jesus" (vs. 19).

The needs God supplies are concrete and specific. About our *need for harmonious human relations* Paul writes that because "the Lord is at hand"

[53] Starkey, *James Bond's World of Values*, pp. 15-16.

(vs. 5), a living part of every situation, there is only one way for the Christian to behave: "Let all men know your forbearance" (vs. 5), "magnanimity" (NEB), "courtesy" (KT), "gentleness" (PT).

There is *need of poise in the face of provocation.* Because in everything we can let our "requests be made known to God" through "prayer and supplication with thanksgiving," we are to "have no anxiety about anything" (vs. 6). Strong words, from a prisoner facing death! And tested words: "I have learned, in whatever state I am, to be content" (vs. 11). Needed words in our age of anxiety, when "the ulcer is the wound stripe of civilization" and the heart attack the accolade for having "arrived." Freedom from anxiety is God's gift, a part of his sufficiency, "the peace of God, which passes all understanding" (vs. 7)—considerations of ease and success, on which our normal expectations of "peace" are based, cannot fathom it.

There is the *need for a healthy mental climate.* The life we live in our minds is closely related to our overt behavior. "Whateveer is true, . . . honorable, . . . just, . . . pure, . . . lovely, . . . gracious, . . . any excellence, . . . anything worthy of praise" (vs. 8)—these are not mere sentimentalities. They are nurtured by *doing* the gospel as we have seen it embodied in the great apostle (vs. 9).

So, from beginning to end, this tonic passage points to the reality that "my God will supply every need of yours." What other conclusion can there be than the doxology, "To our God and Father be glory for ever and ever. Amen" (vs. 20)?

Now Life Has Meaning: Mark 14:3-9

Loss of meaning has become our pervasive malady. Life's round is "the rat race," work, "the salt mine." We are told our new way of getting rich is to buy from one another things we do not want, at prices we cannot afford, on terms we cannot meet, in response to advertising we do not believe! The end of struggle, regardless of success or failure, is death which levels all. Its denial of meaning nothing in life can erase. So runs the lament.

Christ puts meaning back. He links even death to good news, as this brief glimpse into the gospel demonstrates. "She has anointed my body beforehand for burying," he says. "And truly, I say to you, wherever the gospel is preached in the whole world, what she has done will be told in memory of her" (vss. 8-9). That tightly he links "burying" and "gospel," death and good news. With him, life has meaning which even death cannot erase.

He restores meaning in the face of all that defeats personhood. Interpreters differ as to whether this is another version of the incident told by Luke (7:36-50) of a similar anointing by "a woman of the city, who was a sinner." Whoever this woman may have been, it seems clear that her life had been a meaningless, dreary round to which Jesus had brought new luster and purpose, and that this restoration of the joy of living motivated the extravagant outpouring of her precious gift.

It is instructive to think of parallel anointings within the biblical record. Mark portrays this as a private anointing of Jesus for his kingly role, possibly so conceived by the woman who poured the ointment "over his head" (vs. 3), as in the anointing of kings.

Its contrast with another secret anointing, of Jehu (II Kings 9:1-16), is striking. The prophet Elisha calls Jehu out of a council of "the commanders of the army" and in solitude anoints him king. Returning to the council Jehu, pressed by his comrades for the meaning of the visit, puts them off with light words about this "fellow and his talk," and when their curiosity is sufficiently whetted, announces the anointing. This triggers a bloody rebellion led by the military junta. By contrast, Jesus, anointed, talks of his own death, and the good news which will emerge from it. Is there a similar contrast, in our time, between the anointing to martyrdom of two leaders of the civil rights movement—Malcolm X, advocate of violent power, and Martin Luther King, Jr., apostle of non-violent love? At any rate, Jesus found meaning even in his own death and showed the way to meaningful life which death cannot blot out.

He *restores meaning in the face of lovelessness.* If this woman has any connection with the one in Luke's account, she had been toyed with by many who sought to possess but not to love her. Jesus brought new meaning through a love which valued without seeking to possess. She was no longer a thing, desired only for the satsifaction she could render. She had become a person, prized beyond her ability to *earn* admiration or *merit* love. Thus cared for, her life had recovered its lost glow. In our crass time, which has reduced "love" to a synonym for sexual acts, he can restore the lost meaning of love as *agape:* "God shows his love for us in that while we were yet sinners Christ died for us" (Rom. 5:8).

He *restores meaning in the face of cynicism.* Some witnesses of this scene grumbled at the waste of treasure that should have been "given to the poor" (vs. 5). Jesus, understanding the woman's motive—extravagantly overflowing love—declared: "She has done a beautiful thing to me. For you always have the poor with you, and whenever you will, you can do good to them; but you will not always have me" (vss. 6-7). This was no fatalistic acceptance of poverty. It was a refusal to let general poverty become an excuse for suppressing love's occasional act of costly devotion. Cynically some would neglect the poor because they are always with us and must be accepted. Others would make the poor an escape from love's extravagant self-giving. To both Jesus brings personal understanding and concern that can awaken our drab lives to meaning.

KINGDOMTIDE

"In the New Testament . . . the Spirit's presence is the assurance that the glory of the Divine Kingdom will come in its fulness . . . . This New Testament conception of the 'guarantee' . . . , the 'firstfruits' . . . , means that the doctrine of the Holy Spirit is associated in the closest possible way with the Kingdom of God . . . . But the majesty of the Kingdom still lies in the future, and the promise awaits fulfilment. For the New Testament Christian the time between Easter and the Second Coming was the time of the Church, the Divine-human community ruled by the dynamic power of the Holy Spirit. The very presence of the Spirit was the guarantee that God's Kingdom would come in its fulness of glory. Eschatology is inexorably linked with the doctrine of the Spirit." [1]

Because this is true, the season of Kingdomtide is the proper outgrowth of the season of Pentecost. Those who would either advocate or deplore its observance—seeing in it only a time of exhortation keyed to a purely "social gospel" message—miss its scriptural and theological depth. As this lectionary provides for its celebration, the lessons of the respective Sundays proclaim

[1] McArthur, *The Evolution of the Christian Year*, p. 147.

that God rules in all of life now, and uphold the Christian hope of his fuller reign yet to come.

This climactic season brings the whole weight of the New Testament kerygma into vital relation to expanding areas of human concern: the disciple's fealty to Christ, recognized in the Festival of Christ the King—last Sunday in August; industrial relations as focused by Labor Sunday; educational excellence, timely interest as schools reopen; Christian education and its needs, exemplified in Church School Rally Day; the church ecumenically one, yet sadly fractured, as seen at its divided altars in the united act of World Communion Sunday; the need to underwrite peace in an organized world community, poignant appeal of World Order Sunday; our communion with all who are in Christ, whether in the Church Militant or the Church Triumphant, of which All Saints' Day makes us newly aware; the claims of our common humanity upon our shared resources, pressed by Community Fund efforts across the nation; and that loving response to God's goodness which Thanksgiving Day expresses. The one great theme of the Kingdom of God weaves these otherwise heterogeneous emphases into a New Testament unity and makes them related episodes in the one drama of the liturgical year as Kingdomtide completes its cycle.

FIRST SUNDAY IN KINGDOMTIDE

Liturgy of the Kingdom
I Chronicles 29:10-18

By derivation our word *liturgy* implies service in a double sense—our service of worship before God, and our service of love and helpfulness to our brother man. This noble passage is high liturgy in the first sense, as the Chronicler brings his epic of David, the ideal king, to a climactic summation in noble farewell to his people (chapters 28–29), concluding with this kingly prayer in which David leads the devotion of the assembly. In the full splendor of his kingship, surrounded by his people pledging their gifts to "the treasury of the house of the Lord" (vs. 8), David acclaims God as the supreme Sovereign. Here, at its best, is liturgical celebration of God's kingdom. And reverberating all through the implications of this prayer, one hears rich overtones of the other meaning of liturgy as service among men.

In the great king's confession of faith we hear the truth that *God is the source of all rule* (vss. 10-11). "Thine, O Lord, is the greatness, and the power, and the glory, and the victory, and the majesty"—this is sonorous liturgical rhetoric, but it is far more. It is the king's recognition that all rule is delegated, and that God is the ultimate source of orderly life among men. David has vastly extended the borders of Israel, but he recognizes that all achievement rests on a Source beyond himself; "for all that is in the heavens and in the earth is thine; thine is the kingdom, O Lord, and thou art exalted as head above all." In this insight there is no room for the chauvinism that cries, "Our country, right or wrong"; or the demagoguery that declaims, "The voice of the people is the voice of God"; or the cynicism that growls, "When I have won, no one will ask, Who was right? but only, Who was strongest?"

The roots of all right rule are sunk in the reign of God, where alone they can secure just and stable welfare for all.

In the great king's thanksgiving we hear the truth that *God is the source of all wealth* (vss. 12-16). "For all things come from thee, and of thy own have we given thee"—the familiar offertory sentence rings out from the heart of a kingly recognition that we can *give* nothing to God; we are pensioners *returning* what is *his* by right. The evidence of this is the transitory nature of our life as "strangers," "sojourners," who live through insubstantial days "like a shadow" soon gone (vs. 15). Even the provision for the temple so dear to the king's heart comes not from human hands, but from God (vs. 16).

The overtones of human service are not far to seek. If we are pensioners, we cannot afford to disdain a sharing of the benevolence on which we depend. One sees the reality more sharply when it is silhouetted against the dark backdrop of our common attitudes. A grower who has received $18,000 in government subsidies opposes Federal assistance to the poor, saying: "The Bible says a man should work." The wife of a grower who got $29,000 in crop price supports protests that, "Giving causes loss of pride." Strange words from pensioners! Which is what we are! It has been well said that those who sit at the Lord's table ought to have manners enough to pass the bread.

In the great king's intercession we hear the truth that *God is the source of all right motives* (vss. 17-18). He reads the motives of king and commoner alike (vs. 17). So we supplicate him for fidelity of purpose and thought. The kingdom of God is not programs, projects, vast enterprises, of which we can boast that we are "building the kingdom," but personal response to God's sovereign rule. So David prays, "Shape the purpose of your people's heart and direct their hearts to you" (vs. 18 JB); "keep the mind and purpose of thy people ever in this spirit; direct their hearts to thyself" (MT). And so David's greatest Son was to say,

> "How blest are those who know their need of God;
> the kingdom of Heaven is theirs" (Matt. 5:3 NEB).

For knowing their poverty, they keep open to God, on whom they utterly depend and who alone can direct their hearts to himself.

Kingdom of the Victorious One
Revelation 19:1, 4, 6-8

One of Albert Camus's memorable characters, a doctor passionately fighting a plague, asks a question that rises from the deep uneasiness of the mind of our time: "Since the order of the world is shaped by death, mightn't it be better for God if we refuse to believe in Him and struggle with all our might against death, without raising our eyes toward the heaven where He sits in silence?" [2] The doctor's idealism is better than his theology. For while the highest in religious and humanitarian ethics demands the struggle

[2] Albert Camus, *The Plague* (New York: The Modern Library, 1948), pp. 117-18.

against death, biblical religion knows nothing of a God withdrawn in impassive silence in a distant heaven.

The Bible itself is one epic story of struggle—God's warfare against all that defiles, tyrannizes, and defeats man. The conflict begins in Eden, comes to one of its crucial episodes in the struggle against Pharaoh, endures through Olympic contests with the Baal gods, passes through the deep valley of the Exile, and reaches its climax at Golgotha. God stands not only as Creator and Judge, but as Savior whose share in man's lot involves him in the suffering and the tragic exertion. So Job discovers. So the Cross reveals. So the dramatic warfare of Revelation portrays.

Fittingly this Epistle for the First Sunday of Kingdomtide pictures the Kingdom of God in no passive, static, quiet, immobile terms, but as the consummation of the age-long struggle against evil. Through its cosmic drama, the book of Revelation portrays in symbolic action what no amount of our more mundane, pedestrian prose could say. The writer is a Christian sharing in the first sufferings of the Church under Rome's bloody purge, himself a lonely exile on the island of Patmos. Out of the heart of that titanic engagement with the powers of darkness, in which numbers of those dear to him have been martyred, he writes faith's vision of God's conquest of evil.

The early chapters of Revelation have told of Christ's death and resurrection, through which a new creation is assured. His new community of faith will replace Babylon, this book's symbol for the very kingdom of evil itself, of which Rome is the current embodiment. In a series of scenes laid in heaven, we are shown the martyrs who have come through death to salvation, singing their praises to the victorious Lamb, this book's Christ symbol; we see their number brought to completion, to which heavenly action can respond; we learn that the martyrs are given new life and the destroyer of the earth is himself to be destroyed; and at last Babylon is wiped out, freeing the earth of a society incarnating all that is at enmity with Christ and the faithful souls he gathers. It is at this point in Revelation's dramatized philosophy of history that the celebration of victory in today's lection emerges. If we may translate its poetic glories into propositional statements, it speaks three truths about God's kingship.

First, God's rule is his victory over ultimate evil. "Salvation and glory and power belong to our God" (vs. 1). "Fallen, fallen is Babylon the great!" (18:2) has rung as a dirge through the preceding chapter, a picture of the subjection of proud power, the despoiling of wealth, and the utter desolation of a once teeming metropolis. This, the exile on Patmos dares to believe, is the inevitable outcome of evil in every age, and in his age the fate of Rome. The cry of the martyrs, "O Sovereign Lord, holy and true, how long before thou wilt judge and avenge our blood on those who dwell upon the earth?" (6:10) has now been answered. They can sing.

We give thanks to thee, Lord God almighty, who art and who wast,
that thou hast taken thy great power and begun to reign (11:17)

The cry of the suffering "How long?" has sounded through the world from the time of the psalmist until now. Kingdomtide celebrates God's victory in the midst of the struggle. Fight we must, but those who struggle as followers of the Prince of Peace and Love fight on the winning side.

Second, God's rule is embedded in ultimate reality. Concerning the identity of "the twenty-four elders and the four living creatures" who worshiped before God's throne (vs. 4) it is not possible to be definite. The mythical "living creatures" have a clear association with like figures in Ezekiel, and before that with Babylonian signs of the zodiac, suggesting the points of the compass and the origins of the winds. They are associated too with the angelic beings of Isaiah's vision in the temple. They are elemental to the cosmic universe and nearest to God in the traditional pictures of a heavenly host. The twenty-four elders may represent the twelve tribes of Israel plus the twelve apostles of our Lord although numerous other identifications are suggested by careful scholars. Detailed identification is not crucial; what this exalted poetry is saying is clear: God's rule is so deeply embedded in reality itself that the elemental forces of the universe and the highest circles of spiritual insight unite to praise him.

Third, God's rule is celebrated in his union with the company of his faithful witnesses. Christ the Lamb and his Bride the Church are about to be united in marriage (vs. 7). The Church is not the kingdom of God; it must never be confused with it. That way lies ecclesiastical arrogance and apostasy. Yet the Church has an intimate union with Christ and his kingdom, and the devotion of the faithful adorns the Bride in the celebration; she is clad in "fine linen" which "is the righteous deeds of the saints" (vs. 8). Thus the dedication of the martyrs is not lost. It has its place of significance in the ultimate victory of God as he comes in his kingdom.

Is all this remote from us moderns? Let a leading contemporary journalistic analyst, Harrison E. Salisbury, answer with his description of our apocalyptic time:

The problems which overhang the world have never been more dangerous. If we escape nuclear suicide we may drown in a sea of humanity; suffocate in a poison-filled atmosphere; succumb to pollution of the seas and despoilation of the land; descend into robotry with the aid of chemicals and electrodes or perish at the edict of a non-human computer.[3]

In such a time there can be no retreat from our part in the struggle, but there is strength in the faith that we share with a God who does not sit silent in heaven. He is in the struggle, and the victory is his.

Festival of Christ the King
Matthew 25:31-40

One beautiful and proper designation of the First Sunday of Kingdom-tide is "The Festival of Christ the King." For such a festival this is a most appropriate gospel lesson. For it declares that all nations stand under Christ's

[3] From "The World in the Year 2000," appended to Andrei D. Sakharov, *Progress, Coexistence and Intellectual Freedom* (New York: W. W. Norton, 1968), p. 157.

kingly judgment (vss. 31-33). His rule is universal. What we see in him lays claim to all men. Speaking for the Asian peoples, M. M. Thomas comes very near the heart of this affirmation as he writes:

> We have reacted against a loose use of the idea of the Kingdom of God and sought to define the gospel as the kingship of Christ, as the news of the crucified and risen Jesus Christ. But it is clear that the new creation in Christ, the world renewed in Jesus Christ, or the Kingdom of Christ is also an essential constituent part of the gospel; so that Dr. Paul Lehmann has recently defined the Christian gospel as the politics of God "to make and to keep human life human." [4]

Christ's kingly rule, so defined, knows no geographic, ethnic, or creedal boundaries. He comes "to make and keep human life human" in the face of rampant dehumanizing forces. When he comes in this capacity, "before him will be gathered all the nations" (vs. 32).

Christ's kingly judgment expresses his grace (vs. 34). Many a man asks, "How can Christians claim that Christ judges all men? Are we so narrow that great souls like Confucius, Gautama, and their saintly disciples are lost? If that is what the gospel offers, it is strangely inverted good news!" Joachim Jeremias, ablest of the scholarly interpreters of the parables of Jesus, sees in this the answer to the question as it arose in the first generation of Christianity: "Will the heathen be lost?" Jeremias paraphrases Jesus' reply:

> The heathen have met me in my brethren; for the needy are my brethren; he who has shown love to them has shown it to me, the Saviour of the poor. Therefore, at the Last Judgement, the heathen will be examined concerning the acts of love which they have shown to me in the form of the afflicted, and they will be granted the grace of a share in the Kingdom, if they have fulfilled Messiah's law (James 2:8), the duty of love. [5]

Since all men meet him in his brethren, "one of the least of these" (vs. 40), no man is lost for want of contact with him. To men of "all the nations" he extends the invitation "inherit the kingdom prepared for you from the foundation of the world" (vs. 34).

His grace is accepted by those who are at one with him in love (vss. 35-40). The test is not intellectual: Did you give assent to orthodox doctrines about me? It is not ecclesiastical: Were you a faithful member of the Church? It is love's test of human help extended in love to Christ through his most obscure and impoverished brethren. Those who meet that test are in the kingdom, and those who fail that test—however proper they may be on other counts—are not in the kingdom (vss. 41-46). It is as plain as that.

Economist Barbara Ward makes the parable dreadfully contemporary in discussing the crippling poverty of the developing nations:

> Why at the moment when we can incinerate this planet have we also been given the means to feed the human race and lift it up? If this is not the apocalyptic

[4] M. M. Thomas, *The Christian Response to the Asian Revolution* (London: SCM Press, 1966), p. 96.

[5] Jeremias, *The Parables of Jesus,* p. 209.

moment, at which in some sense we as Christians are supposed to look, I don't know how much more apocalyptic you want us to be . . . . Christians alone straddle the whole spectrum of rich nations, and therefore Christians are a lobby or can be a lobby of incomprehensible importance . . . And if we don't do it, and we come ultimately before our Heavenly Father, and he says, "Did you feed them, and did you give them to drink, did you clothe them, did you shelter them?", and we say, "Sorry Lord, but we did give 0.3% of our gross national product," I don't think it will be enough.[6]

SECOND SUNDAY IN KINGDOMTIDE

Kingdom of the Committed
I Kings 18:21-39

Asked if she believed in astrology, a famous film actress replied, "I believe in everything a little bit." Modern as she was, she had assumed an antique, grotesque posture: the one-foot-in-each-security straddle. In ancient Israel, it was King Ahab's stance—and his downfall. Because Baal gods were reputed to give timely rain and fruitful fields, Ahab adopted their rites in the interest of national prosperity. Because Yahweh had been the ancient source of Israel's nationhood, Ahab played it safe by naming his children with names based on Yahweh's name. Not daring commitment to any real faith, he made his cautious bid for a sure thing—believing in everything a little bit.

His modern counterparts want present indulgence and a secure future, a happy marriage and "the Playboy philosophy," world peace and a race for nuclear supremacy, sound education and schools run by the immature, a dynamic faith and no binding religious disciplines.

To all such, Elijah flings down the gauntlet: "How long will you go limping with two different opinions?" (vs. 21). So colorful were his words that translators try vainly to capture their luster. "How long do you mean to hobble on this faith and that?" (MT). Inwardly divided, we are outwardly crippled! But "the people did not answer him a word." For the frightening truth is that the apostasy of the uncommitted thunders in their cautious silence when decision is demanded.

In heroic contrast stands the solitary conviction of Elijah. He articulates the faith, challenging Baal's 450 priests who enjoy the aggressive patronage of Ahab's queen (vs. 22). Seven thousand in the land, who have given Baal no obeisance (19:18), comprise a ready congregation for Yahweh when once a vocal leader has championed the cause. In the meantime they share in the betrayal through silence. How vital is Elijah's courageous commitment!

Not inappropriately, this fiery prophet is associated with other fiery occasions. Legend remembers how he cursed with fire the king's guard sent to bring him to the royal presence (II Kings 1:9-12). It recalls how he was parted from his associate, Elisha: "Behold a chariot of fire and horses of fire separated the two of them. And Elijah went up by a whirlwind into heaven. And Elisha saw it and he cried, 'My father, my father! the chariots of Israel

[6] From the Official Report of the World Conference on Church and Society (Geneva: World Council of Churches, 1967), p. 19.

and its horsemen!' And he saw him no more" (II Kings 2:11-12). Fitting tribute! This man of conviction had been a surer strength to the nation than all its armed forces. No "limping with two different opinions" for him! In *his faith,* the nation found *its faith* again.

His faith proved true; the God of the universe did sustain his committed stand. The test by fire was unmistakably appropriate. It put Baal, nature-god, to a nature-test. The episode ends the drought which Elijah had predicted in the name of "the Lord the God of Israel" (17:1)—a dire threat to Baal whose main business it was to assure the spring rains essential to agriculture in an otherwise quickly arid land. Confronting Ahab (vss. 17-19), Elijah had made it clear that the issue was more than a question of drought; it was the query, Who sends the rain? Does Baal have that power? The god who answered with fire would be understood to control the rain and all the gifts of the fields.

The tense drama of the scene on Mount Carmel, the ingenuity of the test, the frenzy of the priests of Baal, the biting sarcasm of the prophet, and the miraculous burst of flame, make this one of the most colorful scenes in all literature. Norman H. Snaith speculates that the flame may have been ignited by a stroke of the terrible lightnings that end an oriental drought, adding that, more importantly, it came at the exact time to respond to Elijah's prayer. Such a scholar as S. Szikszai ventures that "the details of the contest of Mount Carmel reveal the growth of the miraculous element in the tradition, but the essential historicity of the contest can hardly be denied." [7] This was a crucial turning point in the march of Israel toward secure monotheism. It is a landmark in advance to the conviction that our God is Lord of no segment of life, but of *all* of life in *all* the universe.

God's Reign and Our Wealth
I Timothy 6:6-19

"I put to you the duty of doing all that you have been told, with no faults or failures, until the Appearing of our Lord Jesus Christ,

> who at the due time will be revealed
> by God, the blessed and only Ruler of all,
> the King of kings and the Lord of lords" (vss. 14-15 JB).

Like all meaningful proclamations of God's kingship, this one turns its back on generalities and abstractions to settle down squarely in the midst of every-day duties. All that precedes and follows it has to do with riches, true and false. The theme, then, is God's reign and our wealth. Kingdomtide asserts Christ's Lordship over many specific areas of life, from one Sunday to another, beginning here where the conflict is often fiercest.

False teachers tone down the tension by pretending "that religion is a way of making a profit" (vs. 5 JB). The modern promise of popular religionists runs, "Prayer will *get* you what you want"—as if it had nothing to do with learning to *change your wants!* There is, indeed, "rich profit, pro-vided that it goes with a contented spirit" (vs. 6 MT). Faith as a trick of the

[7] Article on "Elijah the Prophet," *Interpreter's Dictionary of the Bible,* II, 89.

mind restlessly set on some ulterior "success" is hereby dismissed as an illusion. The "profit" or "great gain" is not a matter of worldly wealth at all. This profit cannot be grasped in the hand. "Empty-handed we came into the world, and empty-handed, beyond question, we must leave it" (vs. 7 KT). Contentment is not in multiplied means but in disciplined desires; "if we have food and clothes, that should be enough for us" (vs. 8 GNMM).

To measure life in any other terms is to be trapped. "People who long to be rich are a prey to temptation; they get trapped into all sorts of foolish and dangerous ambitions which eventually plunge them into ruin and destruction" (vs. 9 JB). "Trapped" is the apt word here—witness the frustrations, escapes, and addictions that bedevil the posh suburb and the privileged campus. Reduce slick advertising to its basic axioms, and you get such assumptions as: "It's the *surroundings* that give life its meaning . . . . You deserve the best; you owe yourself easy-chair comfort. Forget the discomforts of others and live it up." People whose presuppositions give such appeals persuasive power are so trapped that parallel ads for drugs to relieve tension offer release!

Turn, then, to the true riches: "pursue justice, piety, fidelity, love, fortitude, and gentleness" (vs. 11 NEB). The catalogue makes heavy demands in an age when much urban wealth is based on real estate holdings in segregated areas where considerations of *justice* would slash cherished profits to the bone; or when the permissiveness of "the sexual wilderness" and the tandem polygamy of epidemic divorce contradict real *fidelity*. Yet the demand for these Spartan standards of discipline is clear: "aim at righteousness" (RSV), "aim at integrity" (MT).

Riches, so understood, are based on faith: "Fight the good fight of the faith" (vs. 12). "Fight" speaks not of belligerency, but of intense contest: "Run your best in the race of faith" (GNMM); "Enter the great contest of faith" (AT). Faith is not surrendered because its way is hard; hardship is part of the contest. We are called to stand firmly on "the good confession" (probably the baptismal confession of faith) and to remember that Jesus also made such a confession "before Pontius Pilate" (vss. 12-13). JB emphasizes the parallel of the two confessions by balancing the way the Christian "spoke up for the truth in front of many witnesses" with the way in which Jesus Christ "spoke up as a witness for the truth in front of Pontius Pilate." If our courage for sacrificial witness needs bolstering we are reminded that "the appearing of our Lord Jesus Christ" is inherent in the Christian expectation. He "appears" in our daily choices and in the final judgment.

Compared with most of the world's people, past and present, we are "rich in this world" (vs. 17). So the closing charge is for us "not to be haughty," "not to be contemptuous of others" (PT)—not to feel that we *have* more because we *deserve* more. We can set secure hope, not "on so uncertain a thing as money" (NEB), but "on God who richly furnishes us with everything to enjoy." The truly rich are "rich in good deeds" (vs. 18), "open-handed and generous" (MT). "Their security should be invested in the life to come, so that they may be sure of holding a share in the life which is permanent" (vs. 19 PT). Good investment counsel!

The Best Messenger: Luke 16:10-15

Everyday proverbs often mint the substance of experience into the coin of words. Take, for instance, the saying, "Money talks." Repeating it, we may fall into the cynical mood of that old-world proverb, "Money never goes to jail," or of its companion, "When money talks, truth is silent." Hard happenings in business, politics, and world affairs underscore that dark estimate. But it is also true that money can be sent on errands of goodwill, so that vast sweeps of experience are compressed into the Yiddish proverb, "Money is the best messenger."

And right use of money demands decision on our first loyalty. "No servant can serve two masters," said Jesus. "You cannot serve God and mammon" (vs. 13), or in NEB's plain talk, "You cannot serve God and Money." You can serve God *with* money, or you can serve money *as* god; but in either case there must be a choice.

Luke observes that the Pharisees scoffed at this saying because they "were lovers of money" (vs. 14). Their piety had something in common with that of John Ward, a member of Parliament who was one of the first owners of a tract of land near Dagenham, England, on which a Ford plant has now been erected. He bought it cheap because it was mostly flooded, then used his influence to get it drained at public expense. Among his papers a delving historian found a prayer informing God of his holdings in Middlesex and Essex counties and asking him to preserve the two counties from any disaster. Then he continues: "As I have a mortgage in Hertfordshire, I beg of Thee likewise to have an eye of compassion on that County; for the rest of the counties, Thou mayest deal with them as Thou art pleased."

Who does not see that John Ward's praying was not a practice of true religion, but its denial? It reinforced his self-centeredness and got in the way of anything God could have wished to do in his life. It set him to "lobbying for special favors in the courts of the Almighty." It dulled his conscience concerning his responsibilities to his fellowmen and to society. It must surely have helped to limit his personal growth—which may have something do do with the fact that the ambitious Mr. Ward died in debtor's prison. God could not honor his prayer, so like that of the Pharisees "who were lovers of money."

So says this lection. Money is the best messenger; only a prior choice of loyalties can give it the best message to carry.[8]

THIRD SUNDAY IN KINGDOMTIDE

Letting Reality In: Isaiah 6:1-8

Like a series of locks letting in the waters that lift a ship, worship lets in reality by which men live as more than victims of events. Isaiah is a memorable example. A young nobleman oppressed with sorrow at the death

---

[8] Adapted from "Faithful in Little and in Much," church school lesson material contributed by the author to *The Adult Student.*

of his beloved king, he got a new grasp of the meaning of history as it unfolded around him. In its vast drama he saw the role he was called to play. The insight shed its light on long years of activity, but it began in a quiet hour of worship in the temple. One majestic line gives its keynote: "In the year that King Uzziah died I saw the Lord" (vs. 1).

To be *always* active is to be *seldom* active about what matters most. *Trying harder* achieves true ends only when we have *stopped trying* long enough to let reality in. In a series of articulate movements Isaiah's experience can guide us into worship with that transforming potential.

Worship begins with august Reality beyond ourselves. The depressed young Isaiah shared in a temple service which took him out of himself. He saw his own situation and that of his people in a new light. The contemplation of God active in history gave new meaning to all that was transpiring.

What began by taking him out of himself brought Isaiah back to himself. He saw his life in clearer perspective. He sensed what the need of the nation laid upon him to do. He glimpsed where the God of truth was leading. Having been *taken out of himself* and *brought back to himself,* he ended by *outdoing himself.* Through years that followed, his grasp of truth continued as he played his heroic part in the affairs of his people. Such alternation between reality beyond us and response within us characterizes all true worship.

"I saw the Lord." The words reflect our need. Irwin Edman records a correspondence in which a student reflects inner insecurity that drives him to an urgent quest for life's meaning. In one letter, he wonders if he may not really be *seeking God.* His professor replies that this hunger within him really *is* God. Our yearnings do not originate in us; they are a response to reality beyond us. We could not seek the Highest if he had not already been dealing with us. As the eye is an organism's adaptation to light, our search for God is a response to Reality that is *there.* As in all true worship, Isaiah felt a presence, august and fearsome. Before God even the angels must cover their faces. His voice shook the thresholds (vss. 1-4). In like manner, our worship begins in adoration of God which takes us out of ourselves to him.

To face his holiness is to know our shame. Isaiah drew back from his vision of God, crying: "Woe is me! For I am lost; for I am a man of unclean lips, and I dwell in the midst of a people of unclean lips; for my eyes have seen the King, the Lord of hosts!" (vs. 5). In all real worship, adoration leads to confession. What other force can give us such realism in self-examination? Not patriotism; it exalts us as citizens of a great country, and encourages us to think our country's greatness is our own. Not education; it leads us to identify ourselves with the cultured minority, as if a degree had transferred us to another class of being. There is hope for a man when he learns to say, "Woe is me! For I am lost"; but apart from great worship the lesson is not likely to be learned. Nor can it be therapeutic apart from worship's assurance of forgiveness and cleansing (vss. 6-7).

From adoration and confession, worship proceeds to personal call. There is new insight into life's meaning, aided by sharing the cumulative treasury of historic faith. The Scriptures, the affirmation of great convictions, and the contemplation of the present in this enlarged and corrected perspective, lead us to see more clearly what claim is laid upon us. Like Isaiah, we hear a call, "Whom shall I send, and who will go for us?" (vs. 8a).

Drawn out of ourselves by the call of meaning and responsibility, we are brought back to ourselves to respond. "Here I am! Send me" (vs. 8b). Those in every age who worship truly echo Isaiah's answer. Call is focused in decision. Surrender is prelude to victory.

Agents of Reconciliation
II Corinthians 5:17–6:2

The gospel has seldom been summarized as succinctly as in Paul's words, "God was in Christ reconciling the world to himself, not counting their trespasses against them, and entrusting to us the message of reconciliation" (5:19). That recognizes the twofold truth that our life is disrupted but has come under a healing power, and that to be Christian is to face an explosive world as agents of reconciliation.

Our disruption needs no proof. We are painfully at odds with one another as, for instance, when a National Advisory Commission warns that "our nation is moving toward two societies, one black, one white—separate and unequal," and adds that this threatens "the future of every American." [9] Our alienation darkens the life of universities, labor relations, and many a home.

In no small degree, it grows out of our inability to accept ourselves. The phenomenon of organized "hate groups" within our common life expresses our painful self-loathing. In his book, *Man Against Himself*, psychiatrist Karl Menninger has helped us see how much of our sickness, to say nothing of our accident-prone behavior, stems from unconscious feelings that we are in the wrong and need to be restrained or punished. When our self-accusation becomes sufficiently pathological, we seek to escape it by projecting it on others, pushing into the world around us the hates that began within us.

Underlying it all is our alienation from God. Our lack of self-acceptance may well spring from our inability to accept our ancestry. A man hates himself because he knows himself an extension of his father, whom he hates. Back of the unaccepted forebears stands the Father of all. Our sense of meaninglessness speaks our alienation from him, as do our anxieties and our guilt.

Into all this comes the message of reconciliation, starting at the point of our root alienation—"be reconciled to God" (5:20). Christ comes into our lives accepting us as *persons*, valuable in our own right, dealt with in unqualified love. Through his forgiving death he shows us forgiveness for all the worst that we can do or be, thus accepting us in spite of all that we have most despised and dreaded in ourselves. Since he brings God to us, this acceptance leads to a new relation to God (vs. 21). Reconciled to him, knowing he has accepted us, we can accept ourselves. The guilt and conflict within us are healed. When at last we can live at peace with ourselves, we can extend our acceptance to one another. Loving with wholeness, we can

[9] *Report of the National Advisory Commission on Civil Disorders* (The New York Times Company, 1968), p. 1.

plant love in the relationships where once we planted only tension. So we are made "ambassadors" through whom God makes his appeal (vs. 20).

Why does this not happen more dependably in our experience? Is it because we seek the *fruit* of the Christian reconciliation—the repair of human relations by ethical precept—before we have its *root*? Paul did not argue the Christian message as a philosophical structure. He did not press it as a moral demand. He affirmed it as an undeniable datum of experience: "If any one is in Christ, he is a new creation; the old has passed away, behold, the new has come" (5:17). The new relation to God was so real that there was no room to question the new relation to himself and all men. He was living in "a new creation."

A convert from Hinduism, who traveled widely in America, said there was one question which churchmen everywhere kept asking about his experience in India: "Do you think Christianity has anything to offer that is really better than what you found in Hinduism?" The prevalence of the question can mean only that we are unsure of our faith. It is formal, external, a set of ideas; not a deeply experienced reality. Who that has known the reconciliation in Christ—"a new creation"—could ask that incredulous "Do you really think Christianity has anything to offer . . . ?"

So the entreaty is addressed to us, "not to accept the grace of God in vain" (6:1). Between alienation and reconciliation there is only one step: in Paul Tillich's expressive phrase, "accept the fact that you are accepted." The "now" in which that happens "is the day of salvation" (6:2).

But Sacrifice Is Absurd! Mark 10:28-31

"But sacrifice is absurd," protests the opportunist, seeing the whole meaning of existence in seizing what he can as soon as he can. Sacrifice is indeed absurd, says Jesus in these swift sentences. But for another reason: whatever you give up for the sake of God's good news comes back to you multiplied.

In the light of the specifics of the passage we understand the closing sentence, "But many that are first will be last, and the last first" (vs. 31). In itself, Joachim Jeremias reminds us, the saying is a generalized catchword similar to saying, "How easily fortune changes overnight." Attached to various contexts in the Gospels (Matt. 19:30; 20:16; Luke 13:30), it takes its meaning in each case from its setting. It is a recurring biblical idea. The Old Testament puts it poetically:

> The bows of the mighty are broken,
> but the feeble gird on strength.
> Those who were full have hired themselves
> out for bread,
> but those who were hungry have ceased
> to hunger (I Sam. 2:4-5a).

Luke, interpreting God's action in Christ, attributes to Mary the hymnic lines:

> He has put down the mighty from their thrones,
> and exalted those of low degree (Luke 1:52),

portraying these reversals of power as acts of the God of justice and grace. Mark records dedication to such inversion of position as part of the disciple's call: "If any one would be first, he must be last of all and servant of all" (Mark 9:35). In the setting of this lection, the saying takes on still another shade of meaning.

The rich man has declined the kingdom invitation, unable to dare what it demands. Jesus remarks, "How hard it will be for those who have riches to enter the kingdom of God!" (vs. 23). Peter has responded. "We have left everything and followed you" (vs. 28). Having sacrificed so much, what do we get? We have left a good fishing business to follow (1:18, 20). All of this world's good we might have had, we have given up. Jesus replies that in the long run it will be no sacrifice; you will receive back, even in this present life, far more than you gave up—to say nothing of eternal life in the age to come (vss. 29-30).

This saying reflects the need and experience of the early church. Separation from synagogue, family, and non-believing friends was the common lot. When martyrdom was not exacted, prejudice and various exclusions were. What the faithful gave up came back to them again. They "had all things in common" (Acts 2:44; 4:32), and when this venture in communal living passed, they shared generously one with another. Excluded from some circles, they found a far more satisfying fellowship in the warm-hearted brotherhood of the primitive, persecuted church. Paul reflects its familylike intimacy in greeting both Rufus, in Rome, and "his mother and mine" (Rom. 16:13).

Though it spoke to the early Christians, it spoke from the experience of Jesus. When his family came to claim him, he replied: "Whoever does the will of God is my brother, and sister, and mother" (Mark 3:35). His family was as vast and inclusive as that! Small interests must let go to make room for the broadest relationships—a family as big as humanity. You can give up much, but sacrifice is an absurd idea. It all comes back multiplied.

Is it not true for us? Eugene V. Debs found this larger family through the conviction he expressed with memorable eloquence at his trial: "While there is a lower class I am in it, while there is a criminal element I am of it; while there is a soul in prison, I am not free." Wilfred T. Grenfell gave up much for his hard life of service in Laborador, yet he insisted there was no sacrifice. What he gave up was temporary; what he won had enduring worth. Near the end of his exposed, exciting, creative career, he wrote: "Christ's religion to me is primarily for this world, and the New Jerusalem is to come down from Heaven onto this earth and we are to be the Washingtons and Nelsons. We are to save that city—and we are to have all the fun of really creating it." [10]

How like Jesus! ". . . a hundredfold now in this time . . . and in the age to come eternal life." With such a Lord, "sacrifice" is absurd.

---

[10] Grenfell, *What Christ Means to Me*, p. 40.

FOURTH SUNDAY IN KINGDOMTIDE

The Dark and the Stars
Obadiah 1:1-4, 15-17a, 21

Asked if he could condense his life's research in one volume, historian Charles A. Beard replied that he could do better; he could sum it up in four sentences: Whom the gods would destroy they first make mad with power. The bee fertilizes the flower it robs. The mills of God grind slowly, but they grind exceeding small. When it is dark enough, you can see the stars.

These motifs run through the short Book of Obadiah: the destruction of the power-mad kingdom of Edom; the enrichment of Israel's insight into God's unifying judgments—insight born of the agony of subjugation; the judgments that slowly work themselves out in the movement of world affairs; and in the darkness of bloody warfare the glimpse of the bright kingdom of God that will yet come. The last line of the book offers a foregleam—"and the kingdom shall be the Lord's" (vs. 21*b*). Much of our talk of the kingdom of God is too placid to convey the dynamics of a kingdom snatched from rebellious hands. This lection helps us see the stars—God's rule—amid the darkness of man's resistance.

The setting is a typical brothers' quarrel between neighbor peoples. "Thus says the Lord God concerning Edom" (vs. 1) sets the locus of all that follows—an ancient blood feud. When Israel entered Canaan, Edom was an established monarchy. David conquered and garrisoned this neighbor, slaying all its male population, and on this conquest Solomon built his wealth. Edom was not only rich in ore, but through it ran the trade highway to the Gulf of Aqaba, protected by the fortress of Sela. Under the divided kingdom, Judah was unsuccessful in putting down an Edomite revolt, though it was reconquered under Amaziah and Azariah. Later securing her freedom again, Edom came under Assyrian vassalage until the Babylonian conquest in 604 B.C. When Jerusalem fell in 586 B.C., the Edomites happily assisted in crushing their ancient enemy, as vss. 11-14 record. The hatred between the peoples has many Old Testament reflections, typical of which is the cry of the psalmist.

> Remember, O Lord, against the Edomites
>   the day of Jerusalem,
> how they said, "Rase it, rase it!
>   Down to its foundations!" (Ps. 137:7).

Old Testament imagery pictures it as a quarrel between brothers. Obadiah condemns Edom "for the violence done to your brother Jacob" (vs. 10), suggesting the identification of Edom with Esau, as Israel identified herself with Jacob. The closing assurance is that "Mount Esau" will again be ruled (vs. 21). We read elsewhere of "Esau the father of the Edomites" (Gen. 36:9); of "the descendants of Esau (that is Edom)" (Gen. 36:1); and are told flatly, "Esau is Edom" (Gen. 36:8). Poignantly the bloody strife of peoples thus stands in the Old Testament lore as a brothers' feud. Brothers in vulnerability, we who live under the nuclear balance of terror may see overselves in the same picture.

Into this darkness comes the light of God's promised judgment. He will judge proud Edom, thinking itself invulnerable in its rock fortress and upon its impregnable heights (vss. 3-4). God's retribution against human pride finds concrete expression here: "The pride of your heart has deceived you" (vs. 3). That is always a possibility for great nations, doubly so for the self-proclaimed "super-nation."

Not only proud Edom is to be judged, but "all the nations" (vs. 15). History's weary law of retribution, "burn for burn, wound for wound, stripe for stripe" (Exod. 21:25), is to work its effects on "all the nations round about" (vs. 16).

> As you have done, it shall be done to you,
> your deeds shall return on your own head (vs. 15).

The reprisals of history visit destruction upon the destroyers. So Jesus said, "All who take the sword will perish by the sword" (Matt. 26:52). Power finally exhausts the powerful.

Yet through this darkenss can be seen the glimmering light of God's kingdom.

> Saviors shall go up to Mount Zion
> to rule Mount Easu;
> and the kingdom shall be the Lord's (vs. 21).

"Saviors" may be, as the Septuagint reads it, "those who have been saved," giving substance to the translation, "Victorious, they will climb Mount Zion" (vs. 21 JB). The vision of Edom's subjection is sweet—victors from Mount Zion shall rule Mount Esau! But in the end "the kingdom shall be the Lord's." The chain of vengeance leading to more vengeance must be broken, even as Jesus said (Matt. 5:38-42).

"The day of the Lord" (vs. 15)—his day of just rule among the nations—provides the light beyond this darkness. Obadiah saw it only dimly, yet he did see that the contest is more than a test of strength between nations.

> For dominion belongs to the Lord,
> and he rules over the nations (Ps. 22:28).

Thus into our darkness—for we are counterparts of Israel and Edom—comes the vision that must not die, that "the kingdom of the world has become the kingdom of the Lord and of his Christ, and he shall reign for ever and ever" (Rev. 11:15).

So New Life Takes Shape
Colossians 3:1-15

You were buried with him in baptism, in which you were also raised with him through faith in the working of God, who raised him from the dead (2:12).

This recalls the contention of Henry E. Horn, that we could find strong help in the nurturing of a style of life appropriate both to the modern world and to the Christian gospel if we took the "shape" of baptism more seriously. He takes us through baptism as the early church practiced it on the island of Rhodes.

> Converts would . . . face away from the font toward the West, still dark, and renounce the powers of darkness—a particularly fearsome thing to do when they knew that this made them outlaws. Next, they went down into the water and were submerged three times into the life of Christ, gasping "I believe" before each submersion. Then they were brought up the Easter stairs toward the rising sun, anointed with the oil of the Holy Spirit of God, and given new robes as symbols of the new life.[11]

Three distinct actions in this service, Horn adds, make clear not only the "shape" of baptism but the nature of the new life in Christ. Paul is amplifying exactly this insight in the lection before us.

New life begins to take shape *as we renounce the powers of darkness.* "Put to death therefore what is earthly in you" (vs. 5) is the call to break with old behavior and make way for a new style of life. We have been changed by God's act in Christ, but we still have a choice of our own to make. Paul enumerates besetting vices and temptations which we must shun, giving ethical counsel specific enough to make it clear that he has no notion we should wait until a "situation" arises in the "context" of which to make decisions (vss. 5-9). Some things are to be settled in advance!

We are called to put away "immorality, impurity, passion, evil desire, and covetousness, which is idolatry" (vs. 5); or "greed, which is the same thing as worshipping a false god" (JB)—the worship of the desired object and of the desiring self. Pagans, called to break with the old life, need specifics: renounce "anger, wrath, malice, slander, and foul talk from your mouth"; "abusive language and dirty talk" (JB)—relevant word in a time that gives force to the quip that best-selling writers obey the maxim, "Nothing risqué, nothing gained." Nor can there be any limiting of respect to some accepted in-group, "Here there cannot be Greek and Jew, circumcised and uncircumcised, barbarian, Scythian, slave, free man, but Christ is all, and in all"—which CPV makes contemporary by a slight but justifiable paraphrase: "The pattern for the new man is the same for a Negro and a white man, a church member and non-church-member, foreigner, Mexican, employee, employer, but Christ is everything in everybody."

New life further takes shape *as, in utter risk and dependence we are submerged, gasping, "I believe."* Christ's Lordship takes full control of those who give themselves to him. "For you have died, and your life is hid with Christ in God" (vs. 3). Not only in the death-and-life symbols of baptism by immersion, but in the realities of our daily existence, we die to our old selves and come to life in him. He rules all things. The rule does not belong to such superhuman powers as were reverenced by the Gnostics who troubled the church at Colossae; nor to the values exalted by our modern myths of scientism, nationalism, racism, materialism. Christ is already "our life," and we shall yet know him better and be more fully transformed by his influence (vs. 4).

[11] Horn, *The Christian in Modern Style,* p. 120.

New life takes shape, finally, *as we put on new clothing expressive of the new person we are becoming.* We are to "put on," as if it were the uniform of a recruit, the full attire of virtues that stand opposite to the vices renounced with the powers of darkness (vss. 12-15). The parallel of these new ways to the teachings of Jesus gives the lie to the once-popular notion that Paul built a mystical theology with little heed to the ethical content of Jesus' ministry. Here Paul emphasizes our need to forgive as our Lord has forgiven us, echoing the Lord's prayer and such words of Jesus as, "if you forgive men their trespasses, your heavenly Father also will forgive you; but if you do not forgive men their trespasses, neither will your Father forgive your trespasses" (Matt. 6:14-15). The virtues named are not a chance collection: "Over all these clothes, to keep them together and complete them, put on love" (vs. 14 JB). Because we are called into one body, the Church of Christ, his peace must be allowed to rule us (vs. 15a)—a sad rebuke to all dissension and bitterness in any congregation.

When his Lordship fully shapes our new life, we have ample ground for thanksgiving (vs. 15b).

Your Theology Is Showing
Matthew 7:15-23

How good is your theology? Take a look at your life! So says this stern conclusion of the Sermon on the Mount. The opening line names the subject: "false prophets" (vs. 15)—those who falsely speak in God's name. Beyond those who preach and teach, it includes all who in "the ministry of the laity" are responsible for witness and leadership.

"False prophets" were a problem to the early church (e.g., II Peter 2:1-3). The Letter to the Colossians, from which this Sunday's Epistle is taken, was written to answer and correct the false prophets of Gnosticism, a perverted theology which had a corrupting influence on the lives of its believers. As Paul said to the Colossians, so Jesus is saying here: Take a look at your life; your theology is showing!

Jesus' figure of the tree and the fruit was already familiar in everyday speech, but the new twist he gave it is instructive. In Ecclesiasticus, the figure relates a man's speech to his character.

> The orchard where the tree grows is judged on the
>   quality of its fruit,
>   similarly a man's words betray what he feels.
> Do not praise a man before he has spoken,
>   since this is the test of men (Ecclus. 27:6-8a JB).

Jesus does not deny this, yet as the next paragraph develops the thought, he is dealing more directly with conduct in accord with God's will as the test. With an inverse application of the logic of Ecclesiasticus, he reasons that if you can know what a man *is* by what he says, you can test what a religious teacher *says* by what he does. "Thus you will know them"—false prophets— "by their fruits" (vs. 20).

Paul reverts to this figure: "the fruit of the Spirit is love, joy, peace, patience, kindness, goodness, faithfulness, gentleness, self-control" (Gal.

5:22). Does one who teaches a given doctrine produce these qualities in human relations? If so, it may presumably be a doctrine prompted by God's Spirit. If not, it fails the "fruit test," and is the work of a false prophet. Any Christian, any congregation, may well test its doctrine in this laboratory.

"Jesus Christ is Lord" was the stark creed of the early church (Phil. 2:11; Matt. 16:16; John 6:69; 20:28; I Cor. 12:3; I John 4:15). Here Jesus is remembered as saying that what this creed really means to us must be searched out beyond the words. "Not every one who calls me, 'Lord, Lord' will enter the kingdom of Heaven, but only those who do the will of my heavenly Father" (vs. 21 NEB). In the final judgment—"that day" (vs. 22) —he will not even recognize those who are disobedient to the Father's will, though they may be ever so correct in their creed and their religious works (vss. 22-23). So! You can show what your *creed means* only by what your *life is.*

FIFTH SUNDAY IN KINGDOMTIDE

Lo, All Our Pomp: Nahum 1:1-8

"Who speaks for man?" asks Norman Cousins, in a book vibrant with concern that nations, races, fragmenting groups have ardent spokesmen, though no one is charged with authority to speak for all humanity in the hour of its threatened extermination. "Who speaks for God?" askes Gerald Kennedy, in his book on the prophetic role in modern times. Answer both questions with one name—Nahum. "He is the spokesman of a humanity that had suffered immeasurably under Assyrian ruthlessness. But he is also the spokesman of God." [12]

It is too small a notion of God to suppose he rules only those who are bound to him as his covenant people. He has the last word concerning powerful pagans—for instance, Nineveh, rampant military terror of the ancient world. This is the burden of Nahum's message. The biting specifics bristle in the remainder of the book, but the poetic prologue which provides this lection "sets up a large moral background on the basis of which the special case of Nineveh can be understood as a single illustration of God's punishment of human wickedness." [13]

The prologue presents, in damaged form, a Hebrew alphabetic acrostic poem dealing with the ways of God in a broad sweep of human affairs. He is a "jealous God and avenging" (vs. 2) who will not stand idly by as men worship what is false. Though he is "slow to anger and of great might" (vs. 3), he will not "clear the guilty." "His way is in the whirlwind and storm" (vs. 3b), and he controls all the mighty forces of the natural world (vss. 3-5). In view of his great might, "who can stand before his indignation?" (vs. 6). His judgments are terrible, but his wrath is directed to a good purpose, that

[12] Emil Kraeling, *Commentary on the Prophets* (Camden, N.J.: Thomas Nelson, 1966), II, 231.
[13] *Ibid.*, p. 229.

he may be "a stronghold in the day of trouble" (vs. 7). He punishes his adversaries but faithfully cares for "those who take refuge in him" (vss. 7-8). These familiar Old Testament figures lay the base for Nahum's message against Nineveh. The prophecy that fills the rest of the book vividly illustrates this philosophy that "God is in control of the history of the nations and . . . His moral government manifests itself in the punishment of the brutal tyrant." [14] See what this means in its particulars.

There are good tidings of peace (1:15) for the faithful in Judah, but utter destruction and desolation for the mighty though faithless, cruel Assyrians. In frightful wreckage the proud power falls (chap. 3). Shadows of our own day lie upon the page in the lines,

> hosts of slain,
> heaps of corpses,
> dead bodies without end—
> they stumble over the bodies! (3:3).

Shade of present-day warfare, with its "saturation bombing" and "search and destroy" missions! God is against all this (3:5)—and so is world opinion:

> And all who look on you will shrink from you and say,
> Wasted is Nineveh; who will bemoan her? (3:7).

Change the name of Nineveh to the successive wielders of military might —Italy, Germany, Russia, perhaps the United States—and the force remains unabated.

The ageless story of armed power runs wearily on: eventually it encounters more crushing power—from without, within, or from the burden of its own defenses and paranoid fears.

> All your fortresses are like fig trees
>   with first-ripe figs—
> if shaken they fall
>   into the mouth of the eater.
> Behold your troops
>   are women in your midst.
> The gates of your land
>   are wide open to your foes (3:12-13).

The fall of the mighty leaves few to mourn.

> All who hear the news of you
>   clap their hands over you.
> For upon whom has not come
>   your unceasing evil? (3:19.)

Thus are the powerful viewed by the weaker peoples, no matter how just they appear in their own eyes. Why do others not love our land and admire our power? they ask, forgetting what the centuries ceaselessly declare: great power has few friends.

[14] Julius A. Bewer, *The Prophets* (New York: Harper, 1955), p. 545.

As Will and Ariel Durant observe, in summing up *The Lessons of History,* "A challenge successfully met (as by the United States in 1917, 1933, and 1941), if it does not exhaust the victor (like England in 1945), raises the temper and level of a nation, and makes it abler to meet further challenge." [15] They might also have added, "If in subduing tyrannical power they do not become addicted to it"—for then they fall under a timeless judgment,

> Behold I am against you,
> says the Lord of hosts (3:5).

Because We Belong to Christ
Hebrews 13:1-6

"There are no pre-fab answers in advance of the particular situation in the particular context," [16] wrote James S. Pike in the concluding chapter of his casebook, *You and the New Morality.* Having given "cases" to show there are no "rules" to guide decision-making, he made his nearest approach to concrete guidance in a closing paragraph which declared that "across the board" we need to answer "Yes" "to these things":

> A responsible approach to all decisions.
> The rating of persons above things.
> The valuing of *erōs* love ahead of all other responses.
> Fulfillment and service as the style of life.
> Serious attention to the relevant portions of the
> Code as representing generalizations of human ex-
> perience with common problems.
> Awareness of pertinent factors to be weighed on the
> scales.[17]

Good as these guides may be, they leave perplexed people dangerously exposed to the persuasive power of their own emotions in situations where cool objectivity is all but impossible. This lection reads strangely like situation ethics, "Let brotherly love continue" (vs. 1), though in making "love" the guiding principle it uses the Greek *philadelphia*, not *eros.* Not content to stop there, it goes on to show what this means in specific relationships about which the Christian is called to make up his mind in advance. This decision-making is not confined to the context of the situation; it is the outgrowth of doctrines discussed in the first twelve chapters of this Letter. It consists less of *laws* than of *announcements*: these are things we do because we belong to Christ. Being his, we have prior commitments in four concrete areas.

First, because we belong to Christ we will "show hospitality to strangers" (vs. 2). Because inns of the writer's day minimized safety and

[15] Will and Ariel Durant, *The Lessons of History* (New York: Simon and Schuster, 1968), p. 91.

[16] James A. Pike, *You and the New Morality* (New York: Harper, 1967), p. 131.

[17] *Ibid.,* p. 140.

maximized immoral surroundings, Christians had some responsibility to show brotherly love by hospitality to those who must be away from home. In our days this may still say something to the Christian conscience about those who suffer as refugees or are excluded by race from decent housing. By such care, we are reminded, "some have entertained angels unawares." Biblical angels are simply God's messengers, not necessarily mythical winged figures. The reference here is to Abraham's hospitality to three strangers who turned out to be messengers of God (Gen. 18), and to Lot's sheltering and costly defense of the same anonymous strangers (Gen. 19). Jesus declared that care of the least human brother in such ways was care given to him (Matt. 25:31-46).

Second, because we belong to Christ, we will "remember those who are in prison, as though in prison with them; and those who are ill-treated" (vs. 3). Prison was the only "welfare agency" to which that day's poor might look. This now has something to say about Christian commitment to the alleviation of poverty. The reason is given: "you also are in the body"—that is, we too are mortal, human, exposed to the dangers and reversals that have overtaken them. Our common humanity should make us care for these victims "as though in prison with them"; since "you also are still in the body" (TCNT); "for you like them are still in the world" (NEB).

Third, because we belong to Christ, we will hold marriage sacred and inviolable (vs. 4). Part of the instability of adult life and the insecurity and anomie of youth in our day comes from the loosening of the marriage ties. In a scene in which Thornton Wilder's "everyman" figure, Mr. Antrobus, has asked for divorce on some familiarly shoddy grounds, his wife replies with a kind of reverie:

I didn't marry you because you were perfect. I didn't even marry you because I loved you. I married you because you gave me a promise. That promise made up for your faults. And the promise I gave you made up for mine. Two imperfect people married and it was the promise that made the marriage. . . . And when our children were growing up, it wasn't a house that protected them; and it wasn't our love, that protected them—it was that promise.[18]

"God will judge the immoral and adulterous" (vs. 4b), Hebrews declares, and the Antrobus story demonstrates how the judgment inheres in what happens to our peace, to our children, and to our society, when that protecting promise is depreciated.

Fourth, because we belong to Christ, we will keep our "life free from love of money, and be content with what [we] have" (vs. 5a). Our dependence on *things*, as if they were our only security, is practical atheism, an assumption that there is no God in whom to trust. But we can count on God's covenant assurance, "I will never fail you nor forsake you" (vs. 5b), as it came through Moses to an insecure band of desert wanderers (Deut. 31:6), to Joshua as he undertook his precarious responsibilities (31:8), to the psalmist (Ps. 118:6), and finally to us.

[18] Thornton Wilder, *The Skin of Our Teeth* (copyright 1942 by Thornton Wilder), Act II.

The Therapy of Forgiveness
Matthew 18:15-22

A divided church, fractured families, shattered friendships, troubled communities need help. Though the details of this passage may not be a direct report of the words of Jesus, they do reflect the understanding of his words in the early church. What we read in this lection spells out that understanding of what is clearly his own saying, from the "Q" source: "Take heed to yourselves; if your brother sins, rebuke him, and if he repents, forgive him; and if he sins against you seven times in the day, and turns to you seven times, and says, 'I repent,' you must forgive him" (Luke 17:3-4). Here, then, is an authentic early Christian guide to the steps in reconciling differences that still trouble us.

Step One: private conversation with the brother who has grieved us: "go and have it out with him alone" (vs. 15 JB). To repress it is to build up inner tensions and make reconciliation improbable. To talk about it to others is to do the brother an injustice, leave him in the dark and in no position to make amends, and pave the way for deeper grievances. Step One can be sheer gain: "If he listens to you, you have won your brother over" (vs. 15*b* MT and NEB). If this fails, we go to . . .

Step Two: arbitration by "one or two others" (vs. 16). The law had declared that no charge could be sustained by a single witness; "only on the evidence of two . . . or three witnesses, shall a charge be sustained" (Deut. 19:15). Jesus, however, calls for witnesses not so much to prepare a case against the brother as to help bring the conflicting parties together. "Witnesses" give objectivity, a third party viewpoint, and some lowering of the emotional temperature, with resultant clarifying of thought. If this fails, we go to . . .

Step Three: a report "to the church" (vs. 17) not in gossip or accusation but in continued search for reconciliation. The "church" here intended is the intimate community of believers with whom one habitually meets—"report the matter to the congregation" (NEB). The modern parallel is not so much the large impersonal urban congregation as the prayer group, or some company of believers who meet often for prayer and the sharing of urgent concerns. If even this fails, we go to . . .

Step Four: quiet separation from the offender as from a "Gentile" or "a tax collector"—without recrimination or grudge-bearing, but in recognition that we cannot find common ground and hence need not go on irritating each other. Paul gave the same advice about "those who create dissensions . . . ; avoid them" (Rom. 16:17). Even then, however, the matter is not closed. We are called to maintain the forgiving spirit without limit. Peter estimated a generous scale of forgiveness: "seven times" (vs. 21). Few of us come near that level. Jesus replied that the estimate was false, being finite, a scorekeeping approach. His alternative is a disputed translation; did he say "seventy-seven times" or "seventy times seven"? Either will do, for the point is not the *number*, but the lifting of the whole matter beyond any scorekeeping. To stop forgiving at the seventy-eighth time, or the four hundred ninety-first, is never to have *forgiven* at all, but only to have postponed the day of reckoning.

To reverse the matter is to throw it into clarifying relief. In judging Cain, God also decreed his protection: "If any one slays Cain, vengeance shall be taken on him sevenfold" (Gen. 4:15). Not many generations had passed, however, until Lamech was making the boastful threat embodied in a little song,

> I have slain a man for wounding me,
> a young man for striking me.
>
> If Cain is avenged sevenfold,
> truly Lamech seventy-sevenfold (Gen. 4:23-24).

But to slay the young man is to go beyond all score-keeping. Death is infinite. So our human nature seeks to "defend" itself by limitless vengeance; and the result is endless conflict, destruction, turmoil, inner tension, heartache, tragedy on every side. There is just one answer—a reversal of the whole process by the therapy of limitless forgiveness.

SIXTH SUNDAY IN KINGDOMTIDE

Not Some Religious Act
Micah 6:1-4, 5d-8

"It is not some religious act which makes a Christian what he is, but participation in the suffering of God in the life of the world." [19] So wrote Dietrich Bonhoeffer in one of the most celebrated of his prison letters. Thus he appropriated the test which Micah applied to Israel—one of the most famous definitions of the true relation of men to God.

Micah begins with a dramatic arraignment of the people before the heavenly court. The scene is cosmic, with the mountains and the foundations of the earth as witnesses (vss. 1-2). The very nature of things is to be the judge of the Lord's rightness as plaintiff in a case in which the prophet is called to be prosecutor.

"Not some religious act" done wrongly or left undone has offended God, but a violation of the demands of social justice and business integrity. Those who insist that the Church and its spokesmen stick to "spiritual matters" might be nonplussed, but the indictment alleges that people and leaders alike have been too religious! In the face of injustice and exploitation in the highest circles of state, "the prophets who lead my people astray" (3:5) have withheld their condemnation, crying, " 'Peace' when they have something to eat." The consequence of their betrayal of God and man will be deepening spiritual blindness—"it shall be night to you, without vision" (3:6).

No prophet dare keep silent when evil is abroad, whether in the realm of private immoralities, or social and economic affairs.

---

[19] Bonhoeffer, *Letters and Papers from Prison*, p. 223.

> They covet fields, and seize them;
>   and houses, and take them away;
> they oppress a man and his house,
>   a man and his inheritance (2:2).

Confined to no ivory tower religious observance, the charge has starkly political implications.

> Hear, you heads of Jacob
>   and rulers of the house of Israel!
> Is it not for you to know justice?—
>   you who hate the good and love the evil,
> who tear the skin from off my people,
>   and their flesh from off their bones (3:1-2).

Though the heads of state "give judgments for a bribe" and the priests and prophets support them by silence for the sake of their own comfort, the trouble is widespread among the people themselves. They feel a false security in their supposed favored relation to the Lord, saying, "Is not the Lord in the midst of us? No evil shall come upon us" (3:11). All this lies back of the indictment which Micah now prosecutes (6:1-2).

As the case proceeds, God himself interrogates his people. How has he offended against them? (vs. 3). He has brought them from Egypt, freed them from slavery (vs. 4), that they "may know the saving acts of the Lord" or "understand the Eternal's saving power" (MT).

The people reply with penitence and a groping quest for right action before God. Shall they bring him the required temple sacrifices? (vs. 6). Shall they multiply this orthodox observance a thousandfold? (vs. 7a). Or, copying the pagan practices of their neighbors, shall they offer God what is dearest to them, their children, on a bloody altar? (vs. 7b). Will such religious exercises free them from the estrangement from God brought about by economic and political sins?

No! declares the prophet. The solution is "not some religious act" in a temple set apart. It must be worked out in the midst of human affairs (vs. 8). "What does the Lord require of you but to do justice" (perhaps in the struggle for civil rights?), "and to love kindness" (as in concern about poverty and its victims?), "and to walk humbly with your God?" (such humility as expresses itself in faithful stewardship of natural resources in God's creation?).

This conclusion is echoed in our time by theologian Nels Ferré, who sees religion as "whole-response"—no partial response, as of intellect, emotion, or aesthetic sentiment, but whole-respone of all there is in us—"to what is considered to be most important and most real." [20] By such definition there can be no "religionless" relation to God. There can be false religion which mistakes some perverted or secondary thing for the "most important and most real." Or there can be true religion which comes to full, creative relation to God and one's neighbor. There is no third choice.

[20] Nels F. S. Ferré, *Faith and Reason* (New York: Harper, 1946), p. 4.

Power to Endure: Hebrews 11:1-3, 6

Faith gives substance to our hopes, and makes us certain of realities we do not see" (vs. 1 NEB).

We are dealing here, not with "a complete theological definition of *faith,* but only an affirmation of what faith *does.*" [21] Yet that is much. There is here no notion that "faith in faith" will save us. Not faith, but the unseen, *through* faith, gives us power to endure.

This speaks to the infant church under persecution—and through them to us—urging that we be "confident of what we hope for, convinced of what we do not see," viz., the triumph of God's righteousness over the unjust tyranny of the persecutors. Such functional faith will beget the kind of durability attributed to Moses, who "endured as seeing him who is invisible" (vs. 27). This sense of durability permeates the roll of heroes which the remainder of the chapter comprises, introduced by the line: "For by it [faith] the men of old received divine approval" (vs. 2).

Many of us discard such faith because we mistake description for explanation, supposing that scientific description explains our experience so fully that God and all non-measurable factors are irrelevant. But belief in something beyond the seen is so much a part of us that when religious faith goes out, strange substitutes come in. Then,

Horoscopes and crystal balls are thought to foretell the future, while ouija boards, tea leaves, and lines on the palm of the hand are supposed to be sure guides to impending events . . . . It is estimated that over 30 per cent of the people of France believe in and consult horoscopes and clairvoyants. . . . Probably a roughly similar percentage of Americans do so. . . . It is difficult for a society as a whole to claim an advanced "scientific outlook" when most hotels have no thirteenth floor and many airplanes have no thirteenth row.[22]

These moderns live by the invisible, no less than Moses did, but it is the *impersonal* invisible; it does not make them notable for sturdy endurance. Think, on the other hand, of a figure like Jessie Binford, associated with Jane Addams at Hull House from 1906 and continuing there until its demise in 1963. Interviewed at ninety, she enthused: "The day isn't long enough for all I want to do. I can't begin to tell you of my new interests." She was concerned about the fears of younger people. "The commonest thing I hear in a town like this is a fear of the unknown," she said. "Fear, fear. . . . They're just scared to death." [23] There stands durability, full of pity for sophisticated, supportless, younger, weaker people.

Faith finds power to endure, not by airtight logical proof—e.g., that God created the world. Rather "by faith we understand" it so (vs. 3). This conviction does not come to us out of the world itself; it is a decision reached in faith, though reasons may support it and no reasons are adequate to dislodge it. Only so can we enter the relation to God which he gives to his friends, who believe in him (vs. 6). "The man who approaches God must have faith in two things, first that God exists and secondly that it is worth a

[21] Grant, *Nelson's Bible Commentary, ad loc.*
[22] Eugene Nida, *Religion Across Cultures* (New York: Harper, 1968), p. 25.
[23] Terkel, *Division Street: America,* pp. 377, 378.

man's while to try to find God" (PT). The reward of faith is not some extrinsic benefit, but the consummation of the quest for God. Though our searching cannot "find out the limit of the Almighty" (Job 11:7), he gives himself—and the power to stand firm in him—to those who eagerly seek him. Our quest is not on our own initiative but in response to his love and self-giving in Christ, as all the earlier chapters of Hebrews have argued.

If our prayers and religious quest seek him, we can but remember that he is "Almighty God, *from* whom every good prayer cometh." In a debilitating age, one choice confronts us: faith that endures as seeing him who is invisible, or fears that fill an impersonal universe. We cannot *prove* faith in a personal God, any more than we can prove the trustworthiness of a friend. We find it only by *trusting*.

Mysterious and Able: Matthew 8:23-27

A theologian's paradoxical remark made in another context admits us to the depths of this gospel incident. "There is not," he said, "one theological sentence which can presume to speak truth unless it refers to the reality of God and the impossibility of embracing this reality in theological sentences." [24] We are dealing here with theological material of a high order, portraying the power and presence of God, not in "theological sentences" but in a vivid picture of repeatable experience.

Because of the peculiar topography of the region, the Lake of Galilee is swept by sudden storms. This incident is based on an experience the disciples had with Jesus in one of them, which became precious in the memory of the early church, lashed by storms of persecution. As it stands in Matthew, it bears obvious marks of the uses the early preachers made of it, developing a thesis still valid in the stormy weather into which every life must eventually sail: that Christ, present and concerned for his followers, is mighty to restore the faith of those who turn to him, thus saving in the midst of storms.

Christ is present and concerned for his followers. The story declares this by implied comparison and contrast with Jonah. Of Jesus it says, "the boat was being swamped by the waves; but he was asleep" (vs. 24). Of Jonah we read, "there was a mighty tempest on the sea, so that the ship threatened to break up. . . . But Jonah . . . was fast asleep" (Jonah 1:4-5). Note the contrast. Jonah, in flight from God and his call, slept in apathy and unconcern. Jesus, in the midst of exhausting response to his call, slept in weariness and utter trust. Jonah's flight from God and from Nineveh's need makes the more apparent Jesus' presence, with God, to human need. The longer the church meditated on this, the more its truth grew on them, so that, whereas Mark's earlier account reflected only the disciples' complaint that Jesus did not share their panic—"Teacher, do you not care if we perish?" (Mark 4:38)—Matthew's longer brooding issues in the cry, "Save, Lord; we are perishing" (vs. 25). That was a real cry of the persecuted church at the end of the first century. It is a real cry in the storms that threaten to engulf

---

[24] Dietrich Bonhoeffer as quoted in John A. Phillips, *Christ for Us in the Theology of Dietrich Bonhoeffer* (New York: Harper, 1967), p. 61, note.

us now. Like them, we reach out to a Christ present and concerned for his followers.

Christ is mighty to restore a failing faith. In Mark's earlier account, Jesus rebuked fear and called forth faith *after* the storm ceased, but Matthew's matured reflection places the summons to faith *before* the storm was stilled. It was while the dangerous winds and waters raged about them that the disciples, like us, most needed faith. "Why are you afraid, O men of little faith?" (vs. 26) he demanded, contrasting faith and fear in his characteristic way. Mark's wording of the question even more sharply opposes the two states to one another: "Why are you afraid? Have you no faith?" (Mark 4:40). To our diffused fear of life itself, Jesus said: "Do not be anxious about your life" (Matt. 6:25); ". . . if God so clothes the grass of the field, . . . will he not much more clothe you, O men of little faith?" (Matt. 6:30). In the midst of our fears we need the faith that God's power shown through Christ can command the threatening forces. Like them, we can find in Christ one who restores needed faith. Where arguments fail, his transforming friendship persuades.

Christ saves in the midst of storms. In amazement the disciples exclaimed, "What sort of man is this, that even winds and sea obey him?" (vs. 27). Only one answer was possible for them: he was a man through whom the power of God was brought to bear. Saturated with psalms that had been their prayers and hymns from childhood, these first Christians could not ask the question without remembering the Lord of whom the psalmist sang,

> he made the storm be still,
> and the waves of the sea were hushed (Ps. 107:29).
>
> By dread deeds thou dost answer us with deliverance,
> O God of our salvation,
> who art the hope of all the ends of the earth,
> and of the farthest seas; . . .
> who dost still the roaring of the seas,
> the roaring of their waves (Ps. 65:5, 7).
>
> Thou dost rule the raging of the sea;
> when its waves rise, thou stillest them (Ps. 89:9).

Remembering all this, they called Jesus "Lord" with a majestic depth of meaning. When they retold this tale of the storm on Galilee, it spoke to them not simply of an incident in the storied past, but of a present reality. He whose power stilled the waves was with them in the stormy dangers through which they passed, to replace fear with faith and to save in the midst of the worst the world could hurl at them.

SEVENTH SUNDAY IN KINGDOMTIDE

Men for a Responsible Society
Ezekiel 18:23-32

"Therefore I will judge you, O house of Israel, every one according to his ways, says the Lord" (vs. 30a). Note carefully: "every one." Countering the emphasis on collective responsibility passed from father to son—allowing men to blame previous generations for their moral dilemmas—the prophet proclaimed a message of individual responsibility requiring individual repentance: "Repent and turn from all your transgressions, lest iniquity be your ruin" (vs. 30*b*).

A popular proverb—"The fathers have eaten sour grapes, and the children's teeth are set on edge" (vs. 2)—bypassed personal responsibility. The saying has enough truth to be persuasive. Generations of hot and cold wars that seek to wipe out totalitarianism by totalitarian methods may have something to do with a public atmosphere in which we worry about "crime in the streets" and try to counter it with indiscriminate clubbing and gassing by police. Violence begets violence in a vicious circle bridging generations. Public order rests on justice, not force.

Only personal responsibility accepted can break out of the circle. All souls, of any generation, Ezekiel proclaimed, belong to God, and "the soul that sins shall die" (vs. 4). He pressed his point by means of a three-generation example. First comes a man righteous in all respects, personal and social; "he shall surely live, says the Lord God" (vss. 5-9). But his unrighteous son can claim no exemption from judgment on grounds of good family; "his blood shall be upon himself" (vss. 10-13). When he, in turn, has a son who lives an upright life, "he shall not die for his father's iniquity" (vss. 14-18). So Ezekiel sought to awaken responsible individuals in a responsible society.

Individual responsibility, far from abrogating the social bond, reinforces it. The man of righteous record, departing from his moral ways, is condemned "for the treachery of which he is guilty" (vs. 24). The word translated "treachery" (RSV) lends itself to other readings: "broken faith" (JB), "treason" (Brewer, MT, AT). The irresponsible individual has broken faith with, or committed treason against, a covenant God and a covenant society of which he is a part. Social solidarity is undeniable. The sins of the fathers curse the children to the third and fourth generations, but this absolves no man from the necessity of making his own moral choices. In our day of "retribalization" in a mass society, this warning comes with renewed urgency. Only individual choice, faithfully made, can break the cycle of sin begetting sin, evil leading to evil. To fail the choice is treason.

We complain against this requirement,

> The time is out of joint; O cursed spite,
> That ever I was born to set it right! [25]

Ezekiel upholds God's justice against the charge that "the way of the Lord is not just" (vs. 25). When a righteous man does an unrighteous deed, he must suffer for it; but by the same token, when an unrighteous man reforms, he is saved.

God offers hope to the repentant (vss. 30-31). It is needful that we both reform our behavior and renew our inner motives: "get yourselves a new heart and a new spirit" (vs. 31)—for which both our discipline and God's help are needed. God has promised, "I will take the stony heart out of their

---

[25] William Shakespeare, *Hamlet, Prince of Denmark*, Act I, Scene 5.

flesh and give them a heart of flesh, that they may walk in my statutes and keep my ordinances and obey them" (11:19-20). This theme will recur in Ezekiel: "A new heart I will give you, and a new spirit I will put within you" (36:26). Our repentance and God's renewal belong together. God *gives* the new life, but we must *live* it. He *adopts* us as his children, but we must *act* in the family resemblance. New life comes neither *by* our effort nor *without* it. "Turn, and live" (vs. 32), God calls, and the new life is one of fulfillment in this age and in the Age to come—repentance *ours,* renewal *his.*

Rx for Reconciliation: James 1:17-27

In this passage, fashioned after Old Testament wisdom literature, a teacher of the church offers a set of proverbs in the name of Christ. Among its diverse counsels no stated theme is developed. Viewed in relation to our contemporary need, however, they have a practical unity as a prescription for reconciliation.

Our explosively divided time needs such help. An able journalist studied the disorders of the late 1960s and concluded: "Our crime is not that America is white, but that we do not even know it is. The Negro does. He knows it every time a policeman passes. That is when *power* speaks to him. . . . *Two* nations exist. . . . This is *two* countries; . . . war could arise between the two." [26]

Not only races are divided, but generations; the "haves" and the "have nots"; the "right," the "left," and the uncommitted center. Neighborhoods are divided, as are offices, congregations, families. Describing the character of the wise man, this passage points to the reconciling role of the wise among us now. Three affirmations speak to this need.

First, God's goodness provides the *ground of reconciliation.* Men may disbelieve this truth, saying "I am tempted by God" (vs. 13), but this inverts the fact that "each person is tempted when he is lured and enticed by his own desire" (vs. 14). God gives only good, "and all our endowments are faultless, . . . from the Father . . . , who casts no shadow on the earth" (vs. 17 MT). The figure suggests that God, Creator of the heavenly luminaries, casts no such shadow as they do in their rotation. He gives only light unmixed with darkness. Those who work for good among men are thus working "with the grain of the universe."

Not only so, but God gives us a new beginning in a new life of his own making. "By his own wish he made us his own sons through the Word of truth, that we might be, so to speak, the first specimens of his new creation" (vs. 18 PT). His Word is his act. "And God said" is the biblical formula for each act of *creation.* "And the Word became flesh. . . . And from his fullness have we all received, grace upon grace" (John 1:14, 16)—that is the record of the *new* creation. His Word is his *continuous action in relation to us men,* so that James urges us to "receive with meekness the implanted word, which is able to save your souls" (vs. 21), and to be "doers of the word, and not hearers only" (vs. 22). The word is a message we hear and practice,

[26] Gary Wills, *The Second Civil War* (New York: New American Library, 1968), p. 22.

which carries its own creative power because God acts in and through it. When we play a reconciling role, this creative power is at work in us, as it has been in such figures as St. Francis and all other reconcilers.

Second, a greater readiness to hear than to speak provides the *atmosphere of reconciliation*. "In view of what he has made us then, dear brothers, let every man be quick to listen but slow to use his tongue, and slow to lose his temper" (vs. 19 PT). Bo Reicke suggests that talkative people in the church, full of advices and denunciations, were exciting themselves and others to anger. "Even in our day," he adds, "this excitement to anger is noticeable among demagogues who thunder against existing conditions and against their fellow men." [27] No ministry is more needed than the ministry of listening. Too many of the reconciler's words fall on deaf ears because he has not first fully *heard* what another has said. When one is heard, he is in no small part relieved of his anger, for he has been treated with the respect that careful listening implies.

The notion of "righteous indignation" has no place among the reconciler's therapeutic instruments. "For the anger of man does not work the righteousness of God" (vs. 20). Bold words in the face of the psalmist's "Surely the wrath of men shall praise thee"! (Ps. 76:10). But there is no contradiction; for the psalmist is not lauding wrath as the servant of divine purpose; he is declaring the overriding power of God, even in the face of men's rebellious wrath. The reconciler eschews "righteous indignation" in favor of patient listening that reduces the tensions of others.

Third, obedient, compassionate action provides the *means of reconciliation*. We need to be "doers of the word" (vs. 22). God's truth shows us who we are in the new identity of his new creation, yet apart from practice of this new life we lose it as surely as a man who glances in a mirror quickly forgets how disheveled he was. Reconciliation begins with the correction of our own life—a truth easily forgotten in the heat of contention over the alleged wrongs of others. We need "the perfect law, the law of liberty" (vs. 25) to free us. Jacques Maritain declared that the most searching question we can face is whether we regard freedom as throwing off limitations, or taking them on. Freedom that discards limitations divides men; freedom that limits itself reconciles.

Reconciling action is compassionate. Its "pure religion" sends it on errands of mercy—"to care for orphans and widows in their trouble" (vs. 27 MT). Those who would be reconcilers in a world of vast gulfs between affluence and want must *act* compassionately to relieve distress which breeds frustration, anger, and violent disorder. Such compassionate action is "religion that is pure and undefiled before God" (vs. 27).

Measured by Remainders
Luke 21:1-4

This little cameo says one thing: loyalty to the Highest is not measured by the size of the gift, but by what remains after the giving. "She out of her

[27] Bo Reicke, *The Epistles of James, Peter, and Jude,* Anchor Bible (Garden City, N.Y.: Doubleday, 1964), 37:20.

poverty put in all the living that she had" (vs. 4b). There was nothing left. The others "contributed out of their abundance" (vs. 4a). Though they gave more, more remained. By this gauge, the widow "put in more than all of them" (vs. 3). Far from sentimental praise of small gifts—a perversion to which it has sometimes been twisted—this story measures gifts by the ultimate rigor: How much is *left?* Truest devotion holds least back.

Note what precedes this story. Jesus is assailed by those who have much—worldly goods, intellectual culture, religious unction, social recognition. "The chief priests and scribes with the elders" had questioned his authority (20:1-8), and had attempted to trap him with a loaded question about taxes paid to the hated colonial government (20:19-26). Some Sadducees had propounded a conundrum designed to discredit his teaching on the resurrection (20:27-40). Rich in both creature comforts and sophisticated doctrine, they had little attention left for the Truth when it faced them in Christ. A book reviewer remarks that "men use simple instruments; complex instruments use men." [28] It is so of cultural and religious mind-sets. Simple men can surrender to new truth; those with a rich heritage are tempted to cling so tenaciously to their treasure that they have no room for the best when God offers it.

Such clinging to our privileged place as beneficiaries of the current "knowledge explosion" is assailed by Jan Myrdal, intellectual son of an intellectual family. He speaks fiercely of

the final solution of the Jewish question; the Stalin era, the Churchill decision to bomb the civilians, the colonial wars for blunder and freedom . . . . But I want to underline that it has been the European, the Western intellectuals that have led and fulfilled these actions in every phase. We have written the theories, we have filled the universities with learned men giving rational motivations and reasonable techniques for every crime.[29]

Perhaps this intellectual culture, so attached to its advantages, is not unrelated to the religious culture of those whom Jesus indicted, "who devour widows' houses and for a pretense make long prayers" (20:45-47). Thus, in consecutive paragraphs, Luke records Jesus' condemnation of the hardened affluent and turns to his praise of the devoted poor.

Note also what follows this story. Some had no eyes for the widow's ultimate devotion, seeing only "the temple . . . adorned with noble stones and offerings" (21:5). Jesus saw its overthrow etched against a lurid future—"there shall not be left here one stone upon another" (vs. 6). The external temple would fall, but the inner temple of devotion, so absolute that it held nothing back, would stand eternally. Searching word! When our giving leaves the working remainder unchanged, ours is the devotion of the temple marked for destruction. Reassuring word! When we have given our best and the cause seems lost, ours is the devotion which in God's economy has the new Age in its grip.

[28] Martin Maloney in *Panorama*, supplement to the *Chicago Daily News*, Aug. 31, 1968.

[29] Jan Myrdal, *Confessions of a Disloyal European* (New York: Pantheon Books, 1968) as quoted in *Saturday Review*, Aug. 31, 1968, p. 28.

EIGHTH SUNDAY IN KINGDOMTIDE

He Keeps Faith: Amos 5:18-24

Our time, uncertain about "God-talk," presses the question, What does the word "God" signify? Biblical writers answer that there will always be mystery, yet we know who God *is* by what he *does*. We experience dependabilities so unvaried that in them we are touched by "the near side of God." Amos talked of inescapable judgment and the unyielding claim of justice upon us. A New Testament writer delcares, "If we are faithless, he keeps faith" (II Tim. 2:13 NEB).

What does the word "God' signify? We dare neither evade the question nor presume to answer it fully. But we can point to some dependabilities, apart from which we cannot understand our own life, to which biblical thought points when it talks to God.

First, *we cannot understand our life apart from the experience of being judged.* Amos put it bluntly to a society that expected to escape judgment by being religious. They looked for a "Day of the Lord" filled with favors because they belonged to God and worshiped him. "Why would you have the day of the Lord?" (vs. 18) Amos demanded. "Is not the day of the Lord dearkness, and not light?" (vs. 20). No "religiousness" will exempt the dishonest, the cruel, or the impure. It is like running from a lion only to meet a bear, or fleeing the safety of home to be bitten by a snake (vs. 19).

When we live at odds with conscience, our personal experience echoes Amos. At war with ourselves, we are less at peace with others. Seething with inner turmoil, we project it on our surroundings, making persons the scapegoats of our self-accusation, becoming accident-prone because our inward division makes us fumble or because we are pulled by an unconscious need to be punished.

National life is no exception. Amos promised Israel what events bore out—the doom of unrighteousness despite all pious religious observance. The Germany of Wilhelm II could flaunt the motto, *"Gott mit uns,"* but it could not evade history's debacle. Americans sing,

> Then conquer we must, for our cause it is just,—
> And this be our motto,—"In God is our trust!"

but the singing does not make it so—as Lincoln knew when he denounced our war with Mexico. A prominent American historican recently reviewed our vain attempt to control the forces of history and worried over the "fearful kind of arrogance and pride" that supposes "we are a special people." Amos saw this inexorable reality of judgment as an encounter with God.

Second, *we cannot understand our experience apart from the liberating renewal of being accepted just as we are.* The trained counselor neither retaliates when he is met by anger nor withdraws when he is denounced. He takes these occurrences not as the end of his usefulness but as a necessary stage in its advance. His client's anger must be externalized and expressed before the new clarity can come; he will absorb the abuse and accept the person. Out of the acceptance comes new life.

So said the faith of the New Testament—"Remember Jesus Christ, risen from the dead" (II Tim. 2:8). He absorbed our abuse, though it cost his death, accepting us with forgiveness. He rose from the dead and has brought new life to many. We had lived in disobedience, but something about *him* and his forgiving acceptance claimed us. Easter came true for us. Christ lived anew in our life, and we lived with him.

What does the word "God" signify? If we cannot answer fully, we can say this much: there are dependabilities of judgment and acceptance apart from which we cannot make sense of our life, and in them we see something of who God is by what he does. "If we are faithless, he keeps faith."

Strong in Grace: II Timothy 2:1-13

"You then, my son, be strong" (vs. 1). Good advice! Obvious enough in its way, it leaves one question: *Can* we? If we have only our own force to depend on, the strenuous life into which our age hurls us overdraws our account. Christian faith, however, knows a better source of stamina. Our worldly wisdom may echo the stoicism of Tacitus—"The gods always favor the strong"—but Christians know a God who *gives* strength to the *weak*. "Be strong *in the grace that is in Christ* Jesus" (vs. 1, italics added).

Who can question our need? Standing for the right is no easier in our day—when a brilliant young theologian, gallant for civil rights, is found beaten to death in his hotel room—than it was when the apostle wrote of "the gospel for which I am . . . wearing fetters, like a criminal" (vs. 9). Keeping some clear sense of direction is no easier amid talk of the "death of God" and "the new morality" than it was when Timothy was enjoined to entrust the gospel "to faithful men who will be able to teach others" (vs. 2). Like the soldier who avoids civilian entanglements, the athlete who welcomes the disciplines of his sport, or the farmer who works hard for his share of the crop (vss. 4-6), we face stern necessities and must bear our loads. Christian faith is no pledge of escape. It calls for iron in our spirit: "Take your share of suffering as a good soldier of Christ Jesus" (vs. 3).

There is more than demand, however. There is a strength not our own. The Christian is not left, like the secularist, with no invisible means of support! We can "be strong in the grace that is in Christ Jesus." If we moderns have lost our grip on what "grace" means, it finds fresh images in such novels as Bernard Malamud's *The Fixer*. A Jewish handyman, a poor half-educated nobody, is jailed on a murder charge. Though there is only the flimsiest trumped-up evidence against him, his obscurity and his Jewishness make him a convenient scapegoat. Held without indictment or legal counsel in the solitary confinement of a czarist prison for two anguished years, he resolutely demands justice. At last he is offered his freedom in exchange for his signature on a confession that he committed the brutal murder under goading from other Jews, to obtain the blood of the victim for religious rites. Though it costs more torture—perhaps life itself—he refuses, not only because the lie revolts his sense of right, but because he will not purchase freedom at the price of persecution and pogrom against other innocent people. While he continues to suffer, a multitude of men and women who do not even know him enjoy the strength of their unpersecuted life by grace of his sacrificial endurance.

"In the grace that is in Christ Jesus" we, too, can be strong. How strong one feels in the new freedom that comes when a hard apology has been made and accepted, lifting a weight from conscience and reconciling a broken friendship! How immeasurably greater and more enduring is the renewed power when our breach with life itself is healed by God in Christ Jesus! The apostle knew that strength. Imprisoned for preaching the good news, he could write: "But God's message is not imprisoned!" (vs. 9 AT). Here is strength no force can bind.

Perils of the Unfaithful
Matthew 25:14-30

"But he who had received the one talent, went and dug in the ground and hid his master's money" (vs. 18). He did not steal, he did not squander, he merely hid it. In the apocryphal Gospel of the Nazarenes, this third servant is a wastrel who, using the trust for a fling with flute-players and harlots, deserves the imprisonment he gets. Matthew's authentic report gets back from such obvious moralizing to the issue our Lord was raising: in life's crisis of ever-impending judgment, not wanton indulgence but unfaithfulness to our trust is our peril.

What, asks Joachim Jeremias, would Jesus' own audience have thought he meant by the man who hid his trust? Would the story have stirred their conscience about their own place in a chosen people "to whom so much had been entrusted, but who had not made use of their trust?" [30] Perhaps it was another of his pointed thrusts at the scribes.

God has entrusted them with much: the spiritual leadership of the nation, the knowledge of his will, the key of the Kingdom of God. Now the judgment of God is about to be revealed; now it will be decided whether the theologians have justified or abused God's great trust. . . . Their judgment will be specially severe." [31]

Since God's Word is always present tense, what does he say to us now? Does he point the parable at us who carry the trust of the gospel? A distinguished Canadian churchman confesses: "It has to be recognized that much of the present unpopularity of religious belief is firmly based on the ignorance and incompetence of religious people, and on the theological mismanagement of religious leaders and teachers." [32] Is this true? Is it true of my church? Is it true of me?

Our Lord set his Church to be "God's *avant-garde*," keeping pace with the march of his kingdom. He is at work in human affairs, breaking up old wrongs, bringing in a new day with all its disturbing challenges. But have we taken our place "at the perilous moving edge of change"? The Grand Dragon of the Southern Knights of the Ku Klux Klan seems to believe, gratefully, that we have not. Resigning his post in the Klan because he had concluded

---

[30] Jeremias, *The Parables of Jesus*, p. 61.

[31] *Ibid.*, p. 166.

[32] Donald M. Mathers, quoted in Kilbourn, *The Restless Church*, p. 65.

that "bombing and burning schools" is futile, he declared that he was still for segregation but that the new line of defense was inside the church, where he would now invest his efforts. Is that a fair picture of our buried talent? As a churchman, where do I stand in this judgment?

NINTH SUNDAY IN KINGDOMTIDE

When Now Is Not Enough
Isaiah 55:1-7

The work of the prophet of the Exile who wrote Isaiah 40–55 comes to its close with a promise that the exiles have a future which can give meaning to their lives even in the bitter now.

> Ho, every one who thirsts,
> come to the waters (vs. 1).

That speaks to us still.

A colorless present hems the exiles in. They can see no future, and the satisfactions with which they try to content themselves turn to dust in their mouths, so that the poet-prophet asks,

> Why do you spend your money for that which is not bread,
> and your labor for that which does not satisfy? (vs. 2a).

One need not be a homeless exile to share their plight. Our advertisers like to appeal to us as "the Now generation," for we pride ourselves on "being with it," abreast of the newest at any given moment.

We do not want to look at anything very long—observe the hop-skip-and-jump kind of visual ticaroo in our movies. We change our styles faster than things wear out. In the Roman Empire furniture styles changed every four hundred years; today they change every fifteen. We believe in built-in obsolescence, so that everything is made to not last long. Our philosophy is that what exists now should perish, and the sooner the better. Exits for people, and exits for things! [33]

Like the exiles, we find little satisfaction in these costly late-model baubles on which we spend money and labor.

To save a disappointing present, we must have a purpose that links us to yesterday and tomorrow. The prophet promises deep satisfaction—"eat what is good, and delight yourselves in fatness" (vs. 2b)—to a people who link themselves to the yesterday God gave and to the tomorrow he will give.

> And I will make with you an everlasting covenant,
> my steadfast, sure love for David (vs. 3b).

The reference seems to be the promise in II Sam. 7:8-10, which identifies king and people, saying: "I will appoint a place for my people Israel, and I will plant them, that they may dwell in their own place, and be disturbed no

---

[33] Miller, *Man the Believer*, p. 67.

more." In this continuing covenant, God will be a Father to David's son: "When he commits iniquity, I will chasten him with the rod of men, with the stripes of the sons of men"—as indeed he has been doing through the rigors of the Exile—"but I will not take my steadfast love from him. . . . And your house and your kingdom shall be made sure for ever before me" (II Sam. 7:14-16). The prophet sees the Exile in this larger perspective, with God's love looming beyond this time of discipline. Israel did return, though her sufferings have never come to a full end. She has continued to live by the power of a hope which irradiates each dark present.

We Christians see in the coming of Christ, a "Son of David," and in the expanding influence of Israel's witness through him and the Church he gathered, a fulfillment of the promise,

> Behold, you shall call nations that you know not,
> and nations that knew you not shall run to you (vs. 5a).

Israel's yesterdays are ours, and her hope, expanded in Christ, gives purpose to our life. This enlarged perspective can redeem our *Now*.

But a return is called for.

> Let the wicked forsake his way,
> and the unrighteous man his thoughts;
> let him return to the Lord, that he may have mercy on him,
> and to our God, for he will abundantly pardon (vs. 7).

The exiles, lost in the drabness of purposeless days, and in the attempt to brighten their lives by running after the tinsel satisfaction of Babylon, could find the purposeful link with past and future only by such a return. Perhaps it is so with us. Gerald Sykes paints a startling picture of us as awed by "the new supernatural" to which, he says, we attach religious significance.

> We have found a new supernatural in our own ingenious manufacture, or more exactly in the godlike powers that we unexpectedly and quite unconsciously have conferred upon it. . . . In the United States children usually yield the new supernatural their only real awe, their only real reverence, and seldom shake off their primary allegiance to mechanized marvels.[34]

But we need something more, for as Sykes says elsewhere, "Man wants first to be saved *by* technology, and then he wants to be saved *from* it." [35] From such imprisonment in a *Now* of our own idolatrous making we need to "return to the Lord, that he may have mercy."

Where a Better World Begins
Philemon 1:1-3, 10-16

Unanimous in the cry for a better world, we cannot agree on the route to the shining goal from the wilderness in which we now wander. Paul's letter to Philemon offers a fruitful suggestion.

[34] Gerald Sykes, *The Cool Millennium* (Englewood Cliffs, N.J.: Prentice-Hall, 1967), p. 11.
[35] *Ibid.*, p. 9.

The slave Onesimus had run away, reached the Roman metropolis where Paul was a prisoner, come under Paul's influence, and been converted. Apparently in his flight he had stolen from Philemon his master, and his now awakened conscience called him back to make restitution. He went bearing a letter from Paul, pleading that Philemon receive him as a Christian brother. For Philemon was also among Paul's converts (vss. 19-20), and the apostle did not hesitate to press a duty upon him. In one sentence Paul gathered up the essence of his case: "Perhaps this is why he [Onesimus] was parted from you for a while, that you might have him back for ever, no longer as a slave but more than a slave, as a beloved brother" (vss. 15-16).

Their slavery-ridden world needed reform. Possibly two-thirds of the population were bondsmen, deprived of all civil rights. Before the law they were not persons, but property. Their masters had absolute control, even over life or death. In the face of the massive evil, a lone man like Paul was powerless to revolutionize the system; but he knew a strategic place to start. Whatever the rest of society did, two men—one a master, the other a slave—could begin to see each other as brothers. They could say: Whatever other men do, we shall begin. A better world has our vote. For us, it begins now and begins here.

We cannot personally decide the questions raised by vast social issues demanding settlement in our time. Yet we need not wait until they are resolved, to begin a better world. Even when broad issues are decided, better conditions are often delayed for want of men of integrity and vision to implement the decisions. In making a better world we can take our cue from Paul; we *must* begin where we *can* begin, in the affairs of the two or three nearest to hand.

Paul's plea for personal brotherhood may seem too obvious to be necessary, but our mechanized mass society makes it once more imperative. Albert Schweitzer believed that the renewal of civilization must depend on the coming of persons with "a new tone of mind," who could stand against mass society and win influence over it. They alone, he said, can rescue us from barbarism.

"Brotherhood" that is not *personal* is not *brotherhood*. But brotherhood which does not quicken the conscience and imagination to see through our impersonal society to the persons our dealings affect, is worthless. In this awakening to be fully responsible persons, concerned to change unjust systems, but always sensitive to persons and their needs, a better world must begin—if it begins at all.

Returning to his master, Onesimus exercised great courage. Even the furtive freedom of the fugitive was sweeter than slavery. To restore the loss he had caused Philemon would cost heavy toil. There was no guarantee that he would not be painfully punished for his flight. Yet in meeting what he believed was the demand of integrity he gave a better world his vote. Paul appealed to Philemon to receive him in the same spirit: "I am sending him back to you, sending my very heart" (vs. 12). "So if you consider me your partner, receive him as you would receive me. If he has wronged you at all, or owes you anything, charge that to my account" (vss. 17-18). "Refresh my heart in Christ" (vs. 20). Philemon, Onesimus, Paul—each in his way was deeply involved in the implications of a *duty* based on a *love* that had been *given* them.

What a love it was—and is! God's love prepared the good earth for us, his children, endowed us with the strength and talents out of which we build our lives, and surrounds us every day we live. Jesus' love to unlovely people, climaxed by his forgiving death on the cross, was not an accident in an alien universe; it was a revelation of deepest, most abiding reality.

This love issues in the gospel of another chance—another chance for each of us, because of which we grow gratefully ready to give others another chance. As this spirit grows among us there is another chance for a disrupted world.

Because each had been given a new chance at life, a new relation became possible. Onesimus could not withhold from his master the restitution for the wrong he had done, since God had not withheld the priceless gift of his love, his Son, his salvation. Philemon could not be a hard master, knowing that he stood under the judgment, but even more under the love, of a God from whom he had deserved nothing, yet had received all. Is it not so with us?

Saga of Two Rebels: Luke 15:11-32

Two rebels share this spotlight. The younger son drove his rebellion to complete break, demanding his inheritance and no further contact with his father. The outcome was bitter loss; "he began to be in want" (vs. 14), or "he began to feel the pinch" (NEB). But we miss the point of the parable unless we see that the older brother was at least equally a rebel. For Jesus was addressing religious Pharisees, and by implication, orthodox people in all ages, saying that they are like the older brother.

Polite rebel, he was still at odds with his father. While the family celebrated, he sulked. "He was angry and refused to go in" (vs. 28). "Look, how many years have I slaved for you" (vs. 29 PT), he remonstrated. "Slaved" is the well-chosen word. He would not say "brother," but rather, "this son of yours" (vs. 30). Far from sharing his father's joyful love, he remained, beneath his pious exterior, an unreconciled rebel. Through him, Jesus appealed to religious leaders, as if to say:

Behold the greatness of God's love for his lost children, and contrast it with your own joyless, loveless, thankless and self-righteous lives. Cease then from your loveless ways, and be merciful. The spiritually dead are rising to new life, the lost are returning home, rejoice with them.[36]

Christian witness, the parable implies, begins with facing one's self in painful honesty. In the parable, the sad truth was that, although the younger son had "come to himself," the older son had not. He could still pretend that he was right and his brother wrong. To come to yourself, you have to hunt yourself from one hiding place to another. But there is no effective Christian witness that does not begin with this painful kind of self-knowledge.

The parable dramatizes the responsibility of the church toward returning prodigals. For the younger son in the story, the restored relation with his

[36] Jeremias, *The Parables of Jesus,* p. 131.

father led to new life. He and his father could face the whole sorry situation together. Forgiveness cannot do everything. The squandered inheritance was still gone. The marks of dissipation might remain on his body. The harm done to the moral standards of the community could not be healed overnight. But he was no longer alone. He and his father faced the wreckage together, and together they would work toward the restoration. Forgiveness does not cancel consequences, but it restores a relation in which there is new heart to rebuild.

The father in the parable represents God. But must not God's way be the church's way of standing with the returning prodigals in understanding friendship that puts new heart into the making of a new life? It is fruitless to *talk* about God's forgiveness to a broken person who does not know what it is to be so loved by another human being that he is accepted and valued just as he is. Before our *words* can give winning witness to the forgiving love of God, our *lives* must express the love that spends time and concern in a real giving of ourselves.[37]

TENTH SUNDAY IN KINGDOMTIDE

Renewed or Abandoned?
Ezekiel 37:1-6, 11-14

"Christianity: Renewed or Slowly Abandoned?" The question is posed in the title of an article by a university scholar in a distinguished scientific journal. Much in everyday experience reiterates the judgment that abandonment is on the way. The choice is renewal or extinction. To this option Ezekiel speaks.

Among the exiles in Babylon in the late sixth century B.C., despair reached its depths as news came that Jerusalem had been wiped out. The people despaired, "Our bones are dried up, and our hope is lost; we are clean cut off" (vs. 11)—the phrase "cut off" being the equivalent of "We are dead people." Deutero-Isaiah, in the same idiom, wrote, "He was cut off out of the land of the living" (Isa. 53:8). In that dark hour, Ezekiel did not deny they were dead; he asserted that God could give them new life.

His message took form in a parable conceived in a trancelike state in which the Lord set him "in the midst of the valley . . . full of bones" (vs. 1). Thus he expanded Isaiah's figure:

> Thy dead shall live, their bodies shall rise.
> O dwellers in the dust, awake, and sing for joy (Isa. 26:19),

a promise of renewal for a nation that has labored and "brought forth wind," having "wrought no deliverance in the earth" (Isa. 26:18).

The "valley" or plain in which the scene is laid (vs. 2) resembles a great battlefield covered with the bones of the fallen. As vs. 11 shows, and as scholars like Julius Bewer and Herbert May point out, the bones are meant to

[37] This treatment of the parable is adapted and condensed from a church school lesson contributed by the author to *The Adult Student.*

signify not the physical death of individuals, but the death of the nation. Ezekiel confesses to having had no certainty in his own right that life could return, trusting the matter completely to the competence of God: "Can these bones live?" "O Lord, God, thou knowest" (vs. 3). God then calls him to preach to the bones of a dead Israel, calling them to new life and promising them breath (vss. 4-6). The Hebrew word can mean breath, or wind, or spirit, according to its context, and this fact makes possible the wordplay upon these meanings, that runs through the passage. "I will cause breath to enter you" (vs. 5) is equally well rendered, "I will make the breath of life enter you" (MT). In like idiom the creation story tells us that God "breathed into his nostrils the breath of life; and man became a living being" (Gen. 2:7).

In the vision, this preached message revived the people, bringing the bones together first into reconstituted corpses and then into reanimated beings (vss. 7-10). What the vision dared to anticipate became, in fact, the exiles' experience.

That the Jews did not lose their identity in the Babylonian exile is due to religious leaders, who gradually led them to interpret their national tragedy in a religious manner and inspired them with a penitential spirit and a new hope for the future. One of these men was Ezekiel.[38]

Ezekiel says plainly that "these bones are the whole house [MT: "community"] of Israel" (vs. 11). Though they see no hope for their dead nation, all political and human resources having run out, there is still promise that God will bring them back from the dead (vss. 12-13). By the power of God's resurrection there is new life for the nation and a promise of moral and spiritual renewal in the return to the homeland (vs. 14).

Now, as we face the alternatives, "Christianity: Renewed or Slowly Abandoned?" this speaks a needed word. We need a "prophesying to the bones" which will bring the languishing church together into daring new ventures. Old, cautious ministries cannot win the allegiance of strong, forward-looking men and women. Creative new forms of ministry, parishes of changing "shapes," are emerging. This is vital.

It can issue only in charmingly reconstituted corpses, however, unless there is also vital "prophesying to the breath," opening men to the winds of the spirit and the renewal of the inner life. New Testament faith deals with life-giving realities: the Holy Spirit, conversion, regeneration, death and resurrection. These can bring renewal to the church. Perhaps the miracle of the dry bones can occur again.

Practical Heresy
II John 1:3-4, 6; III John 1:11

These selected verses on the merits of love and a good life, read out of context, are sickishly sweet and boringly bland. Love and be good—ho hum, so what else is new? Add the tart realism of their setting and see!

"For many deceivers have gone out into the world, men who will not

[38] Kraeling, *Commentary on the Prophets*, I, 401.

acknowledge the coming of Jesus Christ in the flesh" (II:7). Try that, for a beginning. It speaks of the Gnostic heresy, which claimed a "higher spirituality." It would not contaminate its ethereal vision with the notion that the God of the universe could be compromised by entering the life of an individual man—least of all a lowly carpenter who died on a cross. Claiming this lofty spirituality, these teachers arrogantly staked out a private claim on God. But, this letter counters, "any one who goes ahead and does not abide in the doctrine of Christ does not have God" (II:9).

The trouble with heresy is that it does not stay in the realm of ideas. This early theological arrogance led to divisive denials of charity in the church. One Gnostic teacher refused the church's call for hospitality to Christian pilgrims in a time when public inns were notoriously unsafe and immoral. He even presumed to excommunicate those who extended charity to Christian brothers in need (III:9-10).

These letters of John deal with church life in the face of such challenges. II John addresses one particular church as "the elect lady" (vs. 1), whose children have, in the main, held true despite the false teaching (vs. 4). Written by a leader of the church, "the elder" (vs. 1), who continues the apostolic witness, it offers no hesitant prayer that God *may* bless the addressed congregation. Rather it assures them that to those who live the truth as love, who accept Jesus "in the flesh," and who walk in uprightness of life, "grace, mercy, and peace *will*" be present as God's gifts (vs. 3).

Addressed to substantially the same denials of Christian belief and practice, the two letters declare that in the face of this otherworldly spirituality which refuses to show elemental kindness and love, the Christian message is starkly simple, involving two basic elements.

First, love is the one great essential (II:5-6). Set that over against the "spiritual theology" of the Gnostics! What does it mean in the last third of the twentieth century? Hear the Fourth Assembly of the World Council of Churches: "The Church is called to work for a world-wide responsible society and to summon men and nations to repentance. To be complacent in the face of the world's need is to be guilty of practical heresy." [39] In the first century "practical heresy" denied hospitality to needy travelers, and in the twentieth century the World Council had before it such facts as these:

The resources of [the world] community are so distributed—80 per cent of them being at the disposal of 20 per cent of the people, living in the main around the North Atlantic—that while one segment of humanity is rich and growing richer, the rest still struggle in varying degrees of poverty. . . . The majority of Christians live in the developed North and if this area is wealthy far beyond the general level of the world society, they profit from this unbalanced prosperity and must in conscience account for their stewardship. . . . All Christians bear heavy responsibility for a world in which it can seem "normal" to spend $150,000 millions a year on armaments, yet difficult to mobilize more than $10,000 millions for the works of economic and social cooperation. [40]

[39] *The Uppsala Report,* Normal Goodall, ed. (Geneva: World Council of Churches, 1968), p. 51.

[40] *Line and Plummet,* by Richard Dickinson for the Committee for Special Assistance for Special Services (Geneva: World Council of Churches, 1968), pp. 103-4.

It was about such facts that the World Council, true to the insight of the early church, proclaimed the dread words, "guilty of practical heresy."

Second, an upright life, more than any claim of secret knowledge, is the evidence of a true relation to God. "He who does good is of God; he who does evil has not seen God" (III:11). The only thing that can save talk of the cross of Christ from being sickishly pietistic, said a speaker at the World Conference on Church and Society, is to

perceive it to be a secular event, a historic event in which the magnitude of God's plan for his world is revealed to the wondering eyes of faith. . . . The cross of Christ reminds us that when we speak of economic, sociological or political problems, we are speaking of men and women whom Jesus Christ regarded as his own brothers once and for all when he accepted the cross.[41]

How good is our theology? Well, how responsible is our life? How well do we face up to the Cross as "a secular event" which makes a difference with bread and butter issues? By that test, are we "guilty of practical heresy"?

Call to Responsible Personhood
John 8:1-11

The fact that this story does not appear in the earliest manuscripts does not make it spurious. It may be an authentic bit of independent tradition.

Its succinct expression of the mercy of Jesus is as delicate as anything in Luke; its portrayal of Jesus as the serene judge has all the majesty that we would expect of John. The moment when the sinful woman stands confronted with the sinless Jesus is one of exquisite drama. . . . And the delicate balance between the justice of Jesus in not condoning the sin and his mercy in forgiving the sinner is one of the great gospel lessons.[42]

Some commentators to the contrary notwithstanding, the scene does not portray Jesus as condoning adultery. He said quite clearly, "Go, and do not sin again" (vs. 11). What had been done was clearly wrong, and a break with the sin was needed. What Jesus would not do was issue a merely legalistic condemnation which looked at a deed and failed to see a person, judged an act and dismissed the struggle of a life. Seeing a whole person, he was unwilling to pronounce judgment. But, by the same token, he was unwilling to condone the deed. "Go," he said, "and do not sin again."

The carnal act was not the only sin. To the righteous Pharisees he said, "Let him who is without sin among you be the first to throw a stone at her" (vs. 7). This sharp thrust at conscience made the Pharisees see themselves with a clarity that silenced and dispersed them (vs. 9). Even by legalists' standards they were far from blameless, and he helped them to a new self-knowledge. His searching of inner motive (Matt. 5:22a, 28) calls Christians

[41] Official Report, World Conference on Church and Society (Geneva: World Council of Churches, 1967), p. 12.

[42] Raymond E. Brown, *The Gospel According to John (I-XII)*, Anchor Bible (Garden City, N.Y.: Doubleday, 1966), 29:336-37.

to account for all sins of mind and motive in a morality deeper than legalism.

The scene gives scant comfort to either the relativist or the legalist in today's controversy over "the new morality." Because it provides a battleground between the champions of contextual ethics and an ethic of rules, Kyle Haselden's succinct summary of his able discussion of the two positions throws light upon its contemporary significance. Haselden wrote:

Legalism tends to make men servile; relativism tends to make men libertine. Legalism makes a shrine out of an event in the past; the new morality hallows a fleeting instant in the present. Legalism externalizes and mechanizes morality; relativism internalizes and subjectivizes morality. Legalism writes hard contracts between men; the new morality cancels all bonds between men, except those directly related to the immediate situation. Legalism precludes the counsel of the Holy Spirit; contextual ethics substitutes the will and mood of man for the counsel of the Holy Spirit. Legalism encourages immorality by its rigidity; the new morality encourages immorality by its imprecision. Legalism tends to ignore men; relativism exalts man as the ultimate arbiter of good and evil.[43]

Jesus' answer to the dilemma was a quiet act: He "bent down and wrote with his finger on the ground" (vs. 6). To look at either the woman or her self-righteous accusers under these circumstances was to make them *objects*, to stand outside looking on, to look at lust or to look at legalistic vindictiveness. Jesus would do neither. This was a depersonalizing situation, and he would see persons, allow persons to emerge. By waiting as he wrote in the dust, he allowed them to rise into personhood and self-understanding.

ELEVENTH SUNDAY IN KINGDOMTIDE

To Recapture Moral Faith
Zephaniah 3:8-13

In the turbulent times made familiar by Jeremiah, a less known contemporary gave us the brief prophetic book of Zephaniah. Its message has the "moral vigor and religious passion" requisite to "any age which needs to learn again the fundamental verities of moral religion, 'the fear of the Lord.' "[44] Ours is such an age, and to us Zephaniah offers elements basic to the recapture of moral faith.

To recapture moral faith *we need realism about judgment.* In Zephaniah's vision of the future, God is calling nations to "wait" for his "decision," "indignation," and "jealous wrath" (vs. 8). In the background of this summons are indictments already returned against idolatry (1:4-6), violence and fraud (1:9), and skepticism concerning God's moral judgment (1:12). Amid our world-engulfing tidal wave of violence, our moral skepticism, and our tendencies to worship the products of our technology, that is a timely word for us.

[43] Kyle Haselden, *Morality and the Mass Media* (Nashville: Broadman Press, 1968), p. 30.
[44] Bewer, *The Prophets*, p. 536.

To recapture moral faith *we need openness to redemption.* In Zephaniah's vision, judgment is redemptive in purpose. The speech of the people will be purified. No longer invoking alien gods, they will worship the Lord alone (vs. 9). Their new faithfulness will be unifying; men will serve God "with one accord." The literal translation might be "shoulder to shoulder," suggesting comradeship; or "with one shoulder," suggesting unity in burden-bearing—"under the same yoke" (JB).

Is hope for a divided people only visionary? Or does it hold promise for our fragmented world society, which cultural pluralism has left with no common faith or values to which to repair? Yes. For God is the Creator, served not only in liturgical words but in secular deeds. Stout verities are inherent in his nature. After demagogues have led us over the precipice of warring divisions, God puts the shattered bits together as we stumble painfully, a little at a time, toward solid bases of human relations taught by hard experience and open-eyed research. So all peoples, from the ends of the earth can be drawn into one universal recognition of God's reality (vs. 10).

To recapture moral faith *we need humility, forerunner of brotherhood.* In Zephaniah's vision there will be a remnant—"those who are left" (vs. 13)—who "shall not be put to shame" (vs. 11). The humble will endure, though

> I will remove your proud boasters
> from your midst;
> and you will cease to strut
> on my holy mountain (vs. 11b JB).

Pride, source of rebellious strutting, is the root of sin. It cannot stand, nor can those who engage in it—even the powerful in their nuclear strut. Those who endure, who hold the future, are "a people humble and lowly" (vs. 12). Does this suggest that the dark-skinned peoples of the poorer nations, only now emerging into independent nationhood, are those to whom the tomorrows belong? Does the way of the Cross, the Man of sorrows, acquainted with grief, indeed hold the hope of the future? If so, there is a requirement of these humble ones, that

> they shall do no wrong
> and utter no lies,
> nor shall there be found in their mouth
> a deceitful tongue (vs. 13).

God will care for them "and none shall make them afraid." Such humility is the forerunner of brotherhood. Where it is present brotherhood can grow; where it is wanting brotherhood is impossible. That is the solemn truth about life and death in an age which has no place to hide, unless in brotherhood.

Here We Find Ourselves
I John 2:24-25, 28-29; 3:1-2

Visitors to Florida's Bok Tower are greeted by John Burroughs' words, "I come here to find myself; it is so easy to get lost in the world." A distracting world pushes us this way and that until ours is the lostness of those who no longer remember who they are. We need quiet retreats to help us restore our identity. Yet they work no miracles. From their serenity we return to pressure, from new resolutions to repeated temptation and fall. We need a better way to find ourselves than any solitary retreat can give. Here is one strong clue to our identity: "Beloved, we are God's children now; it does not yet appear what we shall be, but we know that when he appears we shall be like him, for we shall see him as he is" (3:2).

The Bible's drama begins with man made in God's image, but despoiling it beyond recognition. Near its close the drama reminds us that we are still God's children, that his image can be restored. "To *see* Christ as he really is, and to be *like* him, is the fullest possible description of the Christian salvation: something far superior to speculative knowledge (such as Gnosticism)." [45] What we need is no mere rediscovery of our old failing selves, only to be lost again. We need to find who we are in our fullest potential, under God. Here are three movements—to *see*, to *resemble*, to *know*—at which we should look more closely.

We begin with the last, to *know* in a way "superior to speculative knowledge (such as Gnosticism)." This need triggered the writing of this passage. Gnostics were disrupting the church with their theology of a God too absolute and impassive to be involved in human affairs by coming among us in the *man* Jesus. No doubt he had come in a Christ figure, they said, but in a way so spiritual that Jesus as a man living and dying among us only *appeared* to be human in any fully physical sense. John repudiated such teaching: "Who is the liar but he who denies that *Jesus* is the Christ?" (2:22, italics added). The fully human Jesus "you heard from the beginning" (2:24) through such teaching as is found in the gospels, is the Christ.

This knowledge is not derived from philosophical speculation. We know by recognizing what is before us on the record and in the experience of the Church. Just as "the world does not know (*ginoskei*) us" for what we are as Christian believers, "it did not know him" (3:1). The word *ginoskei* has no necessary implication of secret knowledge, esoteric enlightenment, such as the Gnostics claimed, but lends itself to the translation "acknowledge" (JB) or "recognize" (MT). The Christian is urged to keep alive in himself, "abide in" this recognition of Jesus as brother man through whom God comes to us. Everything vitally real in the Christian life begins in this.

"To *see* Christ as he really is" begins in direct human recognition, but it needs cultivation. We "abide in him," deepening the association by faith, prayer, and loyal service. It is fostered and completed by something he does for us "when he appears" (2:28). To see anyone truly is to share concern and mutual love with him, to enter empathically into his mind and experience. To know Christ thus is to live fully, and it is possible because he —who is utterly beyond us—has first entered into our lives and revealed himself to us. So we know we are children of God, but we cannot tell what more is in store for us. Without having it all spelled out as Gnostic theologies seek to do, we simply venture in faith with him.

"To be *like* him" is the goal to which he leads. We cannot *achieve* it by

[45] Grant, *Nelson's Bible Commentary*, VII, 353.

our work; he *gives* it by contagion. Living in him (2:24), we receive "what he has promised us, eternal life" (2:25). Hearing his word and believing him, we *have* eternal life, *have passed* from death to life (John 5:24). Arthur Miller has one of his characters say, "Everything was always temporary with us. It's like we never were anything, we were always about-to-be." [46] The pathetic line sums up the married life of a couple whose years had been woven out of large dreams, long procrastinations, and trivial accomplishments. In a sense it is the general human story—always temporary, always about-to-be. Out of this tentative existence, never fully *present* in the moment where we stand, Christ leads us into a life in which each moment has the quality of eternity.

This is salvation. It has made peace with the past, for we know we are accepted in spite of what we have been. It has been led into the increasing fulfillment of our possibilities, so that its future is no longer a painful threat. By the contagion of Christ's love it lives *now* with the stability of eternity.

He the Banquet Spreads Before Us
Mark 6:31-44

And taking the five loaves and the two fish he looked up to heaven, and blessed, and broke the loaves, and give them to the disciples to set before the people (vs. 41).

It cannot be accidental that the four acts—taking, blessing, breaking, giving—always associated with the Last Supper (Matt. 26:26; Mark 14:22; Luke 22:19; I Cor. 11:23-24) are here enumerated in language closely paralleling Mark's own upper room account. The tradition of the early church seems to have seen in this episode something closely associated with, and possibly throwing light upon, the Lord's Supper.

That an actual event of wonder to those who participated in it lies back of this account, we need not doubt. It would be strange for a mere parabolic tale to hold the fascination this narrative—the only wonder story told by all four Gospels—held for the evangelists. By the time the tradition was reduced to writing, however, this event had gathered such a cargo of theological meaning that it is fruitless for us to try to reconstruct the original happening. We are better served if we allow the early witnesses to tell us what it meant to them in the light of the community's experience and reflection.

We begin, then, with the setting in which all the Gospels place it. The Synoptics make it the immediate sequel to the murder of John the Baptist, and the Fourth Gospel links itself with this testimony by setting the event immediately after Jesus' discourse on John's witness (5:30 ff.). Thus, in the gospel tradition, this seems to be a banquet in which, the forerunner having completed his work, we have a foretaste of the new Age which God is inaugurating through the ministry of Jesus. Perhaps the link with the Lord's Supper, already noted, is saying that in every Holy Communion celebration we have a renewal of the pledge of God's bountiful rule in our affairs.

Mark notes that when Jesus saw the crowd "he had compassion on them,

[46] Miller, *The Price*, p. 18.

because they were like sheep without a shepherd; and he began to teach them many things" (vs. 34). The figure is familiar in Old Testament usage. Moses is instructed to commission Joshua, in response to the prayer "that the congregation of the Lord may not be as sheep which have no shepherd" (Num. 27:17). Micaiah prophesies the fall of King Ahab by picturing a shepherdless people: "I saw all Israel scattered abroad upon the mountains, as sheep that have no shepherd" (I Kings 22:17). Ezekiel declares that God himself will be the Shepherd of Israel because the kings appointed to tend the flock have left them with "no shepherd . . . scattered over all the face of the earth, with none to search or seek for them" (Ezek. 34:5-6).

In the light of this usage, Mark's report that Jesus saw the throng "like sheep without a shepherd; and he began to teach them many things" amounts to saying that he saw them leaderless, defenseless, awaiting a messianic king, and that he stepped into that office. Mark gives no report of *what* Jesus taught, emphasizing rather the teaching *office*, as if to say that his kingship is of the mind and spirit. Linked as it is with Communion imagery, the story seems to say that in every celebration of the Eucharist Christ serves again as kingly Lord of our minds, spirits, wills.

The incident is reminiscent of Old Testament scenes of providential care. Its very form—a large number to be fed; earnest, rational questions concerning the inadequacy of a pitiful larder; the repeated command to feed the company; the final distribution of the food; and the discovery that it is more than enough—echoes II Kings 4:42-44.

A man came from Baal-shalishah, bringing the man of God bread of the first fruits, twenty loaves of barley, and fresh ears of grain in his sack. And Elisha said, "Give to the men, that they may eat." But his servant said, "How am I to set this before a hundred men?" So he repeated, "Give them to the men, that they may eat, for thus says the Lord, 'They shall eat and have some left.' " So he set it before them. And they ate, and had some left, according to the word of the Lord.

The emphasis falls on the goodness of God's bounty, not on the miraculous power of the prophet. Even more is this true of the feeding of the fleeing Israelites with manna in the desert (Exod. 16:13-33).

In his interpretative treatment of the feeding of the multitude, John recalls that the people subsequently said, "Our fathers ate the manna in the wilderness; as it is written, 'He gave them bread from heaven to eat' " (John 6:31). Jesus replied that this was a gift not from Moses, but from God, who had now given the true bread of life in his Son. He then spoke of his own flesh and blood as the true life-sustaining nourishment, concluding: "This is the bread which came down from heaven, not such as the fathers ate and died; he who eats this bread will live for ever" (John 6:35-58). Linking such words to the story of the feeding of the multitude, John suggests that God's ultimate providence is his giving of that which sustains us eternally—his gift of Christ.

So the evangelists use this story of the feeding of the multitude as a Eucharistic banquet which portrays how, in each celebration, we renew our participation in the life of him who gives us life abundant, overflowing, eternal.

TWELFTH SUNDAY IN KINGDOMTIDE

No Disembodied Faith
Haggai 1:3-9; 2:2-3

Haggai is too brick-and-mortar minded for the contemporary church. One idea obsessed him—to see the ruined temple rebuilt. Single-mindedly pursuing this purpose, he and his colleague Zechariah saw their dream realized. Prophesying in 520 B.C., sixteen years after the return from the Exile, he offered no lofty challenge to ethical reform or spiritual renewal. In a single sentence he gathers the burden of his call: "Go up to the hills and bring wood and build the house, that I may take pleasure in it and that I may appear in my glory, says the Lord" (1:8). Is this too "dated" to command the attention of Christians in our age of spiritual crisis?

Dwight E. Stevenson sets it squarely in the midst of contemporary affairs by analogy to new communities now mushrooming on the growing edges of American cities. These new subdivisions, he points out, "swank residential and shopping communities—consumer neighborhoods—[are] often without any plans for churches." [47] Sharp contrast with earlier American communities in which the builders of the new homes were at pains to cluster them around church and school even when frontier conditions made the financial strain intense! These older communities achieved a unity of life important to all sound values, but in the newer trend

little thought is given to the making of a cultural community; little responsibility is accepted locally for schools, for civic and political integrity, and for churches. . . . Unless we can create a new sense of religious responsibility in the minds of millions now moving into the suburbs, suburbia has become a vast, foreign-missionary field. One could hardly find a more apt situation for the words of Haggai: "Is it a time for you yourselves to dwell in your paneled houses, while this house lies in ruins?" (1:4). The ruins here are sociological, of course, not physical; but the problem is the same. Will the church question lie fatally neglected? [48]

From this, it is appropriate to voice a word in behalf of the "institutional church." Much is being said concerning the values of the "underground church," but they are insufficient to meet crucial world need. Workers in troubled urban centers now stress the importance of "the church on the corner." As an organization in being, it provides a ready-forged instrument for attacking problems, a focal center for social and ethical concern, physical facilities for many a neighborhood project. Effective witness in a mass society does not issue from an amorphous body of goodwill; organization, funds, instrumentalities are vital. Serving massive world need is no guerrilla action for unrelated individuals. A man must belong to a close-knit world agency with roots in his community and ministering arms in far places. No disembodied faith will do.

Haggai called his people to give their faith local embodiment. To their

[47] Dwight E. Stevenson, *Preaching on the Books of the Old Testament* (New York: Harper, 1961), p. 242.
[48] *Ibid.*

plea that times were too hard, he replied that shortsightedness might make them harder still. "You have looked for much, and, lo, it came to little; and when you brought it home, I blew it away. Why? says the Lord of hosts. Because of my house that lies in ruins, while you busy yourselves each with his own house" (1:9). An aggregation of individuals pursuing selfish ends is not a community, and until they put first some shared concerns and priority values their society is doomed.

To their objection that this poor temple, in spite of the best they can do for it, is a negligible thing (2:3), he responded that they need to look away from the immediate present to the potential future, and from their puny resources to the illimitable means at the disposal of the God of history (2:4-9).

We need the sense of history and of divine potential to which the prophet pointed. In his closing oracle he spoke of the dynamic movement of events, in which presently powerful peoples would be overthrown but the Davidic dynasty would be re-established (2:20-23). The throne did not find a new occupant in the sense Haggai implied. But, in history's long sweep, a greater Son of David than he could have foreseen came to fulfill the messianic expectation. In that coming, Haggai and the temple played their part, keeping alive the faith of Israel and the identity of the threatened people who provided a tradition which could flower in the Christ. In God's economy our efforts, even in the religious institution that is far less than ideal, produce outcomes unpredictable from our time-bound stance but invaluable from his eternal perspective.

Faith Lives in Revolution
II Peter 3:8-14

Probably written between A.D. 120 and 150, this letter may be the last New Testament document. Those who maintain its direct connection with Simon Peter do not place it earlier than A.D. 90. Between it and Jesus' resurrection loomed long years of disappointed hope of his swift return. Would the new Age expected with his coming never arrive? Must things always remain as they are—tyranny and injustice forever in the saddle? Can we no longer hope for God's intervention? Christians could not escape such questions.

God delays that expected day, Peter declared, but it will come. For him, a thousand years—to us an eternity—are but a day, and a day—to us negligible—may have the weight of a millennium (vs. 8). Our view of time needs his eternal perspective. His delay is not negligent but merciful, giving us time to prepare for ultimate crisis by repentance and the witness that shares the faith with others (vs. 9).

Our imagery concerning Christ's "second coming" may not be that of the early Christians, but the truth beneath the image remains. Many of us live long tracts of days under conditions routine, if not always placid. Then the brutally unexpected comes crashing in. In his novel, *The Sleep of Reason,* C. P. Snow chronicles the serene days of a successful British elder statesman living in semi-retirement until he is suddenly drawn into the agonizing wake of a revolting crime. But, the crisis past, he returns to the routine life, in which—despite disturbing memories and unquiet episodes—his existence goes on virtually unchanged, reasonable, all but asleep.

Our life is like that. Granted the mercy of untroubled days, we deepen the ruts of our ways until crisis halts us. Unprepared, we muddle through it; and once it is passed we revert to old patterns with no real repentance or radical change of direction. Peter calls us not to waste the mercy of deferred crisis, but to use it in repentance, change, the winning of others to a new life.

The crisis of God's day will come. The apocalyptic imagery of vanishing heavens and a destroyed earth (vs. 10) need not confuse us. Science has its apocalyptic vision of an ultimate end of the world in solar collision or a final Ice Age. Technology threatens the apocalypse of nuclear annihilation. Short of these, Peter depicts the crisis which comes when a way of life, on which we have depended, collapses and we face ultimate judgment in the removal of old dependabilities. Racial upheaval can do that. Obsolescence of the work in which we have found our sense of personal worth can do it. The death of a loved one can plunge us into its abyss. Shattering guilt, agonizing anxiety, our own death, are in their ways so many "ends of the world" for us. Beneath the imagery of Peter's words, the Christian message speaks to this crisis element in our common life.

What sort of persons, then, should we be? (vs. 11). Peter's suggestions claim us by their inherent validity. We need "lives of holiness and godliness" (vs. 11), not satisfied with participation in mass social movements. It is the disciplined who matter in a shattered world. God-oriented lives of health and integrity help to create a climate of right relations among men.

We need to wait for the coming of God's day, and hasten it (vs. 12). His day of judgment and redress of wrongs *will* come. We can live in reluctant foot-dragging, or we can be among those whose earnest desire (RSV note), expectation, prayer, and preparation help God to prepare the conditions of his coming.

We need to live in anticipation of the promised new order of life "in which righteousness dwells" (vs. 13), throwing "the stubborn ounces of our weight" behind a more decent society that accords full dignity to all men as children of God. Valid hope for Christ's new age generates conflict with things as they are.

In our revolutionary time, we can be creative and hopeful; or we can be dull-eyed, missing its significance, resenting its break-up of our settled ways, heedless of its call to repent. God calls us "to be found by him without spot or blemish, and at peace" (vs. 14). Unless the new age begins in new men, it will be the old age over again. There will be only new oppressors, new ingenuities in evading new rules and structures. Faith that makes life new from its roots is the radical need amid the revolutions with which God confronts every life.

Stress, Strain, and Stamina
Matthew 7:24-29

Phillips Brooks spoke the authentic gospel note: "Do not pray for easy lives. Pray to be stronger men! Do not pray for tasks equal to your powers. Pray for powers equal to your tasks." No man can live with Jesus and continue to think of faith as flight from the fierce onslaughts or frustrating attritions of hard experience. In this parable, Jesus refuses to offer easy lives, and points the way to be stronger men.

Ultimate tests—desolating flood and wind (vs. 25)—come to us all. They overtake good men and bad, wise and foolish, those who build on the rock of Jesus' teaching and those who build on the sand of self-indulgence and worldly philosophies. Christian faith is no guarantee against stress and strain; presentation of its verities as insurance against misfortune falsifies the biblical message. Jesus implies in this parable what he has earlier said in plain proposition: God "makes his sun rise on the evil and on the good, and sends rain on the just and on the unjust" (Matt. 5:45). Disciples are promised no escape from storms.

They have a better thing. To live by promise of escape would diminish us, make us weaklings. So Jesus asserts the power of faith to carry us undefeated *through* storm and flood. It begins with hearing his words (vs. 24), which—if it is real hearing—is itself a strength. We *may* hear without comprehension or sensitive concern (Matt. 13:13-16); to hear him so is to hear him merely as a rabbi of long ago. But hearing him *may* awaken our concern and give us new understanding of our own situation, its demands, and its resources. That alone is real hearing, hearing him as *Lord,* hearing which makes true disciples.

Hearing his words thus, we do them. Our whole being is affected. Righteousness springs from inner consent to God's law as the expression of his holiness and love (Matt. 5:20 ff.) New piety grows out of response to him in prayer and trust (Matt. 6:1 ff.). New righteousness of conduct and piety of relationship produce a new style of life in which there is strength to endure all storms.

The parable of the houses is seen truly only when seen as integrally related to the whole sweep of the Sermon on the Mount. Its message is that we stand confronted by God's kingdom which comes not as haven of refuge but as judgment on our attempts to make a life by our self-sufficient effort; that to live in God's new Age is to live by a righteousness born of love answering his love; and that such love comes to maturity in a disciple's obedient companionship with Jesus, the Christ.

He not only *asserts* the power to live with enduring stamina amid storms; he *exemplifies* it. He teaches with authority (vs. 29) won by firsthand knowledge of things he has experienced and incarnated. He announces the kingdom, and in him it begins. He calls us to its ways; and his companionship gives us the power of his forgiving love, to live by them.

THIRTEENTH SUNDAY IN KINGDOMTIDE

Embrace the Purpose of God
Ezra 1:2-4; 3:10-13

The people's jubilant song of praise at the completion of the temple foundation was associated, in the Chronicler's mind, with other high occasions related to ark and temple.

And they sang responsively, praising and giving thanks to the Lord,

> "For he is good,
> for his steadfast love endures for ever" (3:11).

When David brought the ark to Jerusalem (I Chron. 16:34) and when Solomon brought the ark to the temple he had built (II Chron. 5:13), these lines were sung. They form a constant refrain in the praises of Israel (Ps. 100:5; 106:1; 107:1; 118:1-4, 29; 130:7; 136—a litany formed upon it; 138:8; Jer. 33:11). The lection for this Thirteenth Sunday in Kingdomtide might itself be an extended commentary on God's enduring covenant love in working out his purpose in the life of his people.

His purpose included the actions of Cyrus, pagan conqueror. For, according to this report, the restoration of Israel and the temple began in the proclamation of this Gentile overlord (1:2-4). He may not be presumed to have spoken as a devout believer in Israel's God, yet God used his edict in bringing his own purpose to completion. So the Isaiah of the Exile—who portrayed Cyrus as an instrument in the hand of a God he did not know—had declared (Isa. 44:28–45:7). The Persians acknowledged a supreme "God of heaven," with whom Yahweh may be here identified. There policy toward subject peoples was one of tolerant encouragement of the indigenous religions. In pursuance of this policy, Cyrus is seen lending encouragement to the rebuilding of the temple and the recognition of Israel's faith as the official religion in Jerusalem (1:3). The "survivors"—the Jewish community who had held together through the Exile and were now returning—were thus given the sanction to claim support in their venture from the residents of whatever community they were in, in the land of their exile (1:4).

Thus what had been unparalleled national catastrophe was seen in process of becoming a part of the fulfillment of the nation's destiny and mission. As Lord of history, God could use untoward events, saying to a pagan like Cyrus:

> I call you by your name,
> I surname you, though you do not know me.
> I am the Lord, and there is no other,
> besides me there is no God;
> I gird you, though you do not know me,
> that men may know, from the rising of the sun
> and from the west, that there is none besides me;
> I am the Lord, and there is no other (Isa. 45:4b-6).

God's purpose used the forward-looking piety of devout men. By their faithfulness in a dark, uncertain present, they gave support to the dawning of a better future. Long before there was a temple, they erected an altar on the temple site and resumed the practice of regular sacrifices there, continuing the daily worship, the sabbath observances, and the keeping of the ancient festivals for more than a year (3:1-6). Before any masonary took shape, the temple had begun in the heart and life of devout men who gave the future the vote of their faithfulness in a time when the coming of better days hung in a dangerous and precarious balance.

God's purpose continued to use disappointing circumstances to make pos-

sible a brighter day. At the completion of the temple foundation (3:10), we witness a jubilant service of musical praise. Amid this reverent jubilee, some who had known the former temple wept aloud (3:12) at the sad contrast of these pitiful foundations with the former grandeur (Hag. 2:3; Tobit 14:5). The mingled singing and weeping, heard afar (4:13) stands as a symbolic memorial of the mixed human failures and divine achievements of this restoration period.

This strange mixture is seen in the particularism and legalism of Ezra's reforms. The laws he imposed rigorously separated the people of Israel from their neighbors, imposing cultural impoverishment and what seem to us the cruelties of the dissolution of mixed marriages. Yet precisely these rigors preserved the purity of Israel's faith in the midst of pagan influences, prepared a people who could maintain their religious and cultural identity under the punishing pressures of the Macabbean period, and maintained a base from which the Christian mission could be launched. Blessed by the doctrine of "salvation by faith," we decry the legalism to which Ezra's reform led. Yet Paul, who enunciated the doctrine, had to guard against the anarchy to which some enthusiasts pushed it. Law is a necessity of mortal life, though it is not the means of salvation. The God of history ultimately sent One who, by faith, could write his law upon our hearts.

Now to Him Who Is Able
Jude 1:17-21, 24-25

To frightened, despairing people living under threat in any age, the closing lines of this lection speak with courageous assurance. Set these noble words against the background of their time, and they speak with redoubled power.

Most scholars date this letter near the end of the first century, though some put it as early as 70-80 and some as late as A.D. 125. At any time in that span of years some of the readers would remember the burning of Rome, some would have suffered in the persecutions that followed, nearly all would have lost friends and loved ones by martyrdom. The society around them was decaying with the moral rot of paganism. Worst of all, as the letter testifies, a disguised paganism had come into the church. The letter issues an urgent call to resist this perversion of the faith.

With all this to contend with, the writer closes with an ascription of praise that breathes strong confidence in the face of the worst.

Now to him who is able to keep you from falling and to present you without blemish before the presence of his glory with rejoicing, to the only God, our Savior through Jesus Christ our Lord, be glory, majesty, dominion, and authority, before all time and now and for ever. Amen (vss. 24-25).

In its historic setting, that was a way of saying that all times, even the worst, open doors to the best for those who live by faith in God as we know him in Jesus Christ. Though we cannot control events, they are not out of control. Let us break this affirmation down into its constituent elements.

In all times, even the worst, God rules—"Now unto him who is able. . ." This supplies what too many of our exhortations to courage lack: a faith in God's control of events as the basis of our daring. As newspaper columnist who conducted an informal survey on "how working gals save money," concluded that they were not saving. "It seems," the report said, "that money saved is for dreams, and no one is having dreams these days, they're having nightmares. The crux of the nightmare is uncertainty of the future." The column then ended with reminders of other days of foreboding amid frontier hazards and Indian attacks, finally exhorting: "Let's pull ourselves together." [49] Good as this counsel may be, it omits a central element. That the pioneers "pulled themselves together" is not the whole story. They did so by the power of faith in the future, based on faith that a dependable God is in control. To him Jude points, with confidence that he "is able." He has "competence for the responsibilities that are peculiarly his." [50] In the worst times, he rules.

In all surroundings, even the worst, the best is possible—God "is able to keep you from falling and to present you without blemish before the presence of his glory with rejoicing." Strong words in the midst of the moral rot of the time! (Cf. vss. 4, 8, 12.) Still needed in the face of moral relativism ("everybody does it") and fatalism about our nature ("I can't help being what I am"). God is at work on us—the same God who has made saints out of such human stuff in such situations as ours. In a world of degrading influences the powerful force of his love plays on us. For those who belong to him the best is possible.

In all conditions, even the worst, God opens doors for faith. This is no mere pedestrian claim that God has glory and power. It is faith's strong word of personal intent, as if to say, "I give it my vote to be true. I put my whole self behind it." "To him . . . *be* glory, majesty, dominion, and authority, before all time and now and for ever. Amen." Faith is not a set of ideas affirmed; it is loyal intent that God through Christ shall have the full consent of our wills to *be true,* to be trusted in all circumstances, and to have his truth verified by the witness of our lives.

James Barrie once sent a class of Oxford graduates on their way with the fulsome dismissal, "One hopes that you are leaving Oxford feeling that you are hearing a thousand nightingales, could eat all the elephants in Hindustan, and pick your teeth with the spire of the Cologne Cathedral." [51] Such bombast has a hollow ring, if these Oxford men took with them only the Oxford name, the proud tradition, or the ideas to which they had been exposed. But there is ground for large expectations for those whose feet are planted on loyal faith in "him who is able to keep you from falling."

To Bind a Nation's Wounds
Luke 13:22-24, 34-35

In times of divisiveness, Christian faith has a healing mission. See how Jesus entreated the religious capital, where entrenched prejudices cut deepest:

---

[49] This and the foregoing newspaper quotation: Gladys Blair in the *Chicago Daily News,* Oct. 4, 1961.

[50] Albert Barnett, *Interpreter's Bible,* XII, 342.

[51] Margaret T. Applegarth, *Men As Trees Walking* (New York: Harper, 1952), p. 245.

O Jerusalem, Jerusalem, killing the prophets and stoning those who are sent to you! How often would I have gathered your children together as a hen gathers her brood under her wings, and you would not! (vs. 34).

The wounds in our relations run deepest where convictions are strongest. That was Jerusalem's problem. The prophets had challenged religious doctrines in the name of moral insights. No wonder Jerusalem killed them. Jesus was crucified there because he outraged expectations based on precious doctrines. They were looking for one kind of Messiah; he came as quite another. Away with him! Crucify him!

That is still our problem. Communications research shows that we listen to those who agree with what we already believe; Republicans hear Republicans in a political campaign; Democrats hear Democrats. Worse still, we hear what we want to hear: messages *against* fixed prejudices are heard by the prejudiced as *favoring* them. Sociological studies show that the more "religious" a man is, the greater the statistical probability that he is anti-Semitic. Where our cherished convictions are deepest, we need to be most on our guard.

Rejecting the Reconciler, we are left to our own tragic devices: "Behold, your house is forsaken" (vs. 35a). Some commentators see in this a word of doom for the Temple. Others counter that the temple was spoken of as "God's house"; there is no precedent for speaking of it as "your house." If that is correct, NEB's free translation, "Look, look! there is your temple, forsaken by God," is not justified. Is it, then, a poetic way of speaking of missed opportunities, a time of choice allowed to go by? AT's reading suggests this possibility, "Now I leave you to yourselves."

In our attitudes toward men of other races, classes, or ways of thinking, our own life hangs in the balance. Prejudiced judgments close our minds. Closed minds fumble crucial problems. Fumbled problems in revolutionary times spell disaster. Such risks are inherent in the freedom God gives us, for real freedom is freedom to make mistakes, even catastrophic mistakes. God expresses his love by taking our decisions seriously—as those who would give love's help to an alcoholic must sometimes remove their support and let him "hit bottom," since only then can he be receptive to real help toward a new life. So said Jesus, "Now I leave you to yourselves."

Yet God keeps trying to reach us with healing. "How often would I have gathered your children together as a hen gathers her brood under her wings." The figure occurs repeatedly in Old Testament references to God's gathering of his people (Deut. 32:11-12; Ps. 36:7; Isa. 31:5). So God keeps trying to save us. Christ comes to us in times of decision, passes in our refusals or postponements, but is always about to come again, as he said to Jerusalem: "You will not see me until you say, 'Blessed be he who comes in the name of the Lord!' " (vs. 35). Luke, placing this incident before Jesus' triumphal entry into Jerusalem, seems to understand it as referring to the crowd's acclaim on that occasion. Matthew, placing it after the triumphal entry, seems to look toward another appearing of our Lord.

A familiar motto of German piety declares, "We know not what is coming, but we know Who is coming: Christ." In the dark night of the Nazi terror the words took on strong meaning, as embattled Christians saw events as his visitations. He came in history's crushing judgment on the Third Reich. He came in the tests of those bitter times—in the surprising openings of insight. He came in calls to serve, and in undreamed resources of strength when service seemed humanly impossible. And so it can be with us.

"Some one said to him, 'Lord, will those who are saved be few?'" (vs. 23). He rejected such idle dallying with great issues. That is not what faith is about, he seemed to say. No speculations! Only full commitment! "Strive to enter by the narrow door" (vs. 24). Keep open to God's coming, that you may be healed and be numbered among the healers.

FOURTEENTH SUNDAY IN KINGDOMTIDE

Serving the Eternal in the Crises of Time
Isaiah 40:1-5

Classic lectionaries tend to assign this passage to Advent or to the Sunday after Christmas. But it leads aptly from Kingdomtide to Advent, with strong conviction that because God reigns in the world's affairs, we can live in expectation of his action. We have work to do, preparing the way of the Lord in the wilderness of the world (vs. 3), but we do not act alone. God too will act.

> And the glory of the Lord shall be revealed,
> and all flesh shall see it together (vs. 5).

This is strong assurance. Our world lives from one crisis to another on the international scene. Personal life unfolds as a procession of crises in family affairs, difficult decisions, suffering, sorrow, temptation, and guilt. Born of Israel's paramount crisis, the Babylonian Exile, this tested assurance speaks to our crises.

Israel's defeat had brought multiple trauma—homelessness for the exiles, the heartbreak of national defeat, and the dark night of the soul as they pondered the possibility that the disaster of God's covenant people signified his own defeat. The suffering itself is a medium through which God effects his design, the prophet affirmed, and he will use the witness of Israel, his suffering Servant. Jeremiah declared that the exiles' stay in Babylon would not be brief; they must make her welfare their own.

Crisis came on crisis. Having followed Jeremiah's counsel to be at home in—good citizens of—Babylon, they saw their new home threatened. The all-conquering Cyrus loomed on the horizon. Persia rising, Babylon seemed doomed. Into this redoubled crisis the prophet's words reverberated:

> Comfort, comfort my people,
> says your God (vs. 1).

To us, as to them, this poem of assurance speaks of a God whose strong control of history cannot be overthrown. He works out his purpose in judgment and redemption.

In crisis the servant of the Eternal hears a summons. "Comfort my people" is no soft crooning of consolation. "Comfort" is a word of strength, built on the same Latin root as "fortress" and "fortitude." This is a call to fortify, to make strong God's people. There is assurance here that God is in control of historic forces even when his hand cannot be seen. Nations come and go, and all their pomp is trifling dust on the scales, too light to change the price of a purchase (vs. 15). It is Israel's Lord

> who says of Cyrus, "He is my shepherd,
> and he shall fulfill my purpose" (44:28).

He will use the conquest of Cyrus to prepare the way for Israel's return to her own land.

God's control did not fail. Israel did return. The Exile did prove to be a refining fire, giving the faith a new universality, freeing it from dependence on the Temple, establishing it more than ever as a religion of the Word, making of the sufferings a vicarious witness finally culminated in the Cross.

This tonic assurance in crisis does not absolve the faithful from struggle. Amid the evils of our time, as Roy Pearson exclaimed, "peace of mind is not so much an achievement as an accusation." Courage and stamina for the long warfare belong to those who believe that we do not fight alone; "the glory of the Lord shall be revealed."

In crisis the servant of the Eternal accepts an assurance

> that her warfare is ended,
> that her iniquity is pardoned,
> that she has received from the Lord's hand
> double for all her sins (vs. 2).

Israel had received punishment in full. "Soon or late," said Robert Louis Stevenson, "every man sits down to a banquet of consequences." But now "her warfare" was done; her period of conscript service was over, and she was set free again. "Her iniquity is pardoned"; God had spoken from the side of the wronged one—the only side from which reconciliation can come—to say that he had taken initiative to close the gap, heal the breach, restore the peace. Vital word in any human crisis!

Made Worthy of the Kingdom
II Thessalonians 1:3-5, 11-12; 2:1-2, 13-15

This Epistle of transition from Kingdomtide to Advent speaks of God's reign already present in faith, love (1:3-4), and Trinitarian experience (2:13-14); yet coming more fully in what waits in store (1:5; 2:1-2).

Present experience is a preparation, "that you may be made worthy of the kingdom of God" (1:5). Within this perspective suffering can be understood. "You are suffering" for the kingdom (vs. 5), and "your steadfastness and faith in all your persecutions and in all the afflictions which you are enduring . . . is evidence of the righteous judgment of God" (1:4-5). Paul deals here with a familiar understanding of suffering, and it is not all he has to say on the subject. The Thessalonian letters are the earliest writing we have from his pen, and indeed the earliest Christian literature known to us. As such, they leave much more to be said.

We have yet to hear of suffering as sustained by God's love, from which nothing in all creation can separate us (Rom. 8:38-39); or of suffering as the strengthening experience through which we are brought closer to a suffering God whose "power is made perfect in weakness" (II Cor. 12:9); or of suffering endured redemptively for others, sharing Christ's redemptive suffering (II Cor. 1:6; 4:10). Disciplinary suffering, to prepare us for the kingdom, is not a full Christian doctrine of suffering, but it is a beginning.

God works in our dark experiences: "that our God . . . may fulfil every good resolve and work of faith by his power, so that the name of our Lord Jesus may be glorified in you" (1:11-12). We do not work alone; God has a purpose for us, and all that happens may be used as a means of witness to the glory of our Lord.

Not confining himself to work in present experience, our Lord is *coming*. The Christian lives in disciplined faith in Christ's impending appearance in the affairs of our world. From its early date, this letter bears the marks of primitive eschatology; Paul was disturbed by a silly prophecy of Christ's early arrival (2:1-2). Excited speculations on the subject contributed nothing to sane religion. Rather it caused irresponsible idleness among those who saw in it an excuse for taking their duties lightly. Paul repudiated all this. Yet a dimension of expectation inheres in Christian teaching. We do expect God to act in our experience. We do carry on our struggles in the faith that he will win ultimate victory over evil. We do hold it to be unthinkable that we shall go forever in poor, drab ways, never knowing him better. The *forms* of our expectation change, but the *substance* of our hope of his appearing abides. This hope planted holy impatience with injustice in the hearts of black slave preachers. It propels present effort toward revolutionary justice.

We have foretastes of the victory of God, whom we experience in threefold manner as Father, Son, and Holy Spirit. *This is how we know him.* God chose us; the Spirit sanctifies, nurtures, completes us; the glory of the new life has been opened to us by our Lord Jesus Christ (2:14). Our God-talk refers to this threefold experience. For this reason no "God is dead" theology makes sense. A secularistic age may change its metaphysics, but the Christian has a continuing experience of being chosen, called, held under claim; of being nurtured toward a greater completeness of life; and of sharing riches he could not know apart from Jesus Christ. Since this threefold experience is what God *means* in our affairs, God is empirical reality. To say he is dead is to say that experience no longer has meaning or coherence.

We are not worthy of the Kingdom—cannot be, in our own right. But we can be *made* worthy. Suffering can discipline us for it. The vision of God's purpose can increase our faith for it. The hope of his fuller coming can strengthen us for struggle. And all along the way the threefold experience of God can nurture and refine us as candidates for his kingdom.

But First . . . : Luke 17:20-25

"For me, it *has*"—that is the Christian's answer to the query, "When is the kingdom of God coming?" It was given in court by a courageous young believer. To his plea of conscientious conviction against war, the judge sneered, "You talk as if the kingdom of God had already come." "For me, it *has*," said the youth.

So says this Gospel. The kingdom is no external event we could catch on film and display as overpowering evidence to the unbelieving. It is no mere academic theory. It has immediate ethical implications. Talking confidently of its coming, Jesus added that "first he must suffer many things and be rejected by this generation" (vs. 25). Because the kingdom was coming there was something he must do. This runs all through his message. The Sermon on the Mount begins with a kingdom announcement—"blessed are the poor in spirit, for theirs is the kingdom of heaven" (Matt. 5:3)—and proceeds as a description of the style of life of those who live by the power of the coming kingdom. Kingdom eschatology without kingdom ethic is *ersatz* Christianity.

Interest in the coming of the kingdom is appropriate to this transition Sunday when we culminate the season of kingdom celebration and look forward to the season which anticipates Christ's advent. But such interest is more; it is a way of dealing with the question of the meaning of history. Does history *have* a meaning, or are things perpetually at undecipherable sixes and sevens? Is there any room for hope? Are things getting better—or worse? Are we on the way to catastrophe which obliterates all gains and all meaning?

In the language of their time, the Pharisees raised such issues as they asked "when the kingdom of God was coming" (vs. 20). Israel had long speculated on the signs of the coming kingdom.

They gave their imaginations free reign in their portrayal of the catastrophes— "the woes of the Messiah"—which would indicate that God was about to destroy the present world order. Wars, fratricidal strife, social collapse, natural disasters, a breakup of the cosmic order—such were the lurid events they delighted to detail and delineate.[52]

In their way they were asking, Does violently unfolding history have any meaning?

Jesus cut through such speculation. There is no visible timetable to which men may profitably refer, he said; "signs" have no importance (vs. 20). Important events are all around us, but a photographically faithful report of them would not prove the kingdom's coming; men could always explain them in some other way. Will and Ariel Durant were not far from this truth when they ended their study of *The Lessons of History* saying, "The historian will not mourn because he can see no meaning in human existence except that which man puts into it; let it be our pride that we ourselves may put meaning into our lives, and sometimes a significance that transcends death."[53] Though we hold that the kingdom is *true* beyond our mere ability to "put meaning into our lives," we know its truth is apprehended by *faith*, not proven by "signs."

By faith we can know that God now reigns as king. "The kingdom of God is in the midst of you" (vs. 21), "among you" (JB), "now in your midst"

[52] S. MacLean Gilmour, *Interpreter's Bible*, VIII, 300.
[53] Will and Ariel Durant, *The Lessons of History*, p. 102.

(MT). The translation "within you" is almost certainly wrong. "Jesus is not speaking of the *inwardness* of the kingdom, but of its *presence*." [54] It is a modern notion that the kingdom is within men, rather than men within the kingdom. Nowhere else in the Synoptic Gospels is there any reference to the kingdom of God as an inward state. It would be amazing if the only such reference were found in this answer to the Pharisees, who are shown throughout the Gospels as very far from all that the kingdom stands for. The kingdom is here, not in a subjective state, but in the historical fact of what Christ is doing and enabling others to be and do.

We are not to live in perpetual frustration by constantly looking for what lies only within God's providence to date or perform. "Do not go, do not follow" (vs. 23) those who deal in such speculative timetables; they have none of the authentic kingdom style of life in them. See rather, Jesus said, that the kingdom comes in a flash, like lightning. You do not see lightning a bit here and another there, piecing them together into a guess that there has been a lightning flash. It flashes! and the whole horizon lights up. So too does the kingdom of God (vs. 24). It has already come in the work of Jesus, but it is yet to come more fully. There is ethical demand at the heart of the good news: The kingdom is here—live in it.

[54] Vincent, *Word Studies in the New Testament*, I, 401.

SPECIAL DAYS

The moving drama of salvation fills the Christian year with the fascination of events, the "mighty saving acts" in which God comes to us. Its dramatic intensity is further heightened by special days, which began in the early church with the anniversaries of the deaths of local martyrs—or as the first Christians preferred to say, their "birthdays" into eternity. By the time of the Reformation these saints' days filled a complicated calendar.

In the lectionary we are studying, All Saints' Day alone remains of these historic saints' days. The worth of reverent observance of such a day should not be overlooked.

The lives of the saints continually remind us of the great host of witnesses in the faith who have gone before us and who, we believe, are still our examples and our encouragement in the Christian life. They are also a reminder of the continuing existence of the body of Christ—the Church—and of the fact that whether it be militant and on earth or triumphant and in the joy of its Lord in heaven, it is one, holy, catholic church, timeless and composed of God's people of every age.[1]

[1] Edward T. Horn, *The Christian Year* (Philadelphia: Muhlenberg Press, 1957), p. 183.

Special days, in this lectionary, are of three kinds. Some belong to the historic lectionaries of Christendom and are shared ecumenically with the whole Church or with large sections of it: Universal Bible Sunday, Ascension Day, Trinity Sunday, Reformation Day (adopted from the Lutheran tradition), and All Saints' Day. Some provide the means for Christian interpretation and celebration of significant secular observances: New Year's Day or Watch Night, the Festival of the Christian Home (formerly Mother's Day), Independence Day, Labor Day, World Order Sunday, and Thanksgiving Day. A final group are specially ordered for observance in The United Methodist Church: Race Relations Sunday (shared with some other communions), Aldersgate Sunday, and Commitment Day.

The lectionary throws around the special days biblical associations that amplify their dimensions, giving the height and depth of which John Oman spoke:

There is law and there is gospel, and there is gospel in law and law in gospel. There are the rocky steeps of Sinai and the green pastures of Galilee, there are parables by the lake and the sword piercing through the soul on the way to Calvary. Always to be denouncing, always to be pleading, always to be in the depths or in the heights, always to be using the moral whip or always to be supposing that nothing is involved except "my yoke is easy," is just to miss the one great thing in life that is worth preaching about, all its heights and its depth.[2]

To observe this calendar of Special Days, in the context of the Christian year and with the lectionary's biblical richness, is to erect strong safeguards against flatness and impoverishment in our Christian celebration.

UNIVERSAL BIBLE SUNDAY

Dynamics of the Word
Deuteronomy 30:8-20

Century after century, the Bible speaks with amazing freshness to unforeseen situations. Is it the Word of God? Does it *contain* the Word? To such debated questions Karl Barth replied aptly: "A more precise statement of the truth would be to say that the Bible *becomes* God's Word, and when it becomes this for us, then it is so."[3] The thrust of insight by which it speaks to us where we are lays claim on conscience, deepens self-understanding, lights up meaning where there had been dark confusion. In these dynamic moments it "becomes God's Word" which makes a mighty difference.

This section of Deuteronomy exemplifies these dynamics. We see Israel returning to a past time relived. Out of the encounter comes new light for a new day. The literary method adopted is that of a discourse of Moses to the people of Israel, though the situation is not that of Moses' day. The Israel

---

[2] John Oman, *Concerning the Ministry* (New York: Harper, 1937), p. 69. (Paper ed., Richmond: John Knox Press, 1963.)

[3] Karl Barth, *The Preaching of the Gospel* (Philadelphia: Westminster Press, 1963), p. 46.

of Deuteronomy "no longer resembles in any respect the one which was once on Horeb—it has kings, prophets, and is even acquainted with false prophets!" [4] The prophetic religion of a later time here delivers a powerful message to Israel in an hour of new decisions. In so doing, it returns to the springs of the people's life in the Exodus pilgrimage, recaptures the spirit of those savingly creative days, and speaks to the Israel of the new crisis as Moses *would* speak if he could confront them in their dilemma.

In just such ways the Bible returns us to our sources of insight. We renew contact with the life of the people of God in diverse periods and circumstances. We encounter the mind of Christ and his continuing witness in the early church.

In this passage, Moses confronts the people with a choice between Canaanite idolatry and undivided commitment to the Lord who has brought them out of Egypt (vss. 15-20). It was a necessary decision; without it they would confront their pagan surroundings with easy tolerance. There is no possibility of remaining a little open to both God and idols. This issue is posed variously from age to age. In our time the challenge rises from the temptation to worship our technology, or a secularism utterly at odds with our Lord.

The Scriptures bring a life-giving tradition into living touch with a new time in which legalistic application of the old words no longer applies. In this passage, Moses relates legal obedience to national prosperity (vss. 8-10). In the light of the New Testament or of such late Old Testament writings as Job, righteousness and material reward are not nearly so closely linked.

A righteous life may tend to health and wealth; there is much to show that it often does. But frequently it leads also to suffering, even to martyrdom. The welfare of God's people, as measured by the Christian gospel, is not registered at the bank. Its treasures are elsewhere, where moth and rust do not corrupt.[5]

To read the Bible rightly is to find the dynamic thrust of the call to obedience by the aid of the fuller light shed upon it by Jesus and the experience of the new Israel he called.

The Bible speaks in mature terms which a lifetime of study does not exhaust, yet with a directness that makes insight available to all thoughtful men. As Moses says, in this passage, we need not search for some esoteric secret. "The word is very near you; it is in your mouth and in your heart, so that you can do it." (vss. 11-14).

Book of the One Church
Romans 15:4-13

In this passage, the chief topical interest for Bible Sunday lies in the opening sentence: "For whatever was written in former days was written for our instruction, that by steadfastness and by the encouragement of the scriptures we might have hope" (vs. 4). The sentence cannot be honestly studied

---

[4] Gerhard von Rad, article on Deuteronomy in *The Interpreter's Dictionary of the Bible*, I, 837.

[5] Stevenson, *Preaching on the Books of the Old Testament*, p. 45.

apart from its setting, Paul's concern for the solidarity of the Christian community.

Some of the brethren are troubled because others have been flaunting their Christian liberty to disregard Jewish dietary laws (14:13-23). To Paul it is clear that the strong must bear the burden of the weaker brother's conscience, just as "Christ did not please himself; but, as it is written, 'The reproaches of those who reproached thee fell on me'" (15:1-3). In this setting of division on a matter of conscience, Paul declares that the Scriptures—by which, of course, he means the Old Testament writings, the only established canon of his time—have power to reinforce hope, strengthen servanthood, and justify concern for all, even for Gentile pagans.

This emphasizes the importance of the Bible as *the book of the Church*. For the Church is the community of those who bear one another's burdens and spiritual liabilities under the guidance of insight drawn from the Scriptures. By extension, we apply to the Bible as a whole what Paul wrote concerning the Old Testament. Amid differences that spring from our varied creeds and scruples, the Bible—now as in Paul's day—is a ground of unity.

For *it calls us to a common servanthood* shared with our Lord Jesus Christ. Paul calls the early Christians, divided by conscience concerning dietary laws, to unity in the name of Christ, who "became a servant" to the Jews (vss. 7-8). Whether one belonged to those who were sensitive about the old requirements, or to those who proudly and somewhat scornfully made an issue of casting them aside, the example of Christ as servant called him to concern for the other's conscience. The call to servanthood was—and remains—a call to unity.

In our time, a rediscovered servanthood is one of the prime factors in drawing the divided church together. To minister to suffering, we unite across denominational lines. To minister to a cosmopolitan, pluralistic society, we join hands in increasingly comprehensive Councils of Churches. To communicate the gospel through the mass media, we must unite if we would be persuasive. Servanthood unites, and *the Bible is the book of the one servanthood of the one Church.*

Calling to servanthood, *it nurtures us in mission,* that all men may be saved. Paul reminds us that Jesus was servant of the Jews because God had called them as the people through whom all men should be blessed (vss. 8-12). This integrating theme occurs in God's call of, and promise to, Abraham; and it is renewed in his covenants with Isaac, Jacob, and David. It reappears in the universalism of Isaiah and comes to its full flowering in the New Testament. Today the Church draws together for mission. Whether in lands where Christians are a tiny minority, in the teeming inner city, or anywhere that mission comes to poignant re-emphasis, Christians are drawn together across creedal lines. Ecumenicity and mission are parts of each other, and *the Bible is the one book of the one Church in mission for the salvation of all men.*

Calling to servanthood, nurturing mission, the Bible *holds before the Church a unifying hope.* Paul puts it with beauty: "May the God of hope fill you with all joy and peace in believing, so that by the power of the Holy Spirit you may abound in hope" (vs. 13). Servanthood and mission have to do with unity held together in practical tasks, but the Christian hope deals with the depths of the Church's theological belief. To have full vitality, unity depends on common bonds in this depth area.

One thrilling aspect of the growing ecumenical fellowship of recent years has been the way in which the study of the Bible has laid the groundwork for understanding. With the increasingly rigorous use of tested methods of Bible study in both Catholic and Protestant circles, scholars in each group have found that those in the other were dealing with the same problems and arriving at common conclusions. From this study of the writings in which the Christian hope is grounded, respect and fraternity have grown. *The Bible is the one book of the one Church in its discovery of fuller understanding of the one faith.*

To Cultivate Christ's Friendship
Luke 4:16-21

Whoever would cultivate the friendship of Christ must spend time consistently with the Bible. There is no other source material. Apart from this, it is not Christ we know, but a fantasy spun from our predilections. All basic information about him comes from the New Testament. The tradition which he so fulfilled that only by knowing it can we understand him is embodied in the Old Testament. This reciprocal relation between Jesus and the Scriptures shines through the incident in the Nazareth synagogue.

"He opened the book" (vs. 17) is, of course, an incidental phrase. Yet a document as condensed as Luke's gospel wastes no phrases. Something about the way Jesus opened the book—his reverence, expectation, authority—may well lie behind this phrase. More than that, he "opens" the book in the sense that only in him does it find interpretation.

Luke returns to this theme as he reports the post-resurrection experiences with the risen Lord. Of the walk to Emmaus we read, "And beginning with Moses and all the prophets, he interpreted to them in all the scriptures the things concerning himself" (Luke 24:27). He left the disciples saying, "Did not our hearts burn within us while he talked to us on the road, while he opened to us the scriptures?" (24:32). Appearing later, "he said to them, 'These are my words which I spoke to you, while I was still with you, that everything written about me in the law of Moses and the prophets and the psalms must be fulfilled.' Then he opened their minds to understand the scriptures" (24:44-45). What he thus showed them in the culmination of his ministry he points to in its beginning, as he reads a passage central to Old Testament tradition and adds, "Today this scripture has been fulfilled in your hearing" (vs. 21). He opens the book for all who would know it truly.

The passage he read (Isa. 61:1-2) speaks to the need of Israel in the dreary days after the Exile, when Jerusalem's walls still lie in ruins (Isa. 60:10), the city forsaken (60:15), the temple unbeautified (60:13), and the oppressor's hand heavy upon the people (60:14). In God's name Isaiah is offering assurances of a golden age yet to be, in essence a messianic vision. Jesus' reading and announcement that it "has been fulfilled" is a way of saying that the longed-for new Age is here. It begins today. See the vivid specifics in which he pictured his mission.

"The Spirit of the Lord" has "anointed" Jesus "to preach good news to the poor" (vs. 18). The revolutionary reversal of roles between rich and poor, powerful and rejected, is one of Luke's recurring reports of Jesus' teaching. This has both social and theological implications. The rich can be self-reliant in a way the poor cannot. To be poor, in the gospel's sense of the term, is to know one's dependence and throw oneself utterly on God. The good news of Jesus brings promise to, and responsibility for, those who are poor in this world's goods and those who have found their deep need of more than human resources.

"He has sent me to proclaim release to the captives," the message continues. Isaiah seems to have meant captives held in slavery for debt, who under the law must be released in the periodic year of jubilee (Lev. 25:9-10, 39-40). Like the good news to the poor, this has both social and theological meaning. We are captives of our own sinfulness, and Jesus brings forgiveness that releases us from sin and the attendant paralysis of our powers (Luke 5:17-26).

"Recovering of sight to the blind" is a messianic "sign" which appears again in Jesus' reply to John's question from prison (7:21), and in the story of the healing of the blind man who addressed Jesus by the messianic title, Son of David (Luke 18:35-43). In John's reinterpretation of such material, it is explored in terms of our mental and spiritual blindness to which Jesus ministers (John 9:1-41; 8:12).

"To set at liberty those who are oppressed" had political and social meaning for Isaiah, and must continue such connotations for us. Yet it gains a depth dimension as Luke relates it to the gospel. Jesus liberated men from the religious oppression of the over-elaborated religious law of his time.

He came to "proclaim the acceptable year of the Lord"—"the year of the Lord's favor," the beginning of the new Age of God's fulfilled promises. Thus Jesus announced victory in the warfare between God and the forces of evil. He not only opens and interprets the record, he closes and fulfills it (vss. 20-21). In him the promised victory is won. In him the looked-for day arrives. To live fully in that day, we need the reciprocal relation between Jesus and the Bible. He unfolds its meaning, and it helps us to know and understand him.

NEW YEAR'S DAY OR WATCH NIGHT

On Which the Shadow Stands
Ecclesiastes 11:6-9; 12:13

The Scripture readings for the New Year present time in three perspectives. The Epistle assures us that the future lies in the hands of God, that he who is with us in present struggles will give us opportunity to share in his coming victory. The Gospel turns our attention to the present, calling us to act responsibly under God's call. This Old Testament lesson gives us the circumscribed view of the chastened humanist who loves the life of this world but holds no optimistic hopes. Though he makes passing mention of God in a closing line—not unlike the rhetorical flourish at the end of a political address—the real thrust of what he is saying is a call to make the most of the moment because we have no notion of what may yet be. His outlook suggests a couplet Henry van Dyke wrote for a college sundial:

> One hour alone is in thy hands—
> The NOW on which the shadow stands.[6]

A seasoned man of the world, this philosopher whose diary jottings come to us in Ecclesiastes has been saying that life calls us to venture despite its unpredictable issue; for he who awaits advance assurance of success is permanently paralyzed. The future lies veiled in the hand of God (vss. 1-5). We must make the most of *all* times, since we cannot tell whether this time or that is more propitious, or whether they are equally good or bad (vs. 6). His is prudential counsel to live our life an hour at a time, making the most of each as it comes, not fretting about yesterday or tomorrow. This *sounds* like Jesus' injunction, "Do not be anxious about tomorrow, for tomorrow will be anxious for itself. Let the day's own trouble be sufficient for the day" (Matt. 6:34); but its root reasons sharply differ. Jesus' word rests on complete faith in God's loving care (6:25-33). The philosopher of Ecclesiastes—in common with the Greek Stoics, sure that God is distant, unconcerned, and that we must ourselves determine our days—declares the wise will make the most of each day in its own right.

In just such worldly-wise terms Sir William Osler drew an analogy from the watertight compartments built for safety into the structure of an ocean liner. Even so, he said, we must live in "day-tight compartments." Out of a busy life he advised: Live "for the day only, and for the day's work . . . . The chief worries of life arise from the foolish habit of looking before and after." [7]

It is good to be alive, Ecclesiastes reflects (vs. 7), and we should make full use of our allotted time, recognizing that darkness will be long (vs. 8). This may be only a call to make the most of the good days and accept the dark ones, since they are much alike in the end—"all that comes is vanity." Or it may be saying that—since "the living know that they will die, but the dead know nothing, and they have no more reward" (9:5)—the wise will use the light while they have it, aware that their time is short. Reading so, MT translates the final words of vs. 8: "All that comes after death is emptiness."

The young, then, do well to seize their opportunities and treat life as good, yet to hold it as a trust for which they are ultimately accountable (vs. 9). Although we cannot answer life's final questions—Whence? Why? Whither?—to live fully, we can only accept our brief day as a trust to be held under God and used in obedience to him (vs. 13).

This is wise counsel. And yet, apart from a faith that lends some confidence for tomorrow, many a man is trapped by anxiety, since it is im-

[6] *Chosen Poems* by Henry van Dyke, Sylvanora Edition (New York: Scribner's, 1927), p. 325.
[7] Lillian Eichler Watson, ed., *Light from Many Lamps* (New York: Simon and Schuster, 1951), p. 215.

possible to live in such detached composure. For a truer perspective on time, we need the larger faith of the New Testament lessons for this day.

Eternity Interprets Time
Revelation 21:1-6a

The faith of Revelation sees time as interpreted by eternity. The principal action of the Bible unfolds

between two visions that constitute the prologue and the epilogue to the human drama, . . . the vision of paradise lost and vision of the City of God, . . . the vision of what could have been and vision of what will be when the redemptive work of God has been finished. . . . These two visions are like two beacons that illuminate everything that lies in between them.[8]

These verses from Revelation present a highlight of the vision of "what will be when the redemptive work of God has been finished." No more than the vision of a lost Eden is it a thing to pinpoint in time and space. Eden shows the lost potential God intended for each of us—Adam every man, Eve every woman. We read the meaning of our own life in lostness, alienation, brokenness, disruption born of rebellion against God. Thus Eden pictorially reviews our fallen life within time's framework. But the new Jerusalem (vs. 2) projects the potential of the redeemed. Through the long agony of our resistance, it brings us to a final vision of God's victory. Like a navigator locating himself in a vast sea by sightings from sun and stars, we chart our life in time by the light of faith's gaze at eternity.

The vision shows "a new heaven and a new earth" (vs. 1). Into this language of an old cosmology we fit our minds with difficulty; but cosmology only sets the stage for the idea that an old order of life is passing and a new one coming to be. Isaiah's vision of a promised messianic age uses the same figure:

> For behold, I create new heavens
> and a new earth;
> and the former things shall not be remembered
> or come into mind (Isa. 65:17).

The New Testament sees the new Age as embracing the whole creation: "the creation waits with eager longing for the revealing of the sons of God" (Rom. 8:19). "O Lord, let us not desecrate the moon as we have God's green earth," prayed a modern urbanite at a street-side shrine on the day of the first moon landing. So we begin to see in sober reality that all creation is involved in God's struggle for the redemption of his earth-children.

"And the sea was no more" (vs. 1)—the poignant line speaks of God's victory over all that imprisons and threatens his children. It is a multi-layered figure. History is one layer: Israel, as a people desert born and bred, always feared the sea; Israel, a people saved by God's act at the Red Sea, always remembered his victory over the waters. Mythology is a layer:

[8] Suzanne de Dietrich, *God's Unfolding Purpose* (Philadelphia: Westminster Press, 1960), p. 269.

Israel borrowed the myths of a dragon in the deep from her neighboring peoples, to make the sea the lurking place of all evil (Isa. 27:1; 51:9-10). Personal experience is a layer: the seer of this vision was an exile on the island to Patmos, to whom the ceaselessly beating waves were bars and prison walls. Writing "the sea was no more," he declared his faith in God's victory over everything in a people's history, or the cosmic evils, or tragic personal experience, that cramps and despoils life.

God not only wins the victory; he dwells with men (vs. 3). Israel's national life had depended on his historic presence: "My dwelling place shall be with them; and I will be their God, and they shall be my people" (Ezek. 37:27). Likewise, the new Jerusalem would find him no distant victor leaving men to their own devices. His promised presence assures protection and peace.

The vision promises the end of death, sorrow, and pain in this final consummation of our life (vs. 4). This is a glorious extension of Isaiah's hope of the messianic joys: "He will swallow up death for ever, and the Lord God will wipe away tears from all faces, and the reproach of his people he will take away from all the earth" (Isa. 25:8). Whether the seer of Patmos, like Isaiah, saw this happy state as a coming age in history or as a consummation beyond history, he read the meaning of our life now in terms of it. All that threatens is itself doomed, "for the former things have passed away," "the world of the past has gone" (JB), "the old order has passed away" (TCNT and NEB).

Under the rule of Christ, who is "the beginning and the end" (vs. 6a), a new order will come to be—God's new order for his people. The glowing figures that fill the remainder of the chapter say four things: It is an order based on personal character, from which the unworthy exclude themselves (vs. 27). It is an order of broad hospitality to which all nations, races, and creeds are welcome, its gates open in all directions to welcome the twelve tribes of Israel and the converts of the twelve apostles of Christ (vss. 12-14). It is an order providing in rich abundance for human welfare (vss. 15-21). It is an order responsive to the will of God in all things, a city without a temple, since the Lord himself is its omnipresent light (vss. 22-26). Amid earth's struggles, understanding time in the light of such an eternity makes a saving difference.

Decision and Destiny
Luke 9:57-62

The faithful do not relate to time as passive pensioners of God's acts. Jesus calls us to make serious response to the crisis each hour brings. We take it for granted that destiny is compounded from small commonplaces. In more than this platitudinous sense the Gospel links decision and destiny. Our response to Christ is pivotal, as we see in his dramatic confrontation with three kinds of men alike in one thing: like us, they met him with goodwill and some measure of belief.

The first was the *volatile volunteer* (vss. 57-58). Impulsively he offered to follow Jesus. If he came, Jesus said, it must be to a life of homelessness and risk. The mood is one of warning. On another occasion Jesus spoke similarly of some kinds of would-be followers who are like a man who sets out to build a tower without carefully reckoning the cost and is left with unfinished foundations and the shame of a monument to his ill-considered impulsiveness (Luke 14:27-30). Following our Lord opens momentous issues. We do well to undertake it as a calculated risk.

Jesus was wary of easy popularity. Some of his hardest demands are introduced with the note, "Now great multitudes accompanied him; and he turned and said to them . . ." (Luke 14:25). He was not bent on capturing crowds. It is wrong for Christians to set store by *unpopularity*, as if a church which repels men were by that fact attested to be nearer the Kingdom; but when the Christian movement is drawing great numbers it may well examine itself lest it be popular by virtue of standing for very little. Want of discipline attracts the volatile volunteer.

The second confrontation was with the *cautious conscript* (vss. 59-60). No eager volunteer, he was tapped on the shoulder with an urgent personal call. He was quite willing to serve, he replied, but there would be an indefinite delay before he could begin. He needed to remain at home while his father lived; when his father was gone (and the inheritance settled?) he would come and share in the Master's service. He used a colloquial phrase, "bury my father" (vs. 59), to express this possibly very long delay. Picking up the phrase, Jesus made a play on words: "Leave the dead to bury their own dead; but as for you, go and proclaim the kingdom of God" (vs. 60). That is, those who are spiritually dead, unawakened, can take care of these burying chores; you who have been awakened to new life should be among the heralds of good news.

News of God's goodness in the midst of the crises of time demands action *now*, taking precedence over even the sacred ties of family. This is the force of Jesus' saying, "If any one comes to me and does not hate his own father and mother and wife and children and brothers and sisters, yes, and even his own life, he cannot be my disciple" (Luke 14:26). He who forbade us to hate even our enemies did not intend to sow seeds of hatred within families. These strong words state priorities in our loyalty. Nothing —not even the tender ties of home—can rival loyalty to our Lord. Long care of the home farm, long devotion to beautifying a home, can so delay our duty and deplete our resources that the remaining remnant is insufficient for the world's need or for our Lord's service. Jesus measured family on a different scale: "My mother and my brothers are those who hear the word of God and do it" (Luke 8:21).

The final encounter was with the *double-minded disciple* (vss. 61-62). Willing to serve, he wanted to take time first for some elaborate farewells (vs. 61). The phraseology of the conversation sounds so like echoes of Elijah's call of Elisha (I Kings 19:19-21) that we may well turn to that story for light. The older prophet called the younger man, who asked leave to take his farewells. What follows is a leave-taking both elaborate and time-consuming. Elisha, who had been plowing with twelve yoke of oxen, "returned from following him, and took the yoke of oxen, and slew them, and boiled their flesh with the yokes of the oxen, and gave it to the people, and they ate. Then he arose and went after Elijah, and ministered to him." A banquet that consumes all that beef is not prepared in an afternoon! The number of people involved, the lengthy preparation, and the feasting interposed no small delay. With that glimpse of the double-minded disciple's proposed farewell, as interpreted by the ways of his culture and tradition, it is easier to comprehend Jesus' reply.

"No one who puts his hand to the plow and looks back is fit for the kingdom of God" (vs. 62), he said. No gazing back at old associations! No eye over the shoulder for fence-mending activities! Eyes ahead, or you plow a crooked furrow. The counsel is apt for many of us, who would like to be disciples of Christ—and good fellows with many who scorn Christ. Paul took the Lord's command seriously. He wrote: "One thing I do, forgetting what lies behind and straining forward to what lies ahead, I press on toward the goal for the prize of the upward call of God in Christ Jesus" (Phil. 3:13-14).

RACE RELATIONS SUNDAY

Made in God's Image
Genesis 1:1-3, 26-31

This lection sets race relations in the theological context of three related concerns: (a) God creates by his word (vss. 1-3); (b) God creates all men in his image (vss. 26-27); (c) God appoints man to a corporate stewardship over the good earth entrusted to his keeping (vss. 28-31).

By his word God created the world out of the formless void. The narrative bears the marks of Babylonian creation myths which formed the framework of thinking in the day when the late priestly writer set down this interpretation. God's Word has come to men, age by age, in dialogue with the culture in which they live, using the culture, yet criticizing and purifying it. So this writer used the "science" of his time as carrier of an explicitly religious insight—that God was the Creator of all things *ex nihilo*. Science changes, but this central insight remains.

God's Word—"And God said" (vs. 3)—is the agency of his creation. The Babylonian myths also conceived of creation by a word, but for them it was the "powerful word" of magic. In biblical idiom, God's word is his will.

> For he spoke, and it came to be;
> he commanded, and it stood forth (Ps. 33:9).

God created man in his image, in undifferentiated unity save for the distinction between the sexes (vss. 26-27). With Hebrew concreteness, this image includes the body, as well as the spirit, for the biblical conception of the person is an organic unity of body, mind, and spirit. God differentiates male and female in structure and function, and blesses both with fertility as a great good (vss. 27, 31). The late priestly writer who transmitted Gen. 1 is not restrained in his dealing with sex, as was the earlier Yahwist writer from whose pen comes Chapter 2. The early conflict with the excesses of the

Baal fertility cults, which makes the Yahwist pessimistic about sex, had been passed, and the priestly writer could pronounce God's blessing on this aspect of human experience.

While the sexes are differentiated in this creation theology, the races are not. God made man as one creation. Race is not of the essence of our life; it is an accident of conditioning by the circumstances of earthly existence.

The nature of God's "image" is not so "spiritual" as to inhibit Paul's appeal to it in discussing the custom of covering the head in worship. "For a man ought not to cover his head," he writes, "since he is the image and glory of God" (I Cor. 11:7). Nevertheless the image and likeness of God was chiefly notable in "the power of thought, the power of communication, the power of self-transcendence." [9] These powers inhere in God's gift to men of all races, giving to all a common dignity and holiness.

The image is desecrated by the sin which all men share; through Christ it can be restored. The New Testament calls us to "put on the new nature, created after the likeness of God in true righteousness and holiness" (Eph. 4:24), and it is noteworthy that this promise of the restored image comes from the New Testament document which most emphatically assures us that in the restoration we are one new man across all lines of division (Eph. 2:13-16).

God appointed man to a corporate stewardship over the good earth entrusted to his keeping (vss. 28-31). The implications for conservation and the philosophy of stewardship are strong, though in the context of today's theme the stress falls on the fact that this trust is shared by man in corporate unity, not given to any favorites. In an age when development of the poorer areas of the earth has become a life and death issue, this is a vital dimension of the doctrine.

God made his whole creation good. He found distinct values in all things he had made. He expects us to do no less, and in our relations with one another to accord to men of all races the dignity and concern that belong to those made in his image and likeness.

God Has No Favorites
Acts 10:9-15, 34

"And Peter opened his mouth and said: 'Truly I perceive that God shows no partiality'" (vs. 34).

He had arrived at this conclusion over a road men often travel; God had used common human events to open an uncommon insight. A hungry man, weary from a hard journey, fell asleep and dreamed. What more natural than that his dream should have been preoccupied with food? All kinds of food! Since the man was a fisherman by trade, it was not surprising that when this abundance was let down before him, he saw it held in something that looked like a sail (vs. 11). "Like a great sheet," says the RSV, but the Greek warrants "like a great sail" (TCNT), or "like a great sheet of sail-cloth" (NEB).

Not only a fisherman, the hungry dreamer was a Christian of Jewish unbringing. Not surprising that such a man's dream should reflect a problem

[9] Cuthbert A. Simpson, *Interpreter's Bible*, I, 485.

already troubling his mind: Do the old dietary laws apply in the new faith? Not surprising that his dream should dredge up old ideas in new configurations. Had not God given his blessing to his whole creation? Was it not written, "And God saw everything that he had made, and behold, it was very good"? (Gen. 1:31). Thus, out of the events and materials of the common life, God brought together the insight which was his new Word to a man facing responsible choice in a new situation.

Perplexed about its specific meaning, Peter was not long in the dark. The dawning insight was confronted by a new challenge. The dream had dealt with all kinds of *food*, but the real question concerned the unity of all kinds of *men*. A Gentile, one Cornelius, had sent messengers requesting the gospel. Was not this what the dream meant? If God blessed all kinds of food, such as Gentiles ate, must one not believe that he broke down other barriers than the superficial ones of diet? Surely he would put no boundaries around the gospel. *So* Peter understood the matter, and *so* he interpreted it to the waiting company: "You yourselves know how unlawful it is for a Jew to associate with or to visit any one of another nation; but God has shown me that I should not call any man common or unclean" (vs. 28).

What RSV translates, "any one of another nation" (Greek *allophulo*) is read by NEB as "a man of another race." Both readings convey connotations far from exact equivalents of the idea in Peter's mind. "Race," as we use it, is strictly a modern term; the nineteenth century gave it a coloring it had never had before. It is also a loose, inexact term, carrying popular connotations which careful scientists repudiate. But "race" is as near to Peter's meaning as is "nation," for nationalism in our modern sense is also a late invention. The ideas of nation as a political state were far from Peter's mind. *Allophulo*, to him, meant someone *foreign* in the sense of all that most deeply divides— Jew from Gentile, believer from heathen, Christian from Jew. In this sense NEB is right in reading, "A Jew is forbidden by his religion to visit or associate with a man of another race; yet God has shown me clearly that I must not call any man profane or unclean." The modern divisions nearest to the emotion-laden separations with which Peter struggled are those which we associate with "race."

In the light of all this, it is not surprising that Peter should begin his preaching in the home of Cornelius with the words: "Truly I perceive that God shows no partiality, but in every nation any one who fears him and does what is right is acceptable to him" (vss. 34-35). That God does not support our surface distinctions was a teaching not alien to the religion in which Peter had been reared. God had said to Samuel, selecting a future king, "The Lord sees not as man sees; man looks on the outward appearance, but the Lord looks on the heart" (I Sam. 16:7).

God has no favorites (Deut. 10:17). That is a basic platform for Christian race relations. God sees men without such distinctions as we make. That may tell us something about how distorted our sight is! When the Chicago Junior Association of Commerce and Industry announced its ten Outstanding Young Men of 1968, for instance, a newspaper columnist called attention to the fact that neither in that year nor in the one before it had there been a black man among them. That, said the columnist, was not because of a dearth of qualified young black men. He named six by way of illustration: the Rev. Jessie Jackson, a national figure, highly trained, associate of Dr. Martin Luther King, head of Operation Breadbasket; Gale Sayers, nationally famous athlete of exemplary character and performance; Samuel A. Patch, administrator, head of a youth foundation and of a specialized program in ghetto education; John B. Mack III, prominent teacher, leader among teachers; Garland C. Guice, executive director of the Chicago Economic Development Corporation and civic leader; and Dr. James L. Buckner, dentist, founder of a large shopping center, bank director, and leader in other enterprises. Does the ignoring of these men tell us something about our way of seeing? Perhaps we need a change not unlike Peter's in our way of looking at men.

One Family of God: Mark 3:31-35

"Whoever does the will of God is my brother, and sister, and mother" (vs. 35).

That is no obscure word of Jesus. The other Gospels retell the story (Matt. 12:46-50; Luke 8:19-21; John 15:14). This is surprising because it must have shocked the piety of the disciples. Its tension with the commandment, "Honor thy father and mother," would have troubled them. Yet the clarity of its association with Jesus demanded that it be preserved and faithfully reported.

We cannot be sure why his mother and brothers had come to call him (vs. 31). Many interpreters read it in the light of the earlier word that "his friends . . . went out to seize him, for they said, 'He is beside himself'" (vs. 21). This may provide the rationale of the occasion, though the passage does not specifically relate the two events, and the way in which Gospel materials were pieced together does not lead to the assumption that one followed the other in quick succession. All we know is that his family asserted some priority claim upon him and he set the priority elsewhere than on blood kinship.

This must have been a welcome message to the early church. Many had suffered a break with family for the sake of discipleship; many were ostracized from circles once dear to them; most suffered persecution. Yet in the fellowship of the church they found a new family cemented together by common allegiance to Christ. Obedience to the will of God bound them in one family, closer than the ties of blood.

The bond still holds. All that divides society is canceled by the bond that unites us to him. In kinship with him we belong to each other. Looking on those who gather about him, he still says: "Here are my mother and my brothers! Whoever does the will of God is my brother, and sister, and mother."

For all who suffer exclusions of race or class it is a dignifying word. There is truth in T. R. Glover's observation that "four words destroyed slavery: 'For whom Christ died.'" Those words have destroyed many another entrenched evil; we dare not abuse any man so precious to him. When slavery is destroyed, or civil rights legally buttressed, we may still remain a long way from brotherhood. It is time to say, Nine words made us one family: "Whoever does the will of God is my brother."

We are more prone to welcome the divisive than the unifying. One thing he had learned in twenty-two years as a syndicated columnist, wrote Sydney

J. Harris, was "that most people need enemies as much as they need friends; they can define what they are *for* only in terms of what they are *against;* and this is perhaps the most dangerous tendency of the human animal." [10] Jesus calls us away from mere "tendencies of the human animal" to be children of God bound in one family.

FESTIVAL OF THE CHRISTIAN HOME

Homes that Make Hope Secure
Proverbs 31:10-31

Amid conflict of ideologies, threats to freedom, the menace of the machine, and the overarching fear of atomic war, this is an age of terror. Yet with possibilities of one world under law, larger life through better use of growing leisure, liberation from exclusions based on race, this is an age of promise. Out of our homes must come young people who can live creatively among the crosscurrents of such terror and such promise.

One of literature's oldest pictures of great home life emerges in the closing sentences of the Book of Proverbs. "A good wife who can find?" it begins. "She is far more precious than jewels" (vs. 10). What follows is all about a nobly strong wife-mother. Since such a figure is the center around whom home life grows, it is also about homes that make hope secure in any baffling age.

Creative homes, it suggests, are grounded in useful work and careful management. The wife-mother of such a home "seeks wool and flax, and works with willing hands . . . brings her food from afar . . . rises while it is yet night . . . puts her hands to the distaff . . . looks well to the ways of her household, and does not eat the bread of idleness" (vss. 13-15, 19, 27).

With all our labor-saving devices, do we get more done with our time and energy? Must we not find anew the art of doing things together? Our machines have thus far tended to make us individuals, each off on his own project, entertaining himself in his own way with his own circle of friends, losing the sense of corporate life as a family. Yet all that makes for great living depends on the growth of personality through sharing in such a circle of love as rich family life provides. One challenge confronting the Christian home is thus the call to partnership in some work in which a family plans together, toils together, and achieves a goal together.

Disciplined minds and emotions accompany thrifty management in such sharing households. "She considers a field and buys it; with the fruit of her hands she plants a vineyard . . . She makes linen garments and sells them; she delivers girdles to the merchant" (vs. 16, 24). Here is household activity which by its very nature involves more people than the mother who stands at the center of this picture. It is a well-managed activity of many hands. Remarking that she "works with willing hands" (vs. 13), this classic has touched one secret of the difference between the happy and unhappy home. There is no one so dissatisfied as the chronic consumer—passive, expecting to

[10] "Strictly Personal" column, *Chicago Daily News,* Jan. 3, 1967.

be pleased, requiring constant improvement in what is done for him. No one has so sure a foundation for happiness as the producer, who tests his ingenuity, has the joy of expressing himself in the things he creates, and finds satisfaction in using his own product.

Creative homes need understanding love. Of the wife-mother Proverbs says, "She opens her hand to the poor, and reaches out her hands to the needy. . . . She opens her mouth with wisdom, and the teaching of kindness is on her tongue" (vss. 20, 26). The neighborhood gains understanding from her. Her children have the security of her love, not sentimental and effusive, but steady and dependable. She seeks the good in people and brings out the best in all about her.

Homes that make hope secure must base security on self-respect. "She perceives that her merchandise is profitable" (vs. 18), has confidence in herself as a competent person doing a work with value to others. She cares about her appearance, even though she knows that "charm is deceitful, and beauty is vain" (vs. 30); for "she makes herself coverings; her clothing is fine linen and purple" (vs. 22). She is concerned to keep herself fit, so that "she girds her loins with strength and makes her arms strong" (vs. 17). In security of spirit she faces the future. "Strength and dignity are her clothing, and she laughs at the time to come" (vs. 25).

People who live with secure hope in an insecure time can come only from homes based on such self-respect. Parents competent within themselves have enough freedom from self-conscious concerns to love their children with real understanding. Such parents are not forced to seek their gratifications so completely in their children that they try to draw from them the fulfillment of their own disappointed ambitions, so limiting the children's freedom to reach their own potential. Parents who are thus secure in their own self-respect create an atmosphere of relaxed confidence which extends its length-ended shadow into the secure, hopeful life of the growing child.

Home Claims Its Heritage: Ephesians 5:25–6:4

Christian homes have a heritage of resources for durable family living— the love of Christ, which both teaches and sustains. Underlying the sturdy home maxims of this passage is one reality of human motivation: "Be subject to one another out of reverence for Christ" (vs. 21).

Christ's love offers guidance to the kind of love on which we can build creative homes. "Husbands," the Letter enjoins, "love your wives, as Christ loved the church and gave himself up for her" (vs. 25). That speaks to our confusion. Love has become an overworked word as we lose capacity to distinguish devotion from desire, dependence, and outright lust. Much of what we call love is the will to possess. A man who falls in love with a pretty dimple marries a whole person. The result can be traumatic for all concerned. Loving his wife as Christ loved the church, such a man may yet learn how to love with wholeness.

For Christ not only loved his "bride," the church; he "gave himself up for her, that he might sanctify her, . . . that the church might be presented before him in splendor, without spot or wrinkle or any such thing" (vss. 25-27). Our human life was a sorry thing. There was little in us to attract him to us. There was nothing in us he needed. His love was not the outgrowth of our natural attractiveness that made him yearn to possess. He loved with a self-giving love that cost him a cross.

"Even so husbands should love their wives as their own bodies. He who loves his wife loves himself" (vs. 28), for the marriage has produced a new corporate personality. Mystery that it is (vs. 32), this is profoundly true. All self-regarding speculation—What would have happened if I had married someone else?—is folly. Such a question cannot even be intelligently put, not to mention answered; for with the marriage a new reality has come to be, and you can no more project what would have happened if one of its parts had not been what it undeniably *is*, than you can unscramble an egg. "Let each one of you love his wife as himself, and let the wife see that she respects her husband" (vs. 33), since this is the only way to wholeness in the new corporate personality, and it is Christ's way with his church (vs. 32).

Christ's love guides family relations. (a) It offers the key to mutual helpfulness in the marriage partnership: "Be subject to one another out of reverence for Christ" (vs. 21).

(b) It suggests the key to growth and fulfillment within the marriage relationship: "Husbands should love their wives as their own bodies" (vs. 28) —strong words to the lordly male of the ancient world! But as a result of this dimension of Christian relationships Christian women grew into a richness of personality that made them a wonder to their pagan neighbors.

(c) It gives the key to avoidance of one of the most serious love triangles of modern times, not the rivalry of another woman but of a man's work: "Let the wife see that she respects her husband" (vs. 33)—a counsel which could relieve the tension in many a home where a man seeking to meet the demands of a difficult position is faced with the inner conflict, "My wife or my work."

(d) It points to the key to the nurture of children: "Obey your parents in the Lord" (6:1). It has been remarked that if we needed proof of the divine authorship of the Scriptures, we could find it here; no one else would dare address Junior, at least in our time, in the imperative mood! Cultural continuity and social stability depend on the spirit of this command. The youth who will learn nothing from his elders is doomed to make old mistakes over again—and call them "progress."

(e) It places in our hands the key to life's only final satisfaction: "Fathers, do not provoke your children to anger, but bring them up in the discipline and instruction of the Lord" (6:4). All other successes are empty to him who has failed in this; all other failures trivial to him who has succeeded here. About deep need at this point a college girl said: "My folks gave me everything I could have wanted except one thing . . . they forgot to tell me who I was. What's the use of having money and education and friends, if you don't know who has them?"

Catechism on the Christian Family
Matthew 19:1-5, 10-14

The early church gathered teaching material on related topics for catechetical use. In this lection we have such an anthology dealing with divorce, celibacy, and the value of the child. Though neither the mood of our time nor the spirit of the Christian faith is friendly to legalism in such matters, we still need careful thought and clear teaching about them. These swift paragraphs answer our need with a little catechism on the Christian family.

In catechetical fashion, it begins with a question: "Is it lawful to divorce one's wife for any cause?" (vs. 3). The reference is to the law's provision that a man might divorce his wife "if then she finds no favor in his eyes because he has found some indecency in her" (Deut. 24:1), if "she fails to please him because he finds something obnoxious about her" (TMT). The bill of divorcement must declare her freedom to marry again.

This was a merciful provision and marked an advance in ancient custom. But traditional law fell back upon the conditions stated in Deuteronomy, and the scribes debated the nature of the indecency (or *unseemly thing*, KJV) which occasioned the divorce. Rabbi Shammai held it to mean unchastity, Rabbi Hillel simply incompetent housekeeping ("burning the bread") or even the fact that the husband preferred another woman. The results of such interpretations were often disastrous for the status of women and the security of the home.[11]

The tradition reported by Matthew understands Jesus to be protecting the weaker person—the woman in the ancient world—and defending the security of the home. He stands on the high ground of the Genesis conception of male and female created by God as part of his good creation (Gen. 1:27-28, 31). He then quotes from the second creation story, "Therefore a man leaves his father and his mother and cleaves to his wife, and they become one flesh" (Gen. 2:24). RSV translates the quotation simply as "the two shall become one" (vs. 5), since the Hebrew for "one flesh" was not intended to confine attention to the physical. Hebrew had no word for "personality"; it conceived the person in psychosomatic wholeness, the term "flesh" connoting the unified being. Endorsing the view that marriage forms a new entity, all but indissoluble, Jesus throws protection around the stability of the home and the neglected rights of women.

This teaching should not be pressed as a legal mandate; there are times when divorce may be humane. But to neglect the teaching is equally wrong. In a time when divorce is taken lightly, when marriages are even contracted with the glib proviso, "If it doesn't work out, we can get a divorce," the whole matter needs to be set amid the grave implications of this basic Christian stance.

The catechism next raises the question of celibacy. Jesus' view of the indissoluble permanence of marriage brought up a popular cynical reaction: If marriage is inescapable, it's better not to be trapped! Jesus replied that there may be a number of good reasons for celibacy, but this attitude is not among them (vss. 10-12). "For while some are incapable of marriage because they were born so, or were made so by men, there are others who have themselves renounced marriage for the sake of the kingdom of Heaven" (NEB). Those who have foregone the joys of home for the sake of God's service in some demanding cause deserve respect, and those deprived of

[11] Grant, *Nelson's Bible Commentary*, vol. 6, comment on Matt. 5:31-32.

home and marriage by adverse circumstance should have our compassion. No celebration of the Festival of the Christian Home should be unmindful of either group.

A charter of Christian education and infant baptism closes the catechism. The kingdom is not reserved for adults. We enter not as those who have earned the right, but as those who have been given God's grace—"poor in spirit," "meek," pensioners on God's providence. "To such belongs the kingdom of heaven" (vss. 13-14). No matter how mature we become, our entrance into the kingdom can be only that of little children whom God receives.

The Christian home has a mission to nurture children in the faith. Civilization advances by its concern for the child. Divorce, faithless homes, war, poverty, slums, ghettos—all the evils brought about by our hardness of heart—fall most destructively on children. Christ is concerned for them. "Let the children come to me," he said, "and do not hinder them" (vs. 14). This is a Magna Charta for Christian nurture, stable homes, and humane social reform.

ALDERSGATE SUNDAY

Call to a Captive Church
Isaiah 52:1-2, 7-12

In the depth of the Babylonian captivity, the prophet sang this song of hope. Into the moral captivity of the Age of Rationalism, John Wesley came with just such a call. On Aldersgate Sunday, anniversary of rebirth that made Wesley a commanding prophet, it is fitting that the call come again to a church in "suburban captivity"—a state of mind and life that reaches far beyond the perimeters of great cities.

This is a call *to rouse from lethargy born of hopelessness.* The prophet used a poetic figure: Israel as the bride of the Lord, putting on her beautiful garments (vss. 1-2), hers only as part of the dowry given by her husband. She is to put on strength—hers because she belongs to him. In this new strength and dignity she is called to shake herself from the dust, rise, and loose the bonds from her neck. If return from exile depends on Israel's own strength, her case is hopeless. In her Lord's strength it is full of promise.

Aldersgate stands for such a call—whether in Isaiah's sixth century B.C., in Wesley's dreary age, or in any other time of renewal. God, who has been at work in repeated liberations, is at work now. It is for the church to hear and heed.

This is a call *to the joy of a rediscovered message of good news.* While the valley is still dark, the rising sun tips the mountaintop with golden light in promise of a new day. The approaching steps of those who bring good news are similarly full of beauty (vss. 7-10). The watchmen "sing for joy" as they see them approaching. The exiles, depressed with hopelessness and loss of meaning from their frustrated lives, can rediscover the joy and vigor of something great to live for. God cares! Rolling up his sleeve, he "has bared his holy arm" to fight for those who have been rejected outcasts. The "waste places of Jerusalem" are to be filled with singing, as songs of "peace" and "good tidings of good" replace the lethargy of despair.

To our day of existentialist despair, anomie, social apathy, the discouragement of society torn by bitter and violent divisions, this promise of good news comes. The Church is given a message to proclaim. In the act of telling the good news it can rediscover the joy of a dynamic reason for being. "All the ends of the earth shall see the salvation of our God" (vs. 10) only if there is a living people of God through whom his action becomes visible. We are called to be that people. By God's grace we can.

This is a call *to get out of Babylon.* To the exiles the city had become home; its prosperity had become theirs. They were bound to it by ties of marriage and the cultural habits of more than a generation. To leave it would be hard. But with Cyrus sweeping everything before him, it was a doomed city. The only sanity was to "depart, go out thence" (vs. 11), "leave that place" (JB), "get out of there!" (Knight). Resorting to the pictorial imagery of the Exodus, the prophet promised,

> For the Lord will go before you,
> and the God of Israel will be your rear guard (vs. 12),

as in the pillar of cloud and the pillar of fire in the wilderness.

Is there not a parallel call to the church to get out of its compromised position, wrapped in the mores of contemporary culture? Called to be the critic of civilization, we have become its pensioner. The order in which we have been comfortable is marked for change. To remain its custodian and champion is to be doomed. Purifying ourselves from complicity, we must venture forth. When we do, we shall not go in our own strength but in the power of God.

This involves practical steps, such as the disciplining of expenditures in a world fast approaching an ultimate crisis of famine. Wesley's experience at Aldersgate had practical effects. Aldersgate's warmed heart produced a rigorous social conscience. In one of his sermons Wesley said:

Many years ago, when I was at Oxford, in a cold winter's day, a young maid (one of those we kept at school) called upon me. I said, "You seem half starved. Have you nothing to cover you but that thin linen gown?" She said, "Sir, this is all I have!" I put my hand in my pocket; but found I had scarce any money left, having just paid away what I had. It immediately struck me, "Will thy Master say, 'Well done, good and faithful steward?' Thou hast adorned thy walls with the money which might have screened this poor creature from the cold! O justice! O mercy! Are not these pictures the blood of this poor maid?" See thy expensive apparel in the same light; thy gown, hat, head-dress! Everything about thee which cost more than Christian duty required thee to lay out is the blood of the poor! [12]

Through Peace God Gives: Romans 5:1-11

At Aldersgate God gave a new peace; beyond Aldersgate the peace produced new power. When Wesley wrote, "I felt I did trust in Christ, Christ

[12] *The Works of John Wesley,* VII, 21.

alone for salvation: And an assurance was given me, that he had taken away *my* sins, even *mine*, and saved *me* from the law of sin and death," [13] he did not affirm mere subjective inner contentment, but reconciliation to God, to life itself—a whole new set of relationships. This found expression in a capacity to bear with composure struggles once unendurable. Of a similar change Paul wrote, "More than this: let us even exult in our present sufferings, because we know that suffering trains us to endure, and endurance brings proof that we have stood the test, and this proof is the ground of hope" (vss. 3-4 NEB).

Not overwhelmed by exuberant joy, Wesley was tempted to doubt the gift he had received.

Then was I taught, that peace and victory over sin are essential to faith in the Captain of our salvation: But that, as to the transports of joy that usually attend the beginning of it, especially in those who have mourned deeply, God sometimes giveth, sometimes withholdeth them, according to the counsels of his own will.[14]

The joy is of another sort, the unshakable certainty that nothing can separate us from God's love (Rom. 8:38-39). This love "has been poured into our hearts through the Holy Spirit which has been given to us" (vs. 5)—the Spirit which is itself Love and the very life of the church.

None of this is left in the realm of subjective feelings. It is based on the objective fact of things done by God through Christ. We were helpless, but Christ died for us (vs. 6). How strange! No one would die even for a *righteous* man, though one might for a *good* man (vs. 7). The distinction here is between one who is "righteous" in the sense of doing all that law or justice requires—does his duty, gives every man his due—and one who actively promotes the interests of others, entering into a real fellowship with them. In terms which Martin Buber has made current, the "righteous" man deals justly with all men, though it may well be on an I-it basis, while the "good" man adds the I-thou dimension in all his dealings. Before Aldersgate, Wesley was "righteous" according to this definition, but there is little in his early life to indicate he was "good." Nor is there in any of us, so long as we are working out our life by methodical rules to discipline our duty. As to Wesley, so to us, something more must happen.

The *more* is God's mighty act. He "shows his love for us in that while we were yet sinners Christ died for us" (vs. 8)—a historical act of tangible reality. We were enemies of God, living in his "wrath" (vs. 9) for no want of love on his part, but because our enmity estranged the relationship. Yet he acted to reconcile us, making the actual relation the reflection of the forgiveness he had given all along—which we had refused to accept. Through Isaiah God had said: "I will tell of your righteousness and your doings, but they will not help you" (Isa. 57:12). So long as one is trying to buy his way to life by the duties of the "righteous" there is no peace. But when we accept the new relationship he offers, it can be ours. To accept it is, in the language of this passage, to be "justified," to stand in a relation to God and all of life that changes everything.

[13] *Ibid.*, I, 103.
[14] *Ibid.*

When this new fact took control of Wesley, it led to a new outlook, new resources to do what he had found impossible, and a new concern for others that made him one of the pivotal figures of the centuries. This is the change of which Paul wrote—reconciliation which leads to growing salvation as the resurrected Christ lives in us and with us (vss. 9-11). Through the peace God gives, all relationships are changed, new growth begins, new powers work in us.

Not Far from the Kingdom: Mark 12:28-34a

One sharp thrust of Scripture tingled with life and smarted with pain in the mind of John Wesley as he left his room on the momentous morning of May 24, 1734: "You are not far from the kingdom of God" (vs. 34). As the day dawned, he notes in his *Journal*, he had opened his Testament on words full of hope, "There are given unto us exceeding great and precious promises, even that ye should be partakers of the divine nature" (II Peter 1:4 KJV). But just before he stepped out into the day's round, he looked again, and what he found was both auspicious and ominous: "Thou art not far from the kingdom of God." [15] So! The distance was not great, but it was real.

So powerfully did the impression grip him that sixteen years later, coming upon this verse in the writing of his *Notes Upon the New Testament*, Wesley echoed the challenge that had been thrust upon him. "Not far from the kingdom"! "Reader, art thou?" he wrote. "Then go on: be a real Christian; else it had been better for thee to have been far off."

How well he knew! For that night of May 24, at the quiet Moravian service in Aldersgate Street, he had come the rest of the distance. Formerly just Christian enough to be tormented by a restless conscience, he was made Christian enough to enter the joy of a fulfilled self. From his wanderings "not far from the kingdom" he had entered in to share its abundant resources.

When Jesus spoke these words to the scribe, he implied two truths about the man's condition. When the words reached Wesley, those two realities gripped him. Could these truths apply to us?

The first hailed the promise in proximity—"*not far* from the kingdom." The scribe could acquiesce in the best answer to the most crucial question: What is life's key commandment? (vs. 28). He agreed that complete love of God has first priority (vss. 29-30)—knew what life's ruling passion should be. Wesley, likewise, ten years beyond Aldersgate, declared:

The ruling temper of [the true Christian's] heart is the most absolute submission, and the tenderest gratitude, to his sovereign Benefactor. . . . But yet this, far from creating sloth or indolence, pushes him on to the most vigorous industry. It causes him to put forth all his strength, in obeying Him in whom he confides. . . . And as he knows the most acceptable worship of God is to imitate Him he worships, so he is continually laboring to transcribe into himself all His imitable perfections; in particular, His justice, mercy, and truth.[16]

That love is indivisible, for with love of God comes the command, "You shall love your neighbor as yourself" (vs. 31). Such love, the scribe agreed,

[15] *Ibid.*
[16] *Ibid.*, X, 67-68.

"is much more than all whole burnt offerings" (vs. 33). So the prophets always insisted (I Sam. 15:22; Amos 5:24). In our age of secularity, not tempted to substitute love of God for love of neighbor, we often content ourselves with trying to love our neighbor in the fond hope that this will be enough, or that then love of God will take care of itself. Yet either command without the other is warped and anemic.

The second truth is that, if the scribe, or Wesley, was "not *far* from the kingdom," neither was he *in* it. Three years after the great change came, Wesley described the man he had been: diligent

to eschew all evil, and to have a conscience void of offence; redeeming the time; buying up every opportunity of doing all good to all men; constantly and carefully using all the public and all the private means of grace; endeavouring after a steady seriousness of behaviour, at all times, and in all places; and, God is my record, before whom I stand, doing all this in sincerity; having a real design to serve God; a hearty desire to do his will in all things; to please him who had called me to "fight the good fight," and to "lay hold of eternal life." Yet my own conscience beareth me witness in the Holy Ghost, that all this time I was but *almost a Christian*.[17]

Living faithfully by the law, he had not yet received the gift of the gospel.

Jesus patiently explained to another leader, who knew and kept the law, that he stood in desperate need of something more: "unless one is born anew, he cannot see the kingdom of God" (John 3:3). Aldersgate brought that to Wesley, resolving his old quarrel with himself, closing the distance between him and the God he had long sought to love and serve. The prodigious labors, the contagious witness, the miracle of productivity, the durability born of inner peace and joy that filled his years attest the reality of the change. Those who share that gift, he said, know that a new birth is as real to all that is essential to their life as physical birth is to their bodies. And, he added, "as, in natural birth, a man is born at once, and then grows larger and stronger by degrees; so in the spiritual birth, a man is born at once, and then gradually increases in spiritual stature and strength." Until that happens, a man may be so diligently obedient that he is "not far from the kingdom," but he is still not in it.

ASCENSION DAY
(For another treatment of these lections see Ascension Sunday.)

When World Powers Pass
Daniel 7:9-10, 13-14

Behind its poetic imagery, Ascension Day confronts the hard practical issue of power. Our continual temptation is to meet bestial power on its own terms. Seeking to defeat it with its own weapons, we become like it. Hating a violent foe, we become violent. Fighting wars to end militarism, we are captured by our own "military-industrial complex." The faith celebrated on

[17] *Ibid.*, V, 21.

Ascension Day declares there is another way to meet the entrenched powers of evil.

From the depths of a power struggle came the apocalyptic visions of Daniel. By bloody persecution, Antiochus IV Epiphanes sought to force Hellenization of life and religion upon resistant Jews. Daniel reports ecstatic, cryptic visionary experiences which imply that when these bloody empires have passed, God's people will remain.

The earlier verses of this chapter report visions of four beasts representing the four world powers at the time. A lion with eagle's wings represents Babylon, a bear with three ribs in its mouth stands for the kingdom of the Medes, a leopard with four wings and four heads depicts Persia, and a nameless beast with iron teeth and ten horns plus another little horn suggests the empire of Macedonia and Alexander the Great—Antiochus being the tiny added horn!

In this setting, "thrones" of judgment were seen "and one that was ancient of days"—poetic term for God—"took his seat" (vs. 9). His white garments and hair symbolize purity. The trappings—flame, wheels on the throne, a stream of fire—are poetic stage settings adapted largely from the visions of Ezekiel. Beyond an air of mystery and power they should not be pressed for specific content. The vast throng attending (vs. 10)—common imagery of the heavenly host—completes the impression of divine majesty. So "the books were opened." The case was called for judgment.

The beasts were shorn of their power, and the fourth beast was slain, "its body destroyed and given over to be burned" (vss. 11-12). So! The bestial power of the bloody empires is only mortal. Its threat is not final.

Then "came one like a son of man" (vs. 13). That is to say: unlike the kingdoms portrayed by the beasts, he was humane. The idiom, "son of man," means quite simply, like a man, as in the familiar line,

> what is man that thou art mindful of him,
>   and the son of man that thou dost care for him? (Ps. 8:4).

To this humane figure "was given dominion and glory and kingdom . . . his dominion is an everlasting dominion, which shall not pass away" (vs. 14). Under God's judgment imperial power passes, yet the power of the humane remains.

Who is this "son of man" figure? Presented as an individual, he stands in a *representative* capacity, just as did the four beasts. He symbolizes another kingdom, identified as "given to the people of the saints of the Most High" (vss. 22-27). Thus the messianic figure emerges—gentle, humane, representing God's chosen people,

> and his kingdom one
>   that shall not be destroyed (vs. 14)

Jesus' recurring use of this "son of man" title is memorable. Though scholars debate whether he meant himself or one yet to come, the devotional reader of the New Testament inevitably sees the term pointing to our Lord. Asked by the high priest, whether he is "the Christ, the Son of the Blessed,"

Jesus uses the figure in direct answer: "I am; and you will see the Son of man sitting at the right hand of Power, and coming with the clouds of heaven" (Mark 14:62). In such a passage it takes no little maneuvering to derive a meaning which looks beyond himself to another yet to come. Significantly, he borrowed the figure from Daniel:

> and behold, with the clouds of heaven
> there came one like a son of man (v. 13).

To come "with the clouds of heaven"—a poetic image not to be literally pressed—is to come with divine sanction and support.

The early church used this figure to represent Jesus' messiahship. Gentle and humane, as contrasted with the bestial power of the kingdoms of this world, his might would endure indestructibly. The risen One, now seated at the right hand of God, who represents power in its most humane form as the power of love, supplies a fitting figure in which to interpret the meaning of Ascension Day. His kingdom is "the kingdom . . . given to the people of the saints of the Most High" (vs. 27).

Jesus never yielded to our temptation to meet bestial power on its own terms. But He denied its illusion, from the time of the offer of the kingdoms of this world, in his wilderness temptation, until the final issue at the Cross. The bestial power seemed, for a time, to triumph through the Crucifixion. But God was preparing another day of resurrection and ascension, repeating the judgment seen in Daniel, this time moving beyond vision to historic event.

Ascension Day urges the question: Which kind of power will we trust?

How Vast the Resources
Ephesians 1:15-23

"I pray . . . that you may know . . . how vast the resources of his power open to us who trust in him" (vss. 18-19 NEB). We need such resources. Moral confusion envelops us, and we need power to decide rightly. Technology makes many of us obsolete, and we need power to restore purpose to our lives. Weapons stockpiled to defend us draw counter-weapons that make us ever more insecure, and we need some kind of power that will break the self-defeating cycle. Depleted by anxiety, we need power to live with confident calm.

Ascension Day celebrates such power, affirming that Christ overcomes all the dark powers of the world—an assertion about the present and the future, anchored in a fact of history. Christ is raised from the dead and placed as life's supreme authority at God's "right hand in the heavenly places" (vs. 20). He lives on through "the church, which is his body" (vss. 22-23). Beginning as "the march of eleven men," continuing more often under the world's scorn than in its favor, enduring the failures of its sinful members, it prevails as witness to a Power beyond it.

"How vast the resources of his power open to us"—something more than our own puny power is at work.

The tide will lift a rowboat, but the lifting of the rowboat is no true indication of the tide's power; and the man who sees no farther than the edge of his own dock will hardly be aware of the full power of the tide, which lifts with equal ease the navies of the world and whatsoever else floats upon the oceans. Likewise the Christian believer, whose life has been lifted into the heavenly places in Christ, will not know the *immeasurable greatness* of the divine power which has lifted him until he sees it as an instance of *the working of* [God's] *great might which he accomplished in Christ.*[18]

Ascension Day is the church's celebration of that transcendent power, seen in these verses to display four characteristics: (a) It manifests God's power, who "raised him from the dead and made him sit at his right hand in the heavenly places" (vs. 20). (b) It makes Christ judge over all hierarchies of spiritual values (vs. 21). (c) It sets him supreme in all historic times, both the advancing present and the unrealized future (vs. 21*b*). (d) It makes him victorious over all assaults, hardships, and reverses ever to be experienced by "the church, which is his body."

We are called to pray that by faith we may respond to this victory. Pray for the wisdom and knowledge he gives, an appropriation of his history as the meaning of *our* life (vs. 17). Pray that we may make enlightened response to our call to be his body (vs. 18). Pray that we may understand and be ready to enter into the "inheritance in the saints" (vs. 18*b*). Pray for a full trust in his power against all the powers of the world (vs. 19).

Lord of Every Age and Sphere
Luke 24:44-53

Through this story the New Testament says little about the physical universe, much about the meaning of Christ in our experience. At stake is no bodily levitation into the wild blue yonder. The soaring language of faith, rather, seeks a visual symbol of abiding reality: he is Lord of every age and sphere.

Our eternal contemporary, he participates in unfolding events. "You are my witnesses" (vs. 48)—with these words he sent his disciples to begin a process by which he would touch the life of all parts of the world, in all centuries, at every level of human relationship, confronting all manner of issues. Forgetting this commission, we earn the taunt that ours is an "opiate" religion of "pie in the sky." He is the Lord of all of life—the economics of slums, the politics of poverty, the tensions of race, the dynamics of disarmament, the motives of mission—and to this Lordship we are called to bear witness.

Witness is linked with expectation that power will be given: "stay in the city, until you are clothed with power from on high" (vs. 49). Christians must *act,* but when they act they must be obedient servants of a power and wisdom from beyond themselves. Goethe's dictum—those who *act* are always right—requires correction. Helmut Thielicke offers the balancing comment that those who merely *observe* are always wrong. The non-participant is wrong by default. Yet action merely in the light of our own good intentions

[18] Francis W. Beare, *Interpreter's Bible,* X, 632.

may be sadly misguided; the world's needs are too complex and exhausting for us to meet alone.

Our ultimate guide is neither abstract principle nor disembodied spirit, but the concrete reality known to us in Jesus of Nazareth. "These are my words" (vs. 44), he said, referring to his fulfillment of Old Testament expectation, and to his death and rising as a call to new life (vss. 45-47). Amid all speculations about "the historical Jesus," we know a vivid personal character and the main thrust of his teaching. John Knox illustrates the significance of the disciples' memories of him—which have become the church's corporate memory—by analogy with his own experience with his father. Recalling little of his father's explicit *words* and *acts*, he remembered *him* with a concreteness and force that made him a vital, continuing part of his adult consciousness. The disciples, Knox went on, remembered many of Jesus' deeds and sayings, but even more they remembered *him;* and it was through this vivid personal memory that God's love came to them. The doctrine of his Ascension is a perpetual call away from abstractions about a vague "spirit of Christ" to the concreteness of that memory of Jesus, who he was, what he did, how he thought, as our guide in dealing with emerging issues that confront us.

Ascension Day celebrates the truth that he was no mere local figure confined to a specific period of history, but that he is the Lord of every age and sphere. "He parted from them. And they returned to Jerusalem with great joy" (vss. 51-52). Strange paradox—*joy* in the disappearance of one who is Friend, Master, Lord! We can understand it better in the light of his saying, "If I do not go away, the Counselor will not come to you; but if I go, I will send him to you" (John 16:7); or of the recollection that in commissioning them to a world mission he had said, "Lo, I am with you always, to the close of the age" (Matt. 28:20).

He confronts us in every new crisis. When the Methodist Tehological Seminary in Frankfurt was bombed during World War II, Bishop Sommer rebuilt the chapel before undertaking work on any other facility of the school. In great haste he restored the old inscription over the chancel arch: *"Einer ist euer Meister, Christus; ihr aber seid alle Bruder"*—"One is your Master, even Christ; and all ye are brethren" (Matt. 23:8 KJV). Amid Hitler's idolatrous claims, that reminder that only Christ is Lord and that in him our brotherhood is indissoluble must be kept ever in clearest view. So in each new challenge we encounter, he is Lord of every age and sphere.

TRINITY SUNDAY

Momentous Meeting
Exodus 3:1-8b, 10-15

Moses not only found God, he found himself. This incisive story goes beyond human interest narrative to theological interpretation, steps to life-changing encounter with God. We are like the thirteen-year-old boy, homesick on his first extended absence from his parents, who said in one short letter:

Dear Mother and Daddy: The thing that has been bothering me most is very fundamental. I just don't understand why I or anyone else is alive. We are born, we live, and we die—all for no apparent reason. Why do I exist? I feel as if I have no purpose in life at all.[19]

Though we do not ask as insistently as men once did, "How can I find God?" there is desperate urgency behind our quest for purpose in life. Perhaps, as for the boy who felt cut off from the roots of his life in parents and home, the answer to the question of purpose is the rediscovery of our roots. This story speaks forcefully of steps in the momentous meeting with God, in whom we can have rootage.

Step one: the questing second look beneath surfaces. "And Moses said, 'I will turn aside and see this great sight, why the bush is not burnt' " (vs. 3). Is this how God comes to a man? A second look, a curious question, a thoughtful "Why?"—and then God? If so, it is because men are so made that they reach out to the unknown and are called by mystery, and because God is the Rewarder of the penetrating second look. Which is to say there is a bond between such men and God, a bond prior to the man's question.

Step two: reverence before mystery. "Do not come near; put off your shoes from your feet, for the place on which you are standing is holy ground" (vs. 5). In the presence of mystery there may be helplessness, so that a man says, "It is meaningless. It is absurd." Or there may be fear, infesting the unknown with dragons, as men once did the unexplored areas in ancient maps. Or there may be reverence which writes as did Franklin in the unfilled areas, "Here is God." Bonhoeffer has made us scornful of a "God of the gaps," called in to fill out our ignorance as if it were knowledge; but to write "God" where some have written "the meaningless absurd" or "the nameless dread," is to give promise to the future by reverence before mystery.

Step three: obedience to a claim. "And Moses hid his face, for he was afraid to look at God" (vs. 6). God was the supreme Challenger, calling with the agony of a conscience concerned about a people's bondage. "Who am I that I should go . . . ?" (vs. 11). Something beyond himself was dealing with him—but who? How could he know? How could he be sure? What proof was there that this call was not the wild folly it seemed? Only faith's *non sequitur*: "this shall be the sign for you, that I have sent you: when you have brought forth the people out of Egypt, you shall serve God upon this mountain" (vs. 12). Prove the present risk by an event in the future beyond risk! Faith's proof! Adventurer's proof! Brave men's proof! Try, and *then* you will know.

Step four: discovery of a Name. "What is his name?" the people will ask (vs. 13). Answer: " 'I AM WHO I AM' . . . . Say this to the people of Israel, 'I AM has sent me to you' " (vs. 14). Only that! What exists. What is real. Existence itself. Only that? What more can there be? This is the God of the continuous present, the open future, "I WILL BE WHAT I WILL BE" (RSV note). God would give only that, for to know the name is to be able to call upon it, to have an assured claim—and God is not at our disposal.

[19] John Knox, *Life in Christ Jesus* (Greenwich, Conn.: Seabury Press, 1961), p. 94.

"Yet he is not left faceless, abstract. " 'The Lord, the God of your fathers, the God of Abraham, the God of Isaac, and the God of Jacob . . . ': this is my name for ever" (vs. 15). Existence, Reality, Continuous Contemporary, Open Future, I AM, he can be known through others who have made the great adventure and who stand as witnesses. One day he would have another name: "You shall call his name Jesus, for he will save his people from their sins" (Matt. 1:21).

Source, Guide, and Goal
Romans 11:33-36

"Source, Guide, and Goal of all that is—to him be glory for ever! Amen" (vs. 36 NEB). This sets the true mood of all useful discussion of the doctrine of the Trinity. We have made the doctrine an exercise in metaphysics; its true nature is doxology. Paul's outburst in these verses is full of the poetry of praise. We have puzzled over questions: Three Gods, or One? Why talk of Three if there is only One? What is the relation of the Three to one another and to the One? In the poetic phrase, "Source, Guide, and Goal of all that is" the questions melt away. The phrase is not a Trinity formula, yet in its doxology we see one God held steadily in view, as he is Source, Guide, and Goal. More fruitful than analysis of the phrase is a glimpse of what lies back of this doxology.

It shows us *God as Savior known through Christ.* Dealing with the problem of human lostness, Paul breaks into doxology on the heels of the close theological reasoning that has filled the first eleven chapters of the Letter to the Romans. Concluding, "For God has consigned all men to disobedience, that he may have mercy upon all" (vs. 32), the theology declares the good news that God's love moves toward victory in the salvation of all men, not by some universal principle, but by his own free choice.

This does not short-circuit the seriousness of human wrong. Paul sees our plight as desperate. The doxology is responsive to the vision of what God has done with it. Our disobedience stands under the scrutiny of a God whose wrath against sin is real, yet nothing in creation can separate us from his love in Christ Jesus our Lord. To minimize the reality of our lostness because God is merciful would be false; to omit the note of his mercy because we are disobedient would violate all that he has shown us of his nature. It takes no depth of insight to see our lostness; the newspapers daily update its documentation. Our shame is that we know this dark picture so much better than we know God as Savior through Christ.

The doxology also shows us *God as Creator known only in mystery.* Paul is the supreme theologian, and this passage stands at the conclusion of his noblest statement of the Christian message. All the more impressive then is his declaration of the "unsearchable . . . judgments and . . . inscrutable . . . ways" of God (vs. 33). A God we could understand would be less than God. A man who did not try to understand would be less than a man. Seek to know God we must, and mystery is not so much frustration of the search as part of the data.

To reinforce the insight, Paul quotes (vs. 34) the prophet's word in confronting the deep mystery his people faced in their Exile and the impressive triumph of the idolatrous Babylonians.

> Who has directed the Spirit of the Lord,
>> or as his counselor has instructed him?
> Whom did he consult for his enlightenment,
>> and who taught him the path of justice? (Isa. 40:13-14).

God so towered above these idolatrous powers, the prophet declared, that the nations themselves were like dust upon his scales, making no difference in the reading. The figure so impressed Paul that he quoted it in another of his letters (I Cor. 2:16), this time adding that though we cannot penetrate the mystery of the mind of God, we have all that we really need; "we have the mind of Christ."

The doxology shows us *God as Spirit known in commitment*. Dwelling on mystery, Paul remembers (vs. 35) Job's wrestling with the enigma of suffering. To Job's indictment of God's justice, God himself answers:

> Who has given to me, that I should repay him?
> Whatever is under the whole heaven is mine (Job 41:11).

We have nothing to offer God. He is in no way dependent on our acts to complete his goodness. He owes us nothing, yet he gives us all. Job made the only response a man can make.

> I had heard of thee by the hearing of the ear,
>> but now my eye sees thee;
> therefore I despise myself,
>> and repent in dust and ashes (Job 42:5-6).

When we bow in humble commitment we find our peace in him.

God Deals with Our Doubt
Matthew 28:16-20

"And when they saw him they worshiped him; but some doubted" (vs. 17). Not all eyes could see him. Doubt was natural, and the Gospels testify to how slowly the disciples came to their sense that Jesus was in truth the Lord. They met Mary's report of the Resurrection with skepticism—"these words seemed to them an idle tale, and they did not believe them" (Luke 24:11). When the risen Lord met the disciples at table, "he upbraided them for their unbelief and hardness of heart, because they had not believed those who saw him after he had risen" (Mark 16:14). For them, as for us, doubt was the natural response to things too good to be true.

Slowly God dealt with their doubts. Matthew wrote his Gospel after time and experience had done their work. There had been mature reflection on the initial events. They had lived almost a generation by the teachings, within the fellowship, sustained by the power he had given. In the light of ripened experience Matthew remembered this final encounter with Jesus. Through it he told of God's threefold way of coming to resolve our doubts.

He comes first in the authority of Jesus (vs. 18). Their teacher has given them a whole new approach to life. He has reinterpreted the law. He has brought the immanent and already active kingdom. Now they see that all they learned of him has permanent, universal authority. In the beginning he had sent them on mission within the narrow confines of Israel: "Go nowhere among the Gentiles, and enter no town of the Samaritans, but go rather to the lost sheep of the house of Israel" (Matt. 10:5-6). Now, however, they are to make disciples of all nations (vs. 19). His authority is universal. They have begun with the experience of a transforming Friend and have reached a reality so universal that they can only call him Lord.

God comes in the realization that the authority of Jesus is more than human. It is "all authority in heaven and on earth." It is not won, not seized, but "given." It comes from his unity with the Father. Jesus said to Philip, "He who has seen me has seen the Father" (John 14:9). To accord honor and authority to Jesus while affirming the death of God, as some theologies attempt to do, is a contradiction. To take Jesus seriously one must hear him in the whole sweep of his teaching, not at a few selected points. To hear his teaching with wholeness is to be aware of his constant claim that his authority came from beyond himself. His message proclaimed the reign of God, his mighty acts were done "by the finger of God" (Luke 11:20), he lived in loyal dependence on the Father who heard his prayers. In the experience of Christ's Lordship the disciples found him one in will with the Father (Matt. 26:42).

God comes in the extension of their experience with Jesus to that of a Presence—"lo, I am with you always, to the close of the age" (vs. 20). The transforming Friendship was not merely a memory, or a figment of thought; it was the continuously contemporary reality of the Church, so that successive generations are baptised "in the name of the Father and of the Son and of the Holy Spirit" (vs. 19). The life of a Wesley is transformed from dogged disciplinarian to dynamic evangel by the touch of the present Spirit. The faith of a Luther declares that we could not in our own right believe in Christ, save as the Spirit moved us to respond to him. The discipleship of a Niemoeller finds power to survive Nazi imprisonment and solitary confinement by the touch of that present Spirit who opens our minds to the mind of Christ and sustains us with the strength of the Father.

INDEPENDENCE DAY

This Nation Under God
Deuteronomy 1:5, 8-18

Recording the death of Moses and dealing with ideas and a social structure of a time later than the Exodus, Deuteronomy is dated by scholars in the period of Josiah's reform. Yet this lesson introduces the book by saying that "Moses undertook to explain this law" (vs. 5). Here is an instance of how God's Word comes to men.

A new set of problems had emerged for which new insights and directives were needed. Yet the reformers under Josiah were not content to strike out wildly into the unknown by sheer improvisation. They turned again to events vital to the nation's life, in which as a people they had long seen "the mighty acts of God" forming and directing personal conduct and social policy. Their approach was not merely to quote laws or rehearse precedents. They faced the new issues in the light of a reassessment of what the events and covenant relations of other days had taught them. Moses was presented not as legislating but as "explaining." Thus the writer of a later day sought to understand the new situation *as* through the eyes of Moses.

Such is the biblical understanding of how God's Word comes. He speaks, not in fixed rules and propositions or in mystical abstractions, but in events. His word-through-event illuminates emergent issues as we make *the* history *our* history, our way of understanding who *we* are, what *our* life means, and what is required of *us.* "The Lord" becomes "*our* God" (vs. 6). Thus current life is ever under reexamination in the light of significant experience shared by the people of God. What has been Word in a memorable past is seeking to become Word again in interaction with a living present.

Just as events in the Exodus were reappropriated to give guiding insight for the men of Josiah's time, they can be assimilated in our experience to speak afresh in the quandaries that perplex us.

First, God gives the land. "Behold, I have set the land before you; go in and take possession of the land which the Lord swore to your fathers" (vs. 8). The conviction that the good earth is a trust from God is even more evident in JB's reading, "This is the land that I have made over to you"; or in TMT, "See, I place the land at your disposal." The national domain is not our possession to exploit; it is a trust to hold in stewardship. This speaks forcefully on such urgent matters as conservation or the use of our rich resources in a world where 80 percent of the people have a per capita income of less than $500 a year. God calls us to account for our stewardship.

Second, God multiplies and blesses the people. Moses refers to how "the Lord your God has multiplied you," invoking God's continuing blessing "as he has promised you!" (vss. 10-11). Here is a realization that we are dependent on God's blessing, bound by a covenant to use it for the good of all men and all nations. The passage refers to God's promise to Abraham (Gen. 12:1-7; 15:18) with its enunciation of the divine purpose that "by you all the families of the earth will bless themselves" (Gen. 12:3).

Seeing ourselves as "this nation under God," we must see too that the blessing is contingent on obedience to God's purpose (vs. 18). The pioneer nuclear physicist, Arthur H. Compton, raises hard questions about the future under the impact of the undreamed-of new power. Then he prays for the obedient spirit that can make a nation secure:

> Where the mind is without fear and the head is held high;
> Where knowledge is free;
> Where the world has not been broken up into fragments by
>   narrow domestic walls;
> Where words come out from the depths of truth;
> Where tireless striving stretches its arms towards perfection;
> Where the clear stream of reason has not lost its way
>   into the dreary desert sand of dead habit;
> Where the mind is led forward by thee into ever-widening
>   thought and action—
> Into that heaven of freedom, my Father, let my country awake.[20]

Such a prayer is the heart of patriotism "under God."

[20] Arthur H. Compton, *Atomic Quest* (New York: Oxford University Press, 1956), p. 359.

Third, God judges men's acts. Moses, appointing judges, admonished them to be impartial, never lacking in courage to give a verdict which might expose them to unpopularity or danger, adding, as the ground for such fearless exercise of their duty, "Fear no man, for judgment is God's" (vs. 17 TMT). This principle is not limited to the courts. In modern democracy it belongs to all branches, departments, and levels of government, and to the life of the individual citizen who shares the final sovereignty.

This Legacy of Freedom
Galatians 5:13-15

Liberty-with-law constitutes a perennial problem of democracy. "Law and order" can be made a repressive slogan to maintain a rigid status quo. Freedom of expression can be built into an excuse for anarchic fragmentation of community life as each individual "does his thing." Contemporary ethics underscores the same problem. Shall we be dominated by an ethic of rules? Or, casting rules aside, shall we respond to the "situation" in the context of the moment? Paul speaks to these needs: "You, my friends, were called to be free men; only do not turn your freedom into licence for your lower nature, but be servants to one another in love" (vs. 13 NEB). The parts of this proposition demand individual scrutiny.

"*You . . . were called to be free men.*" This is basic. Throughout the Galatian letter Paul has defended this freedom against the attack of teachers who had been urging the Christian converts to return to the Judaic laws as the necessary basis of their life in Christ. Paul's rebuttal has begun with the people's own experience. New life, he reminded them, was given them by Christ and his Spirit dwelling in them, not by a resolute adherence to commandments (3:1-5). Paul has proceeded to argue that it was Abraham's faith in God which originated the covenant laws, not the laws that gave birth to the faith (3:6-18). He concluded the section by declaring that the law has served as a guardian in our immaturity, in order that it might bring us to the freedom that belongs to the new life in Christ (3:23-26). All this is climaxed by the great charter of freedom: "For freedom Christ has set us free; stand fast therefore, and do not submit again to a yoke of slavery" (5:1).

"*Only do not turn your freedom into licence for your lower nature.*" Freedom is real only under restraint. Free spenders learn by sad experience that they have missed the road to economic independence. "Free love," a succession of temporary "affairs," forfeits the freedom to follow any love to its loyal and wonderful depths. Free whims are the enemy of powerful purpose. As Chaplain of the Senate, Peter Marshall prayed, "Help us to stand for something, that we may not fall for everything." The prayer deals with the issue most crucial to freedom.

"*Be servants to one another in love.*" Tersely Paul gives the key to the law-liberty paradox. "The whole law is fulfilled in one word, 'You shall love your neighbor as yourself'" (vs. 14). There is thus no contradiction between the law (Lev. 19:18) and the spirit of Jesus who reaffirmed it (Mark 12:31). Love is the rationale of the law and the essence of liberty. Paul devotes the rest of the Galatian letter to the unfolding of this truth. Neighbor love, he shows, is inclusive: "let us do good to all men" (6:10). It involves special solicitude for wrongdoers: "if a man is overtaken in any trespass, you who are spiritual should restore him in a spirit of gentleness" (6:1). It demands "walking by the Spirit" which does not permit us to "gratify the desires of the flesh" (vs. 16). In the end, the Cross most illuminates the matter: "God forbid that I should boast of anything but the cross of our Lord Jesus Christ, through which the world is crucified to me and I to the world! Circumcision is nothing; uncircumcision is nothing; the only thing that counts is new creation!" (6:14-15 NEB). Only those who bear their share of the sufferings, as well as the victory, of the Lord Jesus can be trusted with this legacy of freedom.

What Truth Makes Free?
John 8:31-36

"You will know the truth, and the truth will make you free" (vs. 32). No line of the Bible is so tediously quoted out of context. Its "hackneyed use . . . in appealing for national or personal liberty is a distortion of the purely religious value of both truth and freedom in this passage." [21]

The truth of which it speaks is not the result of scientific investigation, a free press, or any of the other modern phenomena that come easily to mind. It is the same truth of which Jesus says, "I am the way, and the truth, and the life" (John 14:6). The truth that makes free comes to those who as his disciples "continue" in his word (vs. 31). Modern translations bring out its force: "If you hold fast to my teaching" (Weymouth); "if you dwell within the revelation I have brought" (NEB); "if you make my word your home" (JB). The idea of constant dwelling on his teachings, coming back to him again and again, is emphatic. It rings like a refrain through the New Testament: "Any one who goes ahead and does not abide in the doctrine of Christ does not have God; he who abides in the doctrine of Christ has both the Father and the Son" (II John 9). "If you abide in me, and my words abide in you, ask whatever you will, and it shall be done for you" (John 15:7). Such is the freedom of life in Christ's teaching and Spirit.

How persistently we misunderstand! Frederick C. Grant comments that

To a pagan reader of the second century this saving truth, which makes one free, would be the truth about the cosmos and its origin and supernatural rulers, the soul, its original state and its fall into the realm of matter, its relation to the body, and the method and process of its salvation. The freedom referred to would be freedom from fate, destiny, the influence of the stars, or blind chance.[22]

No neglible matters these, for them or for the modern pagan, whether he be primitive animist or sophisticated reader of horoscopes. Christ set men free from all these fears, but not by revealing esoteric secrets. He frees by the friendship of his transforming Spirit and by the changed outlook that comes by "making his words our home."

---

[21] Brown, *The Gospel According to John*, Anchor Bible, 29:355.
[22] Grant, *Nelson's Bible Commentary, ad loc.*

Like us, those who heard him misunderstood. Ronald Knox translates with the ring of our own idiom: "They answered him, We are of Abraham's breed, nobody ever enslaved us yet" (vs. 33). "Not enslaved," says the modern patriot. "Not enslaved; I can quit when I want to," says the problem drinker. Both are as mistaken as were the ancient boasters.

> Their boast was ill founded, for Egypt, Babylonia, and Rome had enslaved them. Perhaps they mean that, being the privileged heirs to the promise to Abraham, they cannot be truly enslaved, although occasionally God has allowed them to be chastised through temporary subjection.[23]

We weasel out of our entrapments; we're tied up a bit now, but it's not permanent. Nobody can enslave *us!*

In the eloquent speech which led the trapped Jews at fortress Masada to suicide instead of surrender, their leader said: "Long ago we determined to be slaves to neither the Romans nor anyone else, save God." On our human level the resistance to enslavement may be such a road to death. But Jesus is talking on no mere human level. He seeks to liberate us from slavery to sin: "every one who commits sin is a slave to sin" (vs. 34). Sin is habit-forming. It leads to deeper and deeper complications. We cannot extricate ourselves by an act of will, for our wills are themselves diseased. The way out, not of our making, is a transforming friendship with Christ. Association with him changes desire. His new Spirit gives power we could not generate. "The slave does not continue in the house for ever" (vs. 35)—it is the same "continue" as in vs. 31. So! the slave has not continued in Christ's word, has not made Christ's words his home. But when association with the Christ really takes us into the household, we belong to the family of the free.

LABOR DAY

Religion Re-examined
Amos 5:11-15

God is no fussy old ecclesiastic puttering about the temple. He is out in the world of trade. All that is more human and humanizing is his concern. On Labor Day this aspect of Christian conviction is sharply focused, and Amos speaks to us with special force. For Amos the workingman issues an indictment of the official religion of the nation, challenging the sacerdotal in the name of the secular concern of the Lord. His indictment calls for a reexamination of religion as we ask, Are the evils Amos denounced invading our faith too?

Your religion is too closely allied with a comfortable status quo, Amos declared. In God's name he warned of terrible reverses to come. No arbitrary acts of God, he said, they will bring the punishment that might be expected by a covenant people who "trample upon the poor" (vs. 11). The Law (Exod. 22:25) had explicitly forbidden the exaction of interest when one

---

[23] Brown, *The Gospel According to John,* p. 355.

lent money to the poor. Nevertheless, Amos reminded his people that they take "exactions of wheat" from those who have nothing else to pay. They "afflict the righteous." They "take a bribe." "They turn aside the needy in the gate" (vs. 12).

Out of their ill-gotten gain they have "built houses of hewn stone" (vs. 11)—not the loosely piled, less secure field stone, for they have the advantage of advanced quarrying and masonry. Like those whom Isaiah denounced, they "say in pride and in arrogance of heart:

> 'The bricks have fallen,
>   but we will build with dressed stones' " (Isa. 9:10),

supposing that by wealth and sophistication they can outwit human misfortunes and divine judgment. Build such houses as you will, Amos declared, "you shall not dwell in them." Is our religion thus comfortably at ease in alliance with a *status quo* due for radical overhauling?

Your religion is too cautious in the face of evil, Amos went on. The "prudent" man "will keep silent in such a time" (vs. 13)—the words sound out of character for Amos. In KJV's reading, as mandate—"the prudent *shall* keep silent in that time"—they are completely foreign to the prophet's nature and message. Commentators have made various puzzled responses. Emil Kraeling, for instance, sees this as "a marginal remark by a reader of late (Maccabean?) times." At best, it is a kind of "aside" in which the prophet reflects on the time and his own far from prudent role in it.

> No wonder the prudent man keeps silent,
>   the times are so evil (JB).

But there is no place for such caution in the life of a man like Amos. If there is to be silence, let it not be in the presence of men's evils but in waiting before God for his gidance.

> For God alone my soul waits in silence,
>   for my hope is from him (Ps. 62:5).

Only such silence, as prelude to vigorous speech, befits true faith.

Your religion is too confident of divine protection, Amos concluded. He had been warning against seeking God by running to various shrines—to Bethel, Gilgal, or any other fashionable place of worship (5:4-6). God is not to be found in rituals, he declared. "Seek good, and not evil" if you would know his presence (vs. 14); "hate evil, and love good" if you would have his blessing (vs. 15). There are no special favors for the religious. "The Lord, the God of hosts, will be with you" on no such grounds (vs. 14*b*). "Woe to you who desire the day of the Lord!" (vs. 18) Such pious expectations that God will favor those who keep religious observances but neglect justice in economic affairs are doomed to crushing disappointment. "All the sinners of my people shall die by the sword, who say, 'Evil shall not overtake or meet us' " (9:10). No cultic favors, no covenant preference, will save. There is only one way:

> Hate evil, love good,
> maintain justice at the city gate,

then perhaps God

> will take pity
> on the remnant of Joseph (vs. 15 JB).

God's Call: Our Working World
Colossians 3:23-25

What does work mean to us? A necessary evil? A secular game we play? Something safely separate from spiritual supervision? The New Testament sees it as God's call. The little table of ethical counsels found in this passage is plainly about common daily work. It was advice to slaves! Perhaps the embarrassment of that word is the reason the topic sentence (vs. 22) is omitted from the lection. Its address, "Slaves, obey . . . your earthly masters," need not have troubled us. Paul was simply dealing with the labor system as it existed—a slave economy which an obscure Christian minority was in no position to overturn. That did not change the fact that work was to be seen as a sacred calling. Translated into our parallel terms, it might read: "Employees, always cooperate with your human bosses, not for promotion or praise, but with the pure motive which springs from reverence for God" (vs. 22 CPV). Out of this insight, that work is a call of God, emerge the still valid emphases of the successive verses of this short text.

It says to us that *the true motive for work is to serve God through serving men, his creatures, and to participate in the stewardship of his creation.* "Whatever your work is, put your heart into it as if it were for the Lord and not for men" (vs. 23 JB). What would it mean to take industrial relations, business decisions, the politics of the welfare state, the handling of natural resources, and all our daily dollars-and-cents decisions as things to "put your heart into . . . as if . . . for the Lord and not for men"?

This New Testament insight says, further, that the *real reward of work is inherent in the nature of the work itself and the relation with God it establishes.* "Remember that the Lord will reward you; you will receive what he has kept for his people" (vs. 24a GNMM). "Think of Christ as the master you are working for" (vs. 24b AT). Imagine the difference such an approach to work would make in its meaning to us and in the spirit in which the world's business would be done. A famous British surgeon paints this dark picture of the approach he sees the majority of men actually making:

> What is happening is that nobody works for the sake of getting the thing done. The result of the work is a by-product; the *aim* of the work is to make money to do something else. Doctors practice medicine, not primarily to relieve suffering, but to make a living—the cure of the patient is something that happens on the way.[24]

If that is overdrawn, it still strikes uncomfortably near the truth.

[24] Dorothy L. Sayers, *Creed or Chaos?* (New York: Harcourt, Brace and Company, 1949), p. 43.

The New Testament view of work as under God's call offers a concluding insight: that *failure to perform this elementary obligation brings as great condemnation to those in high places as in low, for all alike work under the scrutiny of him who plays no favorites.* "But the wicked man will be punished for his misdeeds, and naturally no distinction will be made between master and man" (vs. 25 PT). The "misdeeds" need not be gross fraud; they may be simply a failure to recognize the true motives of work. The outcome can still be disastrous.

Some years ago a major oil company, opening an office in China, sought a man to head the new branch. They stipulated four qualifications: he must be under thirty years of age, know the Chinese language, have a good education, possess qualities of leadership. A long seach turned up only one such man, a young missionary on a $600 salary. When he declined their offer of $15,000, the oilmen were amazed. Wasn't that enough? they asked. "Your salary is magnificent," he replied, "but your job is too small. I would rather point China toward Christ at $600 than sell oil at $15,000." Perhaps if more men had thought thus of service above salary China might not have become a great danger spot on the world's map.

What Men Live By
John 6:5-14, 26-27

In a wise book written many years ago—*What Men Live By*—Richard Cabot cited four things: work, play, love, and worship, devoting a section of his book to each. The four are related. We cannot here explore the relation of each to Jesus' saying, "Do not labor for the food which perishes, but for the food which endures to eternal life, which the Son of man will give to you; for on him has God the Father set his seal" (vs. 27), but such an exploration would be a fruitful exercise for the thoughtful Christian.

There are two ways to go wrong in the interpretation of this key saying of our Lord's. One is to apply it only to our workaday life, as if it meant only that; the other is so to "spiritualize" it that it omits the work of the secular world altogether. Let us look briefly at each of these errors.

See what we miss if we are overeager to apply these words about "labor" to the immediacies of the day's work. Jesus was confronted by a crowd so intensely interested in him that they all but took him by storm to be their revolutionary leader (vs. 15); but he saw through them. "You seek me," he said, "not because you saw signs, but because you ate your fill of the loaves" (vs. 26). That is: You don't really want me because of my own ideas and meanings. You have no real fellow-feeling with me. You give no basic loyalty to me, or to the things I stand for. You want only what you think you can get from me.

It is like many a man today, supporting Christianity to keep things stable in a revolutionary time, considering the church important as a bulwark against Communism, favoring faith to bolster the *status quo*. We keep seeking Christ for our own ulterior ends, without really opening ourselves to what *he* wants.

Over against this stand the demands for central loyalty to Christ as Lord of all our wants. "This is the work of God, that you believe in him whom he has sent" (vs. 29). "I am the bread of life; he who comes to me shall not hunger, and he who believes in me shall never thirst" (vs. 35). Until we see the passage as moving at this depth we are not prepared to get from it any true meaning in its more down-to-earth dimension.

Yet that other dimension is also real. It was a Carpenter from Nazareth who said, "Do not labor for the food which perishes, but for the food which endures to eternal life"; and when this Carpenter said "labor" we may be sure he did not rule out what labor means in a toilsome world. He raises sharply the question, What are you working for? Are you only interested in the pay? Or the recognition? One of Graham Greene's characters, a world-weary architect, gives one reply to such questioning:

> What I have built, I have always built for myself, not for the glory of God or the pleasure of a purchaser. Don't talk to me of human beings. Human beings are not my country. . . . I haven't enough feeling left for human beings to do anything for them out of pity.[25]

A very different answer was given by a British prime minister, more than a generation ago, as he struggled with a difficult reform program: "If I did not believe that some day the kingdom of God would spread over this earth, I would give up my job today." We need to see our work related to high ends, so that what we labor for is not some passing thing, but goals that "endure unto eternal life."

It is significant that Jesus' words about "labor" grow out of his feeding of the multitude. John relates the miracle to Passover (vs. 4) and to Jesus as the bread of life (vs. 35), using it as symbolic of the Eucharist. Yet this lofty association does not lift it above a relation to Jesus' comments on "labor." When the priority for all our loyalties is established in Christ, with his goals of personal concern and his unwavering service of the kingdom of God, we become servants of the things that last. Then we come to know "what men live by."

REFORMATION DAY

Foundations of Reformation
Nehemiah 8:1-3, 5-8

The scene laid in this lection depicts the focal point of the reform under Ezra, which gave shape to later Judaism. Some of its factors point to priorities of true religion in the Judeo-Christian tradition and to foundation doctrines of the Protestant Reformation—vitalities we need to recover in each generation.

With the end of the Exile, Nehemiah had come to Jerusalem as governor under a commission from the Persian emperor, and had set about rebuilding the city. As Bernhard W. Anderson reconstructs it, the story can be swiftly told.

> During his first term as governor, Nehemiah worked on the wall of Jerusalem and made some attempt at reform. Since he carried only political authority, how-

[25] Graham Greene, *A Burnt-Out Case* (New York: Viking Press, 1961), pp. 57-58.

ever, he was unable to bring about the sweeping religious reforms needed. So he returned to the Persian capital and persuaded the authorities to send someone with proper religious credentials. Nehemiah returned for his second term as governor in 432 B.C., and about five years later came Ezra, the priest, with the Law as a basis for reform.[26]

Open to emendations in chronology and detail, this reconstruction gives the setting of the events that require our study.

The scene before us reports one of Ezra's first official acts. On a solemn feast day, "the first day of the seventh month" (vs. 2), concerning which the Law prescribes that "you shall have a holy convocation" (Num. 29:1), Ezra read the Law he had brought with him, which his reform stressed as its chief contribution. The identity of this law is a subject of much scholarly speculation, but its stress is clear: separatism from the surrounding peoples, resulting in the enforced dissolution of mixed marriages in the endeavor to preserve Israel as a "pure" people.

This drive toward separateness was not unreasoned. Pressure to break down Israel's distinctive culture and to dilute the faith which has been its perennial contribution to the human treasury had been a threat from the beginning of the life in Canaan, evoking bitter contest with the Baal cults. The Exile had made the faith of a defeated and homeless people even more vulnerable. In the strenuous years that followed the return to their homeland, they were exposed to the cruel efforts of Alexander the Great to draw all cultures and faiths into the amalgam of Hellenism. Israel resisted, convinced that it was a people called to be separate and by its separateness to bear continuing witness to the faith that had been the root of its life. In the scene before us, Ezra indoctrinated this people in the Law that preserved its separateness and its witness as a "kingdom of priests."

His reading began with a renewal of the people's relation to God. "And Ezra blessed the Lord, the great God; and all the people answered, 'Amen, Amen'" (vs. 6). There is a suggestion here of the primacy of grace to law. The force of the Law depended on the relation of the people to the Lord, and this in turn grew out of what he had done in saving, preserving, and guiding them as a people called to be his witnesses. The Ten Commandments, a paradigm of the Law, posit this relation as their base. "I am the Lord your God, who brought you out of the land of Egypt, out of the house of bondage" (Exod. 20:2). So here the Law comes to the people in the context of their relation to the Lord, a relation to which they gave their renewed Yes! So be it! "Amen, Amen." Law rests on a relationship born of grace.

As the Law was read, "the Levites helped the people to understand . . . ; and they gave the sense, so that the people understood the reading" (vss. 7-8). Understanding the law and reflecting upon it became the vital core of later Judaism.

In the light of this lesson and its salient points, there is ground for clearer understanding of some lasting emphases foundational to Protestantism:

The priesthood of all believers is perverted when it is made a negative

[26] Bernhard W. Anderson, *Understanding the Old Testament* (Englewood Cliffs, N.J.: Prentice-Hall, 2nd ed., 1966), p. 448.

assertion that each man is his own priest, needing no other to intercede for him. Our priesthood is that *of a people called to maintain an undiluted witness* for our faith amid alien pressures.

Salvation by grace is not a negation of Law, but a profound insight into the nature of our relation to God. Because of what, despite our unworthiness, he has first done for us, we live in grateful covenant obedience.

Just as the Law—understood and loved through a life of study and reflection—was the heart of Judaism, so the Bible—constantly reappropriated —is the foundation of Christian faith and the core of Protestantism.

What Is "Salvation by Faith"?
Galatians 3:23-26

"Salvation by faith" is not only a popular slogan; it is the integrating doctrine of Protestantism. For all that, many a Protestant finds in it a basic problem to which William Hordern points.

An alcoholic once told me how he had been saved from his alcoholism by his Christian faith. . . . It was only when he had dragged himself and his family to the point where they hit, as he put it, "rock bottom," that he turned to God. And as he analyzed it, he said that what had held him back was his desire to be worthy of God before he came to him. . . . We want to be worthy *before* we come to God so that we can deserve what he will do for us. Our self-love drives us to make our-selves worthy, and so we cling to a doctrine of salvation by works.[27]

We can no more "make ourselves worthy" than the alcoholic can rescue himself by resolutions.

In the passage before us, with its keynote, "that we might be justified by faith" (vs. 24), we have a compressed summary of the doctrine. Because it gathers a much more extended line of thinking into these two swift sentences, it will reward detailed analysis.

It begins with the plight of the religious man whose disciplines have become ends in themselves. "Now before faith came, we were confined under the law, kept under restraint until faith should be revealed" (vs. 23). In the days of Jesus and Paul, Judaism was smothered by minutiae—the oral law which hedged all aspects of daily affairs, of which the prescriptions surrounding the sabbath are notorious examples. Although the reform under Ezra had strong reason to stress the law, the forces of the Macabbean period, with the emerging doctrine that the messianic kingdom would come when Israel kept the whole law perfectly for one day, had given law an almost demonic life of its own. Religion is always under the pressure of our tendency to make ends in themselves of the pieties and disciplines that grow out of our response to God's goodness. We look to the mechanism to save us, forgetting that it is *God* who saves. As John Wesley said of Holy Communion, God *uses* such means of grace but is not *dependent* on any means.

Yet the disciplines of religion serve an important purpose. "The law was our custodian" (Greek, *paidagogos*) "until Christ came" (vs. 24); "our schoolmaster to bring us unto Christ" (KJV). Neither "custodian"

[27] William Hordern, *The Case for a New Reformation Theology* (Philadelphia: The Westminster Press, 1959), p. 154.

nor "schoolmaster" adequately translates *paidagogos*. So greatly has our culture changed that we have no fully equivalent term. *Paidagogos,* literally, is "boy-leader." It represents the man, often a slave, who had charge of a boy, taking him to and from school and looking after other details of his life while he remained a minor. Though we get our word "pedagogue" from this root, this man was not a teacher; yet he played an important role in a boy's life and merited respect. Paul wrote elsewhere, "For though you have countless guides (*paidagogous*) in Christ, you do not have many fathers" (I Cor. 4:15). The religion of Israel—its law that kept this witnessing people distinct, rooting their life in a covenant relation to God—had served as *paidagogos* until Christ came. So the disciplines of the religious life may serve us, bringing us to Christ; they must never be allowed to masquerade as *themselves* the saving power.

For it is God who saves; faith links us to him. In the phrase, "that we might be justified by faith" (vs. 24b), we need to see more clearly what "faith" means. It is not faith-in-general—not the faith that supports the credit system, makes checks possible, gives us security that the oncoming driver will keep to the right, and so forth. In the Greek the definite article is used at almost every occurrence of the word in this passage; it is "the faith"—the faith, as Paul has already explained, that made Abraham believe God's promises out of which the whole covenant relation developed. Because Abraham believed God's promises, God was able to do saving things for him and through him. Similarly, through faith in Christ, God is able to work his intention in us. The law and the prophets once showed us God's will; now we see it more fully through Christ. In Paul's experience, the law had been powerless to conform his life to God's will; for law depends on our will to carry out its demands—a will morally sick with sin. The solution came in Christ, who brought us the assurance of God's acceptance, restoring us to a right relation from God's side. So Christ released in us the power of love in response to God's love, which unifies our scattered powers and enables us to become what in our own right we could not be.

Faith relates us to God. "But now that faith has come, we are no longer under a custodian; for in Christ Jesus you are all sons of God, through faith" (vss. 25-26). Faith identifies us with Christ, makes us so at-one with him that, as Paul says, God adopts (4:5) us into the same relation as his Son. In Christ we are led by the Spirit of God, and "all who are led by the Spirit of God are sons of God" (Rom. 8:14). We have always belonged to our Father, because he created us; but when Christ enables us to respond to him fully, not slavishly or rebelliously, we become his sons in a new way and he is able to do in our lives what he had sought to do but could not until the action of Christ opened our whole being to him. God did not wait to be gracious; his love was unqualified from the beginning. But we could not receive what he offered until faith in Christ opened the way.

Crown Rights of the Redeemer
John 2:13-16

One cry of the Protestant Reformation held that no other can usurp "the crown rights of the Redeemer" in his Church. He must be ever sovereign there. By his sovereign power he reforms the Church. By his life in it he renews its life. These motifs supply the key ideas of this Gospel lesson.

His *sovereign authority* is asserted in this account of the cleansing of the temple. John, stressing interpretation of meaning more than chronological history, placed this story near the beginning of his Gospel. The Synoptics, with presumably greater historical accuracy, place it near the end as the event which triggers the Crucifixion. John places it where he does to fix attention on the one matter of "the crown rights of the Redeemer."

Jesus exercies authority over the most sacred religious institutions at the most holy times. The Passover—supreme sacred festival—"was at hand" (vs. 13), and Jesus came to the temple (vs. 14), holiest of places. Under his scrutiny the temple was seen as defiled. John does not raise the issue of dishonesty as do the Synoptics. In their account, Jesus declares, "You have made it a den of robbers" (Mark 11:17); in John, he says, "You shall not make my Father's house a house of trade" (vs. 16). The focus is not on their immoral behavior but on Christ's authority to cleanse his Father's temple. Amid its defilement he appears with sudden fury reminiscent of Old Testament messianic imagery: "The Lord whom you seek will suddenly come to his temple; the messenger of the covenant in whom you delight. . . . But who can endure the day of his coming, and who can stand when he appears?" (Mal. 3:1-2).

Not only does Jesus have the supreme authority in his Church, authority never to be shared by any other; he has power to give it new life. In the ensuing conversation, not a part of this lection but important to its meaning, he talks about his ability to destroy and rebuild the temple. His meaning, when misconstrued, is explained as referring to his body, a reference the disciples understood only after his death and resurrection (vss. 17-22). Because of John's mode of writing, which builds successive layers of meaning about his images, it is important to look carefully at these words.

Note, for one thing, the intermingling of the words "temple" and "body" and the final flat statement that "he spoke of the temple of his body" (vs. 21). Note, again, the use of the two Greek words for "temple"—*hieros* in vss. 13-16 and *naos* in the remainder of the passage. Elsewhere in the New Testament *naos* is the word used in passages where "the body" is under discussion in a symbolic sense. We are told that Christ reconciles us to God "in one body through the cross" (Eph. 2:16), and in the same context that in Christ as cornerstone "the whole structure is joined together and grows into a holy temple *[naon]* in the Lord." (Eph. 2:21). With all this in mind, read again Jesus' words, "Destroy this temple, and in three days I will raise it up" (vs. 19). There is more than a hint that he is suggesting the Resurrection as bringing back his "body the Church" as the resurrected form of the dying temple.

As a Reformation Day Gospel, then, this urges strongly, if symbolically, three vital truths: (a) Christ exercises supreme authority in the church, to be shared with no other; (b) Christ cleanses the church, which is subject to perpetual reformation; (c) Christ renews the Church, which can find a return to vitality at no other source.

ALL SAINTS' DAY

Enter, the Countless Host
Isaiah 51:11-16

And the ransomed of the Lord shall return,
and come with singing to Zion;
everlasting joy shall be upon their heads;
they shall obtain joy and gladness,
and sorrow and sighing shall flee away (vs. 11).

Read at many a graveside, these words have conveyed the promise of God's comfort in all grief and his restoration after all imprisonment, even that of the tomb. With inclusive sweep "the ransomed of the Lord" takes in the living and the dead. Though we assimilate the words to our Christian understanding of God's response to death and bereavement, such assimilation should come only after we have understood them in their own setting. Even in that setting, they brought the sun of hope shining through the dark clouds of Exile.

Who are "the ransomed of the Lord" in this poem? They are those whom God rescues. A ransom is "something given which 'covers' or cancels an incurred claim." [28] Of a man who is subject to death because his unrestrained ox has gored another, the law says: "If a ransom is laid on him, then he shall give for the redemption of his life whatever is laid upon him" (Exod. 21:30). Here the prophet of the Exile sees God as paying such a ransom for his people Israel, who have incurred the status of captives in Babylon.

I give Egypt as your ransom,
Ethiopia and Seba in exchange for you (Isa. 43:3b).

God of history, holding creation in the hollow of his hand, he cares so much for his exiled people that he considers impressive world powers expendable for their release! "The ransomed of the Lord shall return" from their captivity, and "everlasting joy" will be showered upon them, dispelling all sorrow. The promise may run beyond history, but it is given in and for a crisis in history.

Not only will God restore and comfort his people, he will see them through all tests (vss. 12-15). The greatness of God is supreme over any human foe who can possibly menace his people. He has "stretched out the heavens . . . laid the foundation of the earth . . . stirs up the sea so that its waves roar." What human force can stand against this cosmic Champion? A mere "man who is made like grass"? The picture suggests the fall of Antiochus as recorded in II Maccabees. The conqueror had boasted, "When I reach Jerusalem I will turn it into a mass grave for the Jews." But he had not reckoned on the fragility of his life, which disease and a fall from his chariot could wipe out in an instant.

[28] Article on "Ransom" in *The Interpreter's Dictionary of the Bible*, IV, 12.

He who only a little while before had thought in his superhuman boastfulness to command the waves of the sea, he who imagined he could weigh mountain peaks in a balance, found himself flat on the ground, borne in a litter, a visible demonstration to all of the power of God (II Macc. 9:8 JB).

With like contrast between the boasted power of man and the real power of God, the prophet declares that God's ransomed people are held by one who can fulfill his promises in the face of all hazards.

As if that were not enough, the relation is pushed back to the dawn of time. From the beginning of creation God has intended his relation to his people (vs. 16). He has shown them his will, "I have put my words in your mouth"; controlled their history, "hid you in the shadow of my hand"; and made their creation and call part of the same act,

> stretching out the heavens
> and laying the foundation of the earth,
> and saying to Zion, "You are my people."

With the call has come responsibility—"you shall be to me a kingdom of priests and a holy nation" (Exod. 19:6).

These, then, are "the ransomed of the Lord," elsewhere called "the people of the saints of the Most High" (Dan. 7:27). (a) They are the company of God's people, always spoken of in the Bible in the plural. Far from achieving greatness by any act of theirs, they are overwhelmed that God has surprisingly *chosen* them. (b) They are called to no special honors or privileges, but to a life of witness. (c) They are ransomed from all that enslaves, not by their struggle but by God's goodness, in consequence of which they face all threats, confident that whatever may befall them is as nothing in the face of the power of the God who loves them.

> From earth's wide bounds, from ocean's farthest coast,
> Through gates of pearl streams in the countless host,
> Singing to Father, Son, and Holy Ghost,
> Alleluia, Alleluia! [29]

Who Unfeignedly Love Thee
Revelation 7:9-17

A classic collect for All Saints' Day gathers dominant themes from this Epistle for the day and leads us into a consideration of the doctrine of the Communion of the Saints.

O Almighty God, who hast knit together thine elect in one communion and fellowship, in the mystical body of thy Son Christ our Lord; Grant us grace so to follow thy blessed Saints in all virtuous and godly living, that we may come to those unspeakable joys which thou hast prepared for those who unfeignedly love thee; through the same thy son Jesus Christ our Lord. *Amen.*[30]

[29] William W. How, hymn, "For All the Saints."
[30] Collect for All Saints' Day, *Book of Common Prayer*, p. 256.

We celebrate solidarity with God's people from all nations and all the ages, gathered in one body to whom is given victory over martyrdoms and testings, in God's final triumph.

It is an *inclusive company*. In the vivid symbolism of Revelation, four angels hold back the apocalyptic winds of more than earthly storms (vs. 1). God's people are not to be swept away by such hurricanes. There are a symbolic 144,000—twelve thousand from each of twelve tribes of Israel. But beyond this there is "a great multitude which no man could number, from every nation, from all tribes and peoples and tongues, standing before the throne and before the Lamb" (vs. 9). Thus the vision anticipates a successful mission to all the world, which gathers men from all lands, tongues, and conditions in an ecumenical fellowship. The drive to unity is not an innovation of modern times, but a deeply rooted reality. To move toward making our unity visible and effective is to be faithful to the basic Christian call.

It is a *victorious company*. The symbolic language which speaks of "palm branches in their hands" (vs. 9) is drawn from biblical idiom representing praise to God for victory and deliverance given (Lev. 23:40; John 12:13). Celebrating victory, they are conscious that they have not won it by their own efforts. "Salvation," they cry, "belongs to our God who sits upon the throne, and to the Lamb!" (vs. 10). Like the people of God depicted in today's Old Testemant lesson, this is a "ransomed" host. They sing a paean of victory to God, to whom belong "power and might . . . for ever and ever!" (vs. 12).

It is a *tested company*. "These are they who have come out of the great tribulation" (vs. 14). Elsewhere the same words are used to describe the bloody persecution under Nero. These, then, are a company tested by martyrdom. Yet the word "tribulation" is not confined to this one meaning.

The verb that lies behind the noun "tribulation" means "to make into gruel." What is pictured is a process of grinding between an unyielding bottom and an oppressing top. When applied to the Christian life, this means that the Christian stands crushed between the unyielding demands of his totalitarian faith and the oppressive challenge of the world for compromise.

A Christian can therefore speak of life itself as "the great tribulation," using the specific experience of "persecution" as a symbol of it.[31]

These who have met the test victoriously "have washed their robes and made them white in the blood of the Lamb" (vs. 14), which is to say, they have found in Jesus' victory through the Cross the key to their own victory, and have come to share the triumph with him after first sharing his sufferings.

It is a *company through whom God acts*. In the remaining lines of the poetic vision, woven from Old Testament allusions, four assertions are made about this company of the faithful to which we are called: (a) God has chosen them for service; they "serve him day and night" (vs. 15b). (b) God is their defender, not from martyrdom but from ultimate loss; "he who sits upon the throne will shelter them" (vs. 15c). (c) God is their guide; "he will guide them to springs of living water" (vs. 17b). (d) God will give

[31] D. T. Niles, *As Seeing the Invisible*, p. 139.

them joy on the far side of sorrow; he "will wipe away every tear from their eyes" (vs. 17c).

Men of the New Age
Matthew 5:1-12

As Moses brought the law from Sinai, so in the structure of Matthew's Gospel, Jesus' Sermon on the Mount gives the new law for the new Age of God's kingdom or reign. The Beatitudes etch the portrait of the new man for the new Age. On All Saints' Day we turn our attention to this commanding picture as we celebrate the company of those who by God's grace have been brought together from all peoples and times into a kingdom citizenry.

E. Stanley Jones once proposed a way of thinking through the Beatitudes under the Hegelian scheme—thesis, antithesis, synthesis. Strict adherence to this device may force the Beatitudes into an arbitrary mold not intended in their text; yet the pattern does help to disclose relationships among these sayings as a unified sketch of men of the new Age.

"The poor in spirit" (vs. 3) are deeply aware of their own insufficiency; utterly *dependent* on God, they are received into his kingdom, live under his reign. "Those who mourn" (vs. 4) care deeply about the world's plight, becoming a community of the concerned. Sharing God's concern, they *share his strength,* his comfort. "The meek" (vs. 5) are free from self-will, combining the *humility* of "the poor in spirit" with the *concern* of "those who mourn." Meekness is not to be confused with weakness, as one sees in such usage as "Now the man Moses was very meek, more than all men" (Num. 12:3). Few men in history have been as strong as Moses in leadership, conviction, courage, and mighty action in the service of God and the people. His meekness was his freedom from self-will as he gave himself to obedience to the will of God. Charles Rann Kennedy puts the sense of this first triad into an exclamation by the centurion in command at Jesus' crucifixion, as the meaning of the event dawns upon him: "The earth is his, the earth is theirs, and they made it. The meek, the terrible meek, the fierce agonizing meek, are about to enter into their inheritance." [32]

Beginning the second triad, "those who hunger and thirst for righteousness" (vs. 6) are unwilling to settle for any lesser goal. Hunger and thirst drive a man irresistibly; when their goal is righteousness they will be satisfied—will attain their objective and find in it satisfaction which worldly objectives cannot give. All the more necessary, then, that they be among "the merciful" (vs. 7), for the righteous can be fierce in their judgments on those who have not achieved their level of goodness. Since no man is righteous enough to stand on his own merit before God, mercy is essential, that we may "obtain mercy." "The pure in heart" (vs. 8) combine the single-minded drive to righteousness with "the quality of mercy." In Kierkegaard's phrase, "to be pure in heart is to will one thing"—to be single-

---

[32] *The Terrible Meek,* a one-act play by Charles Rann Kennedy (New York: Harper, 1912), p. 39. Copyright 1912 and 1933 by Charles Rann Kennedy. Used by permission of Samuel French, Inc.

minded toward goodness and merciful in the realization of how far short we have fallen.

"The peacemakers" (vs. 9) have no small task. They do not passively wish for peace; they help to create it. Legal or other external arrangements are not sufficient for so great an undertaking; it requires a new atmosphere of human relations. Such an atmosphere grows out of the qualities of life envisioned in the first two triads, combining them all. But peacemakers may expect to be among "those who are persecuted for righteousness' sake" (vs. 10). To join that high company is to be one with prophets (vs. 12) of all ages and to take one's place in the kingdom of God (vs. 10).

Who is sufficient for these things? They are beyond us, but not beyond the God who works in us. If we could achieve the new Age in our own right, it would be our kingdom, not God's. The new law of the new Age, too difficult for us, was not too difficult for Jesus. He both *announced* and *embodied* it. Yet, amid all our failures, he accepts us—and sets us once more at the task of conforming our lives to this new Way. To those who keep close to him he gives power to grow more and more into the new style of life, new men for the new Age.

WORLD ORDER SUNDAY

To Wake From Folly: Micah 4:1-5

Bertrand Russell wrote a startling sentence summary of world history: "Since Adam and Eve ate the apple, man has never refrained from any folly of which he was capable. The End." [33] We are now capable of the folly of extinction of life on earth. Short of ultimate suicide, we can make our wars dreadful beyond the dreams of previous war-weary generations. Men once dismissed the prophetic vision of a peaceful, disarmed world as idealistic folly; now it is a call to wake from folly.

We must needs read it with the eyes of faith. Ancient geology is reflected in its conception of Mount Zion lifted up as the supreme pinnacle of a leveled earth (vs. 1), and ancient messianism speaks through its view of Israel as the leader of nations (vs. 2). Yet timeless wisdom informs its call to a peaceful world based on four requirements.

First there must be law and justice based on the decisions of a judge supreme above the nations (vs. 3a). Unlimited national sovereignty, in which each nation is final judge of its own cause, breeds international anarchy. The prophet declares that only when nations bow to a Judge who can "decide for strong nations" can there be peace. We now know that this requires international machinery, to which the United Nations is an important first step. God works through such human agencies. Biblically understood, events on history's stage are his acts.

Second, armaments must be exchanged for national development— "Swords into plowshares, . . . spears into pruning hooks" (vs. 3b). World hunger is the archenemy of world peace. In the eight years ending in 1966, violence of international importance broke out 164 times. It occurred *within*

[33] Norman Cousins, *In Place of Folly* (New York: Harper, 1961), p. 11.

82 nations, but only 15 times *between* nations. Using the World Bank yardstick—$100 per capita annual income defining very poor nations, $100 to $300 poor nations, and $300 to $750 middle income nations—these outbreaks disrupted 87 percent of the very poor, 69 percent of the poor, and 48 percent of the middle income nations. Among 27 nations with incomes bove $750 per capita, only one case of such violence occurred.[34] Such figures would seem to indicate that colossal expenditures on armaments and driblets for development produce not security, but its reverse. Until we bow to the prophet's vision, peace and order remain distant dreams.

Third, there must be action for common welfare—"every man under his vine and under his fig tree"—if there is to be peace in the world (vs. 4). Nearly half of the world's people eke out an existence on less than $100 per capita per year, two-thirds have less than $300, and only slightly more than one-tenth have as much as $1000 yearly income per capita. In such a world there can be no secure peace, but such abject conditions need not continue. We now have at our disposal, for the first time in history, the means of providing decent comfort for all. The World Council of Churches has called the nations to devote one percent of their gross national product to the aid of the developing nations.

Fourth, there must be a beginning. Many declare that this idealistic dream is wildly impossible; the nations will not implement it. Just such a response on the part of some early scribe, copying this document, probably caused the insertion of the lines,

> For all the peoples walk
> each in the name of its god,
> but we will walk in the name of the Lord our God
> for ever and ever (vs. 5),

for with these lines there is an otherwise mysterious change in style, meter, and point of view. Yet this marginal notation is not completely cynical. It suggests that although others stick to their own national gods and all the divisiveness they represent, "we" at least can be faithful to the larger vision. "We will walk in the name of the Lord over God for ever and ever."

Someone must make a start. Those who see the vision are placed under its mandate. A Quaker, challenged in his peace witness by the assertion that we can disarm only when other men are willing to do so, replied: "Thee wishes to be the *last* man on earth to do the will of God. I am called to be one of the *first*." Let others do as they must,

> but, we will walk in the name of the Lord our God
> for ever and ever.

Our Wars and Our Wants
James 4:1-12

It would outrageously oversimplify the facts to argue from this passage that wars root only in the spirit. The writer intended no treatise on modern

---

[34] Figures from Robert S. McNamara, *The Essence of Security* (New York: Harper, 1968), p. 146.

great power struggles, and his question, "What causes wars?" (vs. 1), was not designed to open a political science treatise. Yet there is worldy-wise shrewdness in this interpretation of human conflict, relevant to all times and to many levels of the human struggle. Although it throws light on family feuds and party strife, it points, too, to how we prepare the volatile spiritual atmosphere which minor events can explosively ignite.

Frustrated wants prepare the way for wars: "You desire and do not have; so you kill. And you covet and cannot obtain; so you fight and wage war" (vs. 2). Your inner conflicts make you more ready to strike out at others: "Your passions that are at war in your members" (vs. 1), "your lusts which are in conflict in your bodies" (AB), "the desires fighting inside your own selves" (JB) create the anarchy of desire which has no law but itself. We want at one time what conflicts with what seems good at another. Worse still, we entertain conflicting desires at the same time, seeking order without justice, success without discipline, love without loyalty, pleasure without principle, wealth without work. It does not unduly extend this principle to relate it to the conflicting aspirations which drive on to conflict among classes or countries.

Bo Reicke translates vs. 2, "You kill and are fanatics but are not able to obtain [anything]," reading *zeloute* (RSV: "covet") as "are fanatics," a rendering of the verb meaning to desire strongly (as in I Cor. 14:39) or to covet jealously, which plays up its root relation to such fanatical desire as produced the Zealot party with its explosive super-patriotism. Reicke comments:

To the words "You kill" the author adds "and you are fanatics." Undoubtedly there is a direct connection between these statements. The sentence may be interpreted as follows: "You drive people to death by being zealots." . . . No military enterprise is meant, but the strong words suggest that the readers are engaged in certain hostile activities, such as riots, sabotage, and the like. Through their fanatic and violent self-assertion the readers may be thought of as driving their Christian brothers to death, since the authorities react to this behavior by suppression and persecutions.[35]

There is a modern analogy in the frantic superpatriotism that equates "what is right for our country" with "what is right for the world" and supposes that any attempt to see the viewpoint of other peoples is tantamount to treason. In our explosive and interrelated age such a mental climate collects a lethal toll.

To this secular problem the Epistle offers a religious answer: You are in conflict because you do not rightly pray! (vss. 2-3). This will be dismissed out of hand by many as too pietistic to be practical, yet the matter deserves a hearing. Prayer is not, as popular religion insists, a way of "*getting* what you want"; it is a way of opening yourself to *correcting* what you want! (vs. 3). Unless it is that, prayer leaves us just where we have been, "men of double mind" (vs. 8), wanting both peace and the self-aggrandizement that makes for conflict, in love with the world (vs. 4) and at enmity with God.

[35] Reicke, *The Epistles of James, Peter, and Jude*, pp. 45-46.

There is a love of the world that is concerned and self-giving (John 3:16); and there is a love of the world that covets to possess it (I John 2:15-17). Loving in this latter sense, we are "unfaithful creatures" (vs. 4); or, reading the Greek more literally, "you adulterers" (AB); or, "you are as unfaithful as adulterous wives" (JB), recalling the Old Testament conception of Israel's idolatry as adultery against Yahweh (Hos. 1:2). From such misplaced love we can only be called to repentance that puts our desires in some proper order of value. All the way from primitive levels where a tribal pictograph for "war" is literally the phrase "we want more cows," to the commercially motivated foreign adventures of modern powers, grasping desires breed strife. Hence the reordering of desire is prerequisite to peace. To correct desire under God's scrutiny is a primary purpose of prayer.

A part of the addictive psychology of conflict is its pleasant over-simplification of issues. Wrong is defined by what our enemy stands for, right by what we espouse. He is entirely wrong; we are perfectly right. This strong passage protests the folly of such thinking: "Whoever defames or judges his brother, defames or judges the law" (vs. 11 AB). We judge others by some standard, in this case "the law." But the law itself (Lev. 19:16; Matt. 7:1-5) strongly condemns judging. So we mock the law in the name of the law. How easy to point out the wrong in others! How hard to see it in ourselves! New eyes that stay at home to examine ourselves are a prime need of the present hour.

The Christian's Style Amid Conflict
Matthew 5:43-48

In the tinderbox of bitterness under Roman occupation, Jesus described a style of life for those who must live amid conflict. Sherman E. Johnson rightly reminds us that his command to love our enemies was addressed primarily to persons and small groups.

Such love is the supreme test of the religious man's character. Jesus never deals with the responsibilities of free citizens in a democratic state. His teaching of course has political implications, but how it should be applied is one of the most difficult problems of Christian social ethics.[36]

Without presuming to arbitrate a problem so complex, on which thoughtful Christians sincerely differ, we must nevertheless face the implications of this Gospel concerning a Christian style of life in an age of conflict.

The Christian style makes the widest good of all men a primary personal concern. Even before Jesus, the Old Testament enjoined love of neighbor (Lev. 19:16-18). Though this was sometimes confined to "the sons of your own people," it could also include "the stranger who sojourns with you," who "shall be to you as the native among you, and you shall love him as yourself" (Lev. 19:34). Before Jesus' time, however, the bitterness engendered by the persecutions of the Maccabean era and the Roman occupation had made love of Gentiles seem hardly possible to the popular mind. The law

---

[36] Sherman E. Johnson, *Interpreter's Bible,* VII, 303.

never explicitly commanded "hate your enemy" (vs. 43), but the human tendency to justify hatred by equating the enemy with all that defies God had woven itself into popular piety:

> Do I not hate them that hate thee, O Lord?
> And do I not loathe them that rise up against thee?
> I hate them with perfect hatred;
> I count them my enemies (Ps. 139:21-22).

Over against this attitude, still evident in our spiritual climate, Jesus set neighbor love with the wide definition given it by the parable of the Good Samaritan (Luke 10:29-37). Going farther, he included a call to love our enemies and pray for those who persecute us (vs. 44). Though he is not writing a political science formula, it is scarcely conceivable that he would reverse or modify his counsel amid our modern international enmities.

The Christian style sets our attitude toward our enemies in the context of God's dealings with us. Unless we love our enemies we repudiate the filial relation to our Father in heaven (vs. 45). He heaps nature's blessings on all alike, asking no questions as to who is worthy. Who *can* be worthy of such goodness as his? In conflict our relation to God is at stake; for it is conflict that tests the law's command: "You shall be holy; for I the Lord your God am holy" (Lev. 19:2) or Jesus' renewal of it: "You, therefore, must be perfect, as your heavenly Father is perfect" (vs. 48). No call to impossible flawlessness, this does demand such uprightness toward others as God shows in his dealings with us. It is conflict which reveals our level of seriousness in our repsonse to him, for if we are only upright and patient when there is no great provocation our uprightness is pure illusion.

The Christian style puts the whole area of conflict in the context of our relation to Christ. If the standard seems impossibly high, it has nevertheless been met in full, as Jesus prayed for those who nailed him to the cross. If we come to him only as guilty in the light of such a standard, he fully accepts us. If we grow complacent in his acceptance, he keeps sending us back again to struggle with the unsoftened demand, "be perfect, as your heavenly Father is perfect." "Perfect," here, is the word *teleioi* translated "mature" in other passages where we are called to "mature [*teleion*] manhood, to the measure of the stature of the fullness of Christ" (Eph. 4:13). Can a Christian life style amid conflict settle for less than the goal of full maturity as we see it in Christ?

COMMITMENT DAY

And Men Decay: Isaiah 5:11-12, 20-24

Oliver Goldsmith might almost have been echoing Isaiah's judgment of his fellow countrymen, as he sang,

> Ill fares the land, to hastening ills a prey
> Where wealth accumulates, and men decay . . .

Isaiah looked out on reckless and acquistive prosperity, as men added "house to house" and "field to field" (vs. 8). Like all such times, it produced softness, indulgence, and escape into heavy drinking.

Other passages from the period reflect the sorry condition:

> And here is mirth and merry-making!—
> men slaughtering sheep and slaying kine,
> men eating flesh and drinking wine,
> feasting because "tomorrow we may die!" (22:13 MT)

Drink was undermining the leadership of those who should have set the spiritual tone, dulling the insight of what should have been the good minds:

> Yet here too men are reeling drunk
> and staggering in their cups;
> prophets and priests are reeling drunk,
> fuddled with liquor (28:7 MT).

In the same period, Amos denounced the women of prosperous Samaria, addressing them as

> you who defraud the poor and are hard on the needy,
> who tell your husbands, 'Let us have wine to drink!' (4:1 MT),

And Micah leveled at those who resisted his warnings the jibe:

> The prophet for such folk
> would be some empty fellow and a liar,
> who promised to prophesy of wine and spirits! (2:11 MT)

Isaiah's denunciations seen in this lection are no incidental emotional outburst. Indicative of the malaise of the time, they may hold a mirror to periods like our own, when again "wealth accumulates and men decay."

Like us, these people were proud that they knew how to make their liquors a part of "gracious living." Their drinking was accompanied by music and feasting (vss. 11-12). This did not guard them against the ageless symptoms of the problem drinker. They were drinking in the morning:

> Woe to those who rise early in the morning,
> that they may run after strong drink (vs. 11a),

and they stayed at it through the day, until drink "inflamed" them.

Not surprisingly, drinking contributed to a blurred incapacity to understand the meaning of their time. "They do not regard the deeds of the Lord" (vs. 12b)—minds preoccupied with luxury and befuddled by drink missed what God was doing in the events of the period. So central was this dulling of sensibility that Isaiah alluded to it in his account of his call.

> Then he said, "Go and tell this people:
> 'Listen and listen—but never understand!
> Look and look—but never see!'
> Make the mind of this people dull,
> make their ears heavy and close up their eyes,

> lest their eyes see, lest their ears hear,
>   lest their minds understand,
> and their health be restored" (6:9-10 MT).

Not that God *intended* his people to be insensitive! But since it was part of the pattern of their life to become dull and unresponsive, he could foresee it and take it into his plan. The prophet was not to be dismayed by it. Characteristic as this blindness is of all sin, Isaiah reflected on the way in which drink compounds it.

Drink was also contributing to an insane inversion of values.

> Woe to those who call evil good
>   and good evil,
> who put darkness for light
>   and light for darkness (vs. 20).

The problem is not limited to the drinking table. Jesus saw such a reversal of values in the Pharisees, no roistering drinkers (Matt. 12:22-32). Once a man has so stood his values on their heads, there is no hope of forgiveness, for the inversion has made repentance impossible. It can happen to any of us, but excess of drink contibutes to such confusion as anyone knows who has worked with an alcoholic who flees to his worst enemy as if it were his only friend. In the ordinary drinker it shows itself as a few drinks lift the level of self-assured complacency just at the points where he is most dangerously fumbling (vs. 21). In a society so conditioned, prowess at drinking becomes a cheap counterfeit measure of virility (vs. 22). The industry which so victimizes its customers finally corrupts the social and political fabric (vs. 23). It all drives on to the ruin of those who "put an enemy in their mouths to steal away their brains" [37] and end by rejecting God's law and despising his word (vs. 24).

Peril to Abundant Life
I Corinthians 3:16-17

In its Social Creed, The United Methodist Church declares: "The use of beverage alcohol imperils the abundant life to which Christ calls us." Believing this to be true, the church has a special obligation to make its witness for a life of abstinence. This Epistle for Commitment Day relates to such a call, yet it must be used with discriminating understanding.

Paul has been dealing with the tests by which the worth of various contributions to the life of the church at Corinth can be assessed. In these two verses he continues that discussion, reminding his readers of the serious responsibility of those who are building nothing less than God's temple. In earlier apocalyptic writings the figure of persons as the temple had been used to say that God will build his own temple and dwell in it. Christian writers called their readers "like living stones [to] be . . . built into a spiritual house" (I Pet. 2:5). Paul is using the figure thus, not likening individual bodies to the temple of God, but seeing the corporate body, the church, as the new temple.

[37] William Shakespeare, *Othello,* Act II, Scene 3.

Yet the physical body is not ruled out. For, returning to the figure, Paul writes, "Do you not know that your body is a temple of the Holy Spirit within you, which you have from God?" (6:19). The individual natural body is thus included, though the churchly body is never absent from the figure. In this lection, the temple in which God dwells is the Christian community. In similar fashion the Letter to the Ephesians speaks of the community, the church, as "fellow citizens with the saints and members of the household of God," a temple "built upon the foundation of the apostles and prophets, Christ Jesus himself being the chief cornerstone," which is made "for a dwelling place of God in the Spirit" (Eph. 2:19-22).

To use the metaphor, "you are God's temple," too directly as designating the physical body, which must not be defiled by drink, is to miss its depth. Yet Paul is certain that this spiritual temple, the church, is directly involved in what men do with their bodies. He is deeply concerned about the incest and sexual immoralities reported among the Corinthian congregation (5:1; 6:12-20). "Every other sin which a man commits is outside the body," he writes, "but the immoral man sins against his own body. Do you not know that your body is a temple of the Holy Spirit within you, which you have from God? . . . So glorify God in your body" (6:18b-20).

In this double context we must read this lection. As Christians we have been claimed as God's own, our fellowship a place of his dwelling. What we do within this body of believers—including what we do with our physical bodies—may destroy the temple in which God dwells. Bodily sins may corrupt our witness, disrupt our fellowship, make us insensitive to his presence. For a Christian thus to misuse his body is a more grievous wrong than for a pagan to do so. For the sake of the fellowship, of our sensitivity to God's leading, and our witness, we need to adopt high standards in bodily, as well as in more specifically "spiritual," matters. One area of concern is the drink that disrupts much of our modern life and that complicates every other social problem. In this belief, United Methodists declare: "We believe that the Christian principle of love for God and neighbor calls us to abstain from the use of alcoholic beverages and to minister to those victimized by their use . . . . The Church must become a healing and redemptive fellowship for those who suffer because of beverage alcohol." [38]

Steady Hands on a Shaken World
Luke 21:23-26

Between Jesus' apocalyptic view of his world and what our eyes tell us about our own, the parallel is too striking to be overlooked. Men around him were so complacently proud of the material successes of their civilization that, even when they visited the temple, his disciples, distracted from the altar and the Spirit, pointed with pride at the great stones, the architectural beauty, the engineering achievement (vs. 5). Hear Jesus reply: "The days will come when there shall not be left one stone upon another" (vs. 6). In sentences like the rumble of cannonade he then spoke of impending catas-

[38] *The Book of Discipline of The United Methodist Church* (Nashville: The Methodist Publishing House, 1968), p. 57.

trophe—nation arrayed against nation (vs. 10), famine and pestilence exacting their toll (vs. 11), Jerusalem despoiled by surrounding armies (vs. 20), distress widespread in the earth (vs. 23), strong men fainting with fear and foreboding (vs. 26). As if to give the scene full cosmic inclusiveness, he exclaimed: "The powers of the heavens will be shaken" (vs. 26b).

The idiom belongs to the apocalyptic literature of his day. Yet underlying any literary device used by a mind so clear and a spirit so true, there must have been a sense of authentic reality. Speaking of a real crisis in his time, he pointed to a perpetual crisis inherent in all times.

Alert eyes must see how aptly he has portrayed our modern plight. A generation that has seen every civilized standard violated gropes in darkness with no universally recognized standards to light the way. Fear stalks, now as then (vs. 26), haunting the trained and penetrating minds, as on the horizon looms the ever-present possibility of nuclear disaster.

Jesus turned from all this, to focus on the purposeful response to which it called. Completing his apocalyptic picture, he enjoined: "Take heed to yourselves lest your hearts be weighed down with dissipation and drunkenness and cares of this life, and that day come upon you suddenly like a snare" (vs. 34). His practical mind would not rest in fatalism. Catastrophe called to men to live up to the role of directive intelligence. Steady hands, always needed, are never in such imperative demand as when all things are shaken (vs. 26).

Men may dissipate in varied ways, as by overwork or lust for wealth. "The cares of this life" are broadly inclusive. A man may so lose himself in a maze of activities and organizations directed to good ends that he ceases to be a thoughtful person, a soul listening for God, and becomes a bundle of machine-like responses to the push and pull of crowded appointments. Including all this, Jesus was sharply specific about one thing—drunkenness: "lest your hearts be weighed down with . . . drunkenness . . . , and that day come upon you suddenly like a snare." Among varied evils broadly named, one, intensely particular, could rob men of steady hands when their world was shaken.

"I have seen liquor make a lot of good men bad," Frank E. Gannett reported, "but I never saw it make a bad man any better." The remark is conservative. He might have added: "I have seen liquor make strong men weak; I never saw it make a weak man strong. I have seen it make successful men failures, brilliant men silly, dependable men irresponsible; I never saw it make a failing man successful, a stupid man wise, or an irresponsible man trustworthy." In a time when society is shaken to the core and we may be facing an ultimate crisis of civilization, an indulgence which produces unsteady men is a luxury too costly to contemplate. Frightful in its direct human toll, its most condemning blight may well be in the indirect result. For there is not a single social problem now menacing our common life which is not vastly complicated when alcohol is introduced into its human equation.

Contemplating his shaken world, Jesus said: "This will be a time for you to bear testimony" (vs. 13). The testimony of sobriety is a part of Christian witness in such a time as ours. Abstinence from alcoholic beverages is of no light importance to individual welfare, but *witness* by abstinence may be a matter of life and death to others.

Jesus did not forget to say that in the worst times God will act. "Now when these things begin to take place, look up and raise your heads, because your redemption is drawing near" (vs. 28). Though our merely human efforts are no assurance of a better day,

there is something God has done that can change the climate of human history. But it is for those who have learned despair. They and they alone know where hope is. "The day of the Lord is darkness and not light" (Amos 5:18). But it is still the day of the Lord, with a cross outlined against the sky.[39]

THANKSGIVING DAY

Dynamic Compact Remembered
Deuteronomy 8:7-18

Our modern self-sufficiency makes Thanksgiving imperative—and diffi-cult. Thanksgiving confronts this mood with dynamic memories. We remem-ber the first Thanksgiving in America, a feast in the wake of famine, celebrating a conviction that against the hazards of their frontier the Pilgrims were not alone. We remember Thanksgivings amid war, depression, and national mourning for the assassination of a young President, when the mood of festival was not easy but the conviction it engendered exerted a redeeming influence.

Such memories awaken motives. They call us back to faith from our brittle aloneness against life. They restore stamina for the long struggle. They cleanse the springs of mutual concern. Of such dynamics Deuteronomy declares:

You must remember the Eternal your God, for it is he who gives you the power of gaining wealth, that he may ratify the compact which he swore to your fathers, as it is today (vs. 18 MT).

Here is a reminder of what we easily forget—that the source of our wealth is quite beyond ourselves. "Why should I give thanks?" a man asks. "Well, you have your home and a rather comfortable life," a friend answers. "Thanks for that? I work and earn what I have." "Where did you get the strength to do it?" The conversation progresses as if it all were new, but its mode of thinking is as old as Deuteronomy:

Beware lest you say in your heart, "My power and the might of my hand have gotten me this wealth." You shall remember the Lord your God, for it is he who gives you power to get wealth (vss. 17-18).

Our satisfaction in the good things of the world can eclipse our aware-ness of their source. Our "tin can culture" quickly loses touch with the roots of our comforts in the good earth. Earlier generations sang,

[39] Paul Scherer, *Interpreter's Bible*, VIII, 369.

He sends the sunshine and the rain,
He sends the harvest's golden grain—

but we see no connection between the elements and any personal Giver. "*It* rains," we say. "*It* rained yesterday." "*It* may rain tomorrow." We lose God among impersonal sources. Then we lose ourselves among impersonal commodities.

We have become what P. A. Sorokin called a "sensate culture." In his creative social thought Sorokin traced the rise of a culture from its dynamic origin in a common idea or faith, to a flowering in a proliferation of artifacts, thence to an increasing preoccupation with the sensate enjoyment of the comforts thus produced, and from there to an ultimate crisis. For at that point, Sorokin believed, the society either rediscovers a dimension of depth and rootage in its ideational source, or it decays and passes off the scene. Which is not unlike the summons of Deuteronomy:

Take heed lest you forget the Lord your God . . . when you have eaten and are full, and have built goodly houses and live in them, and when your herds and flocks multiply, and your silver and gold is multiplied, and all that you have is multiplied (vss. 11-13).

From such a twilight of sensate hypnosis Thanksgiving recalls us to remember the dynamic compact that gave creativity to our common life. Israel found her unity, identity, and reason for living in her self-knowledge in terms of the covenant; and in our own common life the Mayflower Compact and the faith commitmets of the founding fathers not only proved decisive in their time but have provided a frame for our self-understanding as a people. Like Israel, perceiving the covenant relation to God as a call to ministry through which all nations would bless themselves, we have traditionally seen our blessings as a stewardship which prompted the invitation,

Give me your tired, your poor,
Your huddled masses yearning to breathe free,
The wretched refuse of your teeming shore,
Send these, the homeless, tempest-tossed, to me . . .[40]

But that was before we became an affluent "sensate culture." In our new preoccupation, we restrict immigration, turn from sponsoring revolutionary aspirations to their suppression, and in the presence of threatened world famine spend 10 percent of gross national product to keep more men under arms than are supported by all the nations of Western Europe combined. Can we rediscover the sense of covenant purpose that gave dynamic meaning to the creative youth of our society?

Remember the Eternal your God, . . . that he may ratify the compact which he swore to your Fathers (vs. 18 MT).

[40] Emma Lazarus, "The New Colossus," inscription for the Statue of Liberty.

Gratitude-Generosity Complex
II Corinthians 9:6-12

One theme flows through this passage. As Paul put it, "So that you will have abundant means of every kind for all generosity which gives proof of our gratitude towards God" (vs. 11 KT). Or as we might encapsulate it: Generosity flows out of gratitude—and increases it.

Discussing the fund he is raising for the support of needy Christians in Jerusalem, Paul has come to the religious motivation for such giving. God, he says, is the source of all our blessings. He gives the seed and the bread made from it. He also gives the motive for sharing and the satisfaction that sharing brings.

He who gives the seed to the sower and turns that seed into bread to eat will give you the seed of generosity to sow and, for harvest, the satisfying bread of good deeds done (vs. 10 PT).

Every blessing, material or spiritual, is God's gift.

The matter does not end there. God gives according to law-abiding principle. Perhaps quoting a proverbial maxim of the time, Paul continues: "Remember the saying—'Scanty sowing, scanty harvest; plentiful sowing, plentiful harvest'" (vs. 6 TCNT). "Do not forget: thin sowing means thin reaping; the more you sow, the more you reap" (JB). The rule reigns in nature. Paul declares it the law of our dealings with God and our brother. What he carefully avoids saying is that there is a *quid pro quo* under which to give much is to get much. Such a promise, overt or implied, as a motive of stewardship, blatantly misrepresents him. What he does say is plain: God will give you enough to let you be generous—"He will always make you rich enough to be generous at all times" (vs. 11 GNMM). One can be generous on very little.

The law of harvest is as much a matter of open heart as of open hand. The slogan, "Give till it hurts!" has no kinship with Paul's counsel. For some of us, *any* giving hurts. Where the pain threshold in giving so varies, that rule is worse than useless. Paul calls us to give "not with regret or out of a sense of duty" (vs. 7 GNMM)—not shamed into it by social pressure, not trapped into a grudging gift from which there seems no decent escape. Rather we are reminded that "God loves a cheerful giver" (vs. 7). God is able to meet all our needs so fully that we have enough to share with others (vs. 8). There is no claim that he will make us rich; wealth is the margin of resources over expectations, and he who simplifies wants may be wealthy on little. St. Francis, with only a crust to eat at the end of a toilsome day, shared it with a brother monk, looking out on a beautiful landscape, and crying again and again, "O my brother! we are not worthy of such vast treasure." The Little Brother of the Poor had abundance to share, his open hand moved by his open heart.

Paul illustrates his point by recourse to a psalm describing the man who "fears the Lord" and "greatly delights in his commandments" (Ps. 112:1). His blessings, being many, are climaxed by the durability of his *goodness*.

He has distributed freely, he has given to the poor;
his righteousness endures for ever (Ps. 112:9, cf. vs. 3).

The Hebrew here translated "righteousness" has no adequate English equivalent, for it embraces such meanings as religion, piety, goodness, benevolence.
God gives such durable completeness of life to those who sow abundantly.

Real sowing springs from gratitude—and increases it. To give gladly
is to express love for God who has given all we have, both material and
spiritual blessings. Such giving says to God, "Thy love I share." "We love,
because he first loved us" (I John 4:19). Giving born of gratitude increases
the world's treasure of thanksgiving. Our gratitude grows by its own exercise,
and our sharing of God's gifts prompts gratitude in others (vss. 11-12).
Early in the letter Paul has applied this to his own sharing of the gospel
at hazardous cost: "For it is all for your sake, so that as grace extends to more
and more people it may increase thanksgiving, to the glory of God" (4:15).
In this passage he applies it to material gifts for the relief of need. Its
relevance is as broad as the earth and as long as time.

Stormy Justice: Luke 12:16-31

A remark of Barbara Ward's about "stormy justice" is the apt commentary on the parable that launches this lection.

There is no other culture in which there is so stormy a picture of God's justice
falling on those who are neglectful of God's poor. This Judeo-Christian culture has
had this thrust in it. Take that out and what is left? Well, the Lord told us what is
left. What is left is Dives, and we know what happened to him! Or the man who
got everything together in his barn. He's one of my favorite characters—a very go-go
type, because he got everything into the barn and then said: "We'll have an
absolutely way-out evening and everyone will come and enjoy themselves!" And
the Lord said: "Sorry, my friend but you won't be here!" [41]

That, said Jesus, is how matters stand with us when we are materially
affluent and spiritual paupers.

Luke reports the story in the context of a family quarrel over an
inheritance (vss. 13-14). Jesus refused to arbitrate such disputes; they grew
from covetousness, he said (vs. 15). The contenders forgot that life is
more than goods to put in a barn. Get the lion's share of the estate and the
enmity of your brother, and you have gained what the rich man in the
parable gained—a harvest of folly.

There was no accusation of villainy, no implication that he was a
dishonest land-grabber. His only trouble was that of a fool! (vs. 20). He
thought he could congratulate his *soul* on the pleasures of the table! Would
any but a fool suppose a soul could live on what was in the barn? Rich
as he was, he had to leave all that. Then there remained the two-pronged
question: When Eternity calls, who gets what is anchored to Time? When
your soul's food is stored in the barn, what do you live by in Eternity?

In the presence of this common folly, Jesus warned us against anxiety

[41] Address at the Uppsala Assembly of the World Council of Churches,
reported in *The Christian Century*, Aug. 21, 1968, p. 1034.

about creature needs. "Life is more than food, and the body more than clothing" (vs. 23). This expresses one of the recurring thrusts of the gospel. Matthew weaves it into the Sermon on the Mount as amplification of the pronouncement that "you cannot serve God and mammon" (Matt. 6:24-33); the real disciple commits all his concerns to God, serving and trusting him with undivided loyalty. As a follow-up to the parable of the rich fool, the saying makes the same point. The rich man had to choose one thing or the other—goods in the barn, of worth only to his stomach; or God, who could enrich his total existence. If you want full freedom from anxious worry, Jesus said, put your total trust in God (vss. 24-31).

Life is more than livelihood—how that theme keeps coming back! Tested in the wilderness, Jesus settled a pivotal issue of his ministry on the principle that "man shall not live by bread alone" (4:4). To a friend who supposed the one way to serve him was by the perfection of a meal, he said: "Martha, Martha, you are anxious and troubled about many things; one thing is needful" (10:41-42). To the disciples, puzzled that any other interest could eclipse the attraction of the lunch they had brought, he said: "I have food to eat of which you do not know. . . . My food is to do the will of him who sent me, and to accomplish his work" (John 4:32-34).

His reasoning in the matter is lucid. Since God feeds the birds without their worrying, and since we are worth more than the birds to God, we can live in trust (vs. 24). Since our anxiety can add neither a foot to our height nor a day to our life, our worry is wasted (vss. 25-26). So far, we are on something like common ground with the Stoics. But there is another step. All the nations of the earth want the things we worry about—food, clothing, wealth, peace of mind. But only one thing is important—to want what God wants for our lives. When we seek his kingdom, trusting his care about things we cannot finally control, he gives the boon of a fulfilled life (vss. 30-31).

"Is the kingdom of God realism?" asked the title of a memorable book. Yes, this Gospel answers, indeed it is—realism in its completion of the lives of those who make God's reign their dominant trust, and realism in its stormy justice to those who trust what they can store in the barn. To accept the faith is to make hazardous choice between these trusts.